# FOREWORD

When we set out to create Assassin's Creed III, our vision was to develop a revolutionary game, reflecting unequaled ambitions in the series. We knew we could benefit from solid assets which lay to hand:

- ⊙ Highly experienced development studios, which had worked on the franchise for years;

- ⊙ The unconditional creative and marketing support of our mother company Ubisoft;

- ⊙ An almost three-year development window, an increasing rarity in these days of rationalization;

- ⊙ Last but not least, amazing, advanced, end-of-cycle technology, enabling us to start the project at full speed from scratch.

We realized from the off that we had a once-in-a-career opportunity: our chance to create a game with gameplay matched by incredibly high production values, something very special.

And here we are, three years later, proud to present the fruit of our long and intense labor – a game with a breathtaking setting and storyline, a sandbox with unprecedented freedom of movement and action, completely enhanced gameplay backed up by a powerful engine, multiple new features such as naval combat, season cycles, and the list could go on and on.

Having worked so hard to create a new gaming benchmark, we were very keen to make sure that it would launch with a triple-A guide. The decision to work with Piggyback was a natural extension of our long-term partnership in the series. I'm proud to present the best travel guide to our world that you could ever hope for.

The Piggyback team has spared no efforts in making this 100% complete guide. It includes a novel Walkthrough offering annotated screencaps for every step of the adventure, details for all side quests as well as an original "The Story So Far" section to get newcomers to the series smoothly up to speed.

Perhaps more importantly, this is a guide that respects your need to experience both game and story for yourself. It doesn't solve your problems – it shows you how to solve them yourself, at your own pace and in the order that suits you. And this is the beauty of the guide: every page is carefully conceived to help you get maximum enjoyment from *your* game.

**Alex Hutchinson, Assassin's Creed III Creative Director**

Concise recaps, explanations and insights to help all readers – both seasoned Assassin's Creed players and newcomers – to understand the most important story developments and concepts introduced in previous episodes.

This chapter is designed to help you ease into the opening hours of Assassin's Creed III with confidence, focusing on abilities and concepts introduced during the game's first three Sequences.

This chapter will guide you through all Main Missions, with annotated screenshots providing at-a-glance solutions, enabling you to complete the entire adventure (and its Optional Objectives) with a Full Synchronization rating.

This chapter offers everything you need to complete all side missions and gain a maximum 100% Synchronization rating.

# CONTENTS

In this chapter, we take an in-depth look at the many systems that underpin the Assassin's Creed III experience.

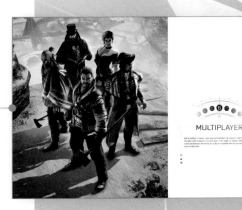

In this chapter, we provide a wealth of explanations, insights and techniques that will help you to play at a competitive level from your very first foray into the engrossing multiplayer mode.

In this **spoiler-heavy** chapter, we offer a short recap of all secrets and unlockables. This is followed by extensive analysis of major events in the Assassin's Creed III storyline.

### Quickstart

You will find a "Quickstart" section overleaf. This offers a visual presentation of the guide's contents, and explains how you can use the guide in an optimal way depending on your personal needs and expectations.

### Index

If you would rather play with a minimum of assistance, the guide's comprehensive Index can be used to jump to topics of interest whenever you need a hint or specific piece of information.

### Vertical Tab

The vertical tab on the right-hand margin of each double-page spread is a navigational tool designed to help you find your way around the guide. The top section lists the individual chapters, while the lower section highlights the part of the chapter you are currently reading.

### Update Notice

We have taken every step to ensure that the contents of this guide are correct at the time of going to press. However, future updates to Assassin's Creed III may contain adjustments, gameplay balancing and even feature additions that we cannot anticipate at the time of writing.

Assassin's Creed III is a true giant of its genre: an action adventure with dozens of side stories and hundreds of unique challenges to master… all of which are fully documented and dissected in the commensurately weighty guide that you hold in front of you. There is a lot of information to digest in this book, and we recognize that each reader will seek specific assistance and analysis to suit their play style. In this Quickstart section, we explain the structure and contents of this guide, and we offer a variety of easy entry points for players of all levels of gaming experience.

We have defined five different player profiles, with each attributed a unique color. We present each chapter below as a double-page spread, upon which you will see icons that repeat the color codes. A full-size icon means that gamers of this profile are advised to read the chapter as a whole. A half-size icon indicates the chapter can be used as a reference source when required.

## THE STORY SO FAR

This is your ideal entry point to the guide, featuring all you need to re-acquaint or familiarize yourself with key developments in the series storyline to date. We offer concise recaps, explanations and insights to help all readers understand the most important narrative concepts and developments in previous episodes.

## PRIMER

The Primer examines and explains the core abilities and play mechanics introduced during the first three Sequences of the adventure. It can be used as a companion to the early sections of the walkthrough, browsed casually for tips and techniques or read in its entirety if this is your first foray into the Assassin's Creed world.

## REFERENCE & ANALYSIS

This is a must-read chapter if you would like to improve your skills and acquire a good understanding of the mechanics that govern the Assassin's Creed III world. Using diagrams, detailed stats (many of which are "hidden" during play) and expert analysis, we take an in-depth look at the many systems that underpin the playing experience – with a particular focus on advanced combat, equipment and managing the Homestead to maximize your income.

## MULTIPLAYER

This chapter provides a wealth of explanations, insights and techniques that will help you to play at a competitive level from your very first entry into the engrossing multiplayer mode.

| Series Newcomer | Story-Focused | Experienced Gamer | Completionist | Multiplayer Fan |
|---|---|---|---|---|
| This is your first Assassin's Creed experience. | Your goal is to complete the main storyline. | You've played at least one Assassin's Creed game before, and you are familiar with its structure. | You've played all Assassin's Creed games to date and will settle for no less than 100% completion. | You are mainly interested in Assassin's Creed III's multiplayer mode. |

Player Experience →

## WALKTHROUGH

The Walkthrough chapter can be used as a travel guide, with step-by-step assistance for the entire storyline, or as a handy reference tool whenever you encounter a problem. All main missions are covered, with a focus on accessible and instant visuals that provide at-a-glance solutions. Players who would like to see the story to its conclusion will find all the advice they need, while those who aspire to a perfect Synchronization rating will benefit from our uncompromising offering of all solutions to Optional Objectives. We also provide helpful page references to other chapters, where you can learn about topics as and when these become relevant to your progression or performance.

## SIDE QUESTS

This chapter is the heart of this book and begins with a Completion Timeline diagram that reveals the order in which the game features are unlocked and offers suggestions for a streamlined path to 100% completion. The pages that follow are packed with walkthroughs, analysis and tips covering every optional activity in Assassin's Creed III, from simple diversions to side stories that will take many hours to complete. You will also find detailed maps of all regions, showing the positions of all collectibles and points of interest. Everything you need to gain a maximum 100% Synchronization rating is here.

## EXTRAS

In this spoiler-heavy chapter (be warned), we offer a short recap of all secrets and unlockables. This is followed by a concise summary of the Assassin's Creed III story, and an extensive section where we analyze established facts and speculate on future developments. If you have any questions about the game's plot and its most intriguing mysteries, this will tie it all together.

## MAP LEGEND & INDEX

If you are keen to play with a minimum of assistance, you can use our comprehensive Index to jump to your topic of interest whenever you need a hint or specific piece of information. The Map Legend features all of the icons that you will encounter in the guide.

# THEMATIC INDEX

Quickstart also serves as a reference tool. Whenever you seek help with a particular question, you may find that your most direct route to the answer lies in this thematic index.

QUICKSTART

THE STORY SO FAR

PRIMER

WALKTHROUGH

SIDE QUESTS

REFERENCE & ANALYSIS

MULTIPLAYER

EXTRAS

MAP LEGEND

INDEX

# THE STORY SO FAR

With four core episodes to date, in addition to ancillary tales shared via handheld games and assorted publications, an integral part of the Assassin's Creed experience is its compelling and densely layered story. Over the following pages, we offer concise recaps, explanations and insights to help all readers – both seasoned and new players – to understand the most important developments and concepts presented in previous installments.

Each Assassin's Creed episode features two parallel yet intertwined tales. In one, Desmond Miles is a barman inexplicably kidnapped in September 2012 by agents of Abstergo, a multinational corporation. Desmond is forced to interact with a remarkable machine: the "Animus". This phenomenally advanced technology immerses its subject in a virtual reality where they can experience hereditary memories stored within their DNA. When Desmond is later rescued, he chooses to continue his adventures in past lives to combat Abstergo, and the clandestine organization that the corporation embodies.

The second story arc, traditionally self-contained within each Assassin's Creed installment, covers the experiences that Desmond has of direct-line ancestors through his interaction with the Animus tech. Seeking powerful artifacts from an advanced race (the "First Civilization") that inhabited the Earth before mankind, Desmond relives momentous events in the lives of distant antecedents – and, in so doing, acquires their extraordinary faculties.

Both narratives dovetail to tell of an ancient struggle between two opposing forces: the Templars, who seek to bring order to the world through absolute control, and the Assassins, who strive to preserve mankind's freedoms. Both factions operate in secret to advance their cause through centuries of conflict, continually vying for possession of First Civilization relics known as "Pieces of Eden". By reliving moments in history via the recent Animus tech, the current-day Assassins and Templars gain insights into events that affect the present.

# ASSASSIN'S CREED ™

## PRESENT

**September, 2012:** Kidnapped by Abstergo and spirited away to a secret laboratory in Italy, Desmond is forced to interact with the Animus.

Desmond explores events in the life of an ancestor during the Third Crusade: Altaïr, a member of the Assassin Brotherhood.

## PAST

Altaïr inflicts a grievous blow to contemporary Templar power by assassinating a sequence of high-ranking Order officials.

He then retrieves a Piece of Eden. This triggers a holographic projection of Earth.

This "vision" features annotations that identify specific locations around the globe, indicating that this artifact may have recorded the locations of further Pieces of Eden or First Civilization temples.

| **Altaïr** (Holy Land, 1191) | Altaïr (Masyaf, 1191-1257) | Ezio (Italy, 1459-1499) | Ezio (Rome, 1500-1507) | Ezio (Masyaf & Constantinople, 1510-1512) |

PAST

QUICKSTART

THE STORY
SO FAR

PRIMER

WALKTHROUGH

SIDE QUESTS

REFERENCE &
ANALYSIS

MULTIPLAYER

EXTRAS

MAP LEGEND

INDEX

STORY RECAP

TIMELINE

CAST &
CONCEPTS

## PRESENT

Not long after Desmond completes the Memory where Altaïr finds the Piece of Eden, he experiences the power of the "Bleeding Effect" for the first time – the process whereby a subject interacting with the Animus assimilates the memories and capabilities of his or her ancestors.

His vision is blurred yet amplified in a manner evoking Altaïr's Eagle Vision (an almost arcane ability that enables him to discern the unseen), enabling Desmond to discover cryptic messages and pictures smeared in blood on the walls and floors of the laboratory where he is detained. These are, in fact, a desperate farewell (and, for the most part, a dire warning) left by one of Abstergo's previous test subjects.

| **Desmond**<br>(Abstergo Laboratory, 2012) | Desmond<br>(Assassins Secret Hideout, 2012) | Desmond<br>(Monteriggioni, 2012) | Desmond<br>(Italy & State of New York, 2012) |

PRESENT

# ASSASSIN'S CREED II

**September, 2012:** Desmond escapes the Abstergo laboratory with the assistance of Lucy Stillman, an Assassin sleeper agent.

Once a feckless youth, and later an expert Assassin embroiled in the conflict with the Templars, Ezio obtains the "Apple", a Piece of Eden, and identifies a secret vault hidden beneath the Vatican.

He then joins a small Brotherhood cell based in a secret hideout.

Using an upgraded version of the Animus, Desmond relives the memories of an ancestor from the Renaissance era: Ezio Auditore. Desmond wants to learn more about the Pieces of Eden, and to exploit the Bleeding Effect to gain a lifetime of advanced Assassin training in a matter of days.

Entering the chamber, Ezio meets with a holographic projection of a First Civilization woman named Minerva. Dismissing the Assassin's questions, she instead speaks directly to Desmond and warns of an imminent Catastrophe that could destroy all life on Earth. She explains that this cataclysm occurred once before, annihilating her kind many thousands of years ago. She claims that her people had been developing a solution and the fruits of their labors are concealed in secret locations around the world.

| Altaïr (Holy Land, 1191) | Altaïr (Masyaf, 1191-1257) | **Ezio** **(Italy, 1459-1499)** | Ezio (Rome, 1500-1507) | Ezio (Masyaf & Constantinople, 1510-1512) |
|---|---|---|---|---|

**PAST**

QUICKSTART

THE STORY
SO FAR

PRIMER

WALKTHROUGH

SIDE QUESTS

REFERENCE &
ANALYSIS

MULTIPLAYER

EXTRAS

MAP LEGEND

INDEX

STORY RECAP

TIMELINE

CAST &
CONCEPTS

## PRESENT

**End of September, 2012:** Having witnessed Minerva's address via Ezio, Desmond emerges from the Animus to discover that Templar agents have arrived to recapture their erstwhile effects. Demonstrating his now outstanding combat skills, Desmond fights to repel the attack and escapes the hideout with his fellow Assassins.

Desmond
(Abstergo Laboratory, 2012)

**Desmond**
(Assassins Secret Hideout, 2012)

Desmond
(Monteriggioni, 2012)

Desmond
(Italy & State of New York, 2012)

PRESENT

15

# ASSASSIN'S
## CREED
## BROTHERHOOD

**Early October, 2012:** Desmond's Assassin cell seeks refuge in a new location in Italy, where they suspect Ezio's Piece of Eden to be hidden.

Following his return from the Vatican, the Templars launch a large-scale assault on Ezio's hometown and, in the ensuing chaos, seize the Apple of Eden.

Desmond immediately returns to his ancestor's life via the Animus with one critical objective: to discover the location of the artifact.

Once he concludes his vendetta against the man responsible for the attack, Ezio retrieves the Apple.

Ezio eventually secures the Apple in a vault beneath the Colosseum.

| Altaïr (Holy Land, 1191) | Altaïr (Masyaf, 1191-1257) | Ezio (Italy, 1459-1499) | **Ezio (Rome, 1500-1507)** | Ezio (Masyaf & Constantinople, 1510-1512) |

PAST

III

QUICKSTART

THE STORY
SO FAR

PRIMER

WALKTHROUGH

SIDE QUESTS

REFERENCE &
ANALYSIS

MULTIPLAYER

EXTRAS

MAP LEGEND

INDEX

STORY RECAP

TIMELINE

CAST &
CONCEPTS

**October 10, 2012:** As soon as Desmond learns the location of the Apple, the Assassins travel there to discover a temple of Juno, another member of the First Civilization. Juno speaks to Desmond alone as he and his companions seek to gain entrance to the vault.

The Apple is "activated" once Desmond lays his hands on it. The artifact seemingly takes control of Desmond and compels him, ostensibly at Juno's behest, to fatally stab Lucy.

Desmond then collapses. In a state of deep shock, he is vaguely aware of being carried into the back of a van. Voices argue over returning him to the Animus, and although he attempts to protest he slips into unconsciousness.

| Desmond | Desmond | **Desmond** | Desmond |
| (Abstergo Laboratory, 2012) | (Assassins Secret Hideout, 2012) | **(Monteriggioni, 2012)** | (Italy & State of New York, 2012) |

PRESENT

# ASSASSIN'S CREED REVELATIONS

**October, 2012:** Believing Desmond's condition to be a consequence of the Bleeding Effect, his Assassin companions place him in a special Animus program in an effort to forestall fatal mental deterioration.

As his body is transported from Italy to a new destination by his unit supervisor, William, Desmond "wakes up" on a strange island. He meets Abstergo's previous test persona, Subject 16, now fully realized in a virtual body, who discloses that Desmond is inside the original Animus test program. Sixteen explains that Desmond's mind has been fragmented, pushed to the brink of irreversible dementia, by the experience of reliving the lives of Ezio and Altaïr. Sixteen informs Desmond that he can maintain his sanity by "finishing" his ancestors' lives. This will enable the Animus software and his beleaguered synapses to somehow separate the two supplementary existences from his core identity – allowing him to awake from his coma. Unbeknownst to his Assassin colleagues, Desmond resumes his exploration of Ezio's and Altaïr's memories.

Puzzled by the revelations he had witnessed yet failed to comprehend after meeting Minerva, Ezio travels to the Holy Land to investigate a secret library created by his predecessor, Altaïr.

To access the library, Ezio must find five unique keys to fit the openings on its imposing doorway. Despite Templar interference, Ezio obtains each key in turn – and, on examining these First Civilization devices, experiences lucid "waking dreams" that narrate events from Altaïr's life.

Inside the secret library he finds no books, but rather Altaïr's skeletal remains and his Apple of Eden. The device bursts into life, using Ezio as the conduit for a message that is in fact intended for Desmond.

| Altaïr (Holy Land, 1191) | Altaïr (Masyaf, 1191-1257) | Ezio (Italy, 1459-1499) | Ezio (Rome, 1500-1507) | Ezio (Masyaf & Constantinople, 1510-1512) |

PAST

## PRESENT

As Altaïr's Apple activates in the secret library, Desmond is transported to a different place. In this otherworldly domain, Tinia – the third member of the First Civilization triumvirate along with Minerva and Juno – relates to Desmond how his people had tried but failed to survive the great Catastrophe revealed at the close of Assassin's Creed II. The last act of the First Civilization was to transmit their collective knowledge to a single underground vault located in what is now the state of New York. Tinia informs Desmond that the answers to his questions lie inside this long-concealed "Grand Temple".

Meanwhile, outside the Animus, the Assassins land in the state of New York. Oblivious to Desmond's travails within the Animus, they are astonished when he begins to regain consciousness.

After taking a moment to consider William, revealed to be his father, Desmond experiences a strange connection with the nearby Apple of Eden, which pulses in response. As they arrive at the location of the Grand Temple revealed by Tinia, the events of Assassin's Creed III begin…

| Desmond<br>(Abstergo Laboratory, 2012) | Desmond<br>(Assassins Secret Hideout, 2012) | Desmond<br>(Monteriggioni, 2012) | **Desmond**<br>(Italy & State of New York, 2012) |
|---|---|---|---|

# TIMELINE

The following timeline presents the most significant events in the Assassin's Creed story and shows how these lead to the opening events of Assassin's Creed III.

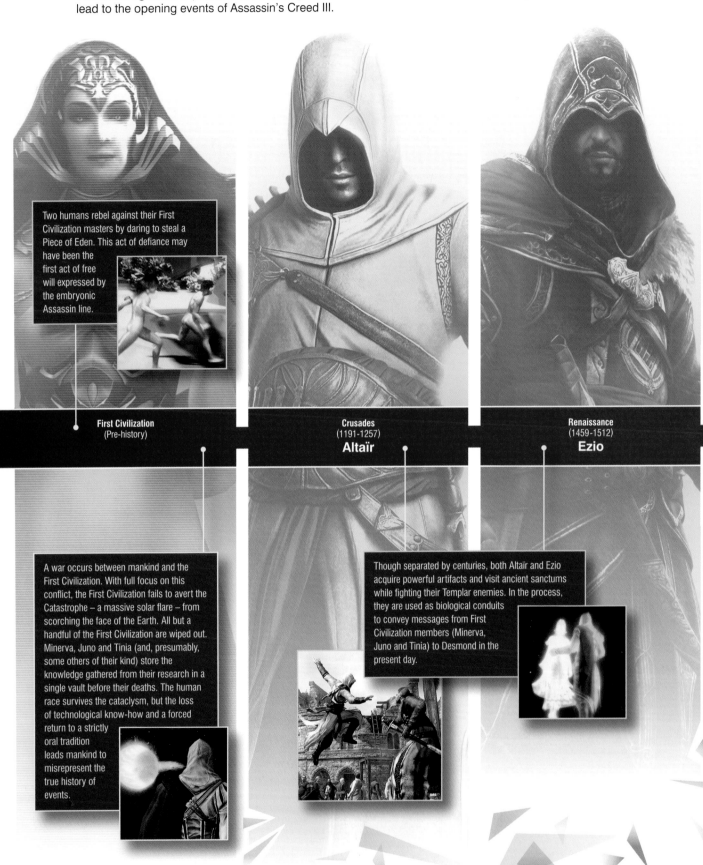

Two humans rebel against their First Civilization masters by daring to steal a Piece of Eden. This act of defiance may have been the first act of free will expressed by the embryonic Assassin line.

**First Civilization**
(Pre-history)

**Crusades**
(1191-1257)
**Altaïr**

**Renaissance**
(1459-1512)
**Ezio**

A war occurs between mankind and the First Civilization. With full focus on this conflict, the First Civilization fails to avert the Catastrophe – a massive solar flare – from scorching the face of the Earth. All but a handful of the First Civilization are wiped out. Minerva, Juno and Tinia (and, presumably, some others of their kind) store the knowledge gathered from their research in a single vault before their deaths. The human race survives the cataclysm, but the loss of technological know-how and a forced return to a strictly oral tradition leads mankind to misrepresent the true history of events.

Though separated by centuries, both Altaïr and Ezio acquire powerful artifacts and visit ancient sanctums while fighting their Templar enemies. In the process, they are used as biological conduits to convey messages from First Civilization members (Minerva, Juno and Tinia) to Desmond in the present day.

III

QUICKSTART

THE STORY
SO FAR

PRIMER

WALKTHROUGH

SIDE QUESTS

REFERENCE &
ANALYSIS

MULTIPLAYER

EXTRAS

MAP LEGEND

INDEX

STORY RECAP

TIMELINE

CAST &
CONCEPTS

**September, 2012:** Kidnapped by Abstergo, Desmond is forced to interact with the Animus to explore the life of one of his ancestors from the Third Crusade: Altaïr.

Desmond eventually manages to escape the Abstergo laboratory and joins a small Assassin cell. By reliving the memories of another ancestor, Ezio, Desmond meets Minerva in the Vatican vault, and learns that Ezio's Piece of Eden is hidden beneath the Colosseum.

American Revolution
(1753-1783)
## Connor

Present
(2012)
## Desmond

Events of Assassin's Creed III.

**October, 2012:** Desmond finds the Piece of Eden in Juno's vault beneath the Colosseum. As he touches the artifact, Desmond is brought under the influence of Juno, and subsequently collapses. His Assassin companions place him in a special Animus program, where Desmond "finishes" the lives of his two ancestors (Altaïr and Ezio) to regain his own identity. Meanwhile, his body is transported by his fellow Assassins from Italy to the US.

The exploration of his ancestors' final memories enables Desmond to meet Tinia – the third member of the First Civilization triumvirate along with Minerva and Juno. Tinia tells Desmond about a single underground vault located in what is now the state of New York. It is in this Grand Temple that the triumvirate claims they stored their accumulated knowledge – information that may enable mankind to avert another Catastrophe. Desmond arrives there at the beginning of Assassin's Creed III.

**December 21st, 2012:** This is the day Abstergo plans to launch a telecommunications satellite containing an Apple of Eden. The Templars conspire to use the Apple to control the Earth's population.

Some cultures prophesize December 21st, 2012 to mark a time of transition, possibly even Armageddon. Could this be the second Catastrophe augured by the First Civilization?

## THE ASSASSIN BROTHERHOOD

The Assassin Brotherhood has been at war with the Templar Order for over two thousand years. The Assassins have intelligence, stealth and surprise at their disposal. They send a lone agent against a legion and halt the march of ten thousand with the death of one. Assassins are sworn to preserve free will and to defend the liberty of all. Their motto – "Nothing is true; everything is permitted" – is their raison d'être, advocating the individual's right to act of their own volition. The Templars' desire to provide peace and stability through the enforced surrender of self-determination is anathema to the Assassins.

Operating in the shadows, the Assassins' modern-day organization is under great pressure, and uses the cell structure of underground resistance groups. Such tactics are essential to avoid the evolved tracking and surveillance techniques provided to the resurgent Templars by the Abstergo corporation.

## ABSTERGO & THE TEMPLAR ORDER

The Knights Templar Order received papal blessing in 1129 and found fame (and infamy) through their military exploits in the Holy Land during the Third Crusade. However, the Templar organization – as represented in the Assassin's Creed canon – is much older. Under various guises and with many different leaders, the Templar Order has sought absolute power to control humanity. Although some individual agents may be corrupt, the Templars should not be viewed as "evil". They consider themselves the custodians of humanity.

Abstergo Industries takes its name from the latin to "cleanse" or "wipe away" and embodies the modern identity of the Templar Order. This front masks a worldwide operation, from telecoms to pharmacology, and enables the Templar Order to access the finest scientific minds, bleeding-edge technology… and political influence.

Abstergo's most valuable asset is the Animus, a device that enables the exploration of genetic memories. Human DNA, it transpires, records the experiences of every living person, with each individual passing their life data to their offspring at conception – a discovery thus far unknown in mainstream science. The Templars deploy the Animus to identify genetic lines that will lead them to the locations of ancient artifacts known as Pieces of Eden, devices with astonishing capacity to influence and indeed control human behavior.

The Templars conspire to obtain an Apple of Eden and conceal this in a telecommunications satellite developed by an Abstergo subsidiary. Once in orbit, they plan to use it to control the Earth's population. The Eye-Abstergo satellite is scheduled for launch on December 21st, 2012.

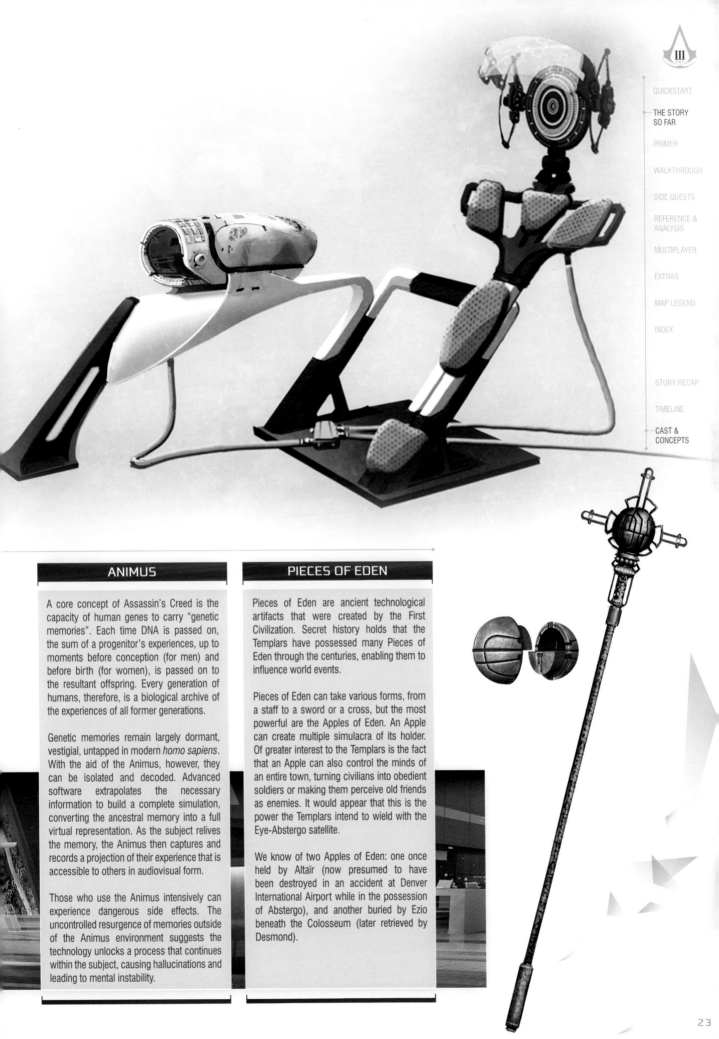

III

QUICKSTART

THE STORY
SO FAR

PRIMER

WALKTHROUGH

SIDE QUESTS

REFERENCE &
ANALYSIS

MULTIPLAYER

EXTRAS

MAP LEGEND

INDEX

STORY RECAP

TIMELINE

CAST &
CONCEPTS

## ANIMUS

A core concept of Assassin's Creed is the capacity of human genes to carry "genetic memories". Each time DNA is passed on, the sum of a progenitor's experiences, up to moments before conception (for men) and before birth (for women), is passed on to the resultant offspring. Every generation of humans, therefore, is a biological archive of the experiences of all former generations.

Genetic memories remain largely dormant, vestigial, untapped in modern *homo sapiens*. With the aid of the Animus, however, they can be isolated and decoded. Advanced software extrapolates the necessary information to build a complete simulation, converting the ancestral memory into a full virtual representation. As the subject relives the memory, the Animus then captures and records a projection of their experience that is accessible to others in audiovisual form.

Those who use the Animus intensively can experience dangerous side effects. The uncontrolled resurgence of memories outside of the Animus environment suggests the technology unlocks a process that continues within the subject, causing hallucinations and leading to mental instability.

## PIECES OF EDEN

Pieces of Eden are ancient technological artifacts that were created by the First Civilization. Secret history holds that the Templars have possessed many Pieces of Eden through the centuries, enabling them to influence world events.

Pieces of Eden can take various forms, from a staff to a sword or a cross, but the most powerful are the Apples of Eden. An Apple can create multiple simulacra of its holder. Of greater interest to the Templars is the fact that an Apple can also control the minds of an entire town, turning civilians into obedient soldiers or making them perceive old friends as enemies. It would appear that this is the power the Templars intend to wield with the Eye-Abstergo satellite.

We know of two Apples of Eden: one once held by Altaïr (now presumed to have been destroyed in an accident at Denver International Airport while in the possession of Abstergo), and another buried by Ezio beneath the Colosseum (later retrieved by Desmond).

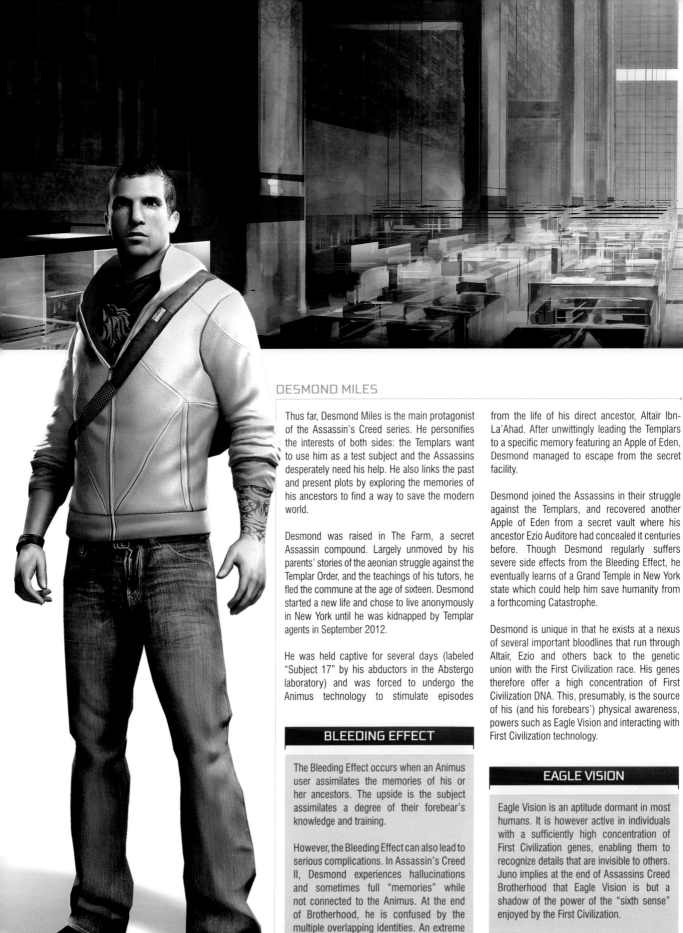

## DESMOND MILES

Thus far, Desmond Miles is the main protagonist of the Assassin's Creed series. He personifies the interests of both sides: the Templars want to use him as a test subject and the Assassins desperately need his help. He also links the past and present plots by exploring the memories of his ancestors to find a way to save the modern world.

Desmond was raised in The Farm, a secret Assassin compound. Largely unmoved by his parents' stories of the aeonian struggle against the Templar Order, and the teachings of his tutors, he fled the commune at the age of sixteen. Desmond started a new life and chose to live anonymously in New York until he was kidnapped by Templar agents in September 2012.

He was held captive for several days (labeled "Subject 17" by his abductors in the Abstergo laboratory) and was forced to undergo the Animus technology to stimulate episodes from the life of his direct ancestor, Altaïr Ibn-La'Ahad. After unwittingly leading the Templars to a specific memory featuring an Apple of Eden, Desmond managed to escape from the secret facility.

Desmond joined the Assassins in their struggle against the Templars, and recovered another Apple of Eden from a secret vault where his ancestor Ezio Auditore had concealed it centuries before. Though Desmond regularly suffers severe side effects from the Bleeding Effect, he eventually learns of a Grand Temple in New York state which could help him save humanity from a forthcoming Catastrophe.

Desmond is unique in that he exists at a nexus of several important bloodlines that run through Altaïr, Ezio and others back to the genetic union with the First Civilization race. His genes therefore offer a high concentration of First Civilization DNA. This, presumably, is the source of his (and his forebears') physical awareness, powers such as Eagle Vision and interacting with First Civilization technology.

### BLEEDING EFFECT

The Bleeding Effect occurs when an Animus user assimilates the memories of his or her ancestors. The upside is the subject assimilates a degree of their forebear's knowledge and training.

However, the Bleeding Effect can also lead to serious complications. In Assassin's Creed II, Desmond experiences hallucinations and sometimes full "memories" while not connected to the Animus. At the end of Brotherhood, he is confused by the multiple overlapping identities. An extreme form of this caused Subject 16 to take his own life.

### EAGLE VISION

Eagle Vision is an aptitude dormant in most humans. It is however active in individuals with a sufficiently high concentration of First Civilization genes, enabling them to recognize details that are invisible to others. Juno implies at the end of Assassins Creed Brotherhood that Eagle Vision is but a shadow of the power of the "sixth sense" enjoyed by the First Civilization.

III

QUICKSTART

THE STORY
SO FAR

PRIMER

WALKTHROUGH

SIDE QUESTS

REFERENCE &
ANALYSIS

MULTIPLAYER

EXTRAS

MAP LEGEND

INDEX

STORY RECAP

TIMELINE

CAST &
CONCEPTS

## SUBJECT 16 / CLAY KACZMAREK

Clay Kaczmarek (Subject 16) was the Assassin captured by Abstergo Industries before Desmond Miles became an Animus test subject.

The fate of Sixteen is a stark warning of the dangers of prolonged, unregulated exposure to the Animus. Having attained the memories of many different ancestors, he suffered extreme forms of the Bleeding Effect. Working against his captors, Sixteen hacked into the Animus and uploaded a "living" digital facsimile of his mind to the machine.

Exhausted, paranoid and suffering from too many overlapping identities, he committed suicide some days later. His final act was to use his own blood to smear messages and symbols on the walls of the Abstergo laboratory in the hope that an Assassin blessed with Eagle Vision – which turns out to be Desmond – might read them.

Subject 16 observed his successor Desmond from his first Animus experiences, looking for opportunities to communicate with him. When the two meet in the Animus test program after the events of Brotherhood, Sixteen guides his fellow Assassin through negating the Bleeding Effect and regaining consciousness in the real world.

The Lost Archive DLC reveals that Sixteen's capture by Abstergo agents was ordered by William Miles. With assistance from sleeper agent Lucy Stillman, Subject 16 was to use the opportunity to gather intelligence within Abstergo's Italian research facility – and, later, to escape. By the time he learned of Lucy's betrayal, the Bleeding Effect had robbed him of his former ability. With no hope of escape, and with initial reluctance, he eventually agreed to Juno's request that he sacrifice himself to aid Desmond Miles.

## SHAUN HASTINGS

The historian in Desmond's Assassin cell structure, Shaun was a university lecturer whose radical views had him ejected from the ivory towers of academia. His intellectual prowess made him an ideal recruit for the Assassins, who needed somebody to reconcile accepted historical accounts with their knowledge of secret Templar influence on world events. Shaun puts his remarkable command of dates, people and cultural minutiae to work and maintains the Animus Database, offering assistance to Assassin agents with real-time research.

## REBECCA CRANE

Rebecca is the technician in Desmond's Assassin cell structure. Her parallel development of the Animus technology has enabled the Assassins to stay abreast of advances made by the Templars. She must often work with stolen and salvaged components to keep her team's equipment functional – testament to her remarkable resourcefulness. A geek and a technophile, Rebecca's interest in hacking, and her mastery of counter-surveillance techniques, enable the Assassins to remain hidden from Templar observation.

III

QUICKSTART

THE STORY
SO FAR

PRIMER

WALKTHROUGH

SIDE QUESTS

REFERENCE &
ANALYSIS

MULTIPLAYER

EXTRAS

MAP LEGEND

INDEX

STORY RECAP

TIMELINE

CAST &
CONCEPTS

## WILLIAM MILES

William Miles is Desmond's father. He raised his son in a concealed remote Assassin community known as The Farm, located in the Black Hills of South Dakota. A senior member of the modern-day Brotherhood, William has the role of supervising Assassin cell structures operating throughout the world. When Desmond collapses at the end of Assassin's Creed Brotherhood, William arrives to assume direct control of his son's unit. He then flies with the unit to a location in Syracuse, NY, identified by the Apple of Eden, which had been found by his son.

## LUCY STILLMAN

A sleeper agent trained by the Assassins to infiltrate Abstergo, and eventually assistant to Warren Vidic on the Animus program, Lucy Stillman helped Desmond to escape the laboratory where he was held prisoner, and assumed command of the Assassin cell formed to guide and assist him. Lucy was killed when Desmond, seemingly under the influence of Juno as he retrieved Ezio's Apple, fatally stabbed her. Juno made a cryptic reference to Templar affiliation just beforehand that suggested Lucy had a hidden agenda.

The Lost Archive, a DLC extension for Assassin's Creed Revelations, offers indisputable evidence that Lucy was actually a *triple* agent. Disillusioned with the Brotherhood, and apparently beguiled by Templar ideology, she conspired with Warren Vidic to feed targeted information to her Assassin handlers on the outside. Desmond's escape from Abstergo was also a ruse: he was actually permitted to escape, under Lucy's supervision, with the Templars confident that they could maintain control of their valuable asset. Vidic's apparent attack on the Assassin hideout (at the conclusion of Assassin's Creed II) was a deft ploy to conceal the transfer of data accumulated by Lucy during Desmond's first experience as Ezio.

## ALTAÏR IBN-LA'AHAD

When Desmond first enters the Animus during the events of Assassin's Creed, he explores the memory of Altaïr Ibn-La'Ahad ("The Son of None"). After inflicting a severe blow to Templar power by assassinating key figures in its hierarchy, Altaïr retrieves a mysterious Piece of Eden, which triggers a holographic projection of Earth. It highlights certain locations around the globe, suggesting this artifact may have recorded the resting places of other Pieces of Eden or First Civilization vaults and temples.

Altaïr dedicates his life to studying the Apple and taking steps to ensure that one of his successors will find the relic. At the age of 91, Altaïr locks himself in his library to pass away, his Apple safely entombed with him. His secret burial chamber remains undisturbed for hundreds of years, until Ezio discovers it and communicates the Apple of Eden's message (from Tinia, a member of the First Civilization) to Desmond in the distant future.

### FIRST CIVILIZATION

Also referred to as "Those Who Came Before", the First Civilization is perceived as an advanced race that inhabited the Earth prior to mankind. They remolded a primitive indigenous species into slaves and workers that would later be known as humans. The First Civilization developed devices (described as Pieces of Eden) which controlled their workforce. Most humans, but not all, are believed to retain the dormant but still receptive neural configuration that subjected their ancestors to enslavement.

The sophistication of Those Who Came Before made them appear godlike to early mankind and they were long worshipped as divine saviors – even after the global disaster that destroyed them. These beings walked among us and gave rise to the many different pantheons and gods of the cultures over which they ruled. Nevertheless, a war eventually broke out between the First Civilization and the human race, who were looking to win their freedom. In their weakened state, the overlords were unable to prevent the calamity that would deny them their existence.

## EZIO AUDITORE DA FIRENZE

Ezio is the second ancestor whose life Desmond explores (in Assassin's Creed II, as well as the Brotherhood and Revelations episodes). A Master Assassin from the Renaissance era, Ezio spends much of his life embroiled in the age-old battle against the Templars. Guided by clues left by Altaïr, Ezio travels to a First Civilization vault hidden beneath the Vatican. There, he encounters a holographic projection of a First Civilization member known as Minerva.

Ezio eventually finds and, later, conceals an Apple of Eden, obtained during his struggles against the Templars, in another vault beneath the Colosseum. He ensures that evidence of its location will only be perceptible to one of his kind.

After opening Altaïr's secret burial chamber in Assassin's Creed Revelations, Ezio completes his role in the First Civilization's scheme, by communicating one last message (Tinia's address) across the centuries to Desmond.

### VAULTS & TEMPLES

The First Civilization vaults and temples visited over the course of the Assassin's Creed story are sealed sanctuaries where Those Who Came Before seemingly worked, each laboring with a different method designed to save the world. Vaults were built underground to avoid the war that raged above (between humans and their masters) and the imminent Catastrophe – the solar flare that scorched the face of the earth.

Following the cataclysm, the few survivors of the First Civilization centralized the knowledge of all vaults into a single Grand Temple: the very destination Tinia instructs Desmond to visit at the close of Revelations. Here, Tinia asserts, Desmond will find answers to all of his questions, and possibly a way to prevent another Catastrophe.

Of what is known, it seems the First Civilization had only intended specific individuals to use their vaults and temples. This is why Ezio could enter the Vatican vault that remained resolutely sealed to his Templar nemesis in Assassin's Creed II. How the Templars have apparently acquired so many artifacts throughout history is open to speculation, but it is certain that the Catastrophe and the war with humans did not allow for an orderly inventory and confinement or destruction of all First Civilization technologies.

III

QUICKSTART

THE STORY
SO FAR

PRIMER

WALKTHROUGH

SIDE QUESTS

REFERENCE &
ANALYSIS

MULTIPLAYER

EXTRAS

MAP LEGEND

INDEX

STORY RECAP

TIMELINE

CAST &
CONCEPTS

## MINERVA

Minerva is the holographic projection of a female entity that speaks to Ezio – or, more accurately, through Ezio – when he enters the Vault beneath the Vatican at the end of Assassin's Creed II. Though seemingly long dead, Minerva was one of the last surviving members of the First Civilization after the Catastrophe annihilated her race many thousands of years ago. She warns of an imminent Catastrophe in Desmond's time, and claims that her kind had been developing a solution, now hidden in secret vaults around the world.

### THE CATASTROPHE

The catastrophe was a solar flare – or coronal mass ejection – that long ago scorched the Earth, flipping the polarity of the planet's magnetic field and exposing all life forms to a lethal dose of radiation. Small pockets of First Civilization survivors attempted to rebuild, but their numbers were too few; with a certain irony, their human creations proved more robust, and usurped their former masters. Erosion and vegetation over time removed any meaningful trace of the First Civilization. Minerva, Juno and Tinia – the First Civilization triumvirate – warn Desmond of an imminent repeat of the Catastrophe.

## JUNO

Juno's contempt for humanity – and enduring fury at its role in the destruction of the First Civilization – is abundantly clear during her soliloquies directed at Desmond as he seeks to retrieve Ezio's Apple at the conclusion of Assassin's Creed Brotherhood. Whereas Minerva and Tinia appear to regard humanity as wayward children, characterized by greed and barbarism, Juno is resolutely unsentimental in her assessment of the species. Interestingly, it may be that she is unique in directly interacting with the modern world through the use of First Civilization artifacts: Juno appears complicit in the death of Lucy by way of the Apple's powers and Desmond's hidden blade. (In The Lost Archive DLC for Revelations, we also learn that it was Juno who persuaded Subject 16 to assist Desmond.)

When Desmond enters the vault where Ezio hid the Apple at the end of Brotherhood, Juno reveals that the Catastrophe was so powerful that the few First Civilization members who survived knew they were doomed. Researching ways to perpetuate their race, they attempted to interbreed with mankind, or at least splice their own genetic code into human DNA. It is this information that offers an explanation for Desmond's abilities and remarkable heritage.

III

QUICKSTART

THE STORY
SO FAR

PRIMER

WALKTHROUGH

SIDE QUESTS

REFERENCE &
ANALYSIS

MULTIPLAYER

EXTRAS

MAP LEGEND

INDEX

STORY RECAP

TIMELINE

CAST &
CONCEPTS

## TINIA

The third in the deified First Civilization triumvirate, Tinia – also known as Jupiter and Zeus – informs Desmond that their long-sealed vaults were each dedicated to researching a single method by which the Catastrophe might have been averted. Minerva, Juno and Tinia tested six methods in total, though none were completed before the solar flare scorched the planet.

Tinia reveals the existence of a single vault where he and his kind stored all of their research results – the Grand Temple that Desmond sets out to explore at the beginning of Assassin's Creed III.

## WARREN VIDIC

The head of research at Abstergo Industries, Dr. Warren Vidic is a leading figure in the company's advances in genetic memory technology. Contemptuous and petulant, Vidic forces the captive Desmond into an aggressive and potentially dangerous schedule of Animus use during the events of Assassin's Creed. Later, once he obtains the data required by his superiors within the Templar hierarchy, Lucy Stillman's direct intervention appears to dissuade Vidic from ordering Desmond's immediate execution.

The Lost Archive DLC that acts as a postscript to Revelations blows this subterfuge wide open: Lucy's loyalties had shifted to favor the Templar Order, and Desmond's escape under her direction was sanctioned by Vidic as a bold ploy to safeguard continued supply of data from their test subject.

Vidic led a Templar attack on the Assassin hideout at the end of Assassin's Creed II, in which Desmond first demonstrated his combat prowess gained through his Animus experiences. Vidic fled the scene when the Assassins made short work of his subordinates – or so it seemed. The Lost Archive DLC suggests that the attack was little more than a maneuver to facilitate the retrieval of invaluable Animus data that Lucy had stolen from the Assassin hardware.

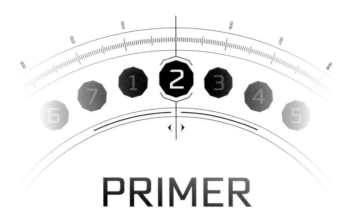

# PRIMER

This chapter focuses on abilities and concepts introduced during the first three Sequences of the Assassin's Creed III story, and acts as a companion to the opening sections of the extensive, step-by-step walkthrough that follows.

Before you continue, we'd like to offer a few brief words on how you might get the most out of this Primer chapter.

⊙ While those who choose to read and consume the Primer in a single sitting will gain a broad understanding of the Assassin's Creed III world and its many features, there's really no harm in skipping straight into the game, with our Walkthrough chapter as your guide.

⊙ As the opening hours of the adventure introduce new concepts and abilities, we provide page references that will enable you to return to this chapter to learn about topics when they become relevant to your progression or performance. This approach means that you can avoid explanations or advice that you might find to be painfully obvious or redundant (of particular interest to readers well-versed in the Assassin's Creed series to date), and easily learn more about fundamental abilities that are rather more complex or broader in scope. Even highly experienced players will benefit from reading about the revised combat system, for example.

⊙ As this chapter examines core abilities pertinent to the first three Sequences, we use Haytham's name alone throughout the document for the sake of simplicity. From Sequence 04 onwards, the Reference & Analysis and Side Quests chapters take over as your primary source of insight, advice and analysis for new features and secondary gameplay challenges. Those who are extremely sensitive to spoilers are advised to avoid both until they reach the appropriate point in the story.

As with previous episodes in the series, Assassin's Creed III begins with a linear collection of main missions that gradually introduce gameplay concepts, abilities and different styles of challenges. For newcomers, the low difficulty of these opening tutorials offers a great opportunity to experiment and get a good feel for the game. More experienced players can treat these sections as a quick refresher course, and complete them with commensurate speed and confidence.

Once you complete the first few Sequences (story chapters), the sandbox begins to open up. In addition to main story missions, you will encounter a vast wealth of side quests, minigames and incidental challenges. The majority of these are purely optional, and are not necessary to complete the central storyline. However, participation will make your character wealthier – and, as a consequence, stronger and better equipped. Engaging in "optional" activities can lead to rewards such as ammo

capacity upgrades, new (and upgraded) weapons and Tools, and even allies that you can call upon – leading to greater tactical flexibility when you face more complicated scenarios later in the story.

One of the principal pleasures of Assassin's Creed III is that you can approach its almost intimidatingly large (but endlessly entertaining) array of side quests and optional tasks whenever you see fit. In time, you can take part in a strategic metagame where you build a trade empire to exploit the spoils of the in-game economy, complete challenges for clubs, hunt collectibles (and wildlife!) over a wide area, craft dozens of items, train acolytes to assist in your adventures (and assign them objectives to complete in a separate minigame), liberate oppressed civilians in two major cities... and the list could go on, *and on*.

Once the world opens up, you will find that all of the game systems that you encounter – from

brief diversions to major side-quest chains – are interconnected in one sense or another. Rather than taking a direct line to the next chapter in the main storyline, then, it's generally far more rewarding to unhurriedly explore other activities that you encounter on the way, or new feature unlocks as they are brought to your attention. There is an astonishing level of variety in Assassin's Creed III, and taking the time to explore it fully will pay off, not just in terms of bonuses, but in terms of the sheer level of enjoyment you can gain from the overall experience.

There is no right or wrong way to approach the many challenges you face – though we do our utmost, in the interlinked Walkthrough and Side Quests chapters, to present an optimal path. That said, we also offer you the tools and advice to pick your own route. Given the rich variety of adventures it offers, Assassin's Creed III is the kind of epic where it is the journey, not the destination, that *really* matters.

Free running and climbing are the skills that lie at the very heart of the Assassin's Creed experience. Though effortlessly scaling buildings or leaping from rooftop to rooftop may seem like demanding feats, you will find that these are not activities that require great finesse with a controller.

Instead, it's your skill as a navigator that really matters: to be able to recognize the pattern of a free run course with a single glance, or instantly identify the fastest climbing route on a tall building. Once you acquire the ability to plan in advance, the physical inputs that enable you to actually guide Haytham on your chosen route become an instinctive activity.

In this section, we look at the many ways that you can exploit Haytham's extraordinary agility and athletic versatility. We also examine alternative forms of travel, such as horse riding: an essential method of crossing great distances at speed.

## WALKING & RUNNING

Use **L** to **move** Haytham, and **R** to **control the camera**. Note how Haytham's movements are made in relation to the direction that the camera is facing. Tilting **L** forward will always cause him to move "into" the screen.

While walking with **L**, hold **A**/**X** to activate the **Fast Walk** function. Haytham will move at a slightly faster pace, and automatically reach out to steer people out of his path or gently push them aside, making it extremely useful for navigating crowds. It is also an essential technique during challenges that encourage or necessitate the use of stealth.

Use **L** + **RT**/**R1** to make Haytham **run**. The degree to which you tilt **L** and the extent to which you hold down **RT**/**R1** governs his movement speed. A slight extension results in a jog; full extension leads to a sprint. Try to avoid colliding with civilians or other NPCs while running, as this can cause Haytham to lose pace as he stumbles or falls.

## CLIMBING

To begin a **climb**, simply run Haytham into a solid surface with obvious handholds within his reach. Experienced Assassin's Creed players should note that it is no longer necessary to press **A**/**X** to achieve this feat. Buildings in urban areas invariably offer several potential climbing routes to a destination (as demonstrated by the dotted line route in this picture); identifying the quickest and most direct of these (solid line) is a talent you acquire with practice. If you do not want Haytham to begin climbing while running, be careful to steer him away from potential start points.

You can actually release **RT**/**R1** once a climb begins, though there's no direct harm in holding it. Use **L** to ascend, traverse to the left or right, or descend. Employing **R** to adjust the camera and see the route ahead is a vital skill.

To begin a **descent** from a standing position on a high vantage point, hold **L** as you approach a suitable edge and Haytham will peer down. Press **B**/**O** to make him drop to a hanging position on the ledge, initiating a climb.

To make Haytham **release his grip** on a surface while climbing, tap **B**/**O**. He will begin to fall to the ground. To perform a "**catch back**" on another ledge as he falls past, press **L** towards the surface.

While climbing, hold **RT**/**R1** and tap **A**/**X** to perform a **Back Eject**. This will cause Haytham to spring away from a surface, automatically grabbing a ledge behind him or dropping to the ground. This is a highly useful move when you accidentally begin a climb with adversaries hot on your heels, as it enables you to skip the awkward pause that ensues when you perform a simple drop.

## FREE RUNNING

Boiled down to its very essence, **free running** is performed by holding 🄻 + 🆁🆃/🆁1, and directing Haytham on a course that he might reasonably hope to follow. In the screenshot here, we illustrate a very simple rooftop route where Haytham will make the requisite jumps and brief climbs as you steer him to his destination.

An essential lesson to learn with free running is that Haytham will only perform jumps when a suitable surface or hand-hold is within his range. Run him to the edge of a tall building, and he will come to an abrupt halt. In the above screenshot, one route leads to an effortless jump; the other a dead stop.

When you need to override Haytham's caution to make a **leap** that lies just outside his default range – or may result in injury – press 🄻 in the required direction, hold 🆁🆃/🆁1, then tap Ⓐ/Ⓧ.

Any jump where Haytham falls a distance greater than a single story can lead to injury. To reduce the damage sustained – and, in chase situations, preserve forward momentum – hold 🄻 in the direction of motion to make him roll on contact with a solid surface.

Urban areas feature a multitude of free run "courses" that begin at ground level. These can be used to ascend quickly and safely to higher elevations, which can be a real boon during pursuits.

Haytham will automatically swing from **poles** (and similar objects) on free run courses while you hold 🄻 + 🆁🆃/🆁1. If you should pause for any reason while he is hanging from a pole, Haytham will need to briefly build up momentum before making the next jump. You can also turn him around to swing and jump in the opposite direction, if required.

III

QUICKSTART

THE STORY
SO FAR

PRIMER

WALKTHROUGH

SIDE QUESTS

REFERENCE &
ANALYSIS

MULTIPLAYER

EXTRAS

MAP LEGEND

INDEX

GAME
PROGRESSION

MOVEMENT &
NAVIGATION

VIEWPOINTS &
MAPS

SOCIAL
INTERACTION

STEALTH

STEALTH
ABILITIES

ASSASSINATIONS

ESCAPING

COMBAT

ENEMY
ARCHETYPES

INTERFACE &
CONTROLS

100%
SYNCHRONIZATION

One drawback to rooftop travel is that some buildings are guarded by **rooftop sentries**. After initial warnings, these adversaries will open fire and potentially give chase. As a rule, it's wise to pay them a wide berth, employing stealth or a detour to avoid conflict.

Whenever you can see a hiding place comprising leaves, hay, branches or a similar "soft" landing position, the quickest and most convenient way to reach a lower level is to perform a **Leap of Faith**. Tilt 🕹 in the direction of the required landing position, hold RT/R1, then tap Ⓐ/⊗ to perform a spectacular swan dive. Though you can perform a Leap of Faith from any position within reasonable range of an appropriate hiding place, the presence of a suitable landing point below is often signposted by the location of birds or bird droppings.

As the 🕹 + RT/R1 combination either initiates a climb or partially "locks" Haytham to a free run course on contact with solid objects, the act of climbing over a fence or equivalent low obstruction can lead him to pause briefly as he hops onto the surface. To **vault** such objects in a more fluid (and slightly faster) fashion, press and hold Ⓐ/⊗ or Ⓑ/Ⓞ as you approach them.

With free running and climbing, route recognition is the key to everything. The real challenge isn't the use of 🕹 to move: it's judicious use of Ⓡ to command the camera, enabling you to identify, plan and adapt your route throughout any given pursuit, escape or journey. In short, the essence of becoming a master at climbing and free running is being able to **read your environment** clearly. As this screenshot illustrates, you shouldn't just see the world in terms of doorways and windows, or barrels, boxes and stalls, but in a more pure sense as ledges and stepping stones that combine to form routes.

01

02

Riding on horseback is the best way to make longer journeys between Boston's districts (◉ 01), and is outright essential once you begin to explore the Frontier. Though later supplanted by the Fast Travel network as a means of travelling quickly while not actively engaged in a mission, taking to the saddle to move between distant waypoints is always significantly faster than travelling on foot.

⊙ Press Ⓐ/Ⓧ to mount a horse, and Ⓑ/Ⓞ to dismount. You can take any horse not occupied by a rider without consequence; those fastened to carts are off-limits.

⊙ Use 🕹 to trot, and hold 🎮/ℝ① to accelerate to a gallop. It's easy to alternate between the two speeds to steer around obstructions. Colliding with civilians leads to nothing more than entreaties and occasional choice epithets, though it pays to avoid Redcoats and other prospective hostiles.

⊙ While galloping, hold Ⓑ/Ⓞ to have Haytham be ready to leap from the saddle; release the button and press 🕹 in the required direction for Haytham to jump. If you pass under a low beam or branch while holding Ⓑ/Ⓞ, Haytham will automatically jump up to grab it

⊙ While in the Frontier, you can also tap Ⓐ/Ⓧ to spur the horse for greater speed; space these out to avoid tiring your steed. This ability is not available in cities.

⊙ Though it's little more than showmanship, tap Ⓐ/Ⓧ while the horse is moving at a walking pace to rear up. This will startle nearby civilians and draw attention to Haytham.

⊙ Select the Horse Whistle tool (see page 57) and press Ⓨ/△ to call Haytham's horse instantly.

Though you will have little direct cause to take to water during the opening hours of play, Haytham is a capable swimmer.

⊙ Use 🕹 to move in water, and hold 🎮/ℝ① to increase Haytham's stroke rate (◉ 02).

⊙ Press and hold Ⓑ/Ⓞ to dive beneath the surface, disappearing from view. You can still move with 🕹, though at greatly reduced speed. This is perfect for evading the gaze of sentries while infiltrating guarded areas via water, or to avoid gunshots during an escape.

⊙ Haytham will automatically switch to wading in shallow water. To climb onto a surface above his position but within his grasp, either hold 🕹 + 🎮/ℝ① and steer Haytham in the appropriate direction, or just tap Ⓐ/Ⓧ in close proximity.

When you first arrive in Boston, the entire map (and, by extension, mini-map) is blank, with the exception of a small area surrounding Haytham's immediate position. You can uncover portions of this obscuring fog simply by moving around. At street level, this will form slim tunnels that barely uncover streets in their entirety, let alone surrounding buildings. The degree of terrain revealed is increased if you explore at higher elevations, but unveiling the entire map by this method would be excessively time-consuming. Fortunately, there is a much easier way.

Boston is dotted with lofty vantages that Haytham can scale, known as **Viewpoints** (03) and marked with a distinctive icon on the main map and mini-map. After reaching the appropriate summit or perch, you can press B/O to have Desmond "Synchronize" with his ancestor's environment.

Synchronizing at a Viewpoint immediately reveals the surrounding terrain, including any points of interest in that vicinity (which, in time, will include side quest start positions and other optional activities).

## MAIN MAP

You can access the main map at any time during active play by pressing ◀/SELECT (04). Haytham's position is represented by the hooded Assassin icon, with the accompanying arrow corresponding to the direction that the camera is facing – not Haytham himself.

Use L to navigate the menu on the left-hand side of the screen. R is used to move around the map, while LT & RT/L1 & R1 enable you to control the zoom level – and, by zooming out entirely, to view a separate map of the entire region. You can view a complete legend for all in-game and map icons by pressing LB/L2. To see a description of an icon on the map, move the cursor over it.

During the early stages of the game, the map menus are incomplete, with further entries introduced as you progress through the storyline. For now, you have access to Filters – which enable you to limit map icons to specific categories to more easily find what you are looking for – and the Collectibles section of the Logbook menu.

Though the main map screen is useful for route planning and gaining an understanding of the distances involved in many endeavors, one of its most useful features is the ability to set a **manual waypoint marker** with A/X. This can be used to explore without losing your bearings, or to break longer journeys into sections – for example, to ensure that a long ride on horseback only follows spacious roads to maximize speed. Using it to highlight a map icon (such as a shop or Viewpoint) will make the site in question appear on the mini-map, even if it is a great distance away. For more complicated and lengthy travels, using such markers can make it much easier to take an efficient route.

### FAST TRAVEL

Though not relevant or necessary during the first two Sequences, you can select icons that mark transitions between maps with A/X to Fast Travel instantly to those locations. As the story progresses, new Fast Travel locations are added to enable swift movement over both long and relatively short distances.

## MINI-MAP

The mini-map shows a small portion of the main map (05). The arrow on the outer edge of the mini-map always points north. The arrow in the center represents Haytham.

All places of interest, points of interactivity and active waypoints within Synchronized areas are marked by icons on the mini-map. Main routes (such as streets, alleyways and dirt paths) are lighter in tone than the dark outlines of the buildings that surround them; a similar color-coding applies in rural areas.

Many icons on the mini-map only appear when they lie within its boundaries. Those representing shops or side quests, for example, shrink and disappear from view as Haytham moves away from them.

Some icons appear at all times. Memory Start locations for main story missions, objective-specific waypoints and manual markers (placed on the main map) are always clearly displayed. If these destinations lie outside of the current mini-map area, the icons will move to the outer rim of the display to indicate their approximate location.

Icons situated at a different elevation to Haytham (such as Redcoats on the streets below as he bounds over rooftops) appear slightly faded on the mini-map.

| KEY MAP ICONS | |
|---|---|
| | Main Mission |
| | Ally |
| | Target |
| | Destination |
| | Enemy |
| | Viewpoint |

Though the opening hour of Assassin's Creed III takes place in relatively small environments, Sequence 02 marks a transition to the vast, open-plan sprawl of Boston. One of the biggest challenges after reaching this milestone is to learn the rules and idiosyncrasies of a quite remarkable sandbox environment, and the behaviors of those who inhabit it. It's also rather important to begin the process at an early stage: the world Haytham arrives in will only grow and become more detailed in time.

Broadly speaking, there are five distinct categories of non-player character in Assassin's Creed 3.

1. **Civilians** make up the vast majority of individuals that you will encounter on your travels, and present no threat to Haytham; indeed, their presence often enables him to hide in plain sight through the essential Blending ability (see page 43). There is no real profit to be had by harming them, and repeatedly attempting to do so (isolated accidents notwithstanding) will actually return you to a previous checkpoint. In areas marked with the ⬔ icon, select groups of civilians will attempt to restrain enemies that seek to harm Haytham, facilitating easy kills or a less complicated escape from combat.

2. **Orphans**, in contrast to often ambivalent civilians, are a nuisance that may test your patience – and yet, the same prohibition on direct acts of violence applies. These groups of small children will beseech Haytham for coins, moving into his path to block his progress (📷 01). They have the potential to disrupt your plans by causing unfriendly eyes to alight on the unfolding spectacle. Fortunately, orphans only operate in fixed zones, and will lose interest outside of those boundaries. Should you attract their attention, your options are as follows:

   ⊙ **Avoid them:** if there is no cause for stealth, just run straight past.

   ⊙ **Pay them off:** the Throw Money ability (see page 45) will bring their pestering or threats to an end.

   ⊙ **Intimidate them:** drawing a weapon may cause orphans to pause, but they will soon resume their irksome onslaught with the realization that Haytham doesn't really intend to use it.

3. **Combatants** include Redcoat patrols (📷 02), rooftop sentries, and a wide variety of mission-specific targets that often attack on sight. Any individual who might potentially enter into combat with Haytham is represented on the mini-map by a red dot. You can avoid needless conflict with the soldiers who patrol Boston and the Frontier by following these simple rules:

   ⊙ Pay all patrols and guards a wide berth. Avoid accidental collisions. If a patrolling Redcoat is barged, he will usually move to rebuke Haytham. Stand still, and the situation need not escalate; run, and it could lead to conflict.

   ⊙ Avoid illegal or excessively extravagant actions while Haytham is in sight of patrols or sentries: these may be regarded as a direct provocation. Common sense will usually suffice, but you'll gradually acquire an appreciation of what you can and can't get away with.

   ⊙ Avoid Restricted Areas marked in red on the mini-map unless you actively need to enter. Trespassing will lead to automatic conflict once Haytham has been identified as an interloper.

4. **Allies** may accompany Haytham in his endeavors during certain missions; they are marked by a blue hexagon that can be seen through solid objects over greater distances, and by a blue dot on the mini-map. You are usually enjoined to protect them at all costs, though many of them are happy to dive into the fray in the event of hostilities. In some instances, allies can be issued the following instructions:

01

02

QUICKSTART

THE STORY
SO FAR

→ PRIMER

WALKTHROUGH

SIDE QUESTS

REFERENCE &
ANALYSIS

MULTIPLAYER

EXTRAS

MAP LEGEND

INDEX

GAME
PROGRESSION

MOVEMENT &
NAVIGATION

VIEWPOINTS &
MAPS

→ SOCIAL
INTERACTION

STEALTH

STEALTH
ABILITIES

ASSASSINATIONS

ESCAPING

COMBAT

ENEMY
ARCHETYPES

INTERFACE &
CONTROLS

100%
SYNCHRONIZATION

⊙ To ask an ally to temporarily stop following Haytham, approach them and press 🅱/◎. Use the same procedure and button to ask them to accompany him once again.

⊙ To request an ally to take refuge in a suitable hiding place – see page 44 – target a suitable position with 🄻🅃/🄻1, then tap 🅱/◎. Press the latter button again in close proximity to their hiding place to ask them to emerge.

5. **Vendors** are individuals that offer some form of service or meaningful interaction (such as a shopkeeper), or represent the start point for a mission or activity. Press 🅱/◎ when a suitable prompt appears to begin.

⊙ When you approach an individual who acts as the trigger for a mission or side quest, certain details appear as an onscreen overlay (such as the name of a mission). Later in the adventure, this will enable you to easily identify optional activities and study their parameters in our Side Quests chapter before you commit to playing them.

⊙ With shopkeepers, pressing 🅱/◎ brings up an interface where you can browse their wares, and buy or sell items.

⊙ You will periodically encounter individuals who are highlighted on the mini-map by the 🗨 icon. Approach them and press 🅱/◎ to have Haytham take part in optional conversations. These are not critical to your progression, but often provide illuminating background information as you learn more about the game world, and the key players in its story.

⊙ The dice icon (🎲) indicates that Haytham can take part in a minigame with a friendly opponent at the location marked on the mini-map.

Much of what you encounter in Boston can be understood as a matter of simple common sense. Those who are charged to uphold laws, for example, will take a dim view of those who disregard them. In time, you'll clearly see how the city functions in a manner akin to a clockwork engine. By observing and coming to understand the rhythms of its mechanisms, such as the way in which soldiers might patrol on cue, you can devise and execute plans to exploit its predictability – and more easily adapt when scripted set-pieces and surprises occur.

Though extraordinarily well-versed in a multitude of combat disciplines, there are many instances where Haytham's interests are best served by avoiding open conflict. You will soon take part in scenarios where stealth is mandatory, or leads to a more rewarding outcome. In this section, we'll look at the many ways in which you can stay out of conflict, keep casualties to a bare minimum, and gradually acquire the ability to infiltrate heavily guarded areas with aplomb.

## LOW PROFILE AND HIGH PROFILE

The first lesson you should learn about stealth in Assassin's Creed III is that if you can't stay out of sight, you should at least do your utmost to be as unobtrusive as possible until you can disappear. There is a clear distinction made between the types of actions you can perform. Those that are described as High Profile – such as sprinting, free running and attacking – are likely to draw attention, whereas Low Profile behavior pretty much entails acting like a nondescript citizen. As a general rule of thumb, actions performed while holding 𝗥𝗧/𝗥𝟭 belong to the High Profile category, and are often incompatible with stealth approaches.

Before we continue, it's worth taking a moment to underline the importance of the (Low Profile) Fast Walk ability (hold 𝗟 + 𝗔/✕) in stealth situations. This makes Haytham adopt a more purposeful stride than the basic walk, but does not attract any greater degree of attention than his default gait. If you need to move in plain sight from one place of concealment to another, this is often the best way to do so.

## SOCIAL STATUS INDICATORS

01

Yellow, down-facing triangles known as Social Status Indicators (SSI) appear above potential hostiles whenever Haytham is arousing their suspicion (📷 01). This is the first stage in a system known as the Detection Loop, which underpins all stealth-based gameplay in Assassin's Creed III. These visual indicators are accompanied by distinctive audio prompts, and appear under the following basic conditions:

◉ If Haytham performs antisocial or extravagant, High Profile actions – such as climbing, free running over rooftops, acts of violence or theft.

◉ Whenever Haytham is seen trespassing in a Restricted Area, marked in red on the mini-map, or if his current objective leads him to a place where his presence is not welcome.

◉ If Haytham is known to potential assailants: some Memories feature situations where guards will attack once they identify him.

◉ Special conditions that determine that certain individuals are set at a high state of anxiety or alertness – for example, a target that you must follow as a mission objective.

The Detection Loop has very distinct stages:

◉ During the first phase, the triangular Social Status Indicators gradually fill with a yellow hue while Haytham remains in range within an enemy's field of vision. Retreating calmly to a safe distance, hiding, or just breaking the direct line of sight between Haytham and potential assailants, will clear the gauge.

When you begin to employ stealth techniques regularly, you'll soon come to appreciate that the first stage of detection is something to respect, but not fear – especially when enemies are distant. In a sense, it represents the kind of casual curiosity or suspicion that can be allayed instantly. On noticing Haytham, a guard might think: "What's his business here?" When you walk calmly out of sight, with no opportunity for real scrutiny, the guard dismisses the thought without hesitation.

◉ Once the gauge is completely yellow, the second stage begins. As it fills with a red hue, potential hostiles will actively pay attention to Haytham, and will often approach him to investigate. The best way to evade this heightened scrutiny is to move out of sight and put at least one additional corner between you and the investigating party or group. Potential hostiles will always move to Haytham's last known location. If they find nothing there, or within the immediate area, they will soon return to their posts or patrols.

◉ When Haytham cannot be seen by an opponent compelled to investigate, the potential hostile is marked by a gray triangle – and the detection process temporarily stalls. As detection meters can be seen through solid surfaces, you can use this feature to judge where best to hide.

◉ When a Social Status Indicator is completely red, Haytham is identified, which will cause all nearby antagonists to attack. If your current objectives specify that he must remain unseen, this will cause immediate Desynchronization – and a return to the last saved checkpoint. Once hostilities commence, all potential adversaries in the vicinity will seek to engage Haytham in combat, or give chase if he attempts to flee the scene. You can resolve the situation by killing all active hostiles, or escaping.

◉ In some situations, particularly when Haytham is trespassing, the initial "suspicion" phase is greatly accelerated – and there are even instances where guards practically attack on sight. In such moments, ensuring that you do not enter their field of view is of paramount importance.

◉ It's worth noting that the detection range of guards is reduced during severe weather, such as heavy rain or thick snowfall.

III

QUICKSTART

THE STORY
SO FAR

PRIMER

WALKTHROUGH

SIDE QUESTS

REFERENCE &
ANALYSIS

MULTIPLAYER

EXTRAS

MAP LEGEND

INDEX

GAME
PROGRESSION

MOVEMENT &
NAVIGATION

VIEWPOINTS &
MAPS

SOCIAL
INTERACTION

STEALTH

STEALTH
ABILITIES

ASSASSINATIONS

ESCAPING

COMBAT

ENEMY
ARCHETYPES

INTERFACE &
CONTROLS

100%
SYNCHRONIZATION

## LINE OF SIGHT

Guards can only see Haytham if he moves into their line of sight: a broad, invisible yet predictable "cone" of vision that extends in the direction they are facing, but not through solid obstacles such as walls or carts ( 02). Guards are not generally blessed with great peripheral vision, and will disregard Haytham over long distances (usually anything greater than 25 meters).

When Haytham is required to follow targets and keep them within sight, different rules apply. In such instances, it isn't Haytham's actual field of vision that is taken into account – it is only required that your targets remain visible to you on the screen, irrespective of what Haytham himself sees. Haytham can be standing facing a wall, yet you can maintain unbroken "visual" contact by positioning the camera with 🔘.

## BLENDING

When in close proximity to two or more civilians, Haytham will automatically "Blend" with them, enabling him to hide in plain sight. In bustling urban areas, Blending is the most common and effortless method of avoiding detection. The process of entering and exiting a Blend situation is always accompanied by visual and audio effects.

⊙ Haytham must be standing still or walking to Blend. While Blending, he is effectively invisible to most potential enemies and individuals that he must follow or avoid.

⊙ Entering a Blend will immediately cancel the first stage of the Detection Loop system, emptying the yellow SSI gauges instantly.

⊙ When Haytham exits a Blend, there is a short period of grace where he remains invisible. You can exploit this to transfer seamlessly between different groups of citizens, or move safely out of sight.

⊙ Illegal or reprehensible actions can immediately break a Blend. In open conflict, citizens will often back away or flee from Haytham as he approaches them, which makes Blending impossible.

⊙ In addition to citizens wandering the streets and ad hoc groups engaged in conversation ( 03), you will encounter situations that are tailor-made for an instant Blend opportunity. Look out for citizens leaning against buildings ( 04), or standing examining wares on market stalls: there is usually a space for Haytham to slide into and effortlessly disappear from view.

## USING CORNERS

If you approach and make contact with the edge of any suitably solid corner, Haytham will press his body against it and peer around to regard the area beyond ( 05). This doesn't render him entirely invisible (anyone approaching from certain angles may see him clearly), but it's a great way to get a clear look at a street or any other open expanse without moving into plain view. To leave this position, just move 🕹 away from the surface.

When Haytham needs to escape a pursuing mob, survey his surroundings without potential violent interruptions, or execute a silent assassination, entering a hiding place is often the best course of action. There are many different varieties of hiding place, which we will introduce after these tips and guidelines:

⊙ Direct Haytham into a hiding place to make him disappear. With "soft" hiding places (such as piles of leaves or hay), you can also enter via a Leap of Faith or a standard jump from above.

⊙ If you can break a clear line of sight between Haytham and his pursuers, entering a hiding place and remaining still will usually enable you to end open conflict. If Haytham is seen entering the hiding place, however, he will immediately leap out: you cannot use them while hostile witnesses can see him.

⊙ Hiding places are refuges where Haytham can survey the surrounding area without fear of detection. If you need to plan an infiltration by observing enemy movements, you can wait inside one and use 🅁 (plus indispensable glances at the mini-map) to study and memorize patrol routes.

⊙ Hiding places are also used for some of the most efficient stealth assassination techniques – a topic we'll come to shortly.

This list of hiding places is not exhaustive, but those that we don't detail here are thematically similar to the ones that we *do* illustrate – and, therefore, easy to identify.

Piles of leaves, soft branches, hay or produce – found on the ground, in a stationary container, or carried in a wagon – are the most common form of hiding place.

Any kind of covered shelter or stall, identified by a billowing white sheet, represents an effective (though relatively uncommon) hiding place.

Benches always offer a spare seat on which Haytham can seem entirely unobtrusive.

In addition to carts carrying produce, you can also jump into the back of covered wagons.

Wells are quite rare, but are an effective hiding position when you find them – and the site of one of the more spectacular assassination animations.

## STALKING ZONES

Stalking Zones are patches of undergrowth or foliage where Haytham can hide (📷 06).

⊙ You must walk, not run, into a Stalking Zone to become concealed. As you cross the boundary where the zone begins, Haytham will automatically adopt a crouching position.

⊙ In many ways, Stalking Zones function similar to Blending with civilians. As long as you remain within their boundaries, Haytham is invisible. However, he enters plain sight the moment he stands up, with no "grace" period to move to another place of concealment. For that reason, ensure that unfriendly eyes are facing elsewhere before you emerge.

⊙ Haytham is also invisible to wild animals in Stalking Zones – a feature that becomes more significant later in the story.

06

# SOCIAL & STEALTH ABILITIES

## THROW MONEY & SMOKE BOMBS

Haytham can utilize the Throw Money ability and Smoke Bombs (once acquired or purchased) to great effect in a variety of social and combat situations. These are categorized as "Tools", and therefore activated by pressing ❿/△. To select either for use, open the Tool Wheel (see page 57) by holding 🆁🅱/🆁2, then use 🅡 to pick your required ability.

The **Throw Money** technique is principally a diversionary tactic. When you use this ability, Haytham will hurl a shower of coins (though only a nominal £10 sum) around his current position (📷 01). All civilians and orphans in range will immediately scrabble for the currency; as the brief spectacle unfolds, any unengaged patrols or sentries will turn to watch the commotion. The effect lasts several seconds.

⊙ In a stealth scenario, using the Throw Money ability has definite drawbacks. It may deal with annoying orphans, but removes immediate Blending opportunities as citizens trade dignity for muddy coins; worse, it draws the very kind of attention that you might hope to avoid.

⊙ As a diversionary tactic, it's rather better: having Redcoats turn to face the ensuing scrum enables you to attend to business you might not want them to witness.

⊙ The most efficient use of Throw Money is to complicate life for pursuing adversaries. If Haytham throws coins as he flees along busy streets, he can form impromptu human barriers that will slow down his opponents. It's especially effective when used to block the entrance to a narrow alleyway.

**Smoke Bombs** are items that can only be purchased, or occasionally looted from slain opponents (see page 47). By default, Haytham can carry a maximum of three at once. Though obviously of utility when escaping combat (creating literal "choke points" in narrow passages works brilliantly), dropping Smoke Bombs incapacitates opponents during battles (📷 02), which makes it possible to assassinate them without resistance.

45

## PICKPOCKETING

Pickpocketing is a risky yet moderately profitable way to acquire funds – at least until overshadowed by other means of moneymaking later in the story.

⊙ To pickpocket a civilian, move close behind them and hold **B**/◎. A circular meter will show the progress of the theft (▣ 03); you must stay in close proximity (and match stride with moving targets)

until the meter is filled to successfully complete the lift. This usually yields a small sum of money, and – unless the civilian turns to discover the crime in progress – rarely arouses their suspicion.

⊙ To continue pickpocketing the same mark in search of additional loot, keep holding **B**/◎ until the theft meter fills for a second time. This almost consistently causes the victim to stop, check their person, and turn in search of the thief. If you can put distance between Haytham and the crime (or, better still, Blend with nearby civilians), you can completely avoid detection – the Fast Walk ability (**L** + **A**/⊗) is perfect for this purpose.

⊙ If Haytham is identified as the culprit, his furious mark will denounce him as a cutpurse – and may even push him briefly before fleeing from the scene. In busy streets, this will lead to a boo of derision, and civilians will back away from Haytham for a time (which makes it impossible to Blend). More pressingly, any patrols or guards within range will immediately engage Haytham in combat. As a rule, it's wise to avoid the activity whenever there are Redcoats nearby.

## WHISTLING

Whenever Haytham is hidden within a hiding place or pressed against a corner, you can push **B**/◎ to have him whistle to attract the attention of nearby guards, who will move to investigate.

⊙ This is obviously a great way to set up Low Profile assassinations, but only if there is a single guard within range.

⊙ If there are multiple targets, whistling might not seem like the most prudent course of action – but it can actually be a simple yet efficient diversionary tactic to draw patrols off course, or pull guards from their posts. If there is no cause to avoid combat, it's a good way to lure opponents to a secluded spot where conflict is less likely to attract the attention of reinforcements.

## LOOTING & HIDING BODIES

04

The aftermath of any confrontation, from silent assassinations to pitched brawls with multiple protagonists, generally leaves Haytham standing over at least one fresh corpse. Though distasteful to some – civilians will be repelled by such behavior, and patrols who witness the act compelled to remonstrate with vigor – the practice of looting slain foes offers a vital way to replenish your stocks of consumable items.

- To loot a body, stand over it and hold **B**/**◎** (📷 04). The action will complete once the onscreen meter has been filled. If you have multiple bodies to search, try holding the button constantly as you move around, releasing **L2** only to conduct each search. This speeds the process up, and prevents instances where you perform other contextual interactions by mistake.

- Most adversaries relinquish practical items (particularly ammunition) and a small sum of currency. The value of what Haytham finds is governed by the rank and station of the former owner.

- If you regularly engage in bouts of looting after battles, you need never waste funds on Cartridges, or needlessly find your pistol empty in a subsequent confrontation.

Many stealth situations call for assassinations that leave a troublesome corpse in plain view for a later patrol to discover. If Haytham will be staying in the vicinity, this might upset carefully laid plans. Tap **B**/**◎** while standing above a corpse to pick it up. Haytham's movement speed will be reduced while he is carrying it. Tap the same button again to drop the body. While it's often enough to just move corpses out of sight, note that you can also drop them into hiding places, Stalking Zones and deep water, disposing of them permanently (📷 05).

05

## INTERACTING WITH ANIMALS

06

More of an atmospheric detail than an ability with practical use, press **B**/**◎** to interact with domestic animals such as dogs, cats, chickens and goats (📷 06).

### EAGLE VISION

07

An ability that defies easy categorization, Eagle Vision has many different applications. After you press **⬆**/**L3** to activate it, Haytham's perception of the world around him changes (📷 07). It enables him to easily identify certain characteristics in the things he beholds in his environment.

- Eagle Vision can be employed to find objects or individuals of note in many missions. Whenever Haytham needs to investigate an area for clues, this uncanny ability highlights where he should look.

- Though of less relevance during earlier Sequences, Eagle Vision also makes clue icons (🔎) visible through certain solid objects.

- There is a distinctive color scheme in Eagle Vision: objective-specific targets are gold; enemies are red; allies are blue; most citizens have no hue at all, save for a white aura surrounding those that offer Blending opportunities. Points of interest (including hiding places, Stalking Zones and areas of special interactivity) are also highlighted by a distinct white glow.

- In heavy rain or snowstorms, Eagle Vision can make it easier to find your way and detect threats, despite its attendant reduced field of view.

01

If stealth scenarios in Assassin's Creed III can be described as a kind of clockwork apparatus, then assassination techniques are the means by which you can break or interrupt the smooth operation of such engines. Whenever there is a need to infiltrate a guarded area, a mixture of sentries and patrols are placed to make it difficult to travel between waypoints without detection. Performing silent assassinations enables you to remove select cogs and wheels, so that a machine designed to prevent your safe passage ceases to function as intended.

There are many different contextual assassination techniques, though they can be separated into two groups: those that are **Low Profile**, thus suitable for stealth situations, and **High Profile** kills that are much more likely to attract attention. As a general rule of thumb, an assassination performed with ✗/□ alone will be low-key in nature, while holding ⊞/⊞ will lead to a more showy and violent killing move.

Before we document the various types of assassination techniques, here are a few useful guidelines:

- ⊙ High Profile assassinations function at a greater range than their more discrete Low Profile equivalents. If a target won't move within range for a stealth kill, and potential witnesses are looking or moving elsewhere, it's often easier to just go for the spectacular kill and hide the body afterwards.

- ⊙ Pay close attention to the highlight (📷 01) that signifies your current target when you perform assassinations, particularly aerial kills. Be sure to adjust Haytham's position and the camera to select the correct opponent.

- ⊙ Haytham will automatically use his Hidden Blade for most assassinations, but will occasionally use his current selected weapon while stalking a target on foot. Use the Weapon Wheel to manually select the Hidden Blade in advance to avoid this: kills with other weapons can be noisier and more protracted.

**Standard Assassination:** Performed while level with a target.

- ⊙ **Low Profile:** Haytham will stab his target discretely, though this will still lead to consequences in plain view of others. It's highly effective when employed from behind on a single sentry or patrolling guard; use the Fast Walk ability to close the gap without creating noise.

- ⊙ **High Profile:** Haytham will leap and knock the target to the ground as he delivers the killing blow. Note that this can be performed while running.

**Double Assassination:** Performed while level with two aligned targets in close proximity.

- ⊙ **Low Profile:** Haytham will reach out and stab both victims simultaneously.

- ⊙ **High Profile:** Haytham will leap and knock both targets to the ground.

**Air Assassination:** Performed from above a target.

⊙ **High Profile Only:** Haytham will leap onto the highlighted victim from above, killing them instantly. This move can take down two targets in close proximity.

**Ledge Assassination:** Performed while hanging from a ledge just below a target.

⊙ **Low Profile:** Haytham will reach out to grab (and stab) the target, then hurl them over the ledge. This is useful if there are other hostiles on the same level that you really need to avoid, but not so great if there are patrols or guards below.

⊙ **High Profile:** Haytham leaps up and knocks his quarry to the ground to perform the killing blow. This is the most efficient technique against solitary rooftop sentries.

**Hiding Place Assassination:** Performed from any kind of hiding place.

⊙ **Low Profile:** Haytham will reach out and simultaneously grab and stab a target within range, then pull them into his place of concealment. (One notable exception: if sitting on a bench, Haytham will expertly stab his quarry and discretely lower them into his previous sitting position – therefore losing his place of concealment.)

⊙ **High Profile:** Haytham will leap out to stab a passing adversary.

**Corner Assassination:** Only available when pressed against a suitable surface.

⊙ **Low Profile:** Haytham quickly rounds the corner, stabs the victim, then pulls them back and lowers them to the floor.

⊙ **High Profile:** Haytham bursts into view to leap on his quarry.

**Stalking Zone Assassination:** Only available when concealed in a Stalking Zone.

⊙ **Low Profile:** Haytham will pull his target into the undergrowth to perform the kill, leaving the body concealed.

⊙ **High Profile:** Haytham will jump out to kill a target within range.

## NON-LETHAL TAKEDOWNS

Some missions have Optional Objectives that specify that Haytham should not kill any adversaries. In these instances, the full repertoire of assassination moves is of little use for those seeking 100% Synchronization – and yet there is one technique that you can use against solitary opponents: switch to Unarmed. If you then sneak up behind a target and tap ❌/⬜, Haytham will silently incapacitate them.

III

QUICKSTART

THE STORY
SO FAR

PRIMER

WALKTHROUGH

SIDE QUESTS

REFERENCE &
ANALYSIS

MULTIPLAYER

EXTRAS

MAP LEGEND

INDEX

GAME
PROGRESSION

MOVEMENT &
NAVIGATION

VIEWPOINTS &
MAPS

SOCIAL
INTERACTION

STEALTH

STEALTH
ABILITIES

ASSASSINATIONS

ESCAPING

COMBAT

ENEMY
ARCHETYPES

INTERFACE &
CONTROLS

100%
SYNCHRONIZATION

It doesn't take a great deal of provocation to incite many of Haytham's potential adversaries to violence, or to fail to evade detection during an attempted infiltration. While fighting for a resolution can be a valid strategy, flight is sometimes a more sensible solution. It's a good idea to at least familiarize yourself with escape techniques during early Sequences, even if your enjoyment of battles usually leads you to be otherwise inclined.

- ⊙ The first step to escaping is naturally to turn tail and run, moving Haytham out of sight of his chasing opponents. At this stage, the Throw Money ability and Smoke Bombs (see page 45) can be highly effective. Enemies will move to block streets as you encounter them, or stand and open fire if you attempt to climb or free run.

- ⊙ Once you move out of view, a large yellow circle on the mini-map (📷 01)

represents the area where Haytham's opponents will actively search for him ( ▼ ). If you can move out of this zone without attracting further attention, or find a secluded place of refuge (like a hiding place, a Stalking Zone or a crowd to blend in) without being seen, the hostiles will eventually give up the chase. If Haytham is spotted by an alert opponent, however, the circle will be reset to his current location – prolonging the pursuit.

- ⊙ Using free run courses and taking to the rooftops can be an effective way to put distance between Haytham and the soldiers on his tail, but sentries posted on top of buildings may spot him from a long distance. Pay these a wide berth if you can. From an elevated position, a Leap of Faith into a hiding place often works well to end a chase.

- ⊙ If you are close to a large expanse of water, taking a plunge and swimming away from the shore is an easy way to escape. No matter how furious your pursuers may be, their ire is always quelled by the prospect of getting their feet wet. Well, once you move out of musket range, that is. If your adversaries open fire, dive beneath the surface immediately.

There are two new methods of escape in Assassin's Creed III that warrant a special introduction. Both function in a similar fashion: they do not end the pursuit, but put an impassable barrier between Haytham and any adversaries immediately behind him. Players who enjoyed the multiplayer modes in Brotherhood and Revelations will recognize these techniques as being identical in spirit to the Chase Breaker device.

Whenever you espy a building with an open door, Haytham can sprint through it to leave his opponents oblivious to his whereabouts.

If you see a gap below a fence section, run Haytham towards it (with RT/R1 held) to have him slide underneath.

# COMBAT

QUICKSTART

THE STORY
SO FAR

PRIMER

WALKTHROUGH

SIDE QUESTS

REFERENCE &
ANALYSIS

MULTIPLAYER

EXTRAS

MAP LEGEND

INDEX

GAME
PROGRESSION

MOVEMENT &
NAVIGATION

VIEWPOINTS &
MAPS

SOCIAL
INTERACTION

STEALTH

STEALTH
ABILITIES

ASSASSINATIONS

ESCAPING

COMBAT

ENEMY
ARCHETYPES

INTERFACE &
CONTROLS

100%
SYNCHRONIZATION

Haytham rarely fights a single adversary at a time once his story is well and truly underway, with the vast majority of confrontations pitting him against several opponents at once. A successful confrontation, then, is one that ends swiftly – so introducing ways to beat opponents decisively is a major feature of this section.

As the Assassin's Creed III combat system evolves over the course of the story, introducing new weapons, enemy archetypes and a need for greater tactical nuance, the advice we offer here is designed to cover fundamental necessities and techniques with lasting utility. Once open conflict becomes more demanding in later Sequences, you'll find plenty of essential stats and strategies in the Reference & Analysis chapter.

## COMBAT BASICS

- **Combat Mode:** Once a fight begins, Haytham will automatically adopt a combat stance, and turn to face the enemy you direct him towards. Pay close attention to the highlight that signifies your current target: this shows at all times who you will be attacking. To change this, simply tilt 🕹 in the direction of your preferred target.

- **Attack/Combo Attack:** To launch a melee attack on an opponent, press 🅧/⬜. The amount of strikes required before an opponent falls depends on the weapon type used. Attacking in this fashion is generally only of use when you face few opponents, or a single strong adversary. In battles featuring numerous assailants, you will be far more effective if you employ a counterattacking strategy, a topic that we cover overleaf.

- **Parry:** Hold 🅱/◎ to make Haytham automatically block incoming melee attacks. Early in the story, when you face weak and generic opponents, this makes Haytham effectively invincible, but certain enemy archetypes introduced in later Sequences can break a Parry to create an opening for a follow-up attack.

- **Weapon Swipe:** Press 🅰/🅧 to perform a Weapon Swipe. This temporarily breaks an opponent's guard, enabling Haytham to launch an assault before they recover. This is generally less important in early Sequences, as so few opponents have the ability to deflect the opening blow in a combo. Some adversaries you meet later, however, are effectively untouchable unless you employ this vital "softening up" attack. Performing two consecutive Weapon Swipes on an opponent will cause Haytham to kick their feet from underneath them, rendering them vulnerable to an instant killing blow as they lie on the ground (📷 01).

- **Collecting & Dropping Weapons:** Outside of combat, tap 🅱/◎ to collect or drop weapons. During a fight, you'll need to hold 🎮/R1 while you tap the button to achieve the same result. The safest way to immediately drop an acquired weapon is to use the Weapon & Tool Wheel, or the Quick Inventory function: see page 57.

- **Tackle:** A non-lethal technique, Tackle is employed while sprinting with 🎮/R1 to knock a target to the ground. When Haytham is just behind his quarry, tap 🅱/◎ to make him leap and propel them from their feet (📷 02).

- **Escaping a Battle:** To leave active combat, hold 🎮/R1. This restores standard 🕹 control, enabling you to turn tail and escape. When surrounded, it's prudent to Parry an attack beforehand, then immediately make a break for the widest and most suitable gap. Of course, this isn't purely a technique for bidding farewell to a fight: you can use it to reposition Haytham if you feel that the initial battleground doesn't favor him, or if a nearby location offers a strategic advantage. A narrow alleyway, for example, could limit the effectiveness of enemy marksmen.

### THE LIFE BAR

When Haytham is engaged in open conflict or fleeing his aggressors, the Life Bar (situated to the left of the mini-map) is subject to certain limitations. You should notice the varying levels of thickness that divide it into three segments. Whenever damage is sustained in combat, regeneration gradually takes place after a short delay. However, once a segment has been fully depleted, it will not refill until combat ends.

The use of counterattacking moves is the very fundament of the Assassin's Creed III combat system: without them, and their attendant strategies, battles against large groups of opponents become dispiritingly attritional and difficult. Fortunately, they are relatively easy to master with a little practice at an early stage in the story.

To perform a counter, wait until you see the ▲ icon appear above the head of an opponent. This indicates that they are poised to strike with a melee attack. Tap 🅱/◎ to set up your counter. (Don't hold it – this could result in a basic Parry.)

A successful 🅱/◎ press initiates a temporary slow-motion state where you must tap a second button to choose one of four counter moves (see below). If this window of opportunity passes, both the enemy attack and the counter attempt fail.

If two enemies attempt to attack simultaneously – both marked by the distinctive overhead icon – pressing 🅱/◎ alone will lead Haytham to kill both automatically.

With the basic ground rules established, let's examine the four types of counterattack.

1. **Counter Kill:** Press ❌/▢ to kill an opponent instantly. This is by far the most effective and low-risk way to eliminate adversaries in large groups. Though the incredible power of the Counter Kill is tempered by the later introduction of enemies who can evade or parry it – at least until sufficiently weakened – it's the pillar of sound combat strategy throughout the entire adventure.

2. **Counter Disarm:** Press Ⓐ/⊗ to make Haytham deftly disarm his attacker. If Haytham is unarmed or using the Hidden Blades, he will claim his opponent's weapon as his own; if he is already using another type of weapon, the opponent's weapon will simply drop to the ground. To discard a weapon acquired from an adversary (which, in earlier Sequences, is generally a musket), just select one of your own weapons.

3. **Counter Throw:** Press 🅱/◎ to hurl an opponent aside. You can use 🄻 to influence the throwing direction. Thrown enemies can be finished with a single attack if you can reach them before they clamber to their feet. Propelling enemies from high buildings or into water is also fatal. If there is a balustrade or other form of low barrier in their path, they will often tumble over it.

4. **Special Counter:** Press Ⓨ/△ to make Haytham counterattack with a weapon selected as his current Tool (which, for Haytham, means the pistol or an acquired musket only). When employed against generic soldiers, this might seem like a waste of a bullet, and hardly worth the time required to reload once the battle is over. The true utility of the Special Counter, though, is only revealed when you later face enemy archetypes who are resistant to the Counter Kill move. Where that fails, a pistol-based Special Counter leads to an instant kill, removing a powerful opponent from the field. If you have no suitable weapon selected, or your pistol is unloaded, Haytham will attempt a standard Counter Kill instead.

A Kill Streak is a combat technique whereby multiple opponents can be dispatched with instant-death attacks. This aggressive strategy perhaps makes Haytham more vulnerable to enemy attacks, but enables you to cut down several opponents with unflinching alacrity.

To begin a Kill Streak, Haytham must either defeat an adversary with a combo attack, or perform a successful Counter Kill. During the killing animation, press 🕹 towards the opponent you wish to dispatch next (the one highlighted), then press ❌/⬜ to "stack" a subsequent assault. If successful, Haytham will automatically move and lash out, killing your specified target. During this animation, you can use 🕹 and ❌/⬜ to select the next victim. This can, theoretically, be repeated until

all combatants, save the victorious Mr Kenway, lie beaten on the ground.

Kill Streaks end instantly if Haytham takes damage, or fails to make contact with an opponent – usually because they are too distant to reach. In pitched battles with aggressive antagonists, you can cancel a Kill Streak (or, essentially, start a new one) with a counterattacking move if an enemy seems poised to land a blow before Haytham reaches the next target.

The secret to successful Kill Streaks is to identify a route of opponents that will enable you to kill as many as possible in sequence, adapting your course on the fly as you "join" the moving dots (📷 03). However, as with Counter Kills, it's important to recognize that some opponents are resistant to such attacks. This certainly isn't a problem you'll encounter during the opening hours of the adventure, but it will eventually complicate matters by compelling you to avoid such antagonists to keep a Streak active.

Finally, Haytham's current weapon influences the range and speed of Kill Streak attacks.

## CONTEXTUAL TECHNIQUES

Combat situations often call for Haytham to react to events in specific ways, or enable him exploit certain opportunities for swift, uncomplicated takedowns.

### Escape Grab/Counter

Opponents situated close behind Haytham may attempt to restrain him (📷 04), restricting his movements so that their colleagues can lash out without fear of reprisal. If you are quick, you can press ❌/⬜ to counter and foil the move, generally hurling the assailant to the ground. If you do not react in time, press the same button repeatedly until Haytham wrestles free.

### Environment-Based Kills

It can take four or five strikes to down an enemy with a combo attack, but less in situations where the environment offers Haytham a method of dispatching an opponent immediately. As you grow in confidence in combat situations, you'll gradually begin to recognize and exploit opportunities for context-sensitive takedowns.

If an opponent is driven against a solid surface, Haytham might gain an advantage and dispatch them in one or two blows. Should you notice an enemy close to a drop, Haytham can dismissively kick them over the edge. Even if the resultant fall is not fatal, it temporarily removes an enemy from the fray. Knocking adversaries into deep water, however, is consistently lethal. Any enemy foolish enough to stand between Haytham and

any expanse of blue can be shoved or kicked to their doom; those standing further away can be propelled with the Counter Throw move.

Haytham's surroundings can even affect Counter Kills and Kill Streaks – though as these special animations do not in any sense accelerate the process of defeating an enemy, it's a purely visual feature.

### Human Shield

Whenever Haytham fights against large groups of opponents where many are armed with muskets, there is a danger that they will form firing lines – and, after observing a preparatory drill, fire simultaneously. If successful, this leads to significant injury. Fortunately, there are a handful of ways in which this can be avoided.

Once they move into formation, ▲ icons will appear over the heads of all soldiers in the active line ( 05). From this point onward, you can grab any opponent within range to use as a human shield by pressing Ⓐ/Ⓧ. In the final stage before the firing line finishes its preparations, the camera angle will automatically switch to a perspective that shows their position in relation to Haytham. This is the last-chance saloon: a final opportunity to perform the Human Shield contextual action to survive without damage ( 06).

It can take a few attempts to get a feel for how to react to firing line situations. Don't panic if you tend to fail at first. There's a knack to identifying the danger and positioning yourself close to a suitable shield. What's more, it's not always strictly necessary to have an opponent nearby to avoid injury.

- ◉ Firing lines can be foiled by moving behind cover, which is easier if you break out of combat mode by holding Ⓛ and ℝ𝕋/ℝ1.

- ◉ If you are sufficiently close to the line, a daring option is to hold ℝ𝕋/ℝ1 and sprint directly at them. At extremely close range, their shots will miss – and you can even kill one and cause the line to break before they open fire.

- ◉ With practice, you can still grab an enemy to act as a bullet sponge even when they are rapidly retreating. Hold ℝ𝕋/ℝ1 to break into a run towards the closest candidate, release it as you move within range, then tap Ⓐ/Ⓧ moments afterwards as Haytham slows to a halt.

05

06

The weapons that Haytham can use in early Sequences all have distinct strengths and weaknesses.

#### Sword

- ◉ The sword offers excellent range, which enables Haytham to initiate combos and reach Kill Streak targets over slightly longer distances.

- ◉ It is relatively slow to use, though this is rarely an issue against early opponents.

- ◉ Haytham cannot claim enemy weapons with the Counter Disarm ability while holding a sword.

#### Hidden Blade

- ◉ The Hidden Blade is great for Counter Kills, and notable for the brutal fashion in which Haytham eliminates opponents.

- ◉ Due to its short range, it is less suitable for maintaining long Kill Streaks and combo attacks.

#### Unarmed

- ◉ Unarmed Counter Kills, Kill Streaks and combo-based takedowns are non-lethal, though they do permanently incapacitate the target. If you perform a Counter Disarm while unarmed, Haytham will adopt his enemy's weapon for subsequent attacks.

- ◉ Can be very effective if employed in a pure counterattacking strategy.

- ◉ Haytham cannot Parry attacks while unarmed against armed opponents – you must either counter, or submit to an incoming blow.

#### Pistol

- ◉ Hold Ⓨ/△ to aim the pistol at a highlighted target, then release the button to fire. To cancel a shot with the button still held, tap Ⓑ/Ⓞ.

- ◉ Haytham's pistol is only good for a single shot in active combat, due to its tortuously slow reload time.

- ◉ The pistol is better suited to use outside of open conflict, particularly to eliminate specific adversaries. To aim manually, hold 𝕃𝕋/𝕃1 to enter Precision Mode. Move the cursor over the required target, then press Ⓨ/△ to fire. Precision Mode increases the range of all firearms.

#### Musket

- ◉ Muskets can be taken from enemies during a battle with the Counter Disarm move, or collected from the ground (or a gun rack) by tapping Ⓑ/Ⓞ.

- ◉ Muskets are fired in exactly the same way as pistols (though they have superior range and damage), but also function as melee weapons. They are suitable for all basic moves and counters.

# ENEMY ARCHETYPES

We cover all of the different enemy varieties (and strategies on how to defeat them with ease) in great detail later in the Reference & Analysis chapter. For now, study the following tips and illustrations to identify and exploit the weaknesses of foes that Haytham faces during early Sequences.

British Regular

## BRITISH REGULAR

- ☉ The most common archetype, and ubiquitous during early Sequences, the British Regular is vulnerable to all attacking moves.

- ☉ Armed with muskets, Regulars can form firing lines that require Haytham to move behind cover or utilize a human shield to avoid injury.

- ☉ Regulars are divided into two sub-types: Militia, who only perform single attacks, and Soldiers, who can execute combos.

## SNIPER

- ☉ These soldiers occupy rooftops, and take a dim view of those who enter their exclusive domain.

- ☉ When they detect Haytham, Snipers will open fire with their muskets after an initial warning.

- ☉ Be very careful while under fire from Snipers: a single hit can cause Haytham to fall while climbing or free running. Press 🅛 towards ledges within reach to grab them.

- ☉ In close proximity, Snipers switch to melee combat. They are functionally identical to British Regulars.

## OFFICER

- ☉ Officers can be identified by their rather ostentatious headgear and use of a sword as primary weapon. They usually march at the head of a patrol, and may stop to investigate hiding places that they pass.

- ☉ They can resist Counter Kills, and will foil the opening blow of a combo (and even counterattack if you insist) unless put off-balance with the Weapon Swipe ability.

- ☉ Officers may draw a pistol to shoot at Haytham independently of other antagonists; grab a human shield, take cover or attack them to prevent them from firing.

- ☉ Disarm them, knock them from their feet with two consecutive Weapon Swipes, or use a Special Counter with the Pistol to defeat them instantly in a fight – or simply avoid them until you defeat their allies.

## SNITCH

- ☉ Snitches do not play an active part in combat encounters. Instead, they will flee the scene in an attempt to locate reinforcements.

- ☉ When they run from conflict, Snitches are represented on the mini-map by the ⬡ icon.

Snitch

Officer

ONSCREEN DISPLAY

OPEN CONFLICT
When conflict is triggered, either kill all enemies, hide, or escape the area.

WARNING: Become anonymous to interact.

Start Mission B

**1** **Life Bar:** This shows Haytham's current state of health. Outside of open conflict, it will always regenerate after a short delay. In combat, only individual sections (as delineated by the three distinct segments of the bar) can regenerate. Lose the first two sections, for example, and they will be unavailable until the battle ends.

**2** **Mini-Map:** This illustrates Haytham's immediate surroundings, including essential details such as potential enemies (red dots) and points of interactivity. See page 39 for details.

**3** **Compass:** The arrow attached to the mini-map always points north.

**4** **Weapon:** This shows Haytham's chosen weapon, or his fists if he is unarmed – the primary attack activated with ✗/▢. You can change the weapon you're using at any time with the Weapon Wheel.

**5** **Tool:** Haytham's currently selected Tool – the secondary attack/ action activated with ✓/△. This can be a ranged weapon (such as a pistol), a special ability (such as Throw Money), or a special device (such as Smoke Bombs). You can change the weapon you're using at any time with the Tool Wheel. Additional Tools are introduced as you progress through the story. If a Tool cannot be used, this icon is dimmed.

**6** **Reload Prompt:** If Haytham has an unloaded firearm equipped, this icon lets you know to reload when an opportunity arises.

**7** **Ammunition:** When Haytham is equipped with a pistol or musket, bars surrounding the Tool icon indicate how many shots it can fire before a reload is required. Loaded cartridges are bright white; spent cartridges are grey.

**8** **Controls HUD:** This section of the display highlights contextual actions that can be performed with Ⓑ/◯ and Ⓐ/✗.

### ANIMUS FEEDBACK SYSTEM

The Animus Feedback System (or AFS) regularly posts text on the screen during play, with the nature and relative importance of the message indicated by its position.

**A** **Goals and warnings** appear in the left-hand corner of the screen. These include mandatory tasks and Optional Objectives.

**B** **Micro-tutorials** and **background information** appear in the right-hand corner of the screen. Whenever a ▶/START prompt appears, you can press the button to automatically visit the Animus Database or in-game manual. If Haytham receives items (such as money or ammunition gained through looting), his new acquisitions are also briefly documented in this space.

**C** **Critical messages**, such as a warning of impending Desynchronization, appear in the center of the screen.

QUICKSTART

THE STORY
SO FAR

PRIMER

WALKTHROUGH

SIDE QUESTS

REFERENCE &
ANALYSIS

MULTIPLAYER

EXTRAS

MAP LEGEND

INDEX

GAME
PROGRESSION

MOVEMENT &
NAVIGATION

VIEWPOINTS &
MAPS

SOCIAL
INTERACTION

STEALTH

STEALTH
ABILITIES

ASSASSINATIONS

ESCAPING

COMBAT

ENEMY
ARCHETYPES

INTERFACE &
CONTROLS

100%
SYNCHRONIZATION

## WEAPON & TOOL WHEEL

Hold **RB**/**R2** to open the Weapon & Tool Wheel interface (📷 01). This freezes the action instantly, even if you are in the thick of combat.

⊙ **Weapon Wheel:** Use 🕹 to select your primary mode of attack from the left-hand Weapon list. Early in the story, Haytham can pick from his sword, Hidden Blade and unarmed combat.

⊙ **Tool Wheel:** 🕹 is used to select an item in the Tool section on the right-hand side of the screen.

⊙ **Quick Inventory:** You can use this menu to assign four items to slots which can be equipped instantly during play with the appropriate press of ✛. To add an item to the Quick Inventory, first highlight it with 🕹 or 🕹, then tap the required ✛ direction.

## PAUSE MENU

Though many features of the Pause menu are self-evident, some perhaps warrant a little further explanation.

⊙ The **DNA Tracker** is used to gauge your performance in all main story Memories and Optional Objectives on your way to 100% Synchronization, or as close as you care to reach. You can also use this menu to replay previous Memories: see page 59 for further details.

⊙ The **Animus Database** offers background information and illustrative material for protagonists, major landmarks and many other points of interest. It is updated regularly as you explore the game world and complete Memories. Whenever you see an exclamation point, this indicates the presence of a new or revised entry.

⊙ **Reload Last Checkpoint** & **Restart Memory** only appear while you are participating in a main Memory or side quest. The former moves you back to one of many checkpoints that divide missions into manageable portions; the latter returns you to the very beginning. These can be extremely useful if you are attempting to complete all Optional Objectives.

⊙ **Leave Animus** ends Desmond's current session in the machine (storing his progress up to the last checkpoint), and returns you to the Grand Temple. You can then check his emails on a computer close to the Animus, or engage in optional conversations with his Assassin cohorts. To reenter the Animus, approach it and press any of the primary action buttons.

## DEFAULT CONTROLS SUMMARY

| XBOX 360 | PS3 | SUMMARY |
|---|---|---|
| 🕹 | 🕹 | Used for basic movement; also employed for directing attacks during combat. |
| 🕹 | 🕹 | Used to control the game camera. |
| ✛ | ✛ | Operates the Quick Inventory; used to instantly equip one of four weapons and items. You can customize the available slots via the Weapon & Tool Wheel. |
| Ⓐ | ⓧ | Appears in the Controls HUD; used to perform context-specific actions, but principally to perform manual jumps, the Fast Walk ability, and to break an enemy's defense. |
| Ⓑ | Ⓞ | This is the second button featured in the Controls HUD. As well as being the main button for interactions, it's a regular feature in all areas of the game – particularly climbing (releasing and grabbing ledges) and combat (it's the gateway to the entire counterattacking system). |
| Ⓧ | ▢ | The primary attack button; also used to perform assassinations. |
| Ⓨ | △ | Activates the currently selected Tool. |
| RT | R1 | Hold to switch to High Profile mode, which enables activities such as faster movement, free running and climbing. |
| LT | L1 | Activates Precision Mode, which is generally used to manually aim weapons. You can either hold it for as long as required, then release to return to standard movement, or tap it quickly to toggle it on and off. |
| RB | R2 | Hold to open the Weapon & Tool Wheel, which is used to pick weapons or equipment. Tap it to reload firearms. |
| LB | L2 | Calls allies into the fray. It's only used in specific situations in early Sequences, but grows in significance later in the story. |
| 🔼L | L3 | Activates Eagle Vision. |
| 🔼R | R3 | Forces the game camera to face directly ahead. |
| ▶ START | START | Enters/leaves the Pause menu. When AFS entries appear onscreen alerting you to new Animus Database entries, it can also be used to jump straight to them with a single button press. |
| ◀ BACK | SELECT | Opens the main map. |

## SYNCHRONIZATION

The Assassin's Creed series storyline places its players in the role of Desmond, experiencing the lives of his ancestors through the remarkable virtual reality presented by the Animus. In a strict narrative sense, then, you do not actually control Haytham, for example, but instead direct Desmond as he relives events in the life of his forebear. Desmond's objective is to experience significant moments in Haytham's life with maximum authenticity, and this is where the concept of Synchronization comes into play.

Synchronization is both the measure by which Desmond succeeds in the Animus, and the means by which you can judge your performance in each main Memory and side quest – and, for that matter, the entire game as a whole. Essentially, it's a representation of how much of the game you have completed, 100% Synchronization being the ultimate goal. Almost every mission or task you engage in has a Synchronization score, which is added to your cumulative Synchronization rating after you complete it.

You can view your current Synchronization for individual Memories and total progress via the DNA Tracker tab in the Pause menu.

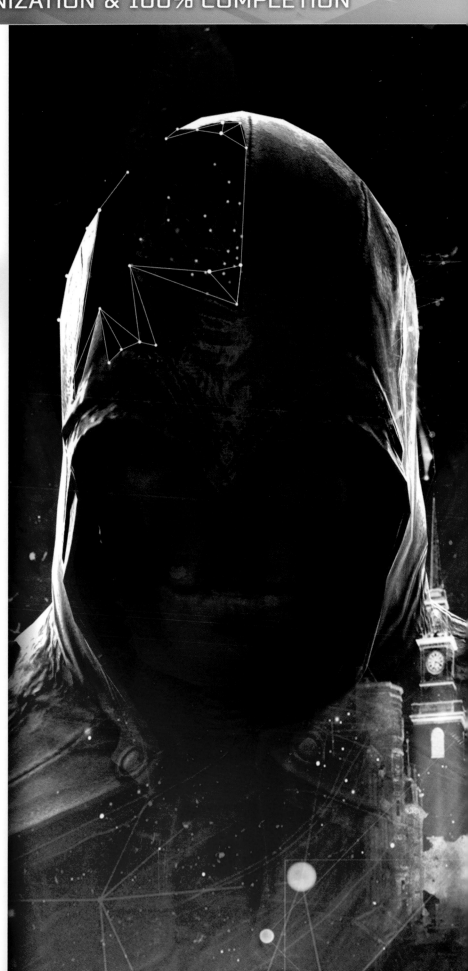

QUICKSTART

THE STORY
SO FAR

PRIMER

WALKTHROUGH

SIDE QUESTS

REFERENCE &
ANALYSIS

MULTIPLAYER

EXTRAS

MAP LEGEND

INDEX

## DESYNCHRONIZATION

While Synchronization is a measure of success, Desynchronization is the consequence of failure. Desmond cannot change the lives of his ancestors, but must experience them with great fidelity. Diverging too radically from the "true" course of events causes Synchronization to be lost.

Desynchronization can occur under the following conditions:

⊙ **Death:** This occurs whenever the Life Bar is reduced to zero. This happens most frequently in combat situations, but is also the result of falls from great heights.

⊙ **Failed objectives:** Failing to comply with key mission parameters will lead to a return to a previous checkpoint.

⊙ **Moving out of bounds:** Attempting to visit a specific locale before the appropriate time, or moving outside the confines of a current mission area can cause a loss of Synchronization. There is a clear visual cue that provides a strident visual warning whenever you approach such boundaries (◉ 01). Take heed, and move away swiftly.

⊙ **Anomalous behavior:** If you attack allies, civilians or domestic animals, Desynchronization will occur if you persist after ignoring an initial message of admonishment. There is, of course, a little leeway. Accidentally striking the wrong individual during a pitched street brawl won't lead to serious repercussions.

In pure gaming terms, if Desynchronization occurs while you are engaged in a mission, you

are returned to a previous checkpoint. These are actually plentiful, dividing individual Memories into manageable portions that call for little in the way of repetition.

While free roaming in the game world, with no active tasks, Desynchronization will restart Haytham in a nearby area with his cause of "death" scrubbed from the record.

## OPTIONAL OBJECTIVES

In addition to mandatory objectives (such as avoiding detection, protecting allies or winning battles), main story missions and many side quests also feature Optional Objectives. Completing a mission might contribute 60% of the Full Synchronization total, but to gain the maximum value, you also need to fulfill the secondary criteria set out in the Optional Objectives.

On one level, these exist to encourage a certain style of play: to make players surrender the assassination abilities and attempt a bloodless infiltration of a heavily guarded area, for example. Others function as a more direct test of your prowess, such as a time limit for the completion of a specific task.

Optional Objectives are not revealed before you start a mission, and are usually introduced at very specific junctures via a pop-up message in the left-hand corner of the screen. Forewarned being forearmed, our Walkthrough and Side Quest chapters detail all of them – and, wherever possible, advice on how they can be beaten.

The main reason to complete Optional Objectives is to increase your Synchronization rating. If this isn't important to you, or you would prefer to return to a challenge later, there is absolutely no penalty for failure. For those who will settle for no less than 100% completion, we would offer the following tips:

⊙ Even if you are trying to play with a bare minimum of assistance, always check the Walkthrough and Side Quest chapters to learn about a Memory's Optional Objectives before you begin. It could be that one condition might be much easier if Haytham has a full stock of Smoke Bombs, for instance, enabling you to prepare in advance.

⊙ If you are poised to fail an Optional Objective, press ▶/(START) and select the Reload Last Checkpoint option to rewind time. If you're playing for perfection, this demands much less effort than replaying the entire mission at a later date.

## DNA TRACKER & MEMORY REPLAY

The DNA Tracker tab in the Pause menu enables you to study your progress in all main missions and side quests to date. In addition to your total Synchronization, you can also check individual Memories to find instances where you are missing an Optional Objective, and replay them if you so wish. The Replay option moves Haytham back in time and places him next to the appropriate Memory Start marker.

⊙ You can leave the Replay at any moment by selecting Abort Memory in the Pause menu.

⊙ Hold **Ⓑ**/**Ⓞ** to jump to the end of cutscenes. Note that certain cinematic sequences (such as short establishing shots or transitions) cannot be skipped.

⊙ Once an Optional Objective has been completed, it cannot be "undone" by replaying a mission. You could conceivably complete one of four in your first attempt, and yet fail that Optional Objective but beat two others on a second playthrough – but it would still remain, along with your new successes.

⊙ Optional Objectives that require you to complete all specified challenges in a single playthrough, however, can only be obtained with a flawless performance.

⊙ You must complete an entire Memory and wait to be returned to the DNA Tracker menu for Optional Objectives to be recorded. Partial playthroughs do *not* count.

GAME
PROGRESSION

MOVEMENT &
NAVIGATION

VIEWPOINTS &
MAPS

SOCIAL
INTERACTION

STEALTH

STEALTH
ABILITIES

ASSASSINATIONS

ESCAPING

COMBAT

ENEMY
ARCHETYPES

INTERFACE &
CONTROLS

100%
SYNCHRONIZATION

# WALKTHROUGH

This chapter has been designed to guide readers through all Main Missions in Assassin's Creed III and, in conjunction with the companion Side Quests chapter, plot a course to a perfect 100% DNA Tracker rating – and, therefore, full game completion.

## ⚠ REFRESHER COURSE

Enter the cave and walk with Desmond's companions until you reach a cinematic interlude. After the second barrier has been opened, move down the steep slope and walk directly ahead to enter the Grand Temple.

Once Desmond is inside the Animus, Sequence 01 (and the Refresher Course Memory) officially begin. Follow the waypoint markers (the green ◉ icon highlighted in the accompanying screenshot), onscreen prompts and Rebecca's spoken instructions to navigate the initial sections of the assault course.

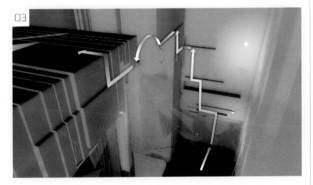

When you reach the first climbing section, follow the route pictured here. For further advice on climbing, see page 35 of the Primer chapter.

### SCREENSHOT ANNOTATION LEGEND

Throughout the Walkthrough chapter, we use annotated screenshots to highlight essential actions or points of specific interest, such as paths you should follow and enemy patrol routes. The following legend details all of the annotations you will encounter, and the simple color code that we employ.

| ANNOTATION | MEANING |
|---|---|
| ➡ | Player character movement |
| ▣▣➡ | Optional player character movement (alternative path or optional challenge) |
| ✕ | Objective/point of interest/point of interactivity |
| ➡ | Enemy movement/patrol route |
| ◯ | Enemy/potential threat |
| ➡ | Ally movement |
| ◯ | Ally |

04

Continue along the linear course until Rebecca introduces the "Optional Objective" concept as you overlook two targets.

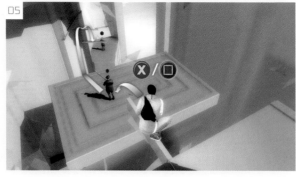

05

Walk to the end of the beam and press ⓧ/□ to perform an air assassination on the first guard, then dispatch the second in a similar fashion.

06

When you reach a beam overlooking a steep slope, perform a manual jump (hold RT/R1 and Ⓛ forward, then press Ⓐ/ⓧ) to reach the next section of the course.

07

Employ a manual jump to cross this large gap safely, then climb the wall to reach the rooftops.

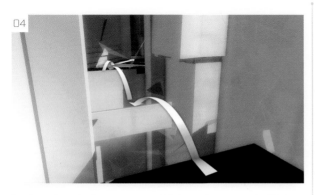

08

Free run over the chimneys, then perform a manual jump to reach the entrance through the archway.

09

Walk along the path until you reach a door, then press Ⓑ/◎ when the prompt appears to enter the world of Haytham Kenway.

01

Walk directly ahead to reach the auditorium, where an attendant will guide Haytham to his seat.

02

During the cutscene, press 👆/L3 to trigger Eagle Vision and identify your target with R.

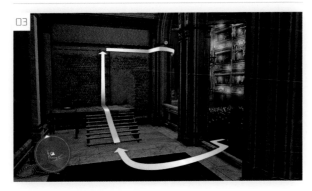

03

When Haytham stands, walk to the left and enter the secluded area at the rear of the auditorium. Climb the ladder, use the ledge to traverse to the right, then move around the corner.

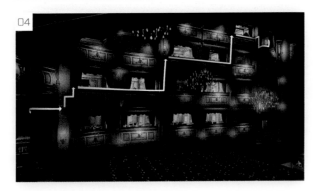

04

Follow the route detailed here to reach a balcony just to the left of the stage, where you can safely climb up. Walk to the highlighted door and unlock it by following the onscreen prompts.

Once backstage, jump from the balcony to reach a small ledge on the "sun and clouds" stage prop.

When the stage prop drops, traverse to the left and climb the ladder.

Climb the ledge to reach the "crescent moon" prop. After another brief plunge, continue left to reach a balcony. Walk into the waypoint to trigger a cinematic.

Follow the waypoint markers to lead Haytham out of the theater. When you reach the crowded doorway pictured here, use the Fast Walk ability to push through. The Memory ends when you reach the building's main entrance.

## MISSION OVERVIEW

| Optional Objectives | Further Reading |
|---|---|
| ■ Limit health loss to 10%.<br>■ Rescue James within 40 seconds. | ■ Read our introductions to free running (page 36) and combat (see page 51). |

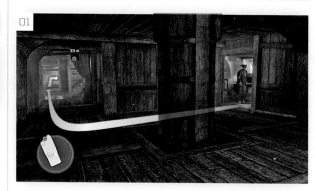

**Day 2:** Leave Haytham's cabin and run to the waypoint at the front of the ship to reach the upper deck. There are some diversions that may pique your curiosity during the short walk: see "Minigames & Optional Conversations" for details.

Approach the second waypoint on the upper deck. After the cinematic ends, you must complete a series of fights that introduce elements of the Assassin's Creed III combat system. An Optional Objective is introduced here; if you fail the damage-based constraint (see "Mission Overview" table), you can use the Reload Last Checkpoint option in the Pause menu to try again. For additional advice to supplement the onscreen prompts, refer to the Combat section of the Primer chapter (page 51). After the third and final bout, accompany the captain to his cabin, then return to Haytham's quarters and interact with the desk to advance the story.

**Day 28:** When play resumes, speak to the sailor at the sole waypoint. When confronted by two avenues of inquiry, head straight for the cook at the back of the galley (pictured). Speak to the nearby James to continue.

Run to the waypoint at the stern, then head to the specified area of the lower deck (highlighted in green on the mini-map). Activate Eagle Vision, then direct Haytham's gaze to regard the barrels highlighted here. Investigate them with Ⓑ/Ⓞ, then return to Haytham's cabin and interact with the desk to advance time.

## MINIGAMES & OPTIONAL CONVERSATIONS

There are two locations below decks where you can play board games, marked with the 🎲 icon. Both games, Fanorona and Nine Men's Morris, are encountered in a variety of locations later in the story (and with wagers to add a little spice to proceedings), so don't feel obliged to take part now. A rule summary appears before you begin a contest.

You can also approach individuals marked by the 🗨 icon and press Ⓑ/Ⓞ to have Haytham strike up a conversation.

05

**Day 33:** During the duel with Mills, use the Counter Disarm move (🅱/◎) when the 🔺 icon appears over his head, then 🅰/❌ when time slows down), then follow up with short combos (see page 51 for further advice). Each time he interrupts Haytham's assault, repeat the process again. Deplete his Life Bar to end the fight. If you want to bring a swift end to the fight, perform a Counter Kill (press ❌/□ when time slows down after a counter).

06

Speak with the captain, then secure the rigging by pressing 🅱/◎ at the locations marked by waypoints; afterwards, attend to the broken rope in the same fashion. Your next task is to deploy the sail from the yard; the route pictured here is marginally faster than others.

07

You must now save James from a surely fatal fall; the Optional Objective offers a very generous time allocation. Follow the route pictured here, and Haytham will do the rest in the resultant cutscene.

08

**Day 72:** Meet the captain at the bow, then climb to the top of the foremast to bring Sequence 01 to a close.

# SEQUENCE 02

## BOSTON

| | |
|---|---|
| **1** | Beacon Hill |
| **2** | Boston Common |
| **3** | Boston Neck |
| **4** | Breed's Hill |
| **5** | Bunch of Grapes |
| **6** | Bunker Hill |
| **7** | Charlestown |
| **8** | Christ Church |
| **9** | Copp's Hill Battery |
| **10** | Crown Coffee House |
| **11** | Faneuil Hall |
| **12** | Fort Hill |
| **13** | General Store |
| **14** | Green Dragon Tavern |
| **15** | King's Chapel |
| **16** | Liberty Tree |
| **17** | Macneal's Rope Yard |
| **18** | Mill Pond |
| **19** | New South Meeting House |
| **20** | North Battery |
| **21** | Old Corner Book Store |
| **22** | Old North Meeting House |
| **23** | Old South Meeting House |
| **24** | Old State House |
| **25** | Paul Revere House |
| ◮ | Exit to Frontier |

NORTH DISTRICT

CENTRAL DISTRICT

SOUTH DISTRICT

## ⚠ WELCOME TO BOSTON

### MISSION OVERVIEW

| Optional Objectives | Further Reading |
|---|---|
| ▪ None. | ▪ Understanding the proclivities and idiosyncrasies of Boston's inhabitants will be of benefit (see page 40). |
| | ▪ You can learn about horse riding on page 38. |

Walk with Charles Lee along the waterfront until you reach the end of the boardwalk, when Haytham's companion will depart to acquire horses. Continue along the road, past the market stalls, then take a right to approach the waypoint marker at the end of the street, as shown here.

After the introduction to the singular Benjamin Franklin, enter the general store and purchase a Normal Sword and Flintlock Pistol as directed.

Leave the store and take the horse provided by Charles Lee, then ride with him to reach the Green Dragon Tavern. Dismount and enter the tavern, then follow Lee upstairs.

### ALMANAC PAGES

The cinematic outside the general store introduces Almanac Pages, the first type of collectible item available in Assassin's Creed III. Though you can track down and chase after the first four of these in Boston during Sequence 02 and 03, we would suggest that you leave this activity until later. Sequence 06 is probably the best time to begin hunting collectibles, for reasons that will become apparent as you progress through the main storyline.

Incidentally, you can return to this general store later in the Sequence (and at any point up until the end of Sequence 03) to engage in two entirely optional but entertaining conversations with Franklin.

### £ MAKING MONEY

For series veterans accustomed to immediately amassing funds in Assassin's Creed games to prepare for later investments, a warning: the money that Haytham can accumulate during these opening Sequences is a relative pittance. Though there is no harm in looting for ammunition (a practice you will be introduced to shortly), you should not use it as a method to raise capital. Later techniques will enable you to earn a fortune for a fraction of the effort.

There is only one side quest of note in the first three Sequences: a Courier Mission situated outside the general store where Haytham meets Ben Franklin. This short diversion is perhaps best saved for a later Sequence.

## MISSION OVERVIEW

| Optional Objectives | Further Reading |
|---|---|
| ■ Kill 10 mercenaries with firearms.<br>■ Do not let Hickey or Lee lose more than half of their health. | ■ Read the Combat section of the Primer: see page 51. |

When the Memory begins, follow the onscreen instructions to shoot the sentry, then scramble up the bank directly ahead. Pick up a musket from the rack highlighted here, then fire on one of the guards at the gate; Lee and Johnson will tackle the remaining soldiers.

Drop the musket, and grab another from the rack; this removes the immediate need to reload. Approach the men engaged in target practice, and shoot one from a safe distance; when the other mercenaries rush you, dispatch them by any means you deem appropriate.

When directed to shoot the explosive barrels, be sure to use the 🔲/🔲 Precision Mode aiming function. Try to get a feel for the process of lining up shots: you'll be using this again shortly. With the gate destroyed, reload and walk through the entrance.

Retrieve the stolen chest (approach it and press 🅱/Ⓞ), then defeat the mercenaries who arrive. You must ensure that Lee and Johnson sustain only limited injuries to complete an Optional Objective, so start with a swift pistol kill and then throw Haytham into the heart of the mêlée.

After the cutscene, loot the bodies to replenish your stock of ammunition (see page 47), then follow your companions. There is another brief battle outside the archway. Once again, start with a firearm kill, then aim for quick takedowns. Pick up a fresh musket before you press forward. Note that you must remain in the circle marked in blue on the mini-map for the rest of this memory.

When you reach this road bordered by crops, be ready for an ambush. Engage the mercenary vanguard up close, then take cover from the marksmen behind the cart, as shown here. Watch them closely, and take note of the intervals between their shots. In each break, grab a musket and use the Precision Mode aiming function for simple kills.

There is one final confrontation before the Memory ends. Once again, dispatch the initial wave with melee attacks, then use a musket to kill the four marksmen; deal with the two on the left-hand rooftop first. After eliminating all assailants, quickly loot bodies to replenish your stock of cartridges before you move to the waypoint.

## MISSION OVERVIEW

| Optional Objectives | Further Reading |
|---|---|
| ■ Eavesdrop on a moving group of guards.<br>■ Do not fail a single eavesdrop.<br>■ Remain undetected during the warehouse infiltration. | ■ Study the Stealth (page 42) and Viewpoints & Maps (page 39) sections of the Primer chapter. A working knowledge of assassination techniques (see page 48) will also be useful. |

**01** Speak with Charles Lee to begin this Memory, then exit via the door downstairs. Haytham is automatically transported to Ben Church's house some way south of the Green Dragon Tavern. Interact with Lee to begin.

**02** Approach the highlighted area to begin the eavesdrop. When prompted, approach the citizens standing against the building on the right-hand side of the street (see picture) to "Blend" and allay suspicion.

III

QUICKSTART

THE STORY SO FAR

PRIMER

WALKTHROUGH

SIDE QUESTS

REFERENCE & ANALYSIS

MULTIPLAYER

EXTRAS

MAP LEGEND

INDEX

03

Take any route you please to reach the next waypoint: a cross on top of the steeple of the church pictured here. Begin your climb in the graveyard to avoid detection (there is a Sniper on a building to the south, though you can soon move out of sight if you are quick), then scale the tower to reach it.

04

The cross is a special location known as a Viewpoint (see page 39). Once Haytham is perched on top of it, press 🅱/◎ to "Synchronize". When the brief cutscene ends, align Haytham with the cart highlighted here, then press 🆁🆃 + 🅰/🆁1 + ✖ and forward on 🄻 to perform a Leap of Faith.

05

Haytham must now listen in on conversations at sites marked on the mini-map to ascertain the location of Ben Church. Though there are multiple eavesdrop opportunities in the green investigation zone, the steps we suggest here should guarantee that you fulfill Optional Objectives. Begin by leaving the hiding place to follow the path specified here.

06

Stand by the produce stall to complete the first of three eavesdrops.

07

From this position, follow the road leading northeast until you reach the next eavesdrop zone close to a church.

08

Take advantage of the highlighted Blend opportunity to snoop without incident.

The final feat of reconnaissance is a little trickier, as it entails following two patrolling soldiers. These can be found in the square by the church mere steps away from the previous eavesdrop. Your targets walk a predictable anticlockwise route around the market area. Blend with nearby civilians, wait until they pass your position, then trail them from a safe distance within the marked zone until the task is complete.

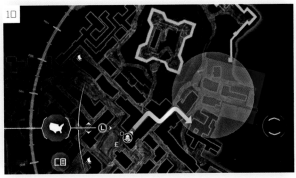

From the site of the last eavesdrop, take the short journey illustrated here to reach the next green investigation zone. It contains a Restricted Area: a zone marked in red where all soldiers will investigate Haytham on sight, and attack if they identify him. Stop when you reach a cart filled with hay.

If you are not interested in completing the stealth-based Optional Objective, you can simply fight your way to the warehouse entrance. Those who would prefer a more subtle approach should stop and watch the street to the right by the hay-filled cart. There is a long guard patrol that you need to avoid for a successful infiltration of the area. When they pass and walk into the nearby alley, wait for five or six seconds, then walk calmly along the route marked in white until you see a stationary guard to your left.

Press against the corner of the building and tap ❌/□ to assassinate the stationary guard, then use the Fast Walk ability (hold Ⓐ/❌) to move to the north side of the warehouse at the heart of the Restricted Area. Approach the doorway and press Ⓑ/◎ to trigger a cutscene. Two guards might notice you and investigate, but they won't have the time to raise the alert if you walk purposefully.

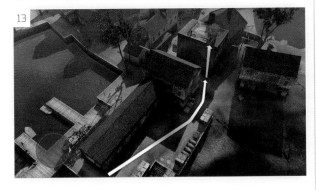

You now have three potential targets to pickpocket in order to obtain the warehouse key. The two on the boardwalks are surrounded by witnesses, but the final one on a rooftop to the west is alone. Climb the ladder and watch his movements. When he presents his back to Haytham, climb up and incapacitate him with a non-lethal takedown (see page 49). It's not *precisely* pickpocketing as directed, but rifling through his pockets as he lies prone yields the same outcome. Return to the warehouse.

Inside the building, you must assassinate Cutter and his associates silently; should Haytham be detected, Church bears the immediate brunt of the forfeit. Switch to the Hidden Blade and approach the guard on the left. When you strike, Lee will follow suit with the adjacent guard. Dispatch Cutter to complete the Memory.

## MISSION OVERVIEW

| Optional Objectives | Further Reading |
|---|---|
| ▪ Limit detection time to a cumulative total of 15 seconds.<br>▪ Perform a Kill Streak of three sequential deaths.<br>▪ Prevent Snitches from calling reinforcements. | ▪ If you have yet to do so, peruse our explanation of Social Status Indicators and the enemy detection system on page 42.<br>▪ The Snitch is a unique enemy archetype. See page 55 for details.<br>▪ You can read about Kill Streaks on page 53. |

**01**

Enter the Green Dragon Tavern to trigger a cinematic; you will be automatically transported to the Memory Start location when it ends. Speak with Charles Lee to begin. After the cutscene, follow Lee to meet with Braddock.

**02**

Trail the patrol from a safe distance. After the first portion of the journey along this road, stay behind Lee to avoid detection. Try to limit your potential visibility by Blending with civilians and hiding behind corners whenever possible.

**03**

Though the onscreen timer that appears may cause a little anxiety on occasion, following Lee's prompts and movements will suffice. Your contribution during stationary moments should be to use 🅡 to maintain visual contact with the patrol where possible.

**04**

Once Lee has engineered a diversion, follow the soldiers into the back alleys. After the cutscene, you must disable Braddock and cut down his men in a fairly frantic fight. If you wish to complete the two Optional Objectives linked to this battle, see the accompanying box-out. When the final soldier falls, approach the beleaguered Braddock to bring the Memory to a close.

## OPTIONAL OBJECTIVES

The closing battle of this Memory introduces two Optional Objectives that can be a little tricky on first attempt. Use the following tips to inform your strategy during the fight. If you are attempting a 100% complete playthrough, don't forget that you can use the Reload Last Checkpoint option to restart the fight if things go awry.

⊙ Target the Snitches first: these opponents do not fight, but will flee a battle to bring reinforcements. Hold 🄻🄸/🅁🄸 to break out of the combat stance and position Haytham accordingly to perform a kill or assassination. Note that Charles Lee may kill one of the Snitches as the battle opens, which makes things a little easier. During this part of the mission, the snitches are marked by a ⬤ icon, which makes them easy to identify.

⊙ The Kill Streak requirement can be satisfied once the Snitches have been disabled. Start with a Counter Kill, then try to pick targets that are likely to attack next (see page 53 for further help). The Memory only ends once you move close to Braddock's position having disabled all other combatants, so it's easy to jump back to the preceding checkpoint if you fail.

## MISSION OVERVIEW

| Optional Objectives | Further Reading |
|---|---|
| ■ Find and kill the General.<br>■ Perform three stealth assassinations from a corner spot.<br>■ Avoid firing line damage. | ■ You can learn about assassination techniques – particularly the new corner assassinations – on page 49.<br>■ This will almost certainly be your first encounter with firing lines. See page 54 for advice on how to avoid injury. |

Enter the Green Dragon Tavern and speak with Charles Lee to begin the Memory. After the cutscene, grab the musket and move unseen to the rooftops on the opposite side of the street as the convoy passes beneath.

Spring the ambush by shooting one of the soldiers beneath your position, then immediately leap into the fray with an air assassination. With the assistance of Haytham's cohorts, the battle is brutal but short.

Haytham must now ride the appropriated cart to infiltrate the Southgate Fort. To avoid detection, you can order his allies to assassinate suspicious soldiers by pressing **LB**/**L1**. Time the strikes to occur when SSI detection meters appear. The first such flashpoint is pictured here.

As you draw level with the house on the left, issue a command to silence the guard dog and the officer who arrives to investigate.

The next group of targets arrives from behind the crops on the right-hand side of the road.

Finally, issue an order to have Haytham's allies eliminate the last group of guards before you reach the fort.

Inside the fort, walk along the path until you see this Officer approach. One of your allies will automatically arrest his curiosity before he can identify the interlopers.

Haytham must complete the next section of the Memory without assistance, remaining undetected as he kills the General and frees three groups of captives. Our walkthrough will explain how to attend to them in the order specified in this screenshot. Follow the route marked here, at a pace no greater than Fast Walk, to move into position for the first step.

Hide in the hay cart as directed here and assassinate the General (who has a rather complicated and variable patrol pattern, as illustrated in the screenshot) from your hiding place with ✖/◻.

Proceed along the route detailed here (along the south wall) until you reach the Stalking Zone. When the Officer's patrol brings him to your position, perform a low-profile assassination from your hiding place. Press ⑧/◎ to free the captives.

From your previous position, approach the second group of captives to the north. Once again, they are guarded by a single patrolling Officer (who you may need to circumvent from the west if he remains stationary at first). Watch and wait from a safe distance, then hide in the cart when he moves behind the crates. Perform a stealth kill when he gets close; you can then free the slaves.

**12**

To reach the final captives, you must climb aboard the ship at the dock. Move into position at the wall as specified in the screenshot diagram, then wait for the Officer's patrol to bring him to your position. When he is highlighted as he nears your position, press ⊗/⬜ to perform a neat and silent corner assassination. (You can also perform a corner assassination from the crates closer to the ship if the Officer is walking away when you arrive.)

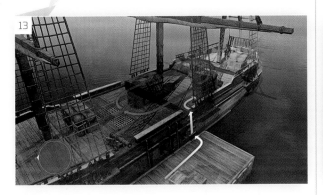

**13**

Scale the side of the ship and watch the patrolling Officer; you are free to ignore the two soldiers stationed at the front of the vessel. When the Officer moves to the stern, where the captives are held, move into position by the crates. When he approaches, perform a corner assassination as before.

**14**

Move up to the next crates, position Haytham at the corner, then tap Ⓑ/◎ to whistle, drawing the guard into position for another corner assassination – completing the related Optional Objective. You can now free the final group of captives.

**15**

With the General killed in advance, you can now focus exclusively on avoiding firing line damage (see page 54) to complete the final Optional Objective. The first firing line occurs as a tutorial; a second scripted firing line takes place as you approach the archway to the north. Those seeking Full Synchronization should be careful to methodically ensure that a suitable human shield is always within range. Use the barrels behind the wagon to climb the wall to reach Silas.

**16**

The Memory ends instantly with the death of Silas. We suggest that you approach and kill him immediately and without fanfare; we have highlighted him in this screenshot to help you to identify your target.

QUICKSTART
THE STORY SO FAR
PRIMER
WALKTHROUGH
SIDE QUESTS
REFERENCE & ANALYSIS
MULTIPLAYER
EXTRAS
MAP LEGEND
INDEX

SEQUENCE 01
SEQUENCE 02
SEQUENCE 03
SEQUENCE 04
SEQUENCE 05
NOVEMBER 15, 2012
SEQUENCE 06
SEQUENCE 07
SEQUENCE 08
DECEMBER 1, 2012
SEQUENCE 09
SEQUENCE 10
DECEMBER 12, 2012
SEQUENCE 11
SEQUENCE 12
DECEMBER 20, 2012

⚠ UNCONVINCED

## MISSION OVERVIEW

| Optional Objectives | Further Reading |
|---|---|
| ■ Limit health loss to 50%.<br>■ Use two breakable objects in a fight. | ■ You can learn about the Fast Travel system on page 39. |

01 Enter the Green Dragon Tavern for a brief meeting with Charles Lee. When you return to the street outside, you can either ride to the Frontier exit at the very south of Boston, or use the Fast Travel system (see page 39). If you arrive in the new area without a mount, use the Horse Whistle to summon Haytham's steed (see page 38).

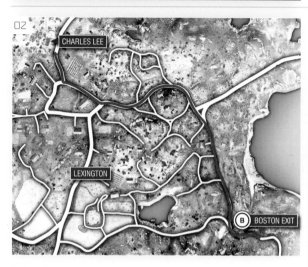

With no Synchronized Viewpoints in the Frontier area, finding Lexington (the settlement where Lee awaits Haytham's arrival) can be a little confounding. Follow the directions on this map.

Speak to Lee to begin the mission, then saddle up and follow him until you arrive at the abandoned campfire.

Follow the fresh trail shown here; note that moving directly along it enables Haytham to walk a little faster than does wading through undisturbed snow.

At the end of the trail is a clearing and, as you approach the crouched figure, a cutscene. When it ends, pursue the woman as she bounds from tree to tree; focus on the orange waypoint marker to more accurately track her movements.

After the next cutscene, a pack of wolves will attack Haytham before he can continue his pursuit: see "Wolf Attacks" for details. When the encounter ends, look for a wooden platform approximately northwest of Haytham's starting position, and activate Eagle Vision (👆/L3) to identify the woman hiding there.

Once again, follow the woman at ground level as she moves through the trees above. When you approach the rocky outcrop shown here, turn right: this is the quickest way to intercept her.

III

QUICKSTART

THE STORY SO
FAR

PRIMER

WALKTHROUGH

SIDE QUESTS

REFERENCE &
ANALYSIS

MULTIPLAYER

EXTRAS

MAP LEGEND

INDEX

After Haytham and Kaniehti:io reconvene outside Concord, perform a Leap of Faith from the ledge to the left of the tree, then enter the tavern at the waypoint.

Blend with drinkers not of the military persuasion within the highlighted zones to successfully eavesdrop on two conversations. A fistfight ensues when Haytham attempts to depart. If you are keen to complete the Optional Objectives tied to this event, see "Tavern Brawl Tactics".

## WOLF ATTACKS

To complete the health-related Optional Objective, you must guide Haytham unscathed through an encounter with three wolves.

- ⊙ Wolves generally stalk Haytham by maintaining a consistent distance that precludes the use of standard combat techniques. When an individual wolf runs to attack, you must follow two onscreen button prompts to kill it without sustaining damage. The timing window is rather tight, so feel free to return to the previous checkpoint if your first attempt doesn't end well.

- ⊙ If you fail the button prompts, tap ✕/□ rapidly to fend off the attack. Being savaged by a wolf drains Haytham's Life Bar quicker than any other attack that you have faced so far, so a single struggle can lead you to fail the Optional Objective.

- ⊙ Wolves can be shot as they circle Haytham, or while walking towards him prior to a charge. After you kill the first wolf, you may have time to kill a second with the pistol immediately and – with a rapid reload and a pinch of luck – dispatch the third before it can run at Haytham.

## TAVERN BRAWL TACTICS

The health-related Optional Objective still stands during the closing fistfight, along with a new challenge to defeat two enemies with context-sensitive attacks.

- ⊙ Don't go on the offensive: focus on parries and counters as you maneuver your opponents into position for takedowns with the scenery items highlighted in the screenshot here.

- ⊙ To perform the contextual attacks, employ the Counter Throw ability (press Ⓑ/◎ twice when an opponent attacks) and use Ⓛ to direct enemies.

- ⊙ Once you have satisfied the Optional Objective, focus on winning the fight with simple Counter Kills.

## MISSION OVERVIEW

| Optional Objectives | Further Reading |
|---|---|
| ▪ Do not kill any guards.<br>▪ Sabotage two cannons. | ▪ If you haven't done so yet, you can read about non-lethal takedowns on page 49. |

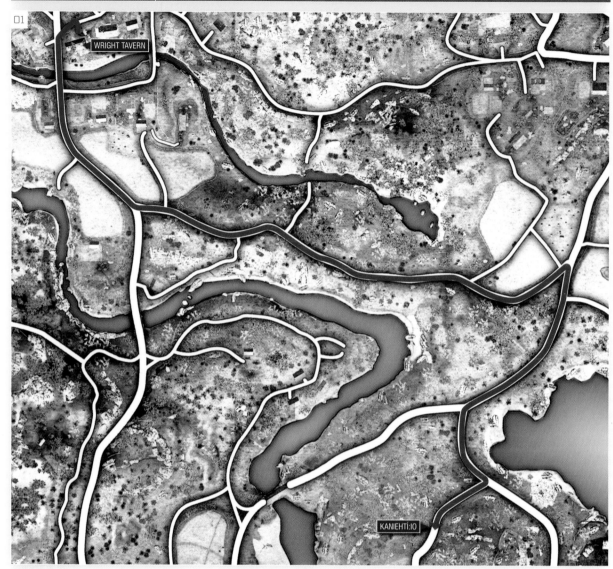

01

WRIGHT TAVERN

KANIEHTÍ:IO

Take a horse and ride to the Memory Start position to the southeast via the route detailed here (a simple journey that follows main trails), then speak to Kaniehtí:io to begin. Note that you cannot unlock Viewpoints in the Frontier at this stage in the story; its mysteries are saved for a later Sequence.

02

100 m

Under cover of the snowstorm, run towards the waypoint marker until you see a cart. Approach the back of it and jump inside, then wait for it to pass through the gate. Detection will lead to instant Desynchronization, so stealth is mandatory for the rest of the Memory.

QUICKSTART

THE STORY SO
FAR

PRIMER

→ WALKTHROUGH

SIDE QUESTS

REFERENCE &
ANALYSIS

MULTIPLAYER

EXTRAS

MAP LEGEND

INDEX

SEQUENCE 01

SEQUENCE 02

→ SEQUENCE 03

SEQUENCE 04

SEQUENCE 05

NOVEMBER 15,
2012

SEQUENCE 06

SEQUENCE 07

SEQUENCE 08

DECEMBER 1,
2012

SEQUENCE 09

SEQUENCE 10

DECEMBER 12,
2012

SEQUENCE 11

SEQUENCE 12

DECEMBER 20,
2012

03

When the cart comes to a halt, drop into the foliage behind it and move slowly to remain concealed. Wait until the guard patrolling the path walks away from Haytham, then carefully climb to the rooftop and approach the eavesdrop area.

04

Move along the rooftop to stay out of sight while eavesdropping on the two soldiers as they stroll through the camp. When they pass the hay-filled cart in the upper area, wait for the nearby guard to look away, then drop into the hiding place. The eavesdrop will end shortly afterwards.

05

Move into the Stalking Zone and select Haytham's fists in the Weapon Wheel. Sneak up behind the nearby guard when his back is turned and perform a non-lethal takedown from behind. You can then retrieve the tactical map from the tent. Completing the Optional Objective to sabotage the cannons also leads you to an easy escape route, so this would be our recommended strategy for all players. Start by creeping towards the second sentry and, once again, disable him with a non-lethal attack from behind. Begin your approach when he looks out to sea. You can then attend to the first cannon (approach it and hold **B**/◎) without fear of discovery.

06

Hop over the small wall by the cannon, then follow the route illustrated here to reach the second. Stand out of sight and wait until the patrolling guard faces Haytham's general position; when he turns to depart, quickly jump over the wall and move into position to disable the weapon.

07

While it is possible to escape the fort on foot by disabling two further guards, it's much easier to simply dive into the sea and swim along the river to the west. When you reach dry land, return to Kaniehtí:io to complete the Memory.

## MISSION OVERVIEW

| Optional Objectives | Preparation |
|---|---|
| ▪ Kill two soldiers without triggering open conflict.<br>▪ Destroy three powder carts. | ▪ Ensure that you have a full supply of cartridges before you start this mission. |

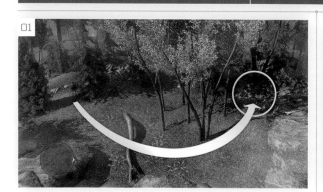

Return to the Wright Tavern in Concord and enter to begin the Memory. After the short (automated) journey on horseback, speak with Kaniehtí:io. When play resumes, follow the route marked here. Hide inside the Stalking Zone, then transfer into the pile of branches (a hiding place) when you are sure that no one is looking your way. There is a checkpoint just beforehand, so it's easy to restart if something goes wrong.

In addition to stationary soldiers, two guards patrol the camp: one on the north side makes regular walks between two positions, while your priority target walks a longer circuit. From your position inside the hiding place, silently assassinate the sentry standing nearby. You can then whistle to attract the attention of another guard, then kill him when he moves within range. These two deaths satisfy the Optional Objective: you can now enter open conflict to disable all guards in the area.

Follow the waypoints to reach Braddock's position. When the cinematic ends, ride off in pursuit of the general; you must stay within range of him to avoid Desynchronization. Use the spur command (tap Ⓐ/Ⓧ) to urge your horse to greater speeds. The new Optional Objective challenges you to destroy three powder carts during the chase. Be ready to shoot them as soon as you move within range, then reload immediately to have a bullet ready for a subsequent opportunity. The first (pictured here) is encountered as you turn to the left at the start of the chase.

The second powder cart is found after you rejoin the track after cutting through the trees.

The third and final target is on the left-hand side of the track shortly after another powder cart falls from above. This marks the home stretch of the chase. After the cinematic, you can deal with Braddock in any manner you see fit.

After another cinematic, Haytham returns to Boston. Entering the Green Dragon Tavern ends the Sequence in a similarly momentous fashion. The story then takes a quick detour back to the present day before Sequence 04 begins. You can use this opportunity to converse with the Assassins for optional conversations, and check the only available terminal to review emails received by Desmond during his time exploring Haytham's memories. When you are ready to continue, approach the Animus and press any button.

# SEQUENCE 04

## ⚠ HIDE AND SEEK

### MISSION OVERVIEW

#### Optional Objectives

- Find all the children without making a mistake.
- Find all the children within four minutes.

01

Follow Ratonhnhaké:ton's friends to the forest outside the settlement. After the cutscene, a game of hide and seek begins. To start the process of finding the children, press ⓑ/◎ to investigate the nearby clue. This reveals three separate (though overlapping) search zones. Scrutinizing each additional clue shrinks the search zone that it pertains to. An easy way to locate clues is to activate Eagle Vision, which makes it possible to espy their general location through solid objects and foliage. When a sufficient number of clues for a specific search zone have been found, the hiding children are highlighted on the mini-map as a waypoint.

02

Once Ratonhnhaké:ton has found his friends, travel to the waypoint marker to begin the next game; this time, it's his turn to hide. Enter a hiding place far from your starting position before the time limit expires to advance the story. Return to the village. Run to the second longhouse and cut through it, pressing ⓑ/◎ rapidly when prompted to move the obstruction. Avoid flames: these will sap Ratonhnhaké:ton's Life Bar in a heartbeat.

03

Interact with the door highlighted by a waypoint marker and, on discovering that it is blocked, run around to the right to get inside the longhouse. Approach the debris covering Kaniehtí:io and press ⓑ/◎ when directed to do so.

### HIDE AND SEEK: SOLUTION

There are two Optional Objectives linked to the game that Ratonhnhaké:ton plays with his friends. If you wish to find them all on the first attempt, and within the time limit, use this annotated map.

A

Crouched by the cliff.

B

Inside a pile of branches.

C

Check this hiding place.

## MISSION OVERVIEW

| Optional Objectives | Further Reading |
|---|---|
| ▪ Do not touch the ground or water. | ▪ Learn more about advanced free |
| ▪ Find three more feathers. | running techniques on page 218. |

**01**

Speak with Ratonhnhaké:ton's friend to begin the Memory, then free run along the tree to jump to an adjoining branch. Climb into the V-shaped section just above, then tap Ⓐ/⊗ when the prompt appears to ascend.

**02**

After the cutscene in the upper branches, free run through the trees to reach the next waypoint marker. Note the appearance of a new Optional Objective.

**03**

As we explain on page 218, free running through trees is a little alien at first, as it's harder to instinctively read the route ahead until you pick up on the distinct "visual language" of these lofty courses. Don't worry: it becomes second nature with practice.

**04**

When you reach the V-shaped section pictured here, jump to the smaller branches to swing down to a branch closer to the ground.

**05**

The restriction on touching ground or water to complete the Optional Objective does not encompass stone areas that are part of the free run course; following the route marked here to reach the log in the river will not lead to failure. At the far side of the log, turn around and return to Kanen'tó:kon to help him up when he falls.

III

QUICKSTART

THE STORY SO FAR

PRIMER

WALKTHROUGH

SIDE QUESTS

REFERENCE & ANALYSIS

MULTIPLAYER

EXTRAS

MAP LEGEND

INDEX

06

Follow the route shown here to reach a cutscene. While free running in trees, Ratonhnhaké:ton will automatically swing around the outside of a tree trunk to reach branches on the opposite side – as illustrated in this picture.

07

The penultimate section of the course leads you to a fallen tree, which can be used to reach the cliff face.

08

Finally, climb the rocks via the path shown here. Approach the nest and press **B**/**◎** to interact with it. When play resumes, you can either collect additional feathers to satisfy the Optional Objective (see box-out), or run directly to the waypoint marker and speak with Kanen'tó:kon to complete the Memory.

## COLLECTING FEATHERS

To complete a final Optional Objective, Ratonhnhaké:ton must collect three additional feathers. Two of these are automatically marked on the map; a third takes a little more investigation to locate.

From your starting position by the hiding place, climb the tree a few steps to the east to find the first feather.

Return to the hiding place where Ratonhnhaké:ton landed and climb the tree to the north.

From the hiding place, run to the northwest until you see the dead tree pictured here. The feather lies at the end of this short free run course.

## MISSION OVERVIEW

| Optional Objectives (Hunting Lessons) | Further Reading | Optional Objectives (Something to Remember) |
|---|---|---|
| ■ Hunt and skin three different types of animal.<br>■ Combine bait and a snare to catch an animal.<br>■ Air assassinate two animals. | ■ You can read our comprehensive guide to hunting on page 242. | ■ Make no more than two collisions. |

01

02

**Hunting Lessons:** As the first part of this Memory is a tutorial for basic hunting techniques, there is no need for additional assistance: just follow the onscreen instructions and prompts as they appear. When the time comes to hunt a deer, use Eagle Vision to find a clue within the green search area. Use the Stalking Zone to approach the animal without being detected, put bait within your place of concealment, then lie in wait and kill your prey when it moves within range.

After skinning the deer and retrieving the catch from the snares, three Optional Objectives appear. Though you only need to collect meat from five animals to complete the Memory, our advice here will focus on satisfying the secondary conditions. From your starting position by the snares, head south and approach the rock pictured here and use it as a starting point to free run through the trees.

03

04

From the trees, look for animals moving below. Creatures that Ratonhnhaké:ton can hunt are highlighted when they move within range for what is, in effect, an air assassination: tap ❌/⬜ to jump down and kill them instantly. Repeat this feat to complete the related Optional Objective. Try to kill a different animal on the second occasion to work towards another challenge.

Catching a creature with bait and a snare is actually very easy. Place the snare first, then take a few steps back to throw bait on top of it. Quickly retreat to a nearby Stalking Zone to await the arrival of an animal. You may find that numerous animals will approach from a surprisingly large radius.

05 Ratonhnhaké:ton can only skin a maximum of five animals to satisfy the Optional Objectives, so you now have two remaining opportunities to complete the "hunt three types of animal" challenge. Start by using Eagle Vision to locate clues within the search zone. Examining these will highlight and identify an animal on the mini-map; if this isn't the animal you seek, move on to the next clue. Once you have located a new variety of animal, approach it very carefully (ideally via Stalking Zones) until you move within range for a successful Bow kill.

With the hunt concluded, move to the waypoint marker. When the bear charges at Ratonhnhaké:ton, press the button prompts that appear onscreen to evade its attacks. You can then run out of the area marked by a red circle on the mini-map to escape it. Return to the village entrance to end the Memory.

06

**Something to Remember:** Enter the village and approach the Clan Mother's longhouse. Speak to her outside, then walk to the waypoint. You must then use 🕹 to move during the events that unfold. Unless you are blessed with swift reactions, conquering the Optional Objective will require that you take the time to familiarize yourself with the course. If you do not beat it on first attempt, you can always return to repeat this short Memory via the Replay function at a later date.

# SEQUENCE 05

## DAVENPORT HOMESTEAD

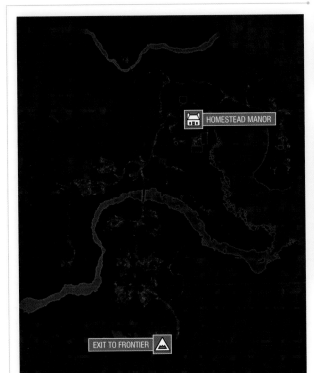

HOMESTEAD MANOR

EXIT TO FRONTIER

## ⬡ A BOORISH MAN

### MISSION OVERVIEW

**Optional Objectives**

- Limit health loss to 50%.

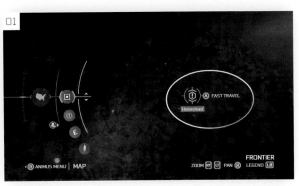

At the start of this Sequence, you must travel to a new region: the Davenport Homestead. You can either move to the map transition on foot, or select it from the main map to Fast Travel instantly. The Homestead is smaller and much easier to navigate than the rugged Frontier wilderness and urban sprawl of Boston. Perform a Leap of Faith from the log directly ahead of your starting position, then follow the trail to reach the Memory Start marker.

Approach the front door of the Manor, and press ⓑ/◎ to begin the Memory. The events that follow are designed to further the narrative, not challenge your gaming prowess, so simply run (and, on occasion, climb) to waypoint markers until Ratonhnhaké:ton awakes in the stable during a storm.

The mission's sole Optional Objective is tied to this fight, so we recommend a cautious strategy based around Counter Kills. Some of the assailants may attempt grabs; press ⓧ/◯ to escape. If you feel that you are likely to fail the Optional Objective, feel free to return to the previous checkpoint to try again. When the brawl ends, and the following cinematic draws to a close, enter the Manor via the front door. Follow the old man when required until the Memory ends.

## MISSION OVERVIEW

| Optional Objectives | Further Reading |
|---|---|
| ▪ Escape within 80 seconds. | ▪ Turn to page 221 to learn about the Notoriety system.<br>▪ You may encounter new enemy archetypes during your stay in Boston. Turn to page 222 to study their strengths and weaknesses. |

You begin in the Manor's basement as Ratonhnhaké:ton recounts his experiences in training. Leave via the front door upstairs, then interact with Achilles. On arrival in Boston, walk with the veteran Assassin until a cutscene begins. Ratonhnhaké:ton now acquires the name Connor, which is the one we will favor from this point on. Follow the waypoint marker to reach the store, then enter. After the conversation with the shopkeeper, return to Achilles.

Walk with Achilles until the unrest escalates in a cinematic. When play resumes, tail the suspicious man through the alleyway, maintaining a safe distance and blending where possible to evade detection.

Once your target turns left, be careful not to move too close; when he climbs the ladder, follow him after he reaches the top rungs. On the rooftop, you can stand behind the chimney to stay out of sight. When the man halts in a position on the opposite side of the roof, a short countdown will begin. Run behind him and perform an assassination before the timer expires.

Connor must now escape the area – or, more specifically, the zone marked in red on the mini-map – and lose any soldiers giving chase. From your starting position, run to the northeast along the rooftop, using the tree as a stepping stone to reach the next building.

If you can make a successful jump to the next building in line, a safe haven awaits: a Leap of Faith into the cart marked here should enable Connor to evade his pursuers. If not, continue to the northeast and dive into the ocean: a consistently foolproof way to evade assailants is to find a solid body of water, then swim to safety.

Connor remains at maximum Notoriety when the Memory ends, which makes the process of reaching the next Memory Start marker fraught with danger. If your escape led you some distance away, there is a trick that you can use to reduce the journey: just select "Leave Animus" or "Quit", then reload. Connor will restart much closer to the marker when you resume. Use Fast Walk and Blending opportunities to reach Sam Adams without incident.

## MISSION OVERVIEW

| Optional Objectives | Further Reading |
|---|---|
| ■ Do not raise your Notoriety to level 3. | ■ Turn to page 220 to read about the Fast Travel system, including information on Boston's underground network of tunnels and the services of Harbormasters. |

01

From your starting position by the hay cart, make your way to the first poster. Assassinate the nearby guard, then approach it and press Ⓑ/◎ to tear it down.

02

Jump into the hay cart and assassinate the soldier standing by it, then move behind the building, as illustrated here.

03

Wait out of sight until the two-man patrol moves behind the fence, quickly run to the poster and tear it from the wall, then partially retrace your steps to find Sam Adams at the center of a marketplace. He will introduce a second method used to reduce Notoriety – though only at a price, which is fortunately waived in this instance.

04

Follow the route outlined here to reach a secret tunnel entrance at the rear of the Green Dragon Tavern, avoiding checkpoints set up in the aftermath of the massacre. All possible points of entry to the area behind the tavern are blocked by guards. To complete the new Optional Objective, we suggest waiting and watching until the two nearby patrols move away, then deal with the pair of sentries on the north side of the building (circled on our map). Start with an assassination, then kill the second with the bow or a Counter Kill, whichever will be quicker. You can then immediately run to the tunnel entrance at the waypoint marker to advance the story before the bodies are discovered. Open conflict that brings all nearby soldiers into the fray will most likely cause you to fail the Optional Objective.

05

Inside the tunnels, follow the route shown here to reach the exit. Approach lamps and press Ⓑ/◎ to mark explored areas: this is useful when you come to chart the Boston Underground to expand your Fast Travel network at a later date.

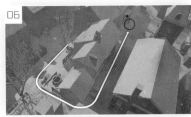

06

Back on the surface, make the short journey to the Printer's Shop and defeat the two guards outside to gain entrance. When the cutscene ends, walk with Sam until the two part ways. Speak to the nearby Harbormaster and select the Davenport Homestead to return for the next main story Memory.

## MISSION OVERVIEW

| Optional Objectives | Further Reading |
|---|---|
| ■ Do not touch the water while rescuing Terry. | ■ You can find a walkthrough for the Homestead Mission that appears after Connor saves Terry on page 193. For a comprehensive guide to Homestead management and the trading system, turn to page 236. You won't be able to access all features at this stage, but the sooner you start, the better… |

Return to the Manor to speak with Achilles; when the conversation is cut short, run outside and interact with the panicked man to begin this Memory. Follow Godfrey until you reach the riverbank.

The Optional Objective for this short but fast-paced memory is to avoid falling or jumping into the river. There is a very specific route that enables you to do just that while keeping track with the beleaguered Terry. This course starts by taking you to the center of the river.

The course then delivers Connor back to the left bank. After running up the slope and past the two fallen trees, jump onto the log that overhangs the river.

Use the log to reach the right-hand side of the river and continue your breakneck pursuit.

If you are making good time, your arrival at the final fallen tree pictured here will coincide with Terry floating below. When the onscreen prompt appears, dive from above to hand the final part of the rescue over to Connor. If Terry has already floated out of range, you cannot complete the Optional Objective – though the Memory only ends if you manually dive into the water. If you wish, you can use this opportunity to return to the previous checkpoint.

You can now either begin the Homestead Mission highlighted in the cutscene, or leave it for later and travel straight to Achilles to continue with the main storyline. When the cinematic ends, return to the Manor for a tutorial on managing the Homestead. After Connor narrates a leap forward in time, travel to the waypoint just beyond the restored Aquila to begin a new and exhilarating Memory…

## MISSION OVERVIEW

| Optional Objectives | Further Reading |
|---|---|
| ■ Sustain no damage before you reach Martha's Vineyard.<br>■ Use the swivel gun to destroy two ships.<br>■ Successfully brace during an attack on three occasions. | ■ You can find an introduction to controlling the Aquila and naval tactics on page 171. |

This Memory acts as an introduction to naval missions in Assassin's Creed III, and offers a comprehensive appraisal of the core mechanics of movement and combat. Begin by speaking to Robert Faulkner, then select the mission icon (①) on the map. As the onscreen instructions and spoken prompts leave little scope for confusion, our advice here will focus on fulfilling the Optional Objectives.

Navigating the channel to reach Martha's Vineyard is easy: just follow the vessel directly ahead. Pay the rocks a wide berth, and be ready to press ⑧/◎ to switch to half sail to avoid the effects of rogue winds and make tight turns (as pictured here).

Once the ambush takes place, use the swivel gun (🔟/🄻) to destroy the smaller vessels. The closer you are to an opponent, the easier it will be to release the trigger while the targeting cursor is red. You need to sink two of the small ships with this weapon to complete the related Optional Objective.

You must employ three successful uses of the "brace" ability to complete the final Optional Objective. Watch the opposing frigate carefully as it moves into position to fire a broadside salvo. When the water between the vessels is tinged with red (as shown here), the frigate is preparing to fire. Press ⊗/◎ as its cannons burst into life to avoid or reduce the damage sustained. Once the secondary objective has been satisfied, sink the frigate to end the Memory.

## ⚠ POWER SOURCE #1

01

Climb the ladder directly ahead, then follow the path to the right.

02

Jump to the scaffold and then the pipe beyond. Free run to the end of the yellow pipe section.

03

Jump to the scaffold through the opening in the wall.

04

Run over the ventilation duct to reach the elevator shaft entrance.

05

Free run through the elevator shaft, then climb the counterweight at the far side.

06

Jump from the V-shaped opening to the construction materials, then make your way through to the next room (as illustrated here).

07

Swing to the lower level via the pole, then run at the corrugated shutter to slide though the gap beneath it.

08

Climb to the very top of the crane arm via the route illustrated here, then jump to the iron girder.

09

Follow this rather perilous course to reach the relative safety of a suspended platform, then climb the lattice wall via the route marked by wires.

Run over to the giant spindle and slide beneath it.

Now run through the metal tube.

Follow the course illustrated here to reach the level above.

Follow the path shown here to reach the suspended girder.

When you reach the exposed upper level, climb to the top of the mechanical arm.

Make your way to the crane arm via this route.

After the brief cutscene, follow Rebecca's prompts to jump and activate the parachute. You should then guide Desmond to the roof highlighted here.

When you return to the Grand Temple, you can insert the Power Source into a special console before you resume your Animus exploits. From your starting position, climb the crumbling staircase pictured here.

Enter the room to trigger a cutscene; when it ends, climb the staircase inside. When you reach the broken walkway, turn left and follow the route illustrated here until you trigger another cutscene. Finally, approach the console to insert the Power Source and go back to the lower level. You can now initiate optional conversations with Desmond's companions and check his emails, if you wish, before you return to the Animus.

## ⓘ ON JOHNSON'S TRAIL

### MISSION OVERVIEW

| Optional Objectives | Further Reading |
|---|---|
| ■ Stay below Notoriety level 2.<br><br>■ Use firearms no more than six times.<br><br>■ Use powder kegs to blow up three caches of smuggled cargo. | ■ Read about the Rope Dart weapon on page 231.<br><br>■ Walkthroughs for the new Homestead Missions – and new trading/crafting opportunities – can be found on page 193 and 244 respectively.<br><br>■ You can embark on new naval missions (see page 176) by speaking with Faulkner at the Homestead, or via a Harbormaster on any map.<br><br>■ As you may have noticed, there are board games and other simple diversions that Connor can participate in. Turn to page 142 to read tips and techniques that will improve your performance. |

01

Before you leave the Homestead to begin this Memory, we strongly suggest that you complete the Silent Hunter mission (starting position highlighted here) to learn how to use your new Rope Dart weapon. It can be found a short walk to the southwest from the Manor; see page 194 for assistance. We would also advise that you familiarize and engage yourself with developing and exploiting the Homestead to increase your income. Starting now will make a big difference later in the story.

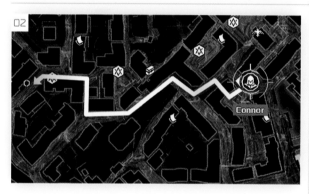

02

When you are ready to begin, Fast Travel to Boston. Make your way to the Memory Start marker at the docks and strike up a conversation with Sam Adams. Walk with him until a cinematic begins. When it ends, assist the indignant Frenchman in dispatching the four soldiers, then make your way to the meeting – tear a poster down if you have reached Notoriety level 1 to travel incognito. Do not tackle any tax collectors that you encounter during the journey, despite the onscreen prompts: you can deal with these later. Dispatching them now would increase your Notoriety.

03

After the cinematic, leave the building and make your way straight to the waypoint at the docks – again, ignore tax collectors and smugglers for now. When you reach the Restricted Area, make your way to the east side of the circle, close to the imposing stone fort. If you approach the first cargo target as illustrated here, you can easily avoid the four stationary guards and single patrolling soldier on the west side of the building.

04

There is no direct prohibition on conflict in this Memory, but our stealth-oriented approach will enable you to fulfill all Optional Objectives with ease. If you do find yourself in combat, be sure to tear down Wanted posters afterwards to keep your Notoriety level under control. Wait until the patrolling soldier approaches the boardwalk, ready Connor's pistol, then emerge from cover and target the powder keg on the ground with Precision Mode aiming (LT/L1), and open fire.

05

As soon as the powder keg explodes, escape via the route detailed here to leave the vicinity before the guards can move to investigate.

There is no powder keg next to the second pile of illegal cargo so, to complete the Optional Objective, pick up the one marked here, then calmly walk it over to the boardwalk. As long as you don't break into a run, the two guards should be oblivious to your presence.

Drop the powder keg beside the cargo, then jump onto the boat to take your shot from a safe distance. As it explodes, turn and leap into the water. Dive beneath the surface (to reduce the chances of detection) as you swim to the next objective marker on the wharf directly ahead.

Climb onto the side of the wharf and observe the movements of the two guards. They move in formation, and will stand for a fairly lengthy duration when they stroll down to the boardwalk. This is your chance to climb up, position a powder keg next to the cargo, and shoot it as before. Immediately jump back into the water, then follow the path shown here to exit the Restricted Area.

With this Memory's principal challenge over, it's now time to finish two final objectives: destroy crates carried by two smugglers (orange circle on our map ), and eliminate two groups of tax collectors (red circles). We've highlighted the easiest targets here, situated in areas that feature few or no additional hostiles.

With tax collectors, start the battle with a suitable assassination. Of the two that we mark on the map, only the site close to the two highlighted smugglers may involve an intervention by a small Redcoat patrol. If you wait until they pass and move out of range, you can fight the tax collectors without additional complications. To keep your Notoriety level down and complete the related Optional Objective, be sure to tear down Wanted posters (which can be found close to both groups of tax collectors) after the battles.

Smugglers are much easier to deal with. Ensure that there are no guards present (there certainly shouldn't be with the sites we recommend), then simply run and barge into them. As the crate smashes to the floor, turn and sprint away to escape the smuggler. They will give chase, but soon lose heart.

## THE ANGRY CHEF

| MISSION OVERVIEW | |
|---|---|
| **Optional Objectives** | **Further Reading** |
| ■ Limit time spent in a single session of open conflict to no more than 15 seconds.<br>■ Limit Chapheau's health loss to no more than 50%.<br>■ Perform five Low Profile assassinations. | ■ The Grenadier is a powerful new enemy archetype. You will also see Scouts appearing in Boston and the Frontier. See page 222 for details.<br>■ There are now a handful of Citizen Missions to complete in Boston, including an Assassination Contract in the North District (see page 137). |

**01** The first stage of this short and intense Memory has Connor trailing in the furious Chapheau's wake as he seeks to remonstrate with British soldiers. The only real difficulty here is completing the challenging Optional Objectives – so this will be our focus in this section. Equip the Hidden Blades immediately: you'll be needing them throughout.

As Chapheau attracts the attention of the first two guards, move behind the most distant of the two and assassinate him, then Fast Walk and dispatch his partner before a fight can break out.

The Redcoats being assailed by the crowd do not attack, so feel free to ignore them. When you reach the next two, follow the same procedure as before. However, you need to be faster this time: get behind the most distant guard and try to assassinate him before the other reaches Chapheau.

The subsequent confrontation is much more testing, but there is a checkpoint just before it begins. Run behind the closest Grenadier and assassinate him, then his companion; you must then defeat the second pair in open conflict before the timer elapses. If you are quick, you can defeat the remaining Regular with a Counter Kill and then assassinate the Grenadier while he is distracted by Chapheau.

As you follow Chapheau through the alleyway, he will exit to the left. When you see two soldiers approaching, take the initiative and assassinate them. If you don't, Chapheau will push one to provoke a fight.

In a later alleyway, watch for two soldiers after Chapheau turns to the right. Once again, sprinting ahead to assassinate them is the safest strategy. After the cinematic, follow the onscreen instructions to direct Chapheau to the appropriate target.

## MISSION OVERVIEW

| Optional Objectives | Further Reading |
|---|---|
| ■ Dump 10 crates of tea in the water.<br>■ Throw three Redcoats into the water.<br>■ Perform a musket air assassination. | ■ You can study the many purposes and potential prowess of Assassin Recruits on page 162. |

01 After starting the Memory, your first objective when play begins is to eliminate the highlighted guards at the docks. This is a good opportunity to call Connor's new Recruit into action. We suggest that you save him for the larger of the two groups, situated on the left-hand side of the ship from your starting position.

III

QUICKSTART

THE STORY SO FAR

PRIMER

WALKTHROUGH

SIDE QUESTS

REFERENCE & ANALYSIS

MULTIPLAYER

EXTRAS

MAP LEGEND

INDEX

02

Once all fifteen targets have been killed, the main section of the Memory begins. As the challenges you face are primarily based around extended combat and situations that will vary on each playthrough, our guidance here will focus on tried and tested tactics. Study our annotated map of the action area. The two men that Connor must protect (Revere and Molineux, blue circles) will each remain on the decks of their respective ships. To the left and right of the two vessels, small gangs of allied soldiers (blue crosses) will attempt to stop the advance of aggressors. Enemies (red lines) will arrive on either jetty, and will attempt to board the ships via the gangplanks, attacking Connor and the men he is enjoined to protect. Finally, crates of tea (white circles) that Connor can throw into the water to satisfy an Optional Objective are mostly found close to the bow on both ships. Your task is to ensure that Revere, Molineux and, indeed, Connor do not fall before the timer expires. This is represented by the total quantity of tea dumped, regularly updated in the upper left-hand corner of the screen.

**General Tips**

⊙ Start the Memory by dumping as many boxes of tea as you can; press Ⓑ/◎ to pick them up, then Ⓐ/⊗ to hurl them into the water. Be careful with your aim: those hurled onto the dock do not count. Moments of calm where this is possible are few and far between later on, so you should aim to clear all ten immediately. You can ignore this step entirely if you do not intend to complete the Optional Objectives.

⊙ To perform the musket air assassination, grab a musket (there are gun racks on the ships), then hop onto the guard rail on either vessel to assassinate an opponent on the dock below. We suggest that you attend to this Optional Objective after you finish with the crates.

⊙ Though the opening battles are quite trivial, the numbers of opponents you face soon increases. If you notice that Revere and Molineux are under attack by several opponents, respond immediately. Later in the battle, focus Connor's energies on protecting whichever of the two has the least health remaining. Officers present the gravest threat to your allies.

⊙ Don't forget to call upon your new Assassin Recruit as events unfold. If you are busy fighting on one deck, you can direct him to attack soldiers on the next ship.

⊙ You can easily hop between the two vessels, but the attacking soldiers will not do the same. Be very careful not to fall into the water: this can be disastrous.

⊙ Though the Optional Objective to throw three soldiers into the water suggests that you must use the Counter Throw ability, you can also just punch or kick them whenever there is no obstruction to prevent their fall. This is far easier to perform if you engage a wave of soldiers on the dock when they first arrive.

## MISSION OVERVIEW

| Optional Objectives | Further Reading |
|---|---|
| ■ Reach Johnson undetected.<br>■ Kill Johnson before a single Native American is killed.<br>■ Perform a swan dive to escape. | ■ Now might be an opportune time to liberate Boston's North and South District from Templar influence: see page 157.<br>■ Boston has two Templar-controlled forts. Conquering these heavily guarded zones is one of the most exciting optional activities in Assassin's Creed III. Our full walkthroughs begin on page 148. |

Fast Travel to the Homestead to find the Memory Start marker, then head to the Frontier to continue. Once again, this is a Memory where a desire to beat Optional Objectives increases its difficulty – but a stealth-based approach is also the most enjoyable way to conquer it. If you prefer action, you can alternatively follow the general path of the route we detail here as you cut a righteous swath to the meeting. Start by following the free run course illustrated here to reach the riverbank.

Cross the log to reach this rock outcrop and watch the guards at the far side of the water. You need to move over to the right, where only one sentry poses any form of threat. Swim into the position marked here when he moves to the leftmost section of his patrol (reeds in water offer the same stealth benefits as Stalking Zones), then stay close to the rocks until he reaches a position above Connor. Wait for a second or two when he turns away, then scramble onto the shore over the rock.

Run up the sequence of steep banks, following the route detailed here. It may seem as if you're approaching a dead end, but that's really not the case.

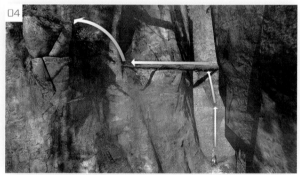

At the top of the bank in the alcove, there is a ledge that, though hard to see, enables you to begin climbing to the top of the cliff.

Unless you have already collected it, you will find a Feather as you cross the log on the penultimate stretch of the cliff ascent.

Be extremely cautious on this section of the climb. There is a guard at the top on a short patrol loop, and the ledge where he looks out over the lake is not at all suitable for an assassination. Stay out of sight until you see him move away on the mini-map, then climb up and hide in the small Stalking Zone for a silent kill on his return. You can calmly walk past the guard crouched by the cliff to the left – if you can resist the sociopathic urge to sneak over and kick him, that is.

Free run through the tree-based course, ignoring the path to the left just beforehand – it leads to a difficult route featuring guards and a two-man patrol.

In the final V-shaped tree section, study the mini-map before you jump to solid ground – the slow, regular stroll taken by the two-man patrol mentioned earlier reaches the edge of this area. If the coast is clear, move forward via the Stalking Zones to approach the house. A cinematic will begin as you draw near.

After the cutscene, a new Optional Objective is given: you must intervene before any Native Americans are killed – and this means that you'll need to be extremely quick. From the Stalking Zone where you begin, wait for the two guards to turn away, then sprint in the direction of the house and follow this free run course. From the final position, perform an air assassination on Johnson. If you fail the Optional Objective beforehand – the timing is extremely tight – select Reload Last Checkpoint to try again.

When play resumes, don't stick around to fight – the reveal of the final Optional Objective should make your next step abundantly clear. From your position in front of the house, sprint down the slope until you reach the top of the cliff, then dive into the water below. Submerge and swim towards the reeds to stay out of sight; as you move away from the Templar guards, the Sequence ends.

THE FRONTIER

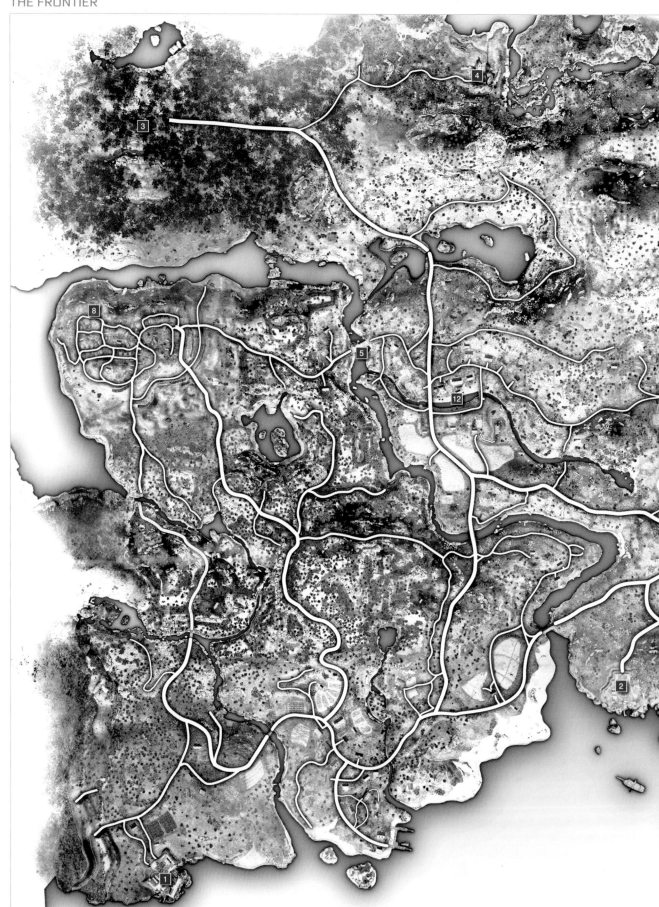

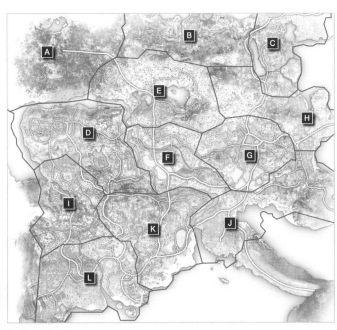

QUICKSTART

THE STORY SO FAR

PRIMER

WALKTHROUGH

SIDE QUESTS

REFERENCE & ANALYSIS

MULTIPLAYER

EXTRAS

MAP LEGEND

INDEX

## Forts:

| 1 | Fort Monmouth |
| 2 | Fort St-Mathieu |
| 3 | Fort Duquesne |

## Landmarks:

| 4 | Connor's Village |
| 5 | North Bridge |
| 6 | Old Belfry |
| 7 | Buckman Tavern |
| 8 | Isaac Potts House* |
| 9 | Johnson Hall |
| 10 | Boston Light |
| 11 | Lexington |
| 12 | Concord |
| ◎ | Exit to Boston |
| ⌂ | Exit to Davenport Homestead |

## Regions:

| A | Black Creek |
| B | Kanièn:keh |
| C | John's Town |
| D | Valley Forge |
| E | Diamond Basin |
| F | Concord |
| G | Lexington |
| H | Great Piece Hills |
| I | Packanack |
| J | Scotch Plains |
| K | Troy's Woods |
| L | Monmouth |

*The west side of Valley Forge is inaccessible until the start of Sequence 09.

## MISSION OVERVIEW

| Optional Objectives | Preparation |
|---|---|
| ▪ Do not trigger open conflict.<br>▪ Reach Prescott's location within two minutes. | ▪ This Memory is much easier to complete if you have Synchronized with Viewpoints in the south and central areas of the Frontier. |

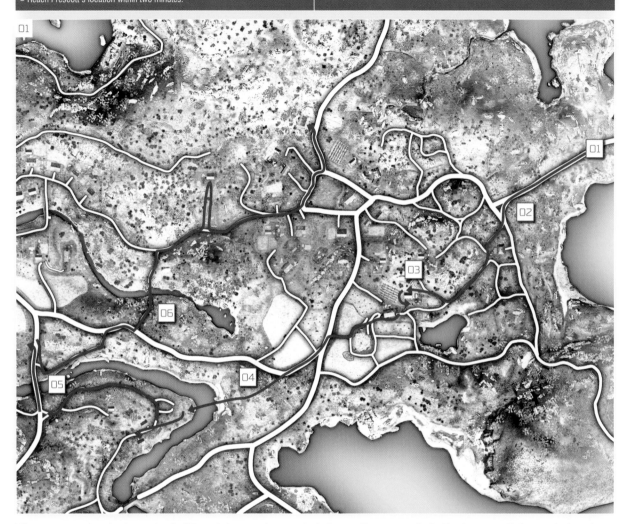

When you are ready to begin, travel to Paul Revere's house at the waypoint in Boston. Play resumes in the Frontier area, with the two sharing a horse. You can tap ⬆/L2 to ask Revere for directions during the journey... or follow our annotated map for precise guidance. Each number corresponds to an important step covered in the walkthrough entries that follow: you start, naturally, at position 1.

It's vital that you avoid Redcoat patrols to complete the main Optional Objective. The first will pass by when you reach the first junction; slow to a trot and move along the left fork until they pass. The next part of the journey requires that you follow a faint trail that can be hard to see at first; look for it in the position shown here. Once behind the house, follow the trail to the southwest.

When you approach the first house, don't ride into the center of town; instead leave the horse and move behind the house as directed here. Check that the coast is clear, then walk around to reach the front door. Approach it and press B/◎. When the cutscene ends, continue along the path. You can cut through the fields to avoid patrols on the roads: keep a keen eye on the mini-map.

04

With this shortcut through the wooded area, you can find a secluded crossing where the water is shallow enough for your horse to wade to the opposite bank. After you pass the first house, the door you must knock is at the front of the next building on your left.

05

Ride on the riverside trail until you reach a bridge. Wait out of sight until the Redcoat patrol crosses, heading in a southerly direction, then gallop over it and approach the first house on the left. Dismount and approach the door. If you have escaped detection until this point, the first Optional Objective is completed here.

06

After the cinematic twist, a new Optional Objective is introduced to add an element of haste to the next section of the journey. Immediately after the cutscene ends, turn 180 degrees on the spot and ride behind the first house on your left to find a narrow trail leading east, as shown on our map. When you arrive at the river, you can cross via the ford illustrated here. After you reach the next door – a journey with no further hazards if you follow the path we suggest – more traditional waypoints are employed to guide you to the final destination. On arrival, enter the house to end the Memory.

## MISSION OVERVIEW

| Optional Objectives | Further Reading |
|---|---|
| ■ Rescue the civilian hostages.<br>■ Kill a group of regulars with a single order on five occasions. | ■ After this Memory, the two final chapters of Sequence 07 spirit Connor away to a new area where you cannot engage in side quests or metagames until you have completed all objectives. If you have activities to attend to (see page 134 for current options), do so before or directly after the events of Lexington and Concord. |

Strike up a conversation with John Parker at the Memory Start marker to begin. When play commences, there is a three-minute time limit to beat. Start by mounting the horse on the right-hand side of the track. The path you travel is the final section of the Midnight Ride journey in reverse order. Stick to the trail, spur your horse at regular intervals for maximum speed, and it is actually a simple journey – despite the chaos unfolding around you.

When you reach the west side of Concord, the first Optional Objective appears. To complete it, ride to the red marker in the south when you reach the junction, and ride behind to the soldiers driving their civilian captives along the path over the small bridge. Press ❌/⬜ to leap off and perform an assassination on the Officer at the rear of the group, then kill his three subordinates. You can then jump back on your horse and race through the remaining waypoints.

The final part of this Memory sees Connor take charge of three firing lines as they seek to repel the advance of the Redcoats from the opposite bank of the river. The opposing soldiers march into the positions marked on the annotated screenshot here. Connor must ride between his soldiers and issue the instruction to fire at the most appropriate moment. Though the process is simple enough at first, the sheer weight of enemy numbers ensures a frantic finale.

To issue a fire order, press Ⓑ/◎ inside the circular zone next to each firing line. Try to time these commands to the precise moment that enemy soldiers move within optimal range. This is usually just after they stop their advance (as shown here), which leads to a perfect result and a strike towards the running Optional Objective tally. Use the mini-map to judge which position requires your most urgent attention: red dots (●) are moving soldiers, red hexagons (⬢) indicate those within firing range, while flashing red hexagons represent those currently firing on Patriot positions. The bar in the top-left corner of the screen indicates the strength of Connor's force, and you must defeat 130 Redcoats to win the skirmish. When it ends, move to the waypoint marker to end the Memory.

III

QUICKSTART

THE STORY SO FAR

PRIMER

WALKTHROUGH

SIDE QUESTS

REFERENCE & ANALYSIS

MULTIPLAYER

EXTRAS

MAP LEGEND

INDEX

## ⚠ CONFLICT LOOMS

### MISSION OVERVIEW

| Optional Objectives | Preparation |
|---|---|
| ▪ Cross Charlestown without taking damage.<br>▪ Air assassinate a Grenadier.<br>▪ Remain undetected while on the ships. | ▪ Once you begin this Memory, Connor is transported to the Bunker Hill region until the end of the Sequence. We advise that you attend to pressing business before you depart, particularly convoys from the Homestead and assigning available Assassin Recruits to missions. You may also decide to stock up on ammunition and other consumable items beforehand. |

01

02

Speak to the soldier at the Memory Start marker to begin. Play resumes in a new region: Bunker Hill. Follow the scout on horseback, then run to Israel Putnam. After the cinematic, begin by following the route illustrated here and climb the first house on the right.

Connor must stay in motion to avoid taking damage from the relentless barrage. Run along the rooftops, taking care to angle your jumps for effortless landings, until you reach the last red brick house in the row.

03

04

Use the tree (to be specific, the right-hand V-shaped section) and low roof to descend to ground level, then cut through the alleyway to the right of the house.

As you exit the alleyway, make a quick dart to the right to move behind the barrels and avoid the Redcoats.

The route illustrated here is quicker than swimming all the way, and features no element of danger. Ignore the waypoint near to the closest vessel for now, and swim to the ship further east. As you approach it, the first Optional Objective ends and two new challenges appear. One compels you to stay undetected; the second (air assassinating a Grenadier) simply complicates the first. Players who prefer action (or wish to leave Optional Objectives until a later date) can ignore our stealth-based walkthrough and fight the soldiers stationed on both vessels instead.

Swim to the boat behind the ship and use it to jump over to the stern. Our annotated screenshot shows the patrol routes of the soldiers on the ship. The target marked in orange is the Grenadier that you must assassinate with a very specific method.

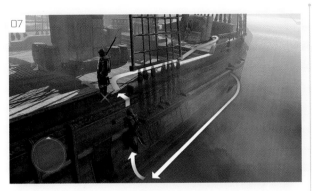

07

08

Climb on the port (east) side of the vessel, then carefully move into the position illustrated here. Wait until the Redcoat stands above you, with the Grenadier facing elsewhere on the opposite side of the ship, then perform a ledge assassination to hurl him into the water. You must then climb up and use Fast Walk to move into position behind the crates at the stern before the Redcoat there finishes his short patrol. This is something that you can accomplish immediately, though you can wait for another full rotation of the "clockwork engine" if you lack confidence.

From your position behind the crates, wait until the soldier ends his patrol at the wheel, then use the Whistle ability to force him to investigate. This will enable you to perform a corner assassination before the Grenadier's patrol brings him into visual range of the act.

09

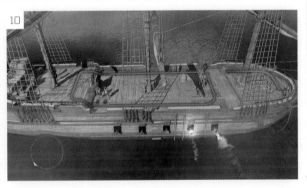

10

Wait and watch the Grenadier. When he sets off on his patrol, climb the mast (start on the pile of crates) and wait until he moves beneath. Perform an air assassination when he reaches the position behind the crates. You can now calmly walk over and plant the explosives at the waypoint marker, then immediately jump overboard.

Swim to the next ship and, once again, use the boat behind the aft section to begin your climb. Traverse to the port side (where the cannons lie dormant) and observe the two patrols carefully. With all soldiers potentially watching others, this is a puzzle with no apparent solution – until you realize that the answer is both bold and bloodless.

11

Wait until the patrolling Officer passes your position, then immediately climb up and Fast Walk to the waypoint marker. Press ❸/◎ as soon as you can to plant the explosives; the Officer may notice but not fully detect Connor at this point. Fast Walk back to the edge of the vessel and dive overboard. Moments later, the explosion will kill all guards instantly. You must now climb back onto the ship and scale the central mast to place a flag. With this final feat accomplished, perform a Leap of Faith into the water and swim towards the shore to end the Memory.

## MISSION OVERVIEW

**Optional Objectives**

- Cross the battlefield without taking damage.
- Limit regular kills to four.
- Air assassinate Pitcairn without being detected.

This Memory begins immediately on completion of Conflict Looms. Mount the horse at the waypoint marker and follow the Patriot until you arrive for Putnam's speech. When play resumes, you must use cover elements and careful timing to cross the battlefield – and, if you wish to complete the Optional Objective, avoid moving under fire. To achieve this, you must make each advance at very specific moments. Look for spoken and visual cues. When you hear cries of "Incoming!" or "Take cover!", the Redcoat lines are poised to fire. As you hide, watch for widespread bursts of muzzle flashes from the Redcoats (pictured here); when these end, it's safe to make a dash to the next position.

This annotated view of the battlefield presents the optimal route between potential cover positions. There is, naturally, a checkpoint at the start of this set piece, so don't hesitate to return to the beginning if you fail the Optional Objective.

Once you pass safely to the left of the main British forces, two patrols will approach your position. You can either fight them, or bypass them altogether by free running in the trees, as shown here.

Once you reach the cliff below the waypoint marker, climb via the route illustrated here. When you reach the top, two new Optional Objectives become active: to perform no more than four regular kills, and to air assassinate Pitcairn without being detected.

From the top of the cliff, enter the Stalking Zone and use it to carefully approach the hilltop camp.

Follow the Stalking Zone as it curves off to the left, then wait and watch the patrolling Redcoat in the area ahead. When his back is turned, cross the gap between the two patches of undergrowth. When he approaches your position, perform a stealth assassination. It's not strictly necessary to kill him, but it simplifies the next steps immeasurably.

Sneak through the undergrowth behind the tents until you reach another break in the Stalking Zone, by a cart full of hay. Watch the camping area until you see an Officer move out of sight, then Fast Walk into the next patch of undergrowth.

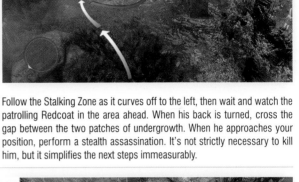

Take up position behind the canvas tent, then perform a corner assassination when the Officer approaches.

You can now free run through the trees to reach a position above Pitcairn and perform an air assassination. Leap from the first bough into the V-shaped section of the next tree, then tap Ⓐ/Ⓧ to climb. Run to the end of the branch, then jump over to the flag pole. From here, all that remains is to target Pitcairn and press Ⓧ/▢ to begin the closing cinematics of Sequence 07.

## FIGHTING PITCAIRN

While most Optional Objectives make Memories more difficult to complete, the stealthy approach to assassinating Pitcairn that we present is easier and quicker than engaging him – and his many allies – in open conflict. If you favor a balls-over-brains approach, it's prudent to dispatch Pitcairn's men before you engage the Templar himself. While he is vulnerable to the Counter Disarm move, note that you cannot complete a combo or Counter Kill, or harm him during a Kill Streak until his life bar has been depleted.

## NEW YORK

NORTH DISTRICT

EAST DISTRICT

WEST DISTRICT

| | |
|---|---|
| **1** | Trinity Church |
| **2** | Trinity School |
| **3** | Wall Street |
| **4** | Smith and Company Brewery |
| **5** | St. Paul's Chapel |
| **6** | Bowling Green |
| **7** | Bridewell Prison |
| **8** | Broad Street |
| **9** | Broadway |
| **10** | King's College |
| **11** | Fort George |
| **12** | HMS Jersey |
| ▲ | Exit to Frontier |

## MISSION OVERVIEW

| Optional Objectives | Important Note |
|---|---|
| ▪ Perform a successful static eavesdrop.<br>▪ Perform a successful mobile eavesdrop.<br>▪ Do not tackle or shove anyone. | ▪ Travelling to New York automatically initiates an unbroken chain of four Memories played in succession, with no opportunities to manage the Homestead or your Assassin Recruits or play other side quests. |

This Memory begins immediately after your arrival in New York. Mount the horse and ride into the city with your guide. After the cutscene, follow the counterfeiter into the alleyway. Blend with the crowd before he turns right, to avoid detection, then press yourself against the corner to watch him from afar. When he resumes his journey after turning suspiciously to regard the alley behind him, you can break into a brief jog to cut the distance.

After he crosses the street to reach another alley, hang back in a crowd by the left-hand corner as a brief fight breaks out. Do not get involved in the scuffle – stay where you are and wait for him to resume his journey.

The counterfeiter will opt for the next alleyway to the left, increasing his pace. Keep up, with the Fast Walk ability, and hide when you reach a wooden fence; he will turn to examine the path behind.

When you reach the position shown here, climb the steep wooden stairs and hide behind the barrels. The counterfeiter meets with an associate, and a new primary goal and Optional Objective are both revealed. Wait until the eavesdrop is complete, hold back a few moments for your target to move away, then jump down and continue your pursuit.

Back on the streets, make your way into the Blend position shown here; your person of interest turns to regard the street behind him before he turns to the left.

In the secluded area, stay behind the fence to avoid detection as the counterfeiter approaches the well. He will jump inside it to avoid two guards. Don't panic: they will not react to Connor, and simply pass him without comment or consequence.

Stay out of sight as your target winds through paths less travelled, and he will eventually convene with an associate in an alleyway. A new Optional Objective is revealed here: you must complete a successful mobile eavesdrop. Make use of Blend opportunities as you find them, and stay to the rear of the circle. In the final long alleyway, hide to the right – as illustrated here – to avoid detection when they turn for the last time.

After the cutscene, Connor must pursue Hickey through the streets, but avoid making physical contact with anyone as he runs if you plan to complete the Optional Objective. The best way to accomplish this is to regulate your use of 𝗥𝗧/𝗥𝟭 to vary your pace as you weave through crowds and past obstructions. Once you leave the alleyway, in the position illustrated above, a group of soldiers will block Connor's direct pursuit of Hickey. To complete the Memory, cut to the left, then take the first right. You can then easily intercept Hickey by performing the Tackle move (𝗕/◎) as he emerges from the alley to the right.

# ⚠ FATHER AND SON

## MISSION OVERVIEW

| Optional Objectives | Further Reading |
| --- | --- |
| ▪ Do not get detected while stealing the mercenary outfit. | ▪ Travelling to New York advances the story by one month instantly, which removes the blanket of snow. Though a large area of the west side of the city is heavily militarized, you can now explore the rest of the region and partake in its many side quests, including Liberation Missions (to acquire new Assassin Recruits – see page 154) and Forts (page 150). We would strongly advise that you Synchronize with local Viewpoints as you pass them. |

Travel to New York, then approach the bench at the Memory Start marker: note that this Memory and the one that follows are automatically played in succession. When Connor and Haytham are reunited, follow the Templar over the rooftops. Haytham stops close to a Viewpoint at one stage; if you pay him a wide berth (as shown here), you can Synchronize with this before you approach him to trigger a (rather fine) cinematic. Afterwards, follow Haytham's lead again until you trigger another cutscene at the bottom of a ladder.

You must now intercept a target at the waypoint to obtain a disguise. From your starting position, follow the route marked here. If you have yet to liberate New York's East District, you may witness an execution. Ignore this for now: you can return to administer justice at a later date.

As you round the corner by the waterfront, look for a hay cart. A group led by an Officer patrols this area, and will stop to examine this hiding place when they pass it. Wait until they move on, heading north.

Your target has a simple movement pattern that takes him between two main positions. Jump into the hay cart, and wait for him to draw near. When he turns away, jump out and quietly assassinate him, then loot him before the patrol returns. This ends this Memory, which transitions instantly to the events of The Foam and the Flames.

## MISSION OVERVIEW

| Optional Objectives | Further Reading |
|---|---|
| ▪ Limit Haytham's health loss to 50%.<br>▪ Do not take any fire damage. | ▪ If you have yet to do so, study the section that begins on page 222 to learn how to identify and defeat more powerful enemy archetypes in combat. |

01

02

Follow Haytham, then quickly dispatch assailants in the brawl that follows to ensure that his health does not fall below 50%. Though most of the combatants are generic mercenaries, there are several that correspond to the Grenadier archetype. If you fail the Optional Objective, it's easy to return to the previous checkpoint – or even restart the Memory if the cutscene that follows the battle has already begun.

Connor must now escape the burning building. Though you can follow Haytham at the start, their paths soon diverge. There is also an Optional Objective that specifies you avoid contact with the flames, though this is one of the easier challenges. Start by climbing up the ramp, then jump into the rafters.

03

04

Cut the corners to avoid the burning wooden beams, then sprint for the V-shaped rafter and jump through.

When you land, turn right and follow the obvious route until the path collapses. Run beneath the burning beams.

05

06

Scale the wall as illustrated here, then follow the onscreen instructions to perform a Back Eject.

Finally, jump over to the wall and climb all the way to the top.

III

QUICKSTART

THE STORY SO FAR

PRIMER

WALKTHROUGH

SIDE QUESTS

REFERENCE & ANALYSIS

MULTIPLAYER

EXTRAS

MAP LEGEND

INDEX

## MISSION OVERVIEW

| Optional Objectives | Further Reading |
|---|---|
| ■ Limit environmental damage to 20%.<br>■ Stay within 500 meters of the schooner.<br>■ Achieve a minimum Kill Streak of three. | ■ Consider investing available funds in upgrades for the Aquila before you begin this Memory: see page 253. If you have neglected naval missions so far, we highly recommend that you play a few now (see page 176). They are hugely entertaining, and doing so now will prepare you for the events of A Bitter End. |

In the battle that follows, avoid the Man-of-War as you sink the smaller vessels. Once they have been removed from the equation, switch to Grapeshot as directed (hold **RB**/**R2**, then select the ammunition from the menu), then perform broadside attacks to destroy its masts, as shown here. When the vessel sits dead in the water, approach it to trigger a cutscene.

The final Optional Objective is to achieve a Kill Streak of three, which must be accomplished before you dispatch all targets marked in red on the mini-map. If you run immediately to the Officer at the stern, it's pretty easy to accomplish this by killing him first, then dispatching his nearby crewmen. It's much harder to do this in the area where two Officers fight together, due to their ability to resist Kill Streak attacks. When the battle ends, walk to the waypoint marker and interact with the door to end the Sequence.

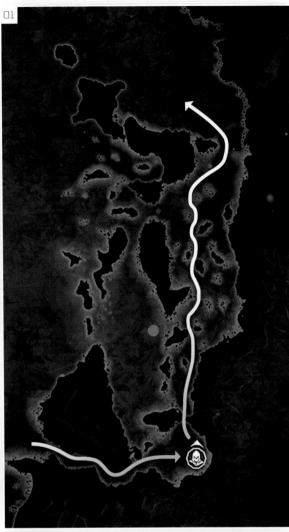

After the events of The Foam and the Flames, Connor is automatically positioned next to Haytham at the Memory Start marker, though don't feel compelled to start immediately: you are free to attend to other affairs beforehand. When you do begin, sail along the narrow channel. Take great care to avoid collisions. Regular short transitions to half sail are enough to navigate with ease until you reach the waypoint. You must now sail after the schooner, and stay within 500 meters to complete the Optional Objective. As before, you will regularly find half sail essential to improve the Aquila's mobility for tight turns, and to counter the effects of rogue winds. Whenever you have the opportunity, employ a brief period of full sail for additional speed. The annotated map here shows a course that will easily enable you to remain within the specified range. When you are directed to take the outside curve, the Optional Objectives end.

## ⚠ ALTERNATE METHODS

### MISSION OVERVIEW

| Optional Objectives | Further Reading |
|---|---|
| ■ Use two guards as human shields.<br>■ Tackle the target from above. | ■ By this stage in the story, the vast majority of optional activities are unlocked and available to play: study our Completion Timeline on page 134 for details. |

Reconvene with Haytham in New York, close to Fort George. When the Memory begins, follow him on the free run course through the burnt-out buildings. In the fight that follows, a new Optional Objective encourages you to use two guards as human shields. This isn't difficult: just move into the center of the area. The volleys of the marksmen highlighted by orange hexagons (⬡) will provide plenty of opportunities to complete the secondary challenge. Keep the camera trained on their position and be ready to react until the Optional Objective has been satisfied, then pull back to the rear of the area for the rest of the fight. When the bodyguards are dead or disabled, run over to the targets.

Sprint in pursuit of the escapee immediately. When you reach the street, move to the right-hand side to prevent the patrol from reacting before Connor passes their position. When your target takes a right into an alleyway, continue straight ahead and take the next right instead.

There are two potential solutions here: those aiming for 100% Synchronization should skip to the "Air Tackle" box-out. If the Optional Objective isn't important to you, just run towards your target as he approaches from the alleyway and hold 🎮/(R1) then press 🅱/◎ to tackle him. After the cutscene, you can propel your reluctant captive towards the waypoint by pressing 🅰/✗ whenever he stops.

### AIR TACKLE

Completing the task with a tackle from above to satisfy the Optional Objective demands a near-flawless run from the beginning, so be prepared for a few restarts before you master the required timing. When you round the corner, run up the wagon and jump to the light fitting, then swing to the beam. Angle the camera to look at the street below, hold 🎮/(R1) then press 🅱/◎ to tackle the escapee as he passes beneath Connor. If you miss this opportunity, all is not lost just yet: swing around the corner, then try again on the next street.

## MISSION OVERVIEW

| Optional Objectives | Preparation |
| --- | --- |
| ▪ Do not touch the ground.<br>▪ Stop the Patriot messengers within three minutes.<br>▪ Stop the Kanien'kehá:ka with non-lethal methods. | ▪ If you have yet to do so, acquire a new pistol: the Double-Barrel Pistol (available in General Stores) or superior will suffice: see pages 229 and 230 for details. We strongly recommend that you have at least a few cartridges in Connor's inventory before you begin.<br>▪ Smoke Bombs may also prove very useful (see page 232). |

**01** To begin this Memory, travel to the Frontier, then meet Haytham at Valley Forge in the west of the region. When the cinematics end, ride to the waypoint in the north. You must now stop the Patriot messengers on the track ahead. Players attempting a perfect playthrough must do so within the specified time limit, and without once touching the ground. The path that Connor must follow is narrow, so pay very close attention to the winding trail – note that the approximate route is marked in green on the mini-map – and limit use of the spur command to straight sections.

**02** The first messenger is attending to his ailing horse on the left side of the track; you should see him approximately twenty seconds after passing through the initial waypoint. Just ride straight over him: there's no need to stop or waste a bullet.

**03** Further along the track, you will encounter three of the messengers riding slowly in close formation. Equip the Hidden Blade, then perform an assassination on the rider to the rear once you move within range; Connor will automatically appropriate his horse. You can then shoot the second and third riders immediately, which is essential: the riders may dismount and attack Connor with firearms. Players who are still using a single-shot pistol can alternatively switch to the bow for the third target.

**04** The final messenger rides with a far greater sense of purpose, perhaps aware of Connor's pursuit. To catch him, try to take a "racing line" on corners and spur your horse when the track allows it. Your target will tumble from the saddle after one shot but, depending on your current preferred firearm, may take another bullet (or an arrow) to finish off. Be very careful to stay on your horse: the related Optional Objective does not end until you reach Connor's village. Pay the red Restricted Area a wide berth during the final leg of the journey.

**05** Ride into the village and approach the final waypoint to trigger a cutscene. When it ends, a third Optional Objective is given: to disable the Kanien'kehá:ka warriors with non-lethal methods. Select Connor's fists as his primary weapon, then exit the village. Run to approach each warrior, then slow down and sneak behind them before tapping ⊗/□ to incapacitate them silently. If you pick your route carefully, you should remain undetected. Should a warrior see Connor, however, drop a Smoke Bomb to incapacitate him before you render him unconscious.

## MISSION OVERVIEW

**Optional Objectives**

■ Neutralize eight platoons with a single cannonball.     ■ Kill two platoons simultaneously with a single cannonball.     ■ Prevent three Patriot executions.

The final Memory of Sequence 10 begins in the south of the Frontier area. After the opening cinematic, play resumes with Connor commanding a cannon emplacement to slow the Loyalist advance while the Patriots retreat. Use 🄛 to aim the cannon, 🄐/⊗ to fire  and 🄡 to pan your view of the battlefield. The annotated screenshot here shows the general movement of the Loyalist soldiers, and the four positions where they will stop and ready their weapons. Loyalist troops with ⬤ icons above their heads are priority targets: they will remain stationary and fire at the Patriots, sapping the "life gauge" in the left-hand corner of the screen. The best general strategy is to focus on the troops to the left, only attending to the single stream on the right during quieter moments.

To complete the Optional Objectives (and the Circus Act Achievement/Trophy for killing 15 guards with a single cannon shot), you must be highly accurate with your marksmanship, taking the cannon's period of flight, and potential movement of troops prior to impact, into account. Each group of eight men moving in close formation represents a platoon. Dispatching two simultaneously is something that is easiest to achieve with the left-hand flow of Loyalists: just position your cannonball between two groups as illustrated here.

03

04

05

You now have three minutes to retreat via a crumb trail of waypoints, but a new Optional Objective rather complicates matters: you must prevent the execution of three Patriots. The first firing line is not far from your starting position. After you cross the river and pass a General Store on your left, look for them in the position marked here. You can simply charge into the Redcoats to avert the execution, but we find it more effective to use a pistol to shoot an opponent during the approach. If you decide to fight the three battles, Counter Kills and Kill Streaks will enable you to save time.

When you pass a large barn with faded red paintwork, the second firing line is in front of the next house on the left.

The final firing line is on the right-hand side of the road, just beyond the field of crops surrounded by a wooden fence. The final waypoint is a short sprint away.

## (!) POWER SOURCE #3

Walk along the corridor until you reach two guards, then disable them when they attack. As in previous excursions outside the Grand Temple, you must interpret the movement of your opponents to react to their attacks.

Approach the elevator; after the cutscene, climb to the top of the shaft. There is only one way up, as illustrated here.

When you reach the opening above, there is a perfect opportunity for a ledge assassination. Jump up and fight the guards. You will need to make regular use of the human shield move from this point forward.

With your back to the elevator, head to the door on the left (marked Conference C) where there are more guards to fight.

When you reach the atrium, stay on the walkway as you dispatch the next group of opponents. Jump through the broken window and approach the first door on the left.

For those who recall the conclusion of Assassin's Creed, activate Eagle Vision after the cutscene with Daniel Cross. Subject 16's messages are still visible in the lab where Desmond was once held hostage.

Kill the two guards in the corridor outside, then chase Cross.

When he leaps through the window, follow him into another area that should be familiar to Assassin's Creed fans. Follow the free run course in a clockwise progression to descend to ground level.

QUICKSTART

THE STORY SO FAR

PRIMER

WALKTHROUGH

SIDE QUESTS

REFERENCE & ANALYSIS

MULTIPLAYER

EXTRAS

MAP LEGEND

INDEX

On the lower level, fight the guards in the immediate area to reduce the number of guns potentially leveled at Desmond, then climb on top of a glass cubicle (or the metal framework above) and activate Eagle Vision to locate Cross; he is marked with a gold highlight. Free run to his position and assassinate him.

When play resumes, you will find that Desmond is now equipped with a gun. Fight your way through the linear path until all guards have been disabled. At this point, a secretary will open a final door. The closing moments of the mission are entirely story-driven, so we'll curtail our involvement here to avoid spoiling any surprises.

If you have inserted the previous two Power Sources (see pages 92 and 114), you can now put the third in its rightful place. Start by running up the steps uncovered by the second Power Source, then take a right. Swing via the poles concealed in the broken ceiling, then take another right to ascend a second set of steps.

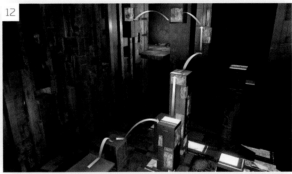

Inside the room with the strange "pillars", those marked with an eerie orange luminescence actually indicate a route to an upper level.

Run through the next room, then swing via the two poles to reach a ledge on the opposite wall. Climb to the top, then walk to the right.

The final step is to use the ledges shown here to traverse to an opening to the right, then approach the console where the Power Source can be placed. Once this has been achieved (via a cutscene), turn left and jump to the lower level, then swing via the pole to return to the main floor area. Check Desmond's emails and speak to his colleagues for new conversations, if you wish, then enter the Animus, to continue.

## ⚠ BATTLE OF THE CHESAPEAKE

### MISSION OVERVIEW

| Optional Objectives | Further Reading |
| --- | --- |
| ▪ Destroy three ships with a single broadside.<br>▪ Destroy two frigates by firing on their powder stores.<br>▪ Counter Kill five enemies. | ▪ If you have yet to invest in upgrades for the Aquila, this is *definitely* the time to do so. See page 253 for details. |

Head down to the Aquila and speak to Faulkner to access the naval map, then select the 🔘 icon to begin this Memory. Sail to the waypoint, being careful to avoid collisions with allied vessels. If you are not invested in Optional Objectives, you can simply adopt an aggressive and efficient strategy to beat this mission. If Naval Missions are not your forte, see page 171 for a variety of useful tips and guidelines. Our walkthrough here is primarily designed to assist players in their quest for Full Synchronization.

The opening battle presents your best opportunity to destroy three ships with a single broadside to complete the Optional Objective – and, indeed, this is something that you must attempt to complete immediately. Sail for the ships directly ahead, then turn when you draw close, to sink three schooners with a broadside. If you intend to obtain Full Synchronization, it's wise to restart if you fail: there is a checkpoint just before the battle begins.

The next part of the engagement features several smaller vessels and a single frigate, which you can destroy by any means you prefer. Once the final ship has been sunk, three frigates will engage the Aquila and its sole remaining ally. To complete the Optional Objective that appears on their arrival, you must destroy two by hitting their powder stores with the swivel gun. As luck would have it, the ship to the right of the formation is vulnerable immediately: sail straight towards it, line up the swivel gun to hit the area marked by a white circle (as shown here), then release when the target is red for an immediate kill. The second is a little more demanding. Pick a ship, hit it with a broadside to weaken its structural integrity, and "scan" it by activating the swivel gun. If it alights on a weak point, steer and aim accordingly. If not, line up another broadside and try again.

Sail into the green circle to locate the enemy ship, then immediately ram the Man-of-War to initiate boarding. Once Connor lands on the deck, remain stationary and defeat the first five opponents that engage him with Counter Kills to complete the final Optional Objective. With this accomplished, run along the deck and charge the firing line to disperse it. Once the initial group of soldiers has been eliminated, engage the captain and kill him to trigger a cutscene. You then have ten seconds to sprint through a short free run course to escape.

## MISSION OVERVIEW

| Optional Objectives | Preparation |
|---|---|
| ▪ Reach the signal tower within three minutes.<br>▪ Remain undetected on the way to the signal fire.<br>▪ Limit health loss to 50%. | ▪ This marks your last opportunity to attend to non-story endeavors until the end of the penultimate main story Memory. Though you are free to continue side quests after the conclusion of the central narrative, players attempting to complete an orderly 100% playthrough should begin wrapping up their affairs before they begin. We also suggest that you have Poison Darts in your inventory, but ensure that you do not use them for now. |

Connor lands on the east side of New York, with the next destination in his story to the southeast. When you are ready to begin, enter the New York Underground at the position marked by the customary ⓘ icon. Take a left turn when you reach a junction and you will eventually arrive at the Center Downtown exit: the official Memory Start position.

There are three Optional Objectives revealed when Connor reaches the surface. Start with the obvious move of assassinating the guard standing beside the well, then scale the building to the southeast and climb the ladder.

From the ladder, turn to the right and sprint over the two flat rooftops to reach a sloped roof just beyond. When you reach the white decorative frontage to this building, you will need to quickly perform a manual jump to leap to the next house in line.

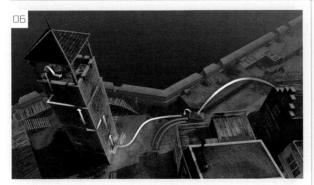

Stick to the right-hand side of the first roof to avoid the guard on the roof to your left: in fact, ignore his SSI meter entirely when it appears. If you run this section smoothly, it doesn't matter for a second. Once you jump to the lower building, run to the right-hand side of the chimney and leap to the branch, then immediately jump to the building ahead.

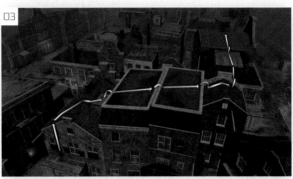

Sprint over the rooftop, then leap through the two V-shaped sections in the tree to reach the next building. Sprint along the right-hand side of the sloped rooftop and perform an immediate Leap of Faith into the hay cart below. There is a guard who moves between this cart and another nearby, so be ready to perform an immediate stealth assassination on landing. If he is further away, wait for his return.

We repeat the guard's precise movements on this screenshot for ease of reference. After his death, the final step is to climb the tower. Once again, this is an instance where you must simply ignore detection indicators and follow the route with speed and at least a modicum of precision. At the top, press Ⓑ/Ⓞ to light the signal fire.

After the signal fire has been lit, move towards the waypoint to begin a climactic showdown. In the fight that ensues, position Connor next to the items highlighted here and press Ⓑ/Ⓞ as your opponent launches an assault, to execute contextual counter attacks. Once you have performed three of these, the closing cinematics of this Sequence will begin.

## ⚠ LAID TO REST

| MISSION OVERVIEW | |
|---|---|
| **Optional Objectives** | **Further Reading** |
| ▪ Limit regular kills to 15.<br>▪ Kill the HMS Jersey's captain.<br>▪ Escape the HMS Jersey without entering open conflict. | ▪ If you followed our advice to acquire and save Poison Darts earlier in the walkthrough, this Memory presents a perfect opportunity to put one to use. See page 231 for information on the unique effects of Poison Darts. |

This Memory begins automatically at the start of Sequence 12. Walk calmly to the waypoint. When play resumes after the momentous cinematic, kill the mercenaries assaulting Connor, then dispatch the second group in the graveyard. You must now reach the HMS Jersey. With Connor at full Notoriety, follow the seemingly unlikely optimal route detailed here to avoid all further conflict and pay the red Restricted Area a wide berth.

From the dock, leap into the water and swim out to the HMS Jersey. Stealth is mandatory from this point in the Memory. Approach the bow of the mighty ship, then follow the climbing route shown here. There are two patrolling guards who may see Connor during the later stages of the climb, but it's easy to move out of sight before they fully detect him.

As the battle with the mercenaries counts for thirteen of your fifteen maximum "regular" kills to complete the Optional Objective, fulfilling both the infiltration and the secondary criteria is a matter of picking your targets carefully. You could, technically, sneak past this guard – but his patrol route might lead him to spot Connor at a later point. Wait until he moves to the south of the ship, climb up, and perform a silent assassination. This also triggers the first checkpoint of the infiltration.

Stop at the top of the staircase and wait for a patrolling guard to stand in the area below. When he turns away, run down and leap from the balustrade to reach a protruding beam, then move out of sight.

III

QUICKSTART

THE STORY SO FAR

PRIMER

WALKTHROUGH

SIDE QUESTS

REFERENCE & ANALYSIS

MULTIPLAYER

EXTRAS

MAP LEGEND

INDEX

Hang outside the window in the specified area to eavesdrop on the captain. Once the conversation is complete, drop back down; note that there is a checkpoint at this stage, should the next steps go awry. Move to the end of the white wooden wall and press Connor against the corner to wait for the arrival of a guard above. When he turns away, jump to the beam directly ahead and traverse to the right.

You must now perform a ledge assassination to remove the stationary guard who faces north. Wait out of sight until the two other patrols marked here are facing elsewhere, then make the kill. Immediately traverse to the right along the wooden ledge.

Continue to the right until you reach the first window, then wait until the guard patrolling outside the captain's cabin walks to the opposite side of the vessel. You should then climb up and move into the eavesdrop position.

Press against the boxes to hide Connor from view during the eavesdrop, then wait for the conversation to finish. When the men leave the cabin, two new Optional Objectives are introduced. If you have no desire to achieve 100% Synchronization, you can now simply dive overboard to end the Memory.

The direct prohibition on detection is essentially maintained by the Optional Objective that specifies against open conflict at this stage. Though the captain does not count as a "regular" kill, the death of even one additional guard will cause you to fail the original Optional Objective. There is no cause for panic, however: with a checkpoint moments beforehand, it's easy to replay this final challenge. Study the annotated map of the pertinent patrol routes on the deck; the captain's path is marked in orange.

Due to the special properties of Poison Darts, they are by far our recommended method of assassination. Stay behind the boxes where you eavesdropped the conversation and wait until the captain approaches the stairs leading to Connor's position, then activate Precision Mode aiming to line up a shot. When he moves within range, tap **Y**/△ to throw the dart, then slip back into cover. The captain will continue to stumble along his patrol route; when he falls dead to the ground, nearby guards will approach his corpse. Once you are sure that no one is watching, dive overboard.

## MISSION OVERVIEW

| Optional Objectives | Important Note |
|---|---|
| ▪ Stay within 50 meters of Lee.<br>▪ Do not shove anyone during the chase.<br>▪ Do not take any fire damage. | ▪ This Memory marks the "point of no return" for side quests and optional activities until the main storyline has been completed. |

Enter the Green Dragon Tavern in Boston, then travel to the investigation zone to the east. Walk along the dock until you pass the second ship on the right, then activate Eagle Vision to identify Charles Lee.

You must now pursue Lee along the dock. This in itself is not especially difficult, completing the two Optional Objectives, however, is much more demanding. Sprint directly ahead until the powder kegs explode (highlighted in red here); directing your initial sprint slightly to the left can sometimes enable you to avoid the effects of the blast.

Free run over the short course to the right of the two soldiers. It may help to hold Ⓐ/Ⓧ for a manual jump at the top to avoid the pole and beam, leaping directly back to the boards below.

Swerve to the right to bypass the next two soldiers.

Move to the outside edge of the boardwalk to avoid the soldiers who run to block Connor's path.

The last step of the pursuit that involves aggressive third parties occurs at the end of the dock: avoid the soldiers by cutting the corner.

III

QUICKSTART

THE STORY SO FAR

PRIMER

WALKTHROUGH

SIDE QUESTS

REFERENCE & ANALYSIS

MULTIPLAYER

EXTRAS

MAP LEGEND

INDEX

07

This next section of the chase is practically a stroll in the park. Avoid civilians, cross the water via the boat, then follow Lee into the ship under construction. At the top of the ramp, take a sharp right and slide beneath the gap.

08

A new Optional Objective specifies that you must avoid contact with flames. After the explosion, scale the wall to the right to reach a beam above, to Connor's left; climb onto it, then swing via the two ropes to land on the platform opposite.

09

When the wooden wall collapses, leap through the new opening. Go through the door and turn left.

10

Though dramatic, the next section of the chase is painless if you maintain your pace and stay to the center of the free run course. At the end, move towards the rope on the left; Connor will automatically cut it and ascend to the upper level.

11

When Lee swings out of sight, run and jump in the direction shown here to follow him. Stay hot on his heels for this short last section of the course, and a cinematic will mark the end of the pursuit. You will require no assistance during the events that follow.

12

**December 20, 2012:** Once the story returns to the present, you have one final opportunity to check emails at the terminal. If you have yet to place any of the three Power Sources, you must attend to this now: see pages 92, 114 and 124 for instructions on how to do so. When you are ready, follow the other Assassins to the vault gate to continue.

## EPILOGUE MISSIONS

After the closing credits, play resumes with Connor outside the Manor. You now have access to three "Epilogue missions" marked by the 🅘 icon. One is in the north of the Frontier in Connor's old village, and another one is on the east side of New York. Both offer cinematics that show developments in the New World, and do not feature direct play.

Once you have viewed both cinematics, a third Memory Start marker appears in Boston. Simply travel to the city to trigger an intriguing cutscene in the Animus "white room". This introduces a new, online-only side quest that you can read about on page 297.

The "Fin." Achievement/Trophy is unlocked when Connor is returned to the streets of Boston, marking the end of the main storyline – but, for most players, the game will be far from over. You can now return to completing all remaining side quests, optional activities and challenges. For the remaining steps in your journey to 100% Synchronization, we now hand over to the Side Quests chapter that lies just over the page.

III

QUICKSTART

THE STORY
SO FAR

PRIMER

WALKTHROUGH

SIDE QUESTS

REFERENCE &
ANALYSIS

MULTIPLAYER

EXTRAS

MAP LEGEND

INDEX

# SIDE QUESTS

This giant and utterly comprehensive chapter documents the steps required to complete **all** optional activities in Assassin's Creed III, from simple diversions to side stories consisting of multiple Memories that will take many hours to finish.

**SPOILER WARNING:** We advise that you avoid browsing this chapter until you complete Sequence 04. While we have taken *every possible* step to avoid storyline spoilers, there are many instances where we must (necessarily) discuss or offer detailed analysis of new or forthcoming gameplay features and developments without prior warning.

## SEQUENCE 04

- Tree-based free running is unlocked.
- The hunting system is introduced, and formally unlocked.

## SEQUENCE 05

- All four sets of Club Challenges can be unlocked (see page 138).
- All Hunting Society missions can be completed (see page 139), and all but two of the Frontiersmen missions.
- Frontier: Convoys appear for the first time (see page 138), and all Viewpoints are available for Synchronization. The region's three Forts can be liberated (see page 144), and two Delivery Requests and a Courier Mission appear (see page 136).
- All Feathers, Trinkets and Chests in the Frontier are available for collection, in addition to four in the newly unlocked Davenport Homestead (see page 200).

- The Boston Underground is available for exploration (see page 164), and the Notoriety system is activated (see page 221).
- Harbormasters are unlocked as Fast Travel positions (see page 200).
- You can start a new Courier Mission and a Delivery Request in Boston (see page 136), and both Forts in the city can be liberated: see page 148.
- All Boston Almanac Pages, Trinkets and Chests can be plundered (see page 202).
- If you have completed "Boy Who Cried Wolf", two Frontiersmen missions are available in Boston (see page 140).
- You can undertake the first Boston Brawlers mission (see page 141).
- The first Assassination Contract appears in the Frontier (see page 137).

- The first Homestead Missions can be completed (see page 193).
- The Accounting Book interface is unlocked, enabling the use of convoys to sell items and crafting to create items (see page 236).

## SEQUENCE 06

- Connor acquires the Hidden Blade and his full stock of Tools (see page 229).
- The first Naval Mission is available (see page 176), along with three Privateer Contracts (see page 180), and you can now deliver up to 14 Trinkets to Peg Leg to unlock and complete the first three installments of the Captain Kidd's Treasure side story (listed under "Naval Locations" in the DNA Tracker): see page 182.
- Upgrades for the Aquila can be purchased from the ledger found by Robert Faulkner and all Harbormasters (see page 253).
- New Homestead Missions are unlocked (see page 193).
- An Assassination Contract appears in Boston (see page 137).
- All enemy archetypes can now be encountered while free roaming: see page 222.

## SEQUENCE 01, 02 & 03

- Courier Mission unlocked in Boston.
- Almanacs introduced, though only a small fraction of pages are made available for collection.

| SEQUENCES | 01 | | | 02 | | | | | 03 | | | 04 | | | | 05 | | | | |
|---|---|---|---|---|---|---|---|---|---|---|---|---|---|---|---|---|---|---|---|---|
| MEMORIES | 1 | 2 | 3 | 1 | 2 | 3 | 4 | 5 | 1 | 2 | 3 | 1 | 2 | 3 | 4 | 1 | 2 | 3 | 4 | 5 |

## SEQUENCE 05

Though Sequence 05 offers an incredible range of new features, young Connor lacks many key abilities and useful pieces of equipment at this stage in the story. It makes sense, then, to wait until Sequence 06 before you embark on side quests and secondary activities.

After you complete Boston's Most Wanted, it's useful to fully explore the Boston Underground and unlock all available Fast Travel positions in the city. This can drastically reduce travel time for all activities in the area. See page 164 for a full guide.

From this point in the story, it makes sense to complete all available Homestead Missions whenever you visit the area. When a Homestead Mission calls for a trip to Boston, New York or the Frontier, leave that step until you visit the map in question for other activities.

## SEQUENCE 06

It pays to start generating lots of money from the Homestead immediately. As you will be short on finance at this stage, conquer Fort Independence (page 149) and Fort Hill in Boston (page 148): this will eliminate taxation on trade in the city, and furnish you with £15,000 from their two Chests. You can optionally conquer the three Forts in the Frontier as well. You should then enlist the services of Myriam at the Homestead (see page 195), then purchase the most expensive animal pelts from her in bulk. Complete the Homestead Mission to recruit Lance (see page 194), and you can then upgrade your convoys and load them with the pelts to sell to Hancock's Store No. 5 in Boston. This is a short convoy journey that will bring massive returns throughout Sequence 06.

Complete the Liberation Missions in the north and south districts of Boston (see page 157) to both reduce the risk rate on convoys, and obtain two new Assassin recruits. To be extra efficient, begin both available Courier Missions and the Assassination Contract for the area before you start: these side quests can all be completed concurrently as you travel around the city. If you purchase all Treasure Maps for Boston, you can also take the time to open Chests and pick up Trinkets and Almanac Pages during your travels. Keep those convoys rolling from the Homestead at all times.

## COMPLETION TIMELINE

In this diagram, the top section reveals the feature unlock progression, while the lower half offers advice and suggestions for a streamlined path to 100% completion. You can use this to plan your approach to optional activities separate to the main storyline, and as a jumping-off point to all guidance in this chapter.

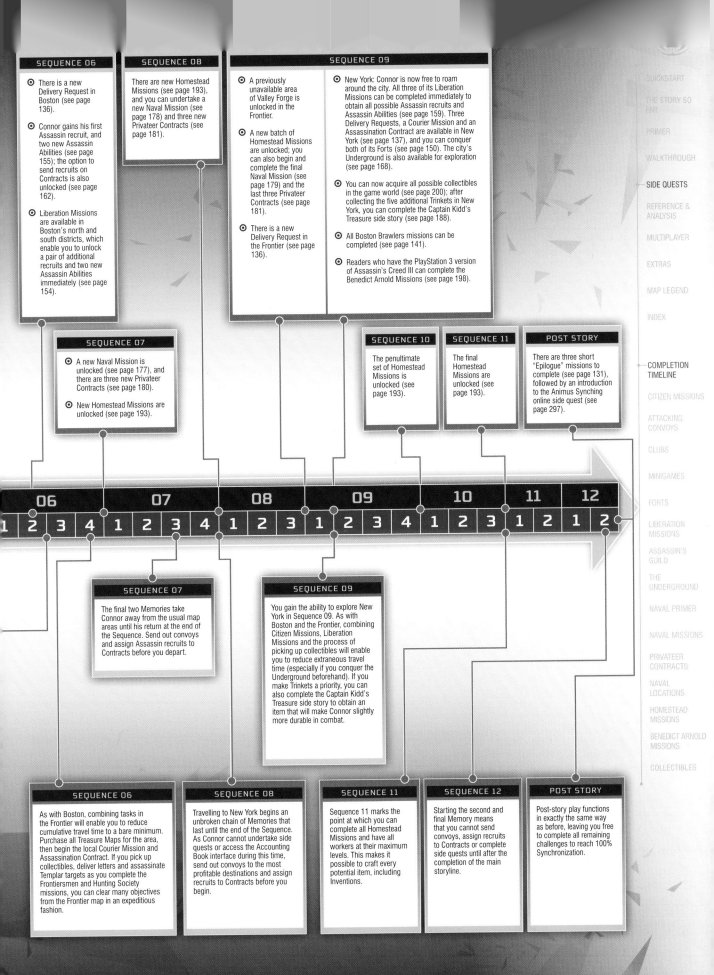

## SEQUENCE 06

- There is a new Delivery Request in Boston (see page 136).
- Connor gains his first Assassin recruit, and two new Assassin Abilities (see page 155); the option to send recruits on Contracts is also unlocked (see page 162).
- Liberation Missions are available in Boston's north and south districts, which enable you to unlock a pair of additional recruits and two new Assassin Abilities immediately (see page 154).

## SEQUENCE 08

- There are new Homestead Missions (see page 193), and you can undertake a new Naval Mission (see page 178) and three new Privateer Contracts (see page 181).

## SEQUENCE 09

- A previously unavailable area of Valley Forge is unlocked in the Frontier.
- A new batch of Homestead Missions is unlocked; you can also begin and complete the final Naval Mission (see page 179) and the last three Privateer Contracts (see page 181).
- There is a new Delivery Request in the Frontier (see page 136).
- New York: Connor is now free to roam around the city. All three of its Liberation Missions can be completed immediately to obtain all possible Assassin recruits and Assassin Abilities (see page 159). Three Delivery Requests, a Courier Mission and an Assassination Contract are available in New York (see page 137), and you can conquer both of its Forts (see page 150). The city's Underground is also available for exploration (see page 168).
- You can now acquire all possible collectibles in the game world (see page 200); after collecting the five additional Trinkets in New York, you can complete the Captain Kidd's Treasure side story (see page 188).
- All Boston Brawlers missions can be completed (see page 141).
- Readers who have the PlayStation 3 version of Assassin's Creed III can complete the Benedict Arnold Missions (see page 198).

## SEQUENCE 07

- A new Naval Mission is unlocked (see page 177), and there are three new Privateer Contracts (see page 180).
- New Homestead Missions are unlocked (see page 193).

## SEQUENCE 10

The penultimate set of Homestead Missions is unlocked (see page 193).

## SEQUENCE 11

The final Homestead Missions are unlocked (see page 193).

## POST STORY

There are three short "Epilogue" missions to complete (see page 131), followed by an introduction to the Animus Synching online side quest (see page 297).

06 07 08 09 10 11 12

1 2 3 4 1 2 3 4 1 2 3 1 2 3 4 1 2 3 1 2 1 2

## SEQUENCE 07

The final two Memories take Connor away from the usual map areas until his return at the end of the Sequence. Send out convoys and assign Assassin recruits to Contracts before you depart.

## SEQUENCE 09

You gain the ability to explore New York in Sequence 09. As with Boston and the Frontier, combining Citizen Missions, Liberation Missions and the process of picking up collectibles will enable you to reduce extraneous travel time (especially if you conquer the Underground beforehand). If you make Trinkets a priority, you can also complete the Captain Kidd's Treasure side story to obtain an item that will make Connor slightly more durable in combat.

## SEQUENCE 06

As with Boston, combining tasks in the Frontier will enable you to reduce cumulative travel time to a bare minimum. Purchase all Treasure Maps for the area, then begin the local Courier Mission and Assassination Contract. If you pick up collectibles, deliver letters and assassinate Templar targets as you complete the Frontiersmen and Hunting Society missions, you can clear many objectives from the Frontier map in an expeditious fashion.

## SEQUENCE 08

Travelling to New York begins an unbroken chain of Memories that last until the end of the Sequence. As Connor cannot undertake side quests or access the Accounting Book interface during this time, send out convoys to the most profitable destinations and assign recruits to Contracts before you begin.

## SEQUENCE 11

Sequence 11 marks the point at which you can complete all Homestead Missions and have all workers at their maximum levels. This makes it possible to craft every potential item, including Inventions.

## SEQUENCE 12

Starting the second and final Memory means that you cannot send convoys, assign recruits to Contracts or complete side quests until after the completion of the main storyline.

## POST STORY

Post-story play functions in exactly the same way as before, leaving you free to complete all remaining challenges to reach 100% Synchronization.

QUICKSTART

THE STORY SO FAR

PRIMER

WALKTHROUGH

SIDE QUESTS

REFERENCE & ANALYSIS

MULTIPLAYER

EXTRAS

MAP LEGEND

INDEX

COMPLETION TIMELINE

CITIZEN MISSIONS

ATTACKING CONVOYS

CLUBS

MINIGAMES

FORTS

LIBERATION MISSIONS

ASSASSIN'S GUILD

THE UNDERGROUND

NAVAL PRIMER

NAVAL MISSIONS

PRIVATEER CONTRACTS

NAVAL LOCATIONS

HOMESTEAD MISSIONS

BENEDICT ARNOLD MISSIONS

COLLECTIBLES

# CITIZEN MISSIONS

The three varieties of side quest in the Citizen Missions category are among the most simple challenges that you face en route to 100% Synchronization. Many of them can be completed before the conclusion of Sequence 06, and the fact that they offer cash rewards on completion can provide capital for a burgeoning Homestead trade empire. Citizen Missions are not "exclusive" quests – that is, Connor can complete their objectives at any time, even during many main story Memories – so we strongly suggest that you accept them as soon as they become available. You can then complete them gradually as you attend to other business. For maximum time efficiency, you can complete Courier Missions and Assassination Contracts while undertaking Liberation Missions: see page 154.

Though all objectives are clearly marked on the main map once you have accepted a Citizen Mission, irrespective of fog, the actual quest vendors are not visible until Connor has uncovered their position. Refer to the maps in the Collectibles section to find their specific locations.

 ## COURIER MISSIONS

On accepting a Courier Mission, four letter icons will appear on the local map. To deliver a letter to a marked individual, simply approach them and press **B**/**◎**. After the final delivery, you will receive a fixed cash payment of £500, and the mission is complete.

| COURIER MISSIONS | |
|---|---|
| **MISSION** | **UNLOCKED** |
| **Central Boston Letters** | Sequence 02 |
| **Frontier Letters** | Sequence 05 |
| **North Boston Letters** | Sequence 05, after "Boston's Most Wanted" |
| **East New York Letters** | Sequence 09, after "Missing Supplies" |

**Notes:**

⊙ All recipients are marked by the ✉ icon, and appear on the map shortly after the mission is accepted.

⊙ Central Boston Letters is the only conventional side quest available as Haytham, and features recipients very close to the start position. North Boston Letters has deliveries throughout the city, but there are no complications to speak of. The same can be said of East New York Letters.

⊙ The letter delivered on the west side of Concord in Frontier Letters is close to potential hostiles who will regard Connor with suspicion once they see him. Fast Walk to make the delivery and then depart without pause unless you don't mind getting into conflict.

 ## DELIVERY REQUESTS

Accepting a Delivery Request provides Connor with a list of items that must be supplied to the civilian that gives the mission. These always consist of five specific types of resources or crafted items in varying quantities. Once Connor has all of the requested stock in his inventory, a specific Delivery Request return icon (📨) will appear in the position of the original request, and you can interact with the civilian to make the delivery and obtain a fixed £1,000 payment. Some of the later Delivery Requests require items that can only be obtained via crafting (see page 244) after making sufficient progress with the Homestead-related side quests (covered later in this chapter on page 193). Though you can *technically* obtain specified trade items and resources by pickpocketing wealthy citizens, this isn't practical: it would take a veritable eternity.

The cash reward for completing Delivery Requests may seem attractive in early Sequences, but we would suggest that you simply accept these quests when you find them, then leave the actual completion of each delivery until much later in the story – or even when you are making the final steps towards 100% Synchronization. With many deliveries, the payment of £1,000 doesn't even cover the base value of the items when sold to a merchant, let alone the ample profits on offer if traded via a convoy.

| LEXINGTON ITEMS | |
|---|---|
| **Items Required** | **Unlocked: Sequence 05** |
| ▪ Beaver Teeth x5<br>▪ Bear Pelt x3<br>▪ Bobcat Pelt x3<br>▪ Cougar Pelt x3<br>▪ Wolf Pelt x5 | Notes: If you intend to complete this side quest at an early stage, note that you can obtain most of these items while completing the Hunting Society missions: see page 139. |

| TROY'S WOOD ITEMS | |
|---|---|
| **Items Required** | **Unlocked: Sequence 05** |
| ▪ Bear Claws x3<br>▪ Bobcat Claws x3<br>▪ Wolf Fangs x3<br>▪ Cougar Fangs x2<br>▪ Elk Antlers x3 | Notes: As with the Lexington delivery, completing Hunting Society missions (or general hunting – see page 242) will provide you with the necessary inventory stock. |

## CENTRAL BOSTON ITEMS

| Items Required | Unlocked: After "Boston's Most Wanted" in Sequence 05 |
|---|---|
| ■ Paper x3<br>■ Hair Accessory x2<br>■ Toy Dolls x2<br>■ Golden Rings x1<br>■ Soap x2 | Notes: Though you can accept this quest at an early stage in the story, three of its items cannot be crafted until Sequence 09. It can be completed once Golden Rings become available during Sequence 10. |

## SOUTH BOSTON ITEMS

| Items Required | Unlocked: After "The Angry Chef" in Sequence 06 |
|---|---|
| ■ Raccoon Pelt x5<br>■ Deer Pelt x5<br>■ Beaver Pelt x5<br>■ Buttons x2<br>■ Fox Pelt x3 | Notes: Buttons cannot be crafted until Sequence 07. As with the Lexington deliveries, it does not make financial sense to complete this at an early stage: the pelts are worth many thousands of pounds if sold via a convoy. |

## VALLEY FORGE ITEMS

| Items Required | Unlocked: Sequence 09 |
|---|---|
| ■ Bear Grease x1<br>■ Deer Marrow x3<br>■ Rabbit's Foot x5<br>■ Elk Heart x1<br>■ Fox Tail x1 | Notes: This Delivery Request can be accepted once the Valley Forge military camp appears at the start of Sequence 09. Ardent hunters will probably have sufficient stock of these items to complete the request immediately – and for a small profit, too. |

## WEST NEW YORK ITEMS

| Items Required | Unlocked: Sequence 09 |
|---|---|
| ■ Salt x1<br>■ Venison x5<br>■ Hare Meat x5<br>■ Elk Meat x5<br>■ Bread x2 | Notes: Only Salt and Bread must be crafted; the three animal products are available through hunting. This contract also leads to a minor profit. |

## EAST NEW YORK ITEMS

| Items Required | Unlocked: Sequence 09 |
|---|---|
| ■ Ales x3<br>■ Ciders x2<br>■ Spirits x2<br>■ Tea x2<br>■ Deer Jerky x2 | Notes: These items must all be crafted, but the required artisan is actually available from Sequence 07 onwards. If you are up to date with all Homestead Missions, you should be able to source them straight away. |

## NORTH NEW YORK ITEMS

| Items Required | Unlocked: Sequence 09 |
|---|---|
| ■ Cough Syrup x1<br>■ Eye Drops x1<br>■ Pomade x1<br>■ All-Purpose Remedy x1<br>■ Stomach Ache Remedy x1 | Notes: Cough Syrup and Eye Drops cannot be crafted before Sequences 10 and 11 respectively. |

## ASSASSINATION CONTRACTS

To all intents and purposes, Assassination Contracts are just a macabre permutation of Courier Missions: it's just that the deadly delivery is performed with ⊗/□ instead, and plunging a Hidden Blade into the back of a recipient is somewhat less socially acceptable. Each Assassination Contract features five Templars to kill within the area where the mission is accepted, and awards £2,000 once the last one has been dispatched.

### ASSASSINATION CONTRACTS

| MISSION | UNLOCKED |
|---|---|
| Frontier's Contracts | Sequence 05, after "Boston's Most Wanted" |
| Boston's Contracts | Sequence 06 |
| New York's Contracts | Sequence 09, after completing "Missing Supplies" |

**Notes:**

⊙ Targets are marked by the ⊕ icon, and appear on the map shortly after the mission is accepted. A red hexagon (⬢) appears above the head of the Templar when you move within visual range.

⊙ Each Templar target yields a small sum of money and – unlike other potential combatants – a resource or trade item when looted.

⊙ The Templars in Boston are situated in deserted alleyways and on roads that do not feature patrols.

⊙ Watch out for patrols when you start the mission in the Frontier. The quest giver is standing just inside the Restricted Area that surrounds Fort Monmouth, so speaking to him won't endear Connor to the nearby patrol. Though the Templars in the Frontier are more suspicious than their peers in Boston, most of them are situated far from patrols. The target south of Concord in Troy's Wood is close to mercenaries guarding a chest, who may kill him on your behalf.

⊙ Most of the Templars in New York are found in alleyways that feature small numbers of guards, with patrols on the surrounding streets. This can lead to large battles (and Notoriety penalties) unless you take the time to be discrete. Try to identify positions where you can lure the Templar to a secluded spot to perform the kill: the whistle ability and corner assassinations work well here. One Templar in the East District, at the approximate center of the city, is located on a rooftop with two Snipers for company.

Templar convoys can be encountered on main trails throughout the Frontier map at any time after Sequence 05, and are highlighted with the ✦ icon. Though you are under no obligation to interfere with them, doing so is a rather profitable endeavor.

Convoys are most frequently protected by humble Soldiers, perhaps accompanied by a single Officer, which means that it's possible to dispatch all guards within less than a minute. Combat can begin once you enter the red Restricted Area that surrounds them, or if you open fire with a ranged weapon. The best attacking strategy is to approach from the rear or above, and open hostilities with assassinations (📷 01). Once you have dispatched the guards, you can approach the rear of a wagon and press **B**/**◎** to rifle through it for a standard £750 reward. You can repeat this with a second wagon on larger convoys for a total reward of £1500: a fair payment for relatively little effort.

Late in the main storyline, you will encounter situations where a Templar convoy consisting of Redcoat troops see Patriot patrols. When hostilities ensue – either without Connor's direct involvement, or after a cunningly timed intervention to act as a catalyst – you may even get to help yourself to the

reward without drawing a weapon. Looting a convoy in this fashion, or by simply neutralizing its escorts with non-lethal unarmed attacks, will lead to the award of the Prince of Thieves Achievement/Trophy.

01

# CLUBS

Clubs are special organizations that offer optional missions for Connor to undertake, and an assortment of "Challenges", separated into three successive tiers, which chart Connor's progress and prowess in thematically appropriate disciplines. Completing each level of Challenges unlocks the next one in line.

Clubs become formally available from the start of Sequence 05, though there is also a small additional task that must be completed before Connor will be approached by a representative of some organizations. Once Connor receives an invitation to join, the first tier of Challenges for that club will be unlocked, and will appear within the Logbook. In a thoughtful move, practically all of Connor's activities prior to an invitation to join a club will be recognized retroactively. The Hunting Society Challenges, for example, will note Connor's hunting feats in Sequence 04.

Three of the four clubs also offer missions for Connor to undertake. Completing these will lead to the reward of Mementos that appear in the Homestead Manor, and count towards 100% Synchronization.

## THE HUNTING SOCIETY

To receive an invitation to join the Hunting Society, you must have hunted and skinned at least one animal. A representative of the society will then approach Connor while he is travelling through the Frontier area. Note that this will not occur immediately at the start of Sequence 05: you may need to leave and return to the area to trigger the approach.

The first tier of Hunting Challenges is unlocked after the introductory conversation, and hunting cabins (⬢) appear in the Frontier: one in the northwest, the other in the south. You can visit either of these locations to accept missions (marked by the ⬢ icon) that are completed in a linear progression.

**Challenge Tips:**

- You can find an assortment of hunting tips and tricks on page 242.
- If you enjoy hunting, the Hunting Society Challenges are probably the quickest and least demanding route to the "In Good Standing" Achievement/Trophy, which is awarded for completing all three tiers of a single club's Challenges. Hunting in the Frontier can be combined with side quests in the area. In addition, the process of picking up Collectibles, and the profits that Connor can make by selling animal products via convoys, can be remarkable.

- The maps in the Collectibles section of this chapter (see page 200) feature annotations that indicate positions where particular varieties of animal are unusually abundant.
- The "Kill 10 animals in close combat" Challenge refers to the process of neutralizing hostile bears, wolves, wild cats or elk in the timed button-press minigame that ensues when they attack.

01

## CHALLENGES & MISSIONS

| QUEST | AVAILABILITY | COMMENTS | REWARDS |
|---|---|---|---|
| Hunting Challenges 1 | Kill and skin a wild animal in the Frontier | Kill five deer.<br>Kill a wolf.<br>Skin 10 animals.<br>Trade Hunting Spoils worth £500.<br>Use bait with a snare to capture five animals.<br>Kill a bear with the Hidden Blade. | - |
| Hunting Challenges 2 | Complete Hunting Challenges 1 | Stealth kill five animals while using bait.<br>Skin 25 animals.<br>Kill 10 animals with the Hidden Blade.<br>Capture 20 animals with snares.<br>Kill 15 animals with the bow. | - |
| Hunting Challenges 3 | Complete Hunting Challenges 2 | Skin every species of animal.<br>Kill five animals from horseback.<br>Trade Hunting Spoils worth a total of £2,000.<br>Kill 10 animals in close combat.<br>Complete your Hunting Map by skinning, or finding clues relating to, all types of animal in each Frontier hunting region and the Homestead (see page 242).<br>Collect 50 Undamaged Pelts. | - |
| The Man-Eater | Starts when you visit a hunting cabin in the Frontier for the first time | Go to the marked area, to the west of the Frontier. Follow the clues in the green search zone to find the bear cave across the river. Enter the cave and carry the corpse at the entrance into the middle of the lair. This will lure the bear out and enable you to kill it. If you engage it via close combat, you will need to follow more onscreen button prompts than usual to defeat the beast. | Unlocks the Bear Memento at the Manor. |
| Feline Feet | Complete The Man-Eater | Go to the marked area in the northwest of the Frontier and activate Eagle Vision to find the Unique Bobcat Tracks on the rocky area. Once it appears, chase it through the gorge and the cave, up to the top of the hill, where you must kill it. If you fail, you will need to restart. If you sprint towards the gorge before the animal starts to run, it's possible to end the chase with a near-immediate kill. | Unlocks the Bobcat Memento at the Manor. |
| The Patriarch | Complete Feline Feet | In the marked area near Connor's village, activate Eagle Vision to locate the deer as a golden target. As you have to get in close, hide in one of the Stalking Zones in the area, taking care not to scare the target away. Once concealed, throw some bait and wait until the deer comes close. | Unlocks the Deer Memento at the Manor. |
| The Pack Leader | Complete The Patriarch | Go to the marked area in the northwest of the Frontier and look for clues in the green search zone. You will have to kill three aggressive wolves to draw out their leader. If you approach them carefully, you can kill the wolves with your bow to prevent them from attacking you. | Unlocks the Wolf Memento at the Manor. |
| Acute Cat | Complete The Pack Leader | The marked area is in the north of the Frontier. To reach the path on top of a cliff, you will need to climb there from the west side (📷 01). Follow the path until you reach a clearing, where the cougar awaits. | Unlocks the Cougar Memento at the Manor. |
| The Elk Bachelor | Complete Acute Cat | Go to the marked area in the Valley Forge region. There are many trees that you can use to make a careful approach, which will enable you to kill your target easily with an air assassination. | Unlocks the Elk Memento at the Manor. |

02

Unlike other clubs, the Frontiersman can be visited at any of their Frontier camps (marked by the △ icon) from the start of Sequence 05. You must begin the first Frontiersman mission to unlock this club's Challenges, and can complete all available missions after the events of "Boston's Most Wanted" in Sequence 05 (marked by the △ icon). The two final Frontiersmen missions take place in Boston: simply enter the highlighted taverns to find the start point.

## Challenge Tips:

⊙ The "Reach five high points" task can be completed simply by synchronizing with Viewpoints.

⊙ The "Dive into water from a height of 50 meters" objective is met by fulfilling the final Optional Objective of the Sequence 06 closing Memory, Hostile Negotiations. If you should miss this, there is another easy way. From the Homestead area transition in the northeast of the map, simply follow the path until you see a fallen tree jutting over the side of the cliff. From here, dive into the water to the left.

⊙ The conversations with Washington that are required to complete the Tier 2 objective occur at very specific junctures. The first of these take place during "Missing Supplies" in Sequence 09, and can be obtained during a Memory Replay if you didn't see them on your first playthrough. After the introductory cutscene, follow Washington and talk to him; this triggers a cutscene outside the house of Isaac Potts. Once this ends, walk with Washington and continue the conversation until he has no new lines to speak. As an aside, this is also a good time to speak with Lafayette if you missed him earlier. The final conversation with Washington takes place after the completion of the main storyline. To find him, travel to Bowling Green on the southwest side of New York: Washington is marked by a "𝕎" icon. Initiate a conversation to complete the Challenge.

⊙ The third-tier objectives that challenge you to fully reveal the Boston, Frontier and New York maps require that you activate all possible Viewpoints and uncover the remaining areas within the Desynchronization boundary. Note that the area "unfogged" as Connor explores is expanded if he is moving at a higher elevation, such as tree-based free run courses and over rooftops.

## CHALLENGES & MISSIONS

| QUEST | AVAILABILITY | COMMENTS |
|---|---|---|
| **Frontiersman Challenges 1** | Complete Sequence 04 and visit a Frontiersman campfire in the Frontier to start the Boy who Cried Wolf mission | ▪ Perform 10 Leaps of Faith. <br> ▪ Reach five Viewpoints. <br> ▪ Discover five Underground Network Entrances (see page 164 for help). <br> ▪ Discover the location of every Fort. <br> ▪ Explore the canopy by traveling 100 meters through the trees. <br> ▪ Collect five Feathers. |
| **Frontiersman Challenges 2** | Complete Frontiersmen Challenges 1 | ▪ Dive into water from a height of 50 meters. <br> ▪ Complete an Almanac (see page 200 for help). <br> ▪ Climb for a total of 1,500 meters. <br> ▪ Discover the location of every Trading Post in the Frontier. <br> ▪ Listen to all of Washington's conversations. |
| **Frontiersman Challenges 3** | Complete Frontiersmen Challenges 2 | ▪ Reveal all of Boston's map. <br> ▪ Reveal all of the New York map. <br> ▪ Reveal the whole Frontier map. <br> ▪ Reach all of the Viewpoints. <br> ▪ Discover all of the Underground Network Entrances in New York and Boston (see page 164). <br> ▪ Visit every Tavern in the Frontier, New York and Boston. |
| **The Boy Who Cried Wolf** | Visit a Frontiersmen campfire | ▪ Once you reach the Frontiersmen camp, activate Eagle Vision and examine a clue on one of the corpses. Kill the wolf to end the mission. |
| **The Sasquatch** | Complete The Boy Who Cried Wolf | ▪ Once you reach the marked area in the northwest corner of the Frontier, analyze clues to narrow the search zone. Enter the cave on the right-hand side of the waterfall to find the Sasquatch. |
| **The Haunted Lighthouse** | Complete The Sasquatch | ▪ Once you reach the marked area near the east border of the Frontier, climb to the top of the Lighthouse and interact with the Fake Ghost. |
| **The Headless Horseman** | Complete The Haunted Lighthouse | ▪ When you reach the marked area to the south of Concord, activate Eagle Vision and look for one of several corpses with sacks over their heads. |
| **Monster of the Sea** | Complete The Boy Who Cried Wolf and talk to the Frontiersmen group in one of the marked Taverns in Boston | ▪ Listen to three of the conversations available in marked areas in the north of Boston, then speak with the widow in the nearby cemetery. Finally, head for the trader's workshop to the south. Activate Eagle Vision and search for the diving equipment. |
| **Unidentified Flying Object** | Complete The Boy Who Cried Wolf and talk to the Frontiersmen group in one of the marked Taverns in Boston | ▪ Go to the marked area in the southwest of Boston, activate Eagle Vision and scrutinize the trees. An umbrella is stuck in one of the branches. In order to reach it, climb the toilet hut and jump on the nearest branch; from there, leap through the trees until you reach the umbrella (◉ 02). |

A representative of the Boston Brawlers will approach Connor after he has beaten up an adversary with his fists alone at any point after the start of Sequence 05. This unlocks the first tier of Challenges. The first mission (marked by the 🏵 icon) becomes available after "Boston's Most Wanted" in Sequence 05, but those that follow cannot be undertaken until Connor returns to New York after completing "Missing Supplies" at the start of Sequence 09.

**Challenge Tips:**

⊙ Killing opponents disabled by a Smoke Bomb is most easily achieved by approaching a sizable group of enemies while incognito: any large patrol will suffice. Drop the device in their midst, and you can then assassinate numerous targets in succession with the Hidden Blade before the cloud dissipates.

⊙ Refer to the section that begins on page 222 to learn how to exploit the weaknesses of all enemy archetypes.

⊙ The "Kill an enemy with every type of weapon" task refers to categories of weapons – not each and every sword, for example – and includes ranged weapons. You will need to use the Hidden Blade, a small weapon (such as the Tomahawk), a normal weapon (a sword), a heavy weapon (an axe), a musket, a blunt weapon (club), a pistol, the bow, a Poison Dart, a Rope Dart and a Trip Mine. See page 226 for further details.

⊙ The Kill Streak challenges are easiest to accomplish against large groups of the Soldier archetype without the added complication of stronger archetypes. Patrols of this kind are rather common in the north of Boston.

⊙ For the Jäger-related task, visit Boston and cause chaos until Connor is at maximum Notoriety. You should then hunt these super-soldiers down one by one as they roam the streets; try to avoid those close to other patrols. When each battle begins, ensure that Connor is unarmed, and use the Counter Disarm move to steal the Jäger's weapon. Launch into an immediate combo while they are defenseless to kill them. Repeat this process a further nine times, and you will complete both the Challenge and Achievement/Trophy at once.

## CHALLENGES & MISSIONS

| QUEST | AVAILABILITY | COMMENTS |
|---|---|---|
| **Brawler Challenges 1** | Complete Sequence 04, then trigger an invitation by defeating an opponent with Connor's fists alone | ▪ Disarm five enemies.<br>▪ Kill five enemies affected by a Smoke Bomb within 10 seconds.<br>▪ Stealth kill 10 enemies without being detected.<br>▪ Kill 25 enemies with the Hidden Blade.<br>▪ Kill 10 Officers.<br>▪ Achieve a five-enemy Kill Streak. |
| **Brawler Challenges 2** | Complete Frontiersmen Challenges 1 | ▪ Fight and kill 10 Grenadiers.<br>▪ Kill an enemy with every type of weapon.<br>▪ Perform five double assassinations. This means assassinating two targets simultaneously.<br>▪ Have your Recruits assist you in combat 10 times.<br>▪ Liberate three Forts (see page 144). |
| **Brawler Challenges 3** | Complete Brawler Challenges 2 | ▪ Achieve a seven enemy Kill Streak (see page 53).<br>▪ Use the Rope Dart to perform a Predator move five times (see page 231).<br>▪ Own every weapon available in the stores (see page 252 for a full list).<br>▪ Disarm and kill 10 Jägers with their own weapon.<br>▪ Defend yourself from a firing line by using a human shield 10 times. |
| **Peter Bunyon** | Complete "Boston's Most Wanted" in Sequence 05, then meet with Harold Ring at the Old Brewery in Boston | ▪ Once you reach Peter Bunyon in the Frontier (Troy's Wood region), quickly dispatch his associates with Counter Kills. Bunyon himself is immune to Counter Kills. Use the Counter Disarm or Counter Throw moves when he attacks, and follow up with combos. |
| **The Sailor** | Defeat Peter Bunyon; complete "Missing Supplies" at the start of Sequence 09 | ▪ The Sailor awaits in New York, on a ship on the west side of the city. Defeat his three friends immediately, then focus on your main target. The Sailor blocks normal attacks and you cannot break his defense. Use the Counter Disarm move and follow up with punches until he falls. |
| **The Smuggler** | Defeat The Sailor | ▪ The Smuggler is found in Boston, in the northern part of the Central District. After you defeated his three allies and dealt some damage to him, another Smuggler appears along with reinforcements. Neither Smuggler can be Counter Killed, but they're susceptible to Counter Disarm and Counter Throw, followed up with punch combos, as usual. |
| **The Stinger** | Defeat The Smuggler | ▪ You will find The Stinger in the Frontier, in the Diamond Basin region. Dispatch the weaker enemies before you take care of The Stinger. He blocks normal attacks and you cannot break his defense, so use Counter Disarm followed by punch combos to wear him down. |
| **The Ropebeater** | Defeat The Stinger | ▪ The Ropebeater is found in the eastern part of Boston. Incapacitate his three allies immediately. The only way to defeat The Ropebeater is to stand next to a table or a barrel and Counter Throw him into one of these obstacles. Repeat this until he falls. |
| **The Merchant** | Defeat The Ropebeater | ▪ You will find The Merchant in the northeast of New York. Quickly eliminate his allies, then use the Counter Throw or Break Defense moves followed by volleys of punches to defeat him. |
| **The Tournament** | Defeat The Merchant | ▪ Return to the Old Brewery in Boston. You will have to fight four groups, each consisting of four members (three weaklings, one resolute and hardy leader). Never get too close to the crowd surrounding Connor, or they will strike him. Each leader offers a unique challenge, though they are all susceptible to the same moves (Disarm and Break Defense).<br>　▪ The Redcoat is strong. Defeat him with Counter Disarms followed by punches, even after he unsheathes a sword.<br>　▪ The Docker will fight you in a small arena, forcing you to pay attention to the crowd.<br>　▪ Against The Surgeon, Connor's vision is blurred and it is harder to see enemies.<br>　▪ Against The Huntress, other women from the crowd will throw Smoke Bombs. When you see one of them starting to run towards you, move away so that you don't get caught in the smoke. |

A representative of this shadowy syndicate will approach Connor after he has pickpocketed more than £100 in funds.

**Challenge Tips:**

⊙ Pickpocketing guards isn't as hard as it sounds. The safest way is to find a position where Connor can perform the lift while Blending, but you can also brazenly lock step with a patrol and pilfer from the soldiers at the rear. Identifying a rich citizen for the second-tier Challenge is usually a matter of finding a civilian in dandy attire (look for long socks and britches) wearing a distinctive tricorne (three-pointed) hat. These must be pickpocketed three or even four times to obtain all of their items.

⊙ If you can't find a guard dog for the related second-tier Challenge in later Sequences, replay the first Memory of Sequence 10, "Alternate Methods". You will encounter an appropriate hound early in the mission.

⊙ The £1,500 benchmark for the third-tier challenge can be completed with relative ease if you regularly loot fallen opponents to replenish ammunition after combat.

## CHALLENGES

| QUEST | AVAILABILITY | COMMENTS |
|---|---|---|
| **Thief Challenges 1** | Pickpocket at least £100 in total during or after Sequence 05 | ▪ Pickpocket £200.<br>▪ Perform 25 air assassinations.<br>▪ Catch a Courier (see page 235).<br>▪ Kill 10 enemies from hiding places.<br>▪ Loot 10 bodies. |
| **Thief Challenges 2** | Complete Thief Challenges 1 | ▪ Escape from open conflict by using blending or hiding 10 times.<br>▪ Steal everything a guard owns three times.<br>▪ Lure away a guard dog using bait three times.<br>▪ Perform 30 stealth kills without being detected.<br>▪ Steal everything a rich citizen owns without being detected. |
| **Thief Challenges 3** | Complete Thief Challenges 2 | ▪ Poison five enemies.<br>▪ Find and empty the 10 chests in New York. See page 200.<br>▪ Win £500 by playing minigames. Checkers and Bowls are probably the easiest games. See the following section for advice and tips.<br>▪ Pickpocket or loot £1,500.<br>▪ Successfully attack and loot a convoy three times (see page 138). |

# MINIGAMES

 FANORONA

**Locations:**

⊙ **Intermediate:** New York (north tavern)

⊙ **Expert:** Homestead, inside the Manor; New York (southwest and center tavern)

**Rules:**

⊙ Your goal is to capture all of your opponent's pieces by moving toward or away from them. When a piece is taken, all consecutive pieces standing behind that piece will also be captured.

⊙ Capturing moves are mandatory. If a capturing move is possible after taking pieces, a player can keep chaining moves until no further captures are possible.

⊙ If no capturing move is available, the player can move one piece to a neighboring empty slot.

⊙ It is forbidden for a piece to move to the same slot twice in one turn.

**Tips:**

⊙ The opening you choose is critical, and has long-term consequences on each game. There are four possible openings: one vertical, one horizontal, and two diagonal. Broadly speaking, the diagonal openings lead to close games, where it takes time to empty the board of its pieces. Conversely, the vertical opening weakens the second line of whoever uses it, leading to shorter games. Finally the horizontal opening is a balanced compromise.

⊙ When you capture multiple pieces in one move, this has the initial advantage of putting you in the lead, but it creates open spaces that your opponent might be able to use to counterattack.

⊙ Sometimes it makes more sense to capture fewer pieces, but move your own piece to a safe position (inside a diamond rather than on a cross), or to a position where it blocks your opponent's potential moves.

⊙ When you reach the end of a game, try to move your remaining pieces towards the center of the board. In the center, you have far more tactical options than on a border or, worse, in a corner.

⊙ To win a game, it can be useful to sacrifice one of your own pieces to force your opponent's pieces towards the outer edge of the board (via an "away" capture), enabling you to corner them.

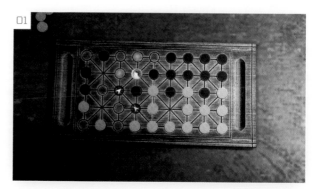
01

## SIX/NINE/TWELVE MEN'S MORRIS

**Locations:**

⊙ **Beginner:** Boston (south tavern)

⊙ **Intermediate:** Frontier (all but one tavern); New York (east tavern); Boston (center tavern)

⊙ **Expert:** New York (south tavern); Boston (north tavern); Homestead (tavern)

**Rules:**

⊙ Your goal is to leave the opponent with less than three pieces or block all possible moves.

⊙ Form "mills" to capture enemy pieces. A mill is formed when three of your pieces are placed in a straight line. Forming a mill enables you to take an enemy piece of your choice that is not already part of a mill.

⊙ Placement Phase: Players place their pieces one after the other in any empty slot on the board. Movement Phase: Players take turn moving their pieces to a neighboring empty slot. Flying Phase: When a player is left with only three pieces, he or she can move them to *any* empty slot on the board.

**Tips:**

⊙ Try to put your pieces on intersections, as this is where you will have the most tactical options.

⊙ Once you have secured an intersection, work your way towards opening two possible mills at the same time. Your opponent will only be able to block one, enabling you to create the mill in the other position.

## BOWLS

**Locations:**

⊙ **Intermediate:** Homestead, outside the tavern and near the harbor; Bowling Green on the southwest side of New York (after the completion of the main storyline)

**Rules:**

⊙ Your goal is to have your bowls stand closest to the "Jack" by the end of each round. The first player throws the Jack, then his first bowl. The turn goes to the player whose bowl is not closest to the Jack. When a player exhausts his bowls, the turn goes to his opponent until the round is finished. The winner of the round gains additional points for every bowl standing closer to the Jack than their opponent's closest bowl. When a player reaches the target number of points, they win the game.

**Tips:**

⊙ You can change the angle of your throw with **🅱/◎**. Lofted shots are ideal to throw a bowl close to the Jack. Straight shots are best used to try and push away an opponent's bowl.

⊙ When you press the **🅰/✕** to throw your bowl, a blue disc appears where you aim, its size oscillating from a large to a small radius. This represents the possible area where your bowl will land. The smaller the radius, the more accurate your throw. Always try to time the second button press to have the smallest possible radius for maximum precision.

⊙ Whenever possible, try to position your bowl between Connor and the Jack. This will make your opponent's life more complicated when trying to adjust his throws. It also means that if he touches your bowl, the Jack is likely to be pushed away.

⊙ With practice, you will gain the ability to knock an opposing bowl out of the way and leave your bowl close to the Jack in a single shot.

## CHECKERS

**Locations:**

⊙ **Intermediate:** Homestead, Harbor

**Rules:**

⊙ Your goal is to capture all of your opponent's pieces or block all his possible moves. You can capture opposing pieces by jumping over them into an empty space.

⊙ Pieces can only move diagonally on black squares, in the direction of the opponent's side of the board. Capturing moves are mandatory. If a capturing move is possible after taking an opposing piece, the player must keep chaining moves until no further captures are possible. A piece that reaches the line furthest from the player becomes a king. A king can move diagonally forward and backward, making it an extremely powerful piece.

**Tips:**

⊙ One of the keys to understand about checkers is that you can force your opponent to perform certain moves by sacrificing your own pieces, as capturing moves are mandatory. Though this can seemingly put you at a disadvantage, forward planning and manipulation of your opponent can enable you to control a game.

⊙ Pieces on the edge and corners of the board have a very limited range of possible movements. In most cases, it is therefore better to occupy squares in a more central position, and to try to trap your opponent on the outside of the board.

⊙ Never be afraid to sacrifice your pieces. All that matters is that you end up in a stronger position later in the game. For instance, sacrificing two pieces to have a chance to capture one but obtain a king is worthwhile in most instances, as a one-piece deficit is easily overcome by the tactical opportunities offered by a king.

## OVERVIEW

| NAME | REGION | LOCATION |
|------|--------|----------|
| Fort St-Mathieu | Frontier | South, close to the New York exit. |
| Fort Monmouth | Frontier | Southwest corner of the map, west of a Harbormaster. |
| Fort Duquesne | Frontier | Northwest of the map, to the north of Valley Forge. |
| Fort Hill | Boston | Easternmost portion of the city. |
| Fort Independence | Boston | Southwest, near the Boston Common landmark. |
| Fort Washington | New York | West, near the docks. |
| Fort Division | New York | Northeast, close the to the Frontier exit. |

Forts are areas marked by large, circular Restricted Areas. Though there is no formal Memory or quest giver that commissions you to conquer these strongholds, liberating all seven Forts is an important step on the road to 100% Synchronization. It also enables you to reduce the taxes levied on convoys that travel to each map (see page 251), and to gain access to a single Chest stored inside.

Each Fort has a large number of Redcoat soldiers within the red boundary. Connor moves to level 2 Notoriety the moment he enters the Restricted Area, which means that any hostile that espies him will immediately move to investigate and, on full detection, attack immediately. Entering open conflict at any point will automatically lead to the sounding of the alarm, which will cause all soldiers in the vicinity to attack. Furthermore, all entrances and exits to the Fort may slam shut, preventing easy access – or, perhaps more pertinently, a simple escape if Connor is sealed inside.

To conquer a Fort, Connor must complete the following steps:

⊙ **Kill the Fort Captain:** This individual is of the powerful Jäger archetype (see page 225), and is marked by a ◉ icon.

⊙ **Ignite the Powder Reserve:** This small building is also marked by a ◉ icon. Interact with the door (**B**/**○**), and a ten-second countdown will begin. Once it elapses, the reserve will explode. Naturally, this causes the surrounding area to erupt in confusion.

⊙ **Lower the Flag:** The final step, only available once the Captain and Powder Reserve have been dealt with, is to approach and lower the British flag (marked by the ◉ icon; again, press **B**/**○**). This ends the Fort liberation immediately, with British troops replaced by Patriots in the closing cutscene. As a small additional bonus, the Fort's icon becomes a new Fast Travel position.

You can kill the Captain and ignite the Powder Reserve in any order you please. However, it's important to note that you cannot interact with a Powder Reserve or lower a flag while in open conflict.

These are the basic ingredients of liberating a Fort, common to all seven sites that Connor visits. However, the manner in which you accomplish each objective is entirely at your discretion. If you would like to brazenly barge through the gates and engage the entire occupying force in a colossal melee, you can do just that.

In this section, we offer stealth walkthroughs for all seven Forts. However, it is important to note that we do not claim to offer *the* stealth walkthrough: there are almost always alternatives, or different permutations. Over the course of near-countless playtests, however, these are the strategies that were most consistently successful. As each Fort can feature variations in the positioning of certain guards, you can never quite know what awaits you inside. If you notice something different, either adapt your strategy accordingly, or Fast Travel out and reenter the area to reset it.

**General Guidelines & Tips:**

⊙ The three Forts in the Frontier can be conquered from the start of Sequence 05. As Connor does not acquire his full arsenal of weapons and Tools until Sequence 06, this is more difficult – but by no means impossible. The Forts in Boston can be liberated once you complete "Boston's Most Wanted" in Sequence 05, while the two sites in New York can be approached after "Missing Supplies" in Sequence 09.

⊙ Always enter a Fort with a full complement of Poison Darts. These are tailor-made for killing Captains, and are requisite for our stealth walkthroughs.

⊙ You must complete all three mandatory steps to conquer a Fort. If you leave the area before you lower the flag, the Fort will be restored to its original state on your return.

⊙ When the alarm sounds, some Captains will run to engage Connor in combat with their troops, while more craven commanders will seek refuge elsewhere in the Fort. If you favor a direct approach to liberation, it's worth noting that killing a Captain will cause some of his nearby subordinates to turn and flee.

⊙ In Boston and New York, you can call on Assassin recruits to aid with the infiltration, and to kill targets on your command – the Marksman ability (see page 155) is particularly effective. Note that using Assassins can lead to unforeseen variations on the behavior and movement of hostiles within a Fort.

⊙ Infiltrating a Fort is easier when it is raining, as this reduces the range of detection of all guards; this is further reduced during blizzards in snowy conditions.

⊙ There are occasional variations in guard positions that occur in accordance with the time of day. Where relevant, our walkthroughs always indicate if it is better to sneak through the perimeter during daylight hours or under cover of night.

⊙ Though you cannot interact with Powder Reserves in open conflict, some Forts have stray Powder Kegs in close proximity. You can shoot these to blow up the Powder Reserve instantly. If you then sprint directly to the flag (assuming you killed the Captain first), you only need kill the hostiles that follow before you can interact with the flagpole.

⊙ Finally, the Chests found inside Forts contain significant rewards, but their locks must be picked manually – and these are the toughest locks you will encounter. After positioning the sticks in the requisite positions (slow, measured rotations lead to faster detection of each "sweet spot"), you must ensure that both remain static as you tap **RT**/**R1** rapidly. The speed at which you press the button is vital. If you do not spring the mechanism within the time limit, you must try again.

Approach the Fort from the east, ideally during daylight hours. Either ignore or neutralize the guard standing by the cliff, then slide down the slope as shown here. As a point of interest, there are cougars in this area. We have noticed several instances where one will actually attack and kill the sentry if you stop and wait out of sight. If you have the patience, this may be a good opportunity to obtain the "Eye Witness" Achievement/Trophy.

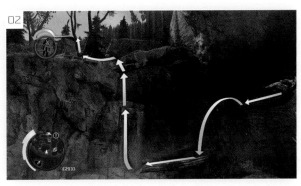

Climb the cliff as directed here. You can kick the guard over the edge, or safely ignore him. Climb the tree and move into the closest V-shaped section.

Follow the route shown here to reach the roof of a lookout tower. Don't worry about the guard in the first tower to the left: he won't notice Connor.

Watch the guard below, then leap down into the hiding place when he moves to the left part of his patrol route. When he returns to the hay cart, assassinate him quietly. (If you are entering at night, there is a chance that there will be other patrols that pass through this area on much longer routes. Use the whistle ability and disable these from the hay cart, one at a time.)

Climb onto the rooftop a short walk to the north then, using the sloped surface and chimney to avoid detection, wait until the Captain moves close to the well. This is your cue to emerge briefly and hit him with a Poison Dart.

Immediately walk back to the south edge of the roof and drop back down behind the logs. If the two guards stationed next to the Powder Reserve investigate the death of the Captain, interact with the door to start the explosion timer, then quickly climb up and position Connor next to the flag. Once the explosion occurs, press 🅑/◎ immediately to lower the British ensign. If the two guards do not investigate the Captain's death, sneak over to the door to start the timer, then hide in the hay cart until the camp returns to a standard routine. You can then wait for a quiet moment to reach the flag.

01

02

Fort Monmouth is easier to conquer at night, as this removes two potentially awkward soldiers from the initial stage of the infiltration. Approach the Fort from the northeast via the route shown here, then stop and observe the two guards on the jetty.

Slip inside the Fort when the two guards begin to walk to the left. Move below the elevated walkway and proceed to the end of the Stalking Zone. Watch the movements of the patrolling Officer, then assassinate the guard close to the cart by pulling him into the undergrowth. When the Officer approaches the Powder Reserve, walk up behind him and perform an assassination. You can then climb up into the Stalking Zone. Take the time to traverse to the left, and climb up when you reach the branch: this means that Connor is shielded from view by the pile of logs as he transitions from the climb to a crouching position.

03

04

There are two potential methods to eliminate the Captain without entering open conflict. The first and perhaps least consistent (marked by a dotted line) is to wait until a soldier patrolling to the left moves out of sight, then strike when the Captain moves to the left of his men: press up against the left corner of the logs, whistle to attract his attention, then perform a corner assassination when he moves within range. The alternative (solid line) is to move to the right of the Captain in the Stalking Zone, then send a Poison Dart once you have him in your sights. Immediately retrace your steps to the Powder Reserve, breaking the line of sight, to stall SSI meters once you move behind the logs: with a little luck, you can drop back down and interact with the door before Connor is detected.

Immediately run back into the Stalking Zone that you passed through when entering the Fort before the countdown expires to hide. Once the chaos and confusion subside and an opening presents itself, make your way to the flag.

## ALTERNATIVE CAPTAIN STRATEGY

There is a very occasional variation that occurs where the Captain will not be addressing his men on the east side of the Fort, but idling with them close to the buildings to the west. This seems more common at dawn and shortly before dusk. They will not move from this position unless you Fast Travel or reload. It's something of a detour to poison the Captain (and entails assassinating the soldier sawing in the lower area), but it's not phenomenally difficult. After you hit the Captain, hide in a Stalking Zone until things calm down.

# FORT DUQUESNE

Approach Fort Duquesne from the northeast. There is a sentry on the cliff to the west once you enter the Restricted Area. The optional route (marked by a striped line) is much shorter, but carries a risk of detection. The longer path to the left is safer. Both routes lead to the same position on the large cut tree trunk.

From the tree trunk platform, use the branches to reach the small roof.

Check to the west and consult the mini-map to ensure that the Captain isn't looking on or approaching, then make your way to a small branch at the end of the route shown here.

From this position, you avoid alerting the guard dog and his handler below. Equip the Poison Darts and, once the Captain moves into view, hit him with a single dart. Immediately turn around and backtrack to the bottom of the ladder.

Walk inside the empty sentry post and watch the Officer feeding the chickens. Sneak into the Stalking Zone just behind him to perform an assassination. You are then free to calmly walk to the Powder Reserve.

Run back to the ladder and climb it to reach the platform above as the explosion timer counts down, then follow the simple free run course shown here to reach the flag behind the building. Press **B**/**◎** immediately as you land to trigger the final cutscene without a single moment of open conflict.

## ⬡ FORT HILL

**01**

We suggest that you have at least three Poison Darts in your inventory for this infiltration. Approach the northwest side of the Restricted Area and observe the two guards stationed outside the entrance shown here. One will move away from the door to walk a short patrol. When he stops, hit him with a Poison Dart from a place of concealment. Once his companion moves to investigate, repeat the feat. (In later Sequences or post-story play, you may find that a Patriot patrol will obligingly dispatch the two Redcoats shortly after you arrive.)

**02**

Go through the entrance and be sure to move no more briskly than Fast Walk pace when you enter the room at the end of the tunnel: there are two guards to your left, though they are facing elsewhere. Take a right and climb up the stairs to reach the Fort's inner courtyard.

**03**

Perform a corner assassination on the guard to your left as you exit the corridor, then go to the nearby Stalking Zone and kill the Redcoat who is busy working; note that this target does not appear at night. Move to, and enter, the hay cart when the next guard turns his back to you, and assassinate him from your hiding place. Walk to the Stalking Zone while the Captain is looking away, and hit him with a Poison Dart when he moves within range. Once he falls, start the Powder Reserve explosion timer, then make your way to the nearby flag for an instant Redcoat eviction once the countdown ends.

III

QUICKSTART

THE STORY SO
FAR

PRIMER

WALKTHROUGH

SIDE QUESTS

REFERENCE &
ANALYSIS

MULTIPLAYER

EXTRAS

MAP LEGEND

INDEX

## FORT INDEPENDENCE

Approach the Fort from the east, kill the Redcoat on the outer edge of the Restricted Area and climb up via the wooden crates. Air assassinate the guard in front of you, then hide behind the wooden boxes. When the patrolling guard spots the body of your victim, whistle to draw his attention and take him down too. Wait until no one is watching, then jump down into the hay cart and dispatch the patrolling Redcoat. You can now climb up via the barrels and hide behind the corner. Whistle to attract the soldier patrolling in the alleyway and eliminate him. Jump to the rooftop and perform a Leap of Faith in the hay cart on the other side of the houses. Stealthily assassinate the Captain from your hiding place when all witnesses are facing elsewhere. Wait until the coast is clear, run up the stairs and head towards the Powder Reserve.

Hide behind the corner and assassinate the lone guard patrolling along the wall, if need be by whistling. Wait until the two guards patrolling on the ground level turn away and quickly go down to blow up the Powder Reserve. Climb back up via the wooden barrels and retrace your steps.

You can now run to the flag by following the path shown here. Having eliminated patrols in this area earlier, you shouldn't encounter any enemies on the way.

01

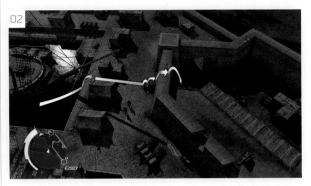

02

Pack plenty of Trip Mines and a full set of Poison Darts for this outing; if you are visiting during the day, you should also ensure that you have an Assassin recruit available. The easiest (and purest) way to complete this Fort is to infiltrate it late at night, with the moon high in the sky. Doing so reduces the number of guards in the area, and means that the Captain is in a much more accessible position. Either way, the optimal stealth approach necessitates a long swim to approach the Restricted Area from the northwest. Swim between the largest ship and the dock to avoid detection.

When the guards patrolling outside walk to the south, slip behind them and climb up on the Fort wall. Immediately perform a Leap of Faith to the haystack below.

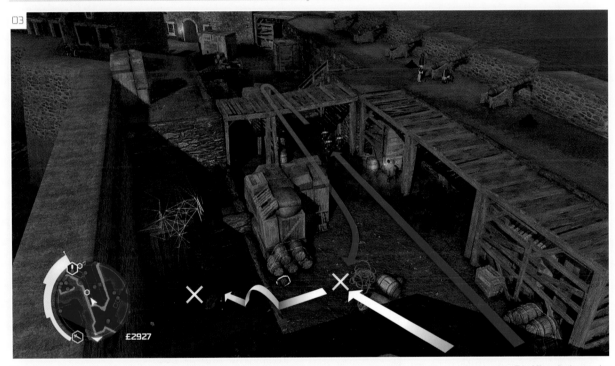

03

Wait for the three patrolling guards to approach Connor's place of concealment. When they turn away, emerge and quickly plant Trip Mines in the precise positions marked here. The first will be triggered by the patrol on their return; the second will ensure that the blast detonates the Powder Reserve. This is the point where the paths of the day and night walkthroughs separate.

## NIGHT | DAY

III

QUICKSTART

THE STORY SO FAR

PRIMER

WALKTHROUGH

SIDE QUESTS

REFERENCE & ANALYSIS

MULTIPLAYER

EXTRAS

MAP LEGEND

INDEX

**04**

After planting both Trip Mines, quickly climb to the upper wall and hide against the edge of the crates, as shown here. When you see the patrol below on their way to your trap, it's safe to move on.

**04**

Having planted the Trip Mines, quickly climb to the right of the Powder Reserve, then drop down and hide behind the stacked crates to avoid the patrol as it makes its return journey.

**05**

Fast Walk past the two oblivious sentries, then head down the steps.

**05**

Pause behind the barrels to ensure that the patrol in the area ahead is not facing Connor, then move into the Stalking Zone behind the sentry. If you can reach this before the Powder Reserve explosion occurs, all should be well. Wait until the patrolling Grenadier and his companion move away, then quietly assassinate the adjacent guard.

**06**

At the bottom of the steps, press up against the wall and watch the area where the Captain is patrolling. When he moves to the far right, assassinate the guard directly ahead. You can then either take a slight risk and stay out in the open to hit the Captain with a Poison Dart once he walks into view, or cautiously retreat behind the corner and poison him when he investigates the body.

**06**

Inside the Stalking Zone, turn to the right and watch the wooden platform. When the Captain moves into view, target him and call a recruit to perform a generic assassination.

**07**

Speed matters here: quickly climb up via the route shown and assassinate the guard with his back to Connor, then Fast Walk to the flag. Be ready to press 🅱/◎ when you reach it, as there is a chance that the two guards further ahead will turn as the commotion surrounding the Captain's demise attracts their attention.

**07**

There is no need for subtlety at this point: just exit the Stalking Zone and make a purposeful sprint for the flagpole via the route shown here, remaining on the left-hand side of the initial rooftops to avoid detection. There is a sentry just before the end of the second row of buildings. Briefly stop to assassinate him prior to the final approach to the flag.

01

Approach the Fort via the unguarded marshland to the southeast. As you near the outer wall, you will notice a small hole in the stockade. You can swim through this without fear of detection.

02

Inside the Fort, ignore the soldier to your left and swim to the guard directly ahead. Perform a ledge assassination.

03

There is a guard who walks a short patrol between the nearby Powder Reserve and a position close to the barrels shown here. Wait until he approaches the Powder Reserve, then leap over the barrels to land in the hay cart. You can then assassinate the guard quietly on the return leg of his journey.

04

Approach the Powder Reserve and interact with the door to begin the explosion countdown. Immediately follow the path shown here to take refuge in the pile of hay. The Grenadier and his companion will move to regard the damage, then split up to investigate the two hiding places. When the Grenadier reaches your position, perform an assassination from inside the hay pile; you can then wait for his companion to return to his original position, and whistle to repeat the same feat.

05

Watch the Officer from your position in the hay pile and wait until he moves away from the cart. This is your opportunity to transfer to the hay cart. Assassinate the Officer on his return. You can now emerge and perform a corner assassination on the next guard in line. Move up to the crates and wait until the two patrolling soldiers further ahead are walking away from you. After a second or two, whistle: this will attract only the soldier to the rear. Perform a corner assassination when he moves within range; you can then eliminate his partner when he returns. If both should move towards you at once, retreat before Connor is detected and try again.

III

QUICKSTART

THE STORY SO FAR

PRIMER

WALKTHROUGH

SIDE QUESTS

REFERENCE & ANALYSIS

MULTIPLAYER

EXTRAS

MAP LEGEND

INDEX

06

07

Wait out of sight at the hay cart and watch through the opening. After the Captain rides by on his horse, and all other soldiers are looking elsewhere, Fast Walk into the grassy, partially fenced-off area to the right.

Move along the "corridor" until you reach the position shown here. Select the Hidden Blade. Wait until the Captain reaches your position, ensure that there are no potential witnesses in the distance, then step out and press ⊗/□ to pull him from the saddle and assassinate him.

08

Finally, climb the nearby ladder and make the short, triumphant walk to the flag to end the liberation.

Introduced in Sequence 06 during the Memory where Connor meets Stephane Chapheau, and formally unlocked after his induction as an Assassin trainee, completing Liberation Missions to free city districts from Templar control offers rewards that have a rather profound bearing on many other activities in Assassin's Creed III.

The most obvious benefit is the acquisition of a new Assassin recruit, which means that Connor can call on more allies to assist him in combat (using "tokens"), or send them on missions to gain money, experience and items through Contracts (see page 162). You also obtain a new Assassin ability, which expands Connor's repertoire of infiltration, distraction and assassination techniques (see "Assassin Abilities"). Last, but by no means least, victory in each district reduces the likelihood that convoys sent from the Homestead to local merchants will be attacked by Templar forces, and also furnishes Connor with a key to all Treasure Chests in that area – removing the need for lengthy lockpicking sessions.

In short, taking the time to complete Liberations is profitable in a multitude of ways. You might assume that such plentiful rewards would entail some form of almighty struggle to obtain, but that's really not the case. To complete the liberation of a district, you must simply complete a set number of Liberation Missions within its borders. These are "ambient" challenges that can occur whenever you approach the ⚘ icon in your travels – even during most main story Memories. In Boston, the North and South districts each have two varieties of local Liberation Missions. In New York, the North, East and West districts all have three distinct mission types within their borders. Completing three of each Liberation Mission variety within a district unlocks a closing Memory (⚘) where Connor can use the Assassin ability of a new recruit to eliminate a local Templar leader.

In this section, we detail the optimal approach to each district, explaining the challenges that each type of Liberation Mission entails, and identify the specific locations that you should target to avoid heavy Notoriety penalties and other such complications.

## GENERAL TIPS

⊙ Use the Liberation Missions filter on the main map to view the boundaries that separate districts in Boston and New York, and to view the locations of all Liberation Missions without other icons obscuring your overview of the area.

⊙ If you fail an individual Liberation Mission, simply travel away from the area to reset the challenge. There are also no penalties for ignoring Liberation Missions that you pass on your way to another objective.

⊙ Completing a single Liberation Mission in a legion permanently removes it from the map. Complete three required missions of a particular variety, and all further instances of that type disappear. You can track your current progress via the Logbook on the main map screen.

⊙ You can vastly cut down on your overall travel time by combining Liberation Missions with other tasks, such as Citizen Missions and hunting for collectibles.

⊙ Once you have completed a single Liberation Mission in an area, you can visit the location marked with the ⚘ icon to speak to Connor's contact (and future recruit) in the district. There are generally two full conversations prior to the liberation of a district, and a further two immediately after the final Memory. These interactions offer more information on the recruit and their reasons for pledging allegiance to Connor. (**MINOR SPOILER:** If you would like to know what became of the boy that witnessed Haytham's exploits in "A Deadly Performance", we suggest that you converse with Duncan Little in Boston North.)

# ASSASSIN ABILITIES

Liberating a district provides Connor with a new recruit and an Assassin ability. These have a wide variety of applications throughout the events of Assassin's Creed III, so it makes sense to complete Liberation Missions as soon as they become available. You can choose Assassin abilities by holding **LB**/**L2** and selecting the required feat from the right-hand menu with **R**. To activate an ability, tap **LB**/**L2**. If a selected ability requires an active target, note that they must be surrounded with the distinctive

"highlight" effect for it to work. You can use the Precision Mode feature (**LT**/**L1**) to specify a particular target.

Note that all abilities are replaced by the Call Backup feature when Connor is in open conflict. This combat-only ability summons an available recruit for every press of **LB**/**L2**.

##  Assassinate

**District:** Boston Central (Story Memory)

**Recruit:** Stephane Chapheau

**Tokens Used:** 1

**Notes:** Assassinate calls a recruit to kill the targeted individual after a short delay; they will usually engage other adversaries that react to their actions, and may enter combat against entire groups if their presence attracts the attention of nearby guards. If a single Assassinate order coincides with the beginning of open conflict, the Assassin will usually stay to fight until they fall or all hostiles have been dispatched. Even if Connor has no part in battles that occur after activating the Assassinate ability, moving in close proximity to fights or bodies may lead to open conflict if guards notice him.

## Riot

**District:** Boston Central (Story Memory)

**Recruit:** Stephane Chapheau

**Tokens Used:** 1

**Notes:** Riot is primarily a diversionary tactic. When used, a Brotherhood agitator will arrive to foment an angry protest in the area of activation, with available civilians accumulating into an angry mob. All potential hostiles in the vicinity will immediately run to contend with the burgeoning riot, which takes them away from sentry posts and patrols to enable easier infiltrations. After a time, events will escalate into an open brawl, with the recruit at its center, where civilians will openly fight the guards; be careful to step away from this, as Connor may be drawn into the mêlée. Naturally, this ability requires the presence of civilians: it is of less utility in low-population areas.

##  Marksmen

**District:** Boston South

**Recruit:** Clipper Wilkinson

**Tokens Used:** All

**Notes:** Boston South is the easiest district to liberate, and yet Marksmen is possibly the most powerful ability at your disposal. To activate it, target an individual that you wish to eliminate, then press **LB**/**L2**. After a short delay, *all* currently available Assassins will open fire, eliminating the specified hostile and up to five targets of opportunity in the immediate vicinity. They will then enter open conflict with all enemies in the area. If conflict is inevitable, this is the most efficient way to begin – and, in many instances, win battles almost immediately.

## Bodyguard

**District:** Boston North

**Recruit:** Duncan Little

**Tokens Used:** All

**Notes:** Tap **LB**/**L2** and all available Assassins will arrive to accompany Connor, walking in his wake. Whenever a hostile enters the "investigation phase" (▼), one of the Assassins will immediately step forward to assassinate him, then depart from the scene. The ability ends when the last Assassin executes an opponent and leaves. While there are exceptions, especially with larger groups of adversaries, Bodyguard essentially prevents situations where Connor is detected by opponents and enters open conflict. To cancel the ability, and refund "unspent" Recruit tokens after the Assassins escape, press **B**/**◎**.

###  Lure

**District:** New York North

**Recruit:** Dobby Carter

**Tokens Used:** 1

**Notes:** This ability calls an Assassin to distract and draw a potential hostile away from their post or patrol by performing a theft. A financial sum (and potential consumable) are immediately awarded to Connor's inventory, but this is a detail. The most important point is that the affected adversary (and any affiliated allies within the vicinity, such as guard partners or patrol colleagues) will immediately chase the recruit as he leads them away from the area. This can even be used when a guard has an active SSI meter as a last-resort gambit to avoid detection. While you can only have one recruit active with the Lure ability at any given moment, it is possible to use it in conjunction with other abilities.

###  Ambush

**District:** New York West

**Recruit:** Jamie Colley

**Tokens Used:** 1

**Notes:** If you are familiar with the use of Trip Mines (see page 232), then you will soon come to recognize this ability as a permutation that explodes with an Assassin payload once detonated. Tap **LB**/**L2** with the Ambush ability selected, and a wide circular marker will appear on the ground. Any prospective adversary – all individuals marked by a red dot on the mini-map – that enter this zone will be attacked immediately by a single recruit. You can place one Ambush marker per active member of Connor's Brotherhood chapter. The best way to use this ability is to defend potential areas of attack, or lay traps to distract or engage opponents while Connor moves elsewhere. Ambush zones are removed (and the token refunded) when Connor moves more than 70 meters away from the zone. To cancel the order manually, stand within the circle and press **B**/**O**.

### Covert Escort

**District:** New York East

**Recruit:** Jacob Zenger

**Tokens Used:** 2

**Notes:** This ability summons a group of available Assassins disguised in military uniforms. In the subterfuge that ensues, Connor will act as a captive as the Assassins pretend to march him to a destination, while actually following his lead. Its primary function is to provide a mobile Blend opportunity and greatly decrease the rate at which opponents detect Connor, both reducing his effective Notoriety and halving the SSI meter fill rate. Even inside a Fort, enemies will only have yellow indicators when they have the Assassin in clear sight. Stationary guards that you encounter while using Covert Escort will stand aside to allow Connor and his "captors" to pass through the entrances without incident; this includes sentries posted outside Forts, and hostiles guarding other Restricted Areas. The only drawback is that you cannot attack while maintaining the subterfuge, and moving outside of the Blend range immediately cancels the active benefits. If open conflict begins, Connor's escorts will fight all opponents within the vicinity. To cancel a Covert Escort, press **B**/**O**.

III

QUICKSTART

THE STORY SO FAR

PRIMER

WALKTHROUGH

SIDE QUESTS

REFERENCE & ANALYSIS

MULTIPLAYER

EXTRAS

MAP LEGEND

INDEX

## SOUTH BOSTON

###  Defeat Escorts

Connor must eliminate four escorts to free two forced conscripts. Combat begins once you move within range; thereafter, the hostiles will attack both Connor and their captives. The mission is failed if both captives die. The most elementary tactic is to sprint behind the escorts and begin with a double assassination, though these targets

are unremarkable: with a Counter Kill to set up a Kill Streak, each battle should end quickly.

If you are liberating Boston South in one sitting, these missions will elevate Connor to a high Notoriety level. As you will mostly operate in areas with sparse patrols, we suggest that you complete all three required missions and also kill the conscription agents. The Martial Law Memory that ends the liberation is very quick to complete, and has the added benefit of clearing Connor's Notoriety.

**1**: Though the escorts and their captives begin in an area close to patrols, you can follow them for a short while until they move to a more convenient ambush position.

**2**: These reluctant conscripts are situated in an area where their captors are unlikely to obtain support.

**3**: There is a reasonably large patrol that may pass this position. Check the mini-map and surrounding area before you commit to the attack.

COMPLETION TIMELINE

CITIZEN MISSIONS

ATTACKING CONVOYS

CLUBS

MINIGAMES

FORTS

LIBERATION MISSIONS

ASSASSIN'S GUILD

THE UNDERGROUND

NAVAL PRIMER

NAVAL MISSIONS

PRIVATEER CONTRACTS

NAVAL LOCATIONS

HOMESTEAD MISSIONS

BENEDICT ARNOLD MISSIONS

COLLECTIBLES

###  Kill Conscription Agents

In this mission type, a civilian is pursued by a conscription agent on horseback. As you near the position, call Connor's steed and ride directly towards the two mounted men. Once the ⬤ icon appears to mark the aggressor, gallop towards them and press ❌/⬜ to perform an immediate horse-to-horse assassination. It's also possible to just sprint over on foot and pull them from their horse just before they gallop away. Approaching all three targets in this fashion enables you to end these chases before they begin.

**A**, **B**, **C**: None of the three marked sites should feature patrols.

###  Martial Law

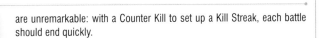

Connor's contact and prospective recruit can be found in the south of the district. After the opening cutscene ends, sneak around to the north corner of the Restricted Area. Jump into the hay cart and assassinate the guard next to it, then jump out and Blend with the crowd or hide in the Stalking Zone. Once you near the Templar addressing the men below, use the new Marksmen ability to eliminate him.

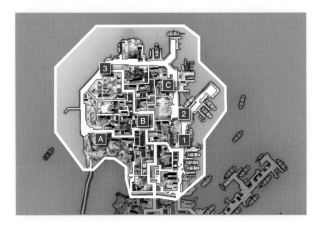

## Protect Merchant

As you approach the mission location, you will see a group of thugs harassing a merchant. Moving in close will lead to immediate combat. Even if you observe events from a distance, combat is inevitable. After a short period of time, one of the thugs – a Grenadier archetype – will automatically run from the scene. You must then catch and kill him with an assassination, while the other mercenaries will give chase and attempt to attack Connor. Complicating matters no end, all patrols in the vicinity will attempt to engage both Connor *and* the mercenaries, which can become quite chaotic.

There are, fortunately, two strategies that make these missions easier to complete. As open conflict is inevitable, it pays to adopt an aggressive strategy and eliminate the primary target immediately. As soon as you approach the icon, sprint in a direct line for the Grenadier standing at the center of the stall and perform a High Profile assassination. This completes the objective instantly. You can now choose whether to stand and fight (and accept some pretty horrendous Notoriety penalties when local patrols become involved), or take flight and lose your pursuers in the streets or, more obviously, sea. An alternative is to attempt to use an Assassin recruit to deal with the Grenadier instead – but be warned that this can lead to mixed results.

**1**, **2**, **3**: These three sites offer Connor a clear path to the Grenadier.

## Free Captives

In these locations, Templar agents have captives secured in stocks. Connor must kill all hostiles in the vicinity, then approach the civilian and press **B**/**◎** to free them. You cannot free the prisoners while in open conflict.

**A**: This is by far the easiest captive to free. Climb the building to the north of the icon, and you can double air assassinate the two Templar guards.

**B**, **C**: These two sites require that you kill numerous Templar guards in open conflict before you can free the captives, but at least the secluded positions mean that it is unlikely that patrols in the surrounding streets will become involved in the altercation. If you wish, it is possible to provoke a patrol and lure them into these areas, then escape to an elevated vantage point and watch the battle between the Templar gang and the local soldiers unfold. If Connor should become Incognito, even though two factions are still fighting, you can actually free the prisoners while the battle is still raging.

## Gangs of Boston

Enter the tavern highlighted by the Liberation Mission Contract marker (**⊗**) to begin the final mission, then travel to the circular Restricted Area in the very north of the city. When you reach the periphery of the red zone, activate the Bodyguard ability as directed. Calmly walk towards the Templar leader, then assassinate him when you move within range.

## Beat Up Merchant

In these sites, approach the group of starving children highlighted by the marker. They will request that Connor beat up two nearby merchants, marked by red hexagons (⬡), to enable them to steal a little food.

**1**, **2**, **3**: These locations feature merchants in areas where there are few (if any) patrols. If you have yet to collect it, there is a Peg Leg Trinket on the stall at position **2**.

## Defend Farmer

Approach the farmer at each site and hear his plea for help with assistance against soldiers determined to exact revenge. A blue circle marks the area that Connor must stay within during the fight that ensues. Two small waves of Redcoats will arrive and attack. You will fail the mission if the farmer's life bar is depleted – though, as with all Liberation Missions, you can simply leave the area and return to reset the challenge. If you are in danger of being overwhelmed, drop a Smoke Bomb – ideally in an area that encompasses the farmer – to facilitate easy takedowns. Note that completing these missions will drive Connor's Notoriety level up rapidly.

**I**, **II**, **III**: Once again, all three marked locations are free of patrols and stationary guards.

## Prevent Evictions

At these sites, you must intervene as tenants meet with bailiffs sent to evict them. Approach the individual marked with a ⬡, and you are given a choice to pay £150 to settle the family's debt: press **B**/**○** to make the bribe when the prompt appears. Alternatively, just rebuff the demand with an attack; you must then defeat his two Redcoat bodyguards. When they fall, the mission is completed. The latter option leads to greater rewards. If you loot the wealthy bailiff he can relinquish over £40 in cash, and high-value trade items or resources. As an aside, players who like to minimize Notoriety maintenance should note that you can actually pay the bailiff, follow him when he separates from the Redcoats, then incapacitate him with an unarmed stealth attack. Looting him enables Connor to retrieve his £150, and help himself to anything else the target is carrying.

**A**, **B**, **C**: You should be untroubled by patrols at these houses.

## Hoarding Provisions

Connor's district contact appears in the northwest of New York. After the opening cutscene, the closing Memory of this liberation involves infiltrating a Restricted Area to deal with the local Templar leader. Head to the waypoint from the main road to the east. When you approach the Grenadiers protecting the path to the house, hide in the convenient Stalking Zone and use the Lure ability to draw them out of position. Simply sprint along the wooden path and assassinate the Templar to free the north of New York from his greed and tyranny.

## Burn Infected Blankets

There are two types of site where you must press Ⓑ/Ⓞ to burn infected bedding. The first is the source of these insidious biological weapons, where you will find a trio of Templars standing next to the bodies of smallpox victims wrapped in the blankets and discussing the process of distributing them. These appear in small Restricted Areas, and necessitate a short fight. Our highlighted suggestions will enable you to avoid these entirely. In the second variety, you will either find the area unattended, or find a civilian with a collection of the blankets. Despite his protestations, you can simply approach them and press Ⓑ/Ⓞ to set them alight.

**I**: Though it lies within a Restricted Area, this site actually has no nearby hostiles. Just walk over to the bodies and blankets, then set them alight.

**II**: This site has a single citizen with a collection of blankets. There is a patrol that may pass close by; when there are no potential hostile witnesses, interact with the blankets to burn them.

**III**: This again features a single citizen, and no nearby patrols.

## Carry Sick Civilian

Complete these simple tasks last, as they leave you close to the final Memory of this liberation. Connor must carry three civilians suffering from the effects of the smallpox outbreak to a makeshift inoculation clinic in the ruins. Press Ⓑ/Ⓞ to pick a patient up, then carry them to the waypoint marker and repeat the button press to lay them down.

**1**, **2**, **3**: All three ailing civilians in these positions lie within 70 meters of the clinic, with no potential complications.

## Put Down Rabid Dogs

These tasks are extremely simple if you use Poison Darts to dispatch the animals humanely, without drama and from a safe distance.

**A**, **B**, **C**: Move into Poison Dart range, then throw the dart when there are no potentially hostile witnesses. With position **A**, approach from the west and turn to run to the north as soon as you throw the dart; there are guards nearby who may react if you linger.

## Protect the Clinic

The Memory Start marker appears close to the clinic where you carried sick civilians; interact with Jamie Colley to begin. You then have thirty seconds to prepare before the attack commences. Enemies can enter the area from paths to the north, south, east and west. While you can set up Ambush zones to have recruits leap out and attack hostiles, you can also place powder kegs at choke points to eliminate groups of opponents as they attack. This short Memory ends after you eliminate the final wave.

## Beat Up an Officer

Connor must kill or incapacitate three escorts (⬡) to automatically subdue an Officer (⬡). These targets will not detect Connor when he is Incognito. The three sites we select here enable you to complete the objectives without initiating open conflict if you use Smoke Bombs.

**1**: Approach this target by running along the alleyway from the east side to meet them as they walk towards you. Drop a Smoke Bomb in their midst, disable the three escorts, and the Officer should capitulate immediately. Try to time your attack to coincide with the point where they reach a crossroads in the side streets, just past a wooden cart.

**2**: The Officer and his men will walk into a deserted side street as you approach. Follow them to the approximate center of this alley to reduce the chance of interventions by passing patrols, then use a Smoke Bomb as before.

**3**: This group can be found in a secluded area, and do not move from their position. Again, start with a Smoke Bomb.

## Prevent an Execution

On arrival in the vicinity of these positions, you will encounter a firing line poised to execute civilians. You must interrupt this and disable all targets marked by ⬡. Using Smoke Bombs or calling on Assassin recruits will enable you to finish each battle in a matter of seconds.

**A**, **B**, **C**: All three execution sites in the northwest of the district occur in secluded areas, so it is unlikely that patrols will intervene once combat begins. The position at **A** features additional soldiers close to the firing line, which makes it slightly more difficult than those that follow. That said, with a well-placed Smoke Bomb, it's possible to eliminate all targets and escape before the smoke clears.

## Plant False Documents

As you approach these positions, a lone civilian will step forward to speak with Connor. Once he has finished, a target – described as a "snitch", though not in the sense of the archetype – will appear in the immediate vicinity. You must follow this hyper-vigilant target from a safe distance, Blending and hiding behind objects whenever possible, in order to wait for a very specific opportunity to sneak up behind them and perform a "reverse pickpocket" (hold **B**/⬤).

**I**: This target will eventually walk out onto a dock. Stay out of sight until he reaches the end, then sprint behind him (slowing to a walk for the last few steps) when a beggar steps out to ask him for change. Perform the reverse pickpocket while he is distracted.

**II**: This target appears on a main street, but soon turns left into an alleyway. When he takes a right, he will stop to relieve himself against a wall. Though there are two guards within sight, you can perform the reverse pickpocket and move away before they detect Connor.

**III**: Stay out of sight (first via a Blend position to the left, then a wooden scaffolding further along) until this target takes a left at the end of the long alleyway. Immediately run to approach him and perform the reverse pickpocket as he speaks to a woman outside a house.

## In the Wolf's Lair

This Memory Start position appears in the northwest of the district once all other requirements have been met; just enter the tavern to begin. After the cutscene, travel to the waypoint. Infiltrating the Restricted Area is just a simple matter of using the new Covert Escort ability to bypass sentries and move straight for your target to assassinate him. There is a strong chance that the subterfuge will fail once you are on board the ship, however. Should this occur, simply kill the marked target in the battle that ensues. You can then dive overboard and swim out of the zone to complete the Memory.

## CONTRACTS

Unlocked in Sequence 06, the Assassin's Guild metagame is both a great source of income and a way to level up your recruits while you are busy doing other things. You get one recruit per completed liberation (see page 154).

Once you have acquired your first Assassin, we advise that you liberate all districts in Boston immediately, and then those in New York during Sequence 09. This will enable you to have a full six recruits working on contracts (and, as a consequence, gaining in experience and rewards) from an early stage in the story. To access the Guild menu simply hold **LB**/**L2**, then press **✗**/**☐**.

The Guild menu features a list of colonies. Select these to study missions that Assassins can be sent on. Every potential mission has specific characteristics:

- ⊙ **Assistance:** The bonus applied to the base Success Rate of each mission in a given colony. This depends on whether or not you have conquered adjacent colonies – more on this shortly.

- ⊙ **Time:** The number of minutes in active play time required to complete the contract. The game clock is frozen whenever an interface screen is open. Assassins sent on contracts are unavailable for gameplay-related duties until they return.

- ⊙ **Difficulty:** A general indication of how hard the mission will be to complete; the more stars (from one to three), the higher the difficulty. This is expressed with greater accuracy in the Success Rate percentage once you assign an Assassin (or multiple Assassins) to a contract.

- ⊙ **Rewards:** The rewards that you will receive on successful completion of the mission.

## THE SUCCESS RATE

Once you have selected a contract, you can assign up to three Assassins to undertake it. After choosing an initial candidate, the Success Rate bar will be filled to show the probability (as a percentage) that he or she will successfully complete it. If it is less than 100%, you can increase it by selecting additional Assassins. Any mission that you begin with a Success Rate rating lower than 100% carries a chance, however slender, that the assignment will fail. Should this occur, the involved Assassin(s) will be injured – and therefore unavailable for a few minutes.

The base Success Rate for a contract depends on its difficulty:

The Success Rate for a contract is then affected by two factors: the level of the Assassins assigned to the contract, and any adjacent colonies that have already been conquered:

| ASSASSIN LEVEL | |
|---|---|
| LEVEL | SUCCESS RATE BONUS |
| 0 | +2% |
| 1 | +5% |
| 2 | +10% |
| 3 | +15% |
| 4 | +20% |
| 5 | +25% |
| 6 | +30% |
| 7 | +35% |
| 8 | +40% |
| 9 | +45% |
| 10 | +50% |
| 11 | +55% |

| BASE SUCCESS RATE | |
|---|---|
| DIFFICULTY | SUCCESS RATE |
| ✱ | 75% |
| ✱✱ | 25% |
| ✱✱✱ | 0% |

| ADJACENT COLONY CONQUERED | |
|---|---|
| DIFFICULTY | BONUS |
| ✱ | +10% |
| ✱✱ | +15% |
| ✱✱✱ | +25% |

## MISSION OUTCOME

When you send Assassins on missions, you will receive a notification once the contract has been completed.

- ⊙ If the expedition was a success, you obtain the mission rewards. If multiple recruits were sent to complete it, they each receive the full XP bonus. When you conquer a new colony, you also receive a bonus to Success Rates for all contracts in neighboring colonies.

- ⊙ With failure, there are no rewards. Assassins that you assigned to the mission are injured, and are temporarily unavailable. You cannot assign injured Assassins to contracts, call them during normal gameplay or send them to save convoys, until they recover.

Each colony begins under Templar control and features six unique main contracts. Once you have completed these, the colony falls under Assassin control, unlocking additional (albeit generic) contracts.

# RECRUIT: TRAINING STRATEGY

III

QUICKSTART

THE STORY SO FAR

PRIMER

WALKTHROUGH

SIDE QUESTS

REFERENCE & ANALYSIS

MULTIPLAYER

EXTRAS

MAP LEGEND

INDEX

COMPLETION TIMELINE

CITIZEN MISSIONS

ATTACKING CONVOYS

CLUBS

MINIGAMES

FORTS

LIBERATION MISSIONS

ASSASSIN'S GUILD

THE UNDERGROUND

NAVAL PRIMER

NAVAL MISSIONS

PRIVATEER CONTRACTS

NAVAL LOCATIONS

HOMESTEAD MISSIONS

BENEDICT ARNOLD MISSIONS

COLLECTIBLES

There are two ways to level up your Assassin recruits:

- By calling them directly on the battlefield – as a rule, they receive around 10 XP per kill or ability use.

- By sending them on contracts, which grants them 40-60 XP on completion, each contract lasting for anything between 2 and 15 minutes.

Both solutions are perfectly viable. The most efficient strategy really depends on your play style. If you like to call your recruits on the battlefield often, you can make them gain a few levels fairly quickly. You could even consider dedicating several minutes of your time just to this: identify large groups of enemies (or even storm a Fort), and let your recruits do the work, assisting them only when they're in danger. Given that the cooldown of the recruit tokens is a mere 30 seconds, you can do this repeatedly, enabling your Assassins to gain sums of XP that will quickly add up. As long as you do not perform the kills yourself, there are no Notoriety penalties.

If, on the other hand, you rarely call upon the services of your recruits, it obviously makes more sense for you to send them out to fulfill contracts.

If you are looking for an optimal development strategy, consider the following approach:

1. Get the full three recruits from Boston as early as possible in Sequence 06.

2. Spend at least a few minutes calling your three recruits on the battlefield, selecting only enemies of the Soldier archetype. They should gain around 10-20 XP per session, so they will quickly reach level 2 or 3 if you're ready to watch over them for 20 minutes or so.

3. Once all three recruits reach at least level 2 or 3, assign them all to the same short and easy ✱ contracts. They will each receive 40 XP (for an overall 120 XP) in only two minutes for the shortest assignments.

4. Once you have completed all of the short ✱ contracts, send your recruits on longer assignments while you complete main story missions. By the time you reach the end of Sequence 08, you should have conquered several colonies.

5. In Sequence 09, enlist the three recruits from New York. At this stage, your initial three Assassins should already be at a high level.

6. From this point forward, use your three initial recruits as "trainers" for the other three: send a trainer with one or two low-level recruits on short ✱ or ✱✱ contracts to vastly accelerate the development of the novices.

7. Once all six recruits are at a fairly high level, you will be in a position to easily complete the ✱✱✱ contracts.

Assassins gain new fighting capabilities to use when summoned by Connor as they rise through the ranks:

## ASSASSIN RANKS

| LEVEL | RANK | XP | MOVES LEARNED |
|-------|------|-----|---------------|
| 1 | Private | 100 | Combo Kill, Air Assassination, Weapon Swipe |
| 2 | Corporal | 200 | Double Assassination, Backstab, Duckfoot Pistol |
| 3 | Sergeant | 300 | Ground Kill, Improved Assassination, Counter Disarm |
| 4 | Officer Cadet | 400 | Human Shield, Improved Combo Kill, Loot |
| 5 | Lieutenant | 500 | Improved Pistol, Counter Throw, New Melee Weapon |
| 6 | Captain | 600 | Special Counter, Resist Combo Kill |
| 7 | Major | 700 | Improved Assassination, Counter Kill |
| 8 | Colonel | 800 | Double Barrel Pistol |
| 9 | General | 900 | Improved Combo Kill, Resist Combo |
| 10 | Field Marshal | 1,000 | Parry Reversal, Smoke Bomb |
| 11 | Assassin | 1,100 | New Weapon, Signature Move |

## SIGNATURE MOVES

| NAME | UPGRADE/ABILITY UNLOCKED |
|------|--------------------------|
| Stephane Chapheau | - |
| Jamie Colley | Slam Attack (requires heavy weapon) |
| Jacob Zenger | Blunt Attack (requires blunt weapon) |
| Duncan Little | - |
| Dobby Carter | Roll & Attack |
| Clipper Wilkinson | Close Range Pistol Attack |

# COLONY CONQUEST

Whenever you conquer a colony by completing its six initial contracts, you receive an Assistance bonus – a boon to the Success Rate of all contracts in neighboring colonies.

## COLONY NEIGHBORING NETWORK

| COLONY | DIFFICULTY | ADJACENT COLONIES |
|--------|------------|-------------------|
| Quebec | ✱ | New Hampshire + Massachusetts |
| New Hampshire | ✱ | Quebec + Massachusetts |
| Massachusetts | ✱✱✱ | New Hampshire + Quebec + Rhode Island |
| Rhode Island | ✱ | Connecticut + Massachusetts |
| Connecticut | ✱✱ | Rhode Island + New York |
| New York | ✱✱✱ | Connecticut + Pennsylvania |
| Pennsylvania | ✱✱✱ | Maryland + New York + New Jersey + Delaware |
| New Jersey | ✱✱ | New York + Delaware + Pennsylvania |
| Delaware | ✱✱ | New Jersey + Pennsylvania + Maryland |
| Maryland | ✱✱ | Virginia + Pennsylvania + Delaware |
| Virginia | ✱✱✱ | Maryland + North Carolina |
| North Carolina | ✱✱ | South Carolina + Virginia |
| South Carolina | ✱ | North Carolina + Georgia |
| Georgia | ✱ | South Carolina |

By taking this network into account, you can conquer the colonies in an order that will enable you to benefit from high bonuses. One effective path is as follows:

1. Quebec
2. New Hampshire (+10% from Quebec)
3. Rhode Island
4. South Carolina
5. Georgia (+10% from South Carolina)
6. Connecticut (+10% from South Carolina)
7. Massachusetts (+30% from Quebec, New Hampshire and Rhode Island)
8. North Carolina (+10% from South Carolina)
9. Virginia (+15% from South Carolina)
10. Maryland (+25% from Virginia)
11. Delaware (+15% from Maryland)
12. New Jersey (+15% from Delaware)
13. Pennsylvania (+45% from Maryland, New Jersey and Delaware)
14. New York (+40% from South Carolina)

Over the following pages, we offer annotated maps and solutions to the challenges you will encounter in the Boston and New York Underground areas.

- We have grayed out all "dead ends" on the maps to make it clear that, unless you are aiming for full exploration of each area, these paths can be safely ignored.

- Letters are used to signify the positions of each exit, and also denote the ideal order of progression in each underground. The destinations of each lettered exit are revealed in the accompanying legend.

- Numbers correspond to the screenshots and advice that follow each map. These cover all puzzles and steps required to explore all essential areas.

- While it is possible to negotiate the dark tunnels with Eagle Vision alone, our walkthroughs presume that you carry the lantern at all times.

- You must complete a lockpick minigame, a "cranks and pulley" or Magic Lantern puzzle at each exit to unlock it as a Fast Travel destination and increase your Synchronization percentage.

- Finally, you should note that there are regular checkpoints throughout the Underground maps, which record each milestone of note – from opening a locked door, to completing a puzzle. To cut down on unnecessary walking, note that you can Fast Travel between unlocked underground exits.

## BOSTON

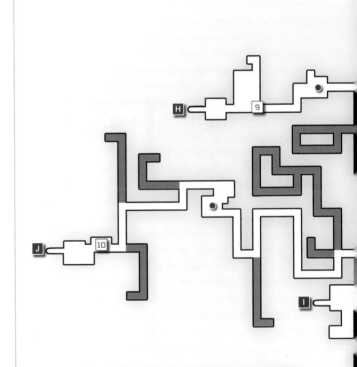

## MAGIC LANTERN PUZZLE SOLUTIONS

Crown Coffee House

South Commons

Boston Gate

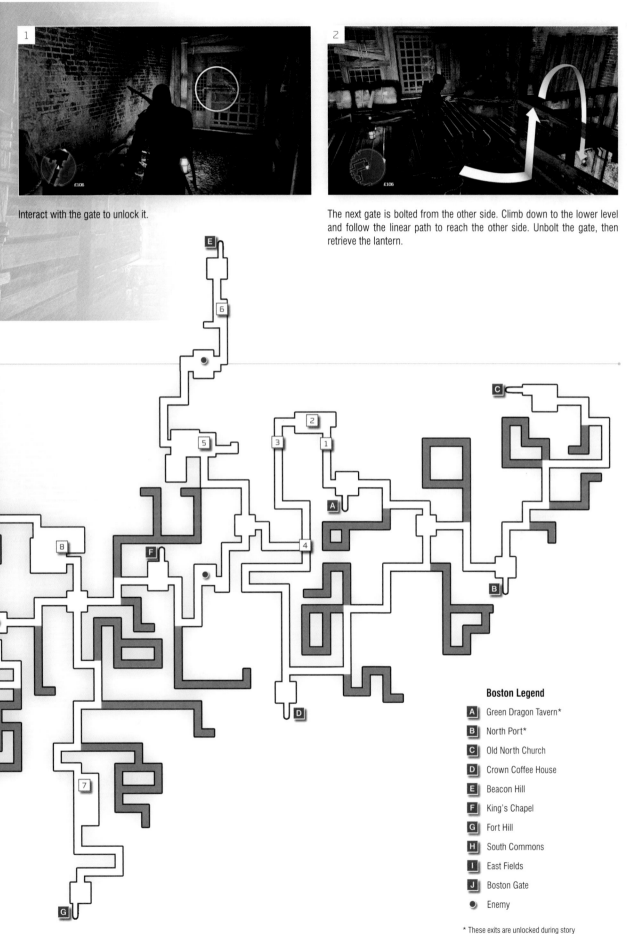

Interact with the gate to unlock it.

The next gate is bolted from the other side. Climb down to the lower level and follow the linear path to reach the other side. Unbolt the gate, then retrieve the lantern.

**Boston Legend**

| A | Green Dragon Tavern* |
| B | North Port* |
| C | Old North Church |
| D | Crown Coffee House |
| E | Beacon Hill |
| F | King's Chapel |
| G | Fort Hill |
| H | South Commons |
| I | East Fields |
| J | Boston Gate |
| ● | Enemy |

\* These exits are unlocked during story events in early Sequences.

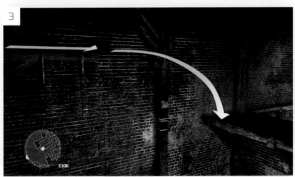

**3**

At the next gate, climb up via the crumbling brickwork on the west wall, then traverse to end of the wooden beam shown here. Hold 🎮/🎮, press 🎮 to the right and tap 🅰/🅧 to jump to the platform. Climb down to open the gate and collect the lantern.

**4**

At this corner, there is a powder keg beside the barrel. Pick this up and position it in front of the red brick wall (as shown here), then stand well back and shoot it to reveal a new entrance. Further south, you must destroy a second wall in the same fashion. This path leads to the Crown Coffee House exit, though you can also reach this from the east side of the map.

**5-1**

Climb down into the lower level as marked here.

**5-2**

Use the posts and wooden beam to reach a wall, as shown here. You will need to perform a manual jump to reach the wall from the final post. Climb to the top and turn to face west. You can now jump via the beam to the pulley, which Connor will use to swing to the next area.

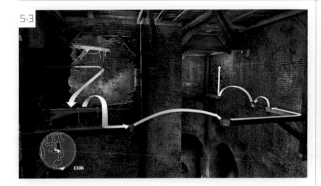

**5-3**

Using the beams on the wall (note that those closest to the camera here are shown from "outside" the playable area), traverse to return to the upper level. Unbolt the gate and collect the lantern.

**6**

After fighting the brigands, climb this wall to reach the Beacon Hill exit.

QUICKSTART

THE STORY SO FAR

PRIMER

WALKTHROUGH

→ SIDE QUESTS

REFERENCE & ANALYSIS

MULTIPLAYER

EXTRAS

MAP LEGEND

INDEX

**7**

At this location, you must climb a wall and avoid the intermittent streams of water that flow from above. The path marked here is the fastest route. Stop in the central midpoint of the climb and time your final ascent to begin right after the flow of water from the right-hand side ends. Climb through the opening on the south wall and jump to the beam, then the wooden partition, then drop down and unlock the gate.

**8-1**

When you reach the door bolted from the opposite side, leave the lantern beside it and drop down through the opening to the north to reach a lower level. Follow the short free run path and climb up to the next room, then unbolt the door.

**8-2**

Place the lantern in the elevator, then use the mechanism to the right to move it to the room above. You can then climb up to follow it.

**8-3**

Leave the lantern where it is and slide beneath the gap shown here. Follow the free run course, using the pulley to swing around the corner, then drop down on the opposite side of the gate. Unbolt it, then collect the lamp and continue to the exit.

**9**

When you reach this position, shoot the powder keg through the gap to unblock the path further ahead.

**10**

Shoot the powder keg to clear the path.

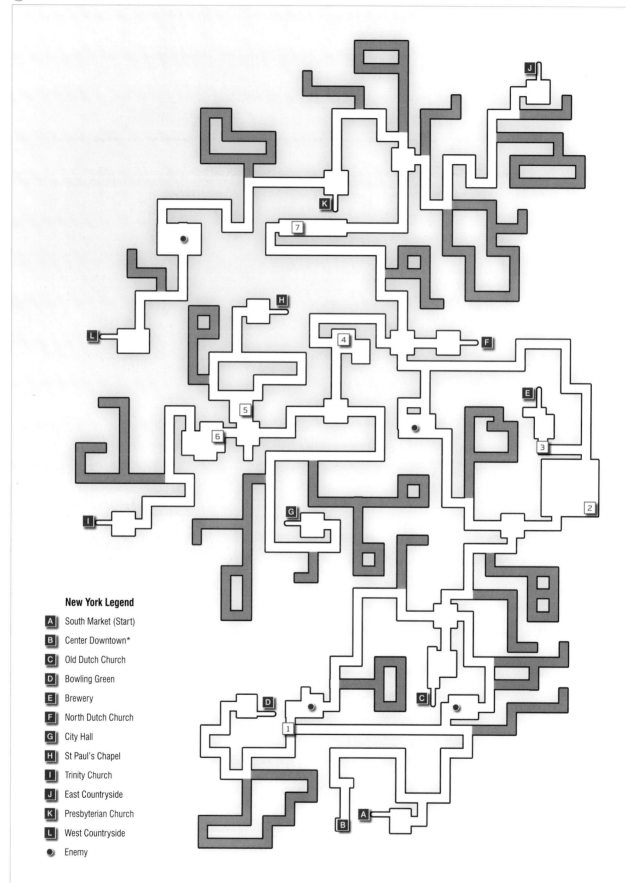

**New York Legend**

A — South Market (Start)

B — Center Downtown*

C — Old Dutch Church

D — Bowling Green

E — Brewery

F — North Dutch Church

G — City Hall

H — St Paul's Chapel

I — Trinity Church

J — East Countryside

K — Presbyterian Church

L — West Countryside

● — Enemy

* This entrance does not count towards full exploration of the New York Underground, and is unlocked as an overground Fast Travel destination during the events of the final Memory of Sequence 11. You cannot visit it beforehand.

| F | H | I |
|---|---|---|
| North Dutch Church | St Paul's Chapel | Trinity Church |

Pick up the powder keg situated a short walk away from this wooden fence, then place it in front of the barrier. Shoot it to open up the long tunnel that leads to the east. At the far end, you will find another powder keg that will enable you to destroy the wall.

In this room, you must free run and climb to reach a platform in the northeast corner, where a replacement lantern awaits.

The path is easy to make out, but there's potential for confusion when you reach this position. You must perform a Side Eject to reach the ledge to the left. Hold **RT**/**R1**, press **L** to the left and tap **A**/**X** to jump. Pick up the lantern and continue onward.

Collect the powder keg to the west of this position and place it in front of this wooden barricade. You can then shoot it to open up the path leading north. At the far end of this long tunnel, there is another wooden barrier that you must again destroy with a nearby powder keg.

Leave the lantern outside the locked gate, then run to the east and climb the rock wall shown here. When the prompt appears, hold **RT**/**R1** and press **A**/**X** to perform a Back Eject. Repeat this until you reach the top.

Traverse along the ledges until you reach this position. Jump over to the wall directly ahead. You now need to perform another Side Eject to reach the ledges to the right. Hold **RT**/**R1**, press **L** to the right and tap **A**/**X** to jump. When you land, perform a Back Eject to reach the next ledge. Jump down to the south and drop to the tunnel below to unbolt the gate and collect the lantern.

5-1

5-2

At the locked gate that prevents Connor from reaching the St Paul's Chapel exit, climb up onto the platform to the east of the doorway. From here, you can shoot a concealed powder keg. Drop through the hole in the wall created by the explosion to unbolt the gate, then move the lantern inside.

To move beyond the next locked gate, climb via the route shown here. Shoot the powder keg to the east, then drop through the hole created to unfasten the bolt. Collect the lantern and move on.

6-1

6-2

Operate the mechanism to the right of the locked gate to lower an elevator platform just beyond it, then climb over to the other side. Unbolt the gate, then place the lantern on the platform.

Climb over the next bolted gate and jump over the water below to reach solid ground to the west. Operate the mechanism to lower a second elevator. As before, unbolt the previous gate, then bring the lantern through.

6-3

7

Climb the wall marked here. Jump over to the wooden beam in the next room, then Side Eject to the right to reach an opening. Drop down on the opposite side to unbolt the final gate and collect the lantern.

This is a slightly more demanding variation on a timed climbing puzzle encountered in the Boston Underground. You must climb via the route marked here, performing the Back Eject move to leap between the ledges on the two walls and avoid the torrents of water. From the beam at the top, leap to the pulley to reach ground level and unbolt the gate.

# ✳ NAVAL PRIMER

III

QUICKSTART

THE STORY SO
FAR

PRIMER

WALKTHROUGH

SIDE QUESTS

REFERENCE &
ANALYSIS

MULTIPLAYER

EXTRAS

MAP LEGEND

INDEX

COMPLETION
TIMELINE

CITIZEN MISSIONS

ATTACKING
CONVOYS

CLUBS

MINIGAMES

FORTS

LIBERATION
MISSIONS

ASSASSIN'S
GUILD

THE
UNDERGROUND

NAVAL PRIMER

NAVAL MISSIONS

PRIVATEER
CONTRACTS

NAVAL
LOCATIONS

HOMESTEAD
MISSIONS

BENEDICT ARNOLD
MISSIONS

COLLECTIBLES

From Sequence 06 onwards, Connor can embark on a number of nautical expeditions. Naval Missions are multi-stage Memories that focus on navigation and naval combat on board the Aquila, and tell a side-story concurrent to Connor's adventures on land. Privateer Contracts are shorter Memories where the Aquila and her crew must neutralize opposing fleets to complete a variety of objectives. Both types of mission can be started via the East Coast map by interacting with Robert Faulkner at the Homestead, or any Harbormaster in other areas.

Before we move on to walkthroughs and tactics for all Naval Missions and Privateer Contracts, we will first offer a variety of valuable explanations, tips and insights on how to captain the Aquila effectively.

## BASICS

The curved meter to the left of the mini-map represents the Aquila's integrity. Collisions with rocks or other vessels, and being hit by enemy gunfire or Rogue Waves without bracing, will all result in damage. If you generate sufficient funds through the Homestead (see page 193), you can invest in upgrades to the ship's hull later in the story. The Aquila's life bar cannot be refilled while she is out at sea, though the crew undertakes full repairs between each mission.

Listening to your crew provides vital information, and isn't just part of an ambient soundscape. We say this now in the knowledge that you will almost certainly disregard their comments at first, but come to respect their contribution when a warning enables you to avoid a collision, or brace to avoid an otherwise deadly broadside. Even when your attention is arrested by a specific target, your crew always has a full 360-degree view of the dangers surrounding the Aquila.

01

While audio cues are useful in many areas in Assassin's Creed III they are perhaps most important during naval sorties, as the crew's comments offer important information on events on and around the Aquila (📷 01).

- ◉ Left of Connor stands Robert Faulkner, who offers warnings of Rogue Winds and Rogue Waves, and will caution his young captain when he sails against the wind.

- ◉ The two men located amidships, on the left and right, are Gunnery Officers. They will inform you when cannons are ready to fire – and protest with strained forbearance if you request a broadside or swivel gun shot while loading is in progress.

### MINI-MAP LEGEND

| | | | |
|---|---|---|---|
| ⬣ | Destination | ⬣ | Allied ships |
| ⬣ | Objective/Target | ❘ | Rogue waves |
| ● | Enemy ships | ⬛ | Wind Direction |

### COMMANDS

| XBOX 360 | PS3 | SUMMARY |
|---|---|---|
| **L** | **L** | Used to steer the ship. |
| **R** | **R** | Used to control the game camera. |
| **A** | **✕** | Half Sail/Full Sail: Increases the speed of the ship. |
| **B** | **○** | Half Sail/No Sail: Decreases the speed of the ship. |
| **X** | **□** | Brace: Connor and his crew take cover from enemy gunfire or Rogue Waves. |
| **LT** | **L1** | Fire Swivel Guns: Hold to aim, release to fire. |
| **RT** | **R1** | Fire Cannons: Hold to focus, release to fire. |

⊙ Sailing at Full Sail makes your vessel faster, but at the cost of reduced maneuverability.

⊙ Sailing at Half Sail is slower, but enables you to steer the Aquila more efficiently.

⊙ Rogue Winds push you in the prevailing direction of the gust, and make it almost impossible to steer into the wind at Full Sail. Indeed, turning the wheel hard right to counter the effects of a Rogue Wind from the right, for example, will still lead to an inexorable drift to the left. To counteract the effects of these temporary gales, call for Half Sail. If time is of the essence, alternating between the two movement speeds can offer a compromise of maneuverability and pace.

⊙ On the mini-map, a funnel-shaped indicator shows the direction of the prevailing wind (Rogue Winds notwithstanding – ⊚ 02). Sailing with the wind makes the Aquila faster; in these instances, the funnel is colored green. When you sail against the wind, the vessel's speed is greatly arrested – as indicated by an orange or red hue.

⊙ Hitting rocks or cliffs will damage the Aquila. Moving too close to the shore can cause the vessel to graze sandbars and reefs, which leads to a reduction in speed.

⊙ Rogue Waves are a phenomena restricted to specific Memories, and require that you brace to avoid damage; the perfect time to do so is usually indicated by an onscreen prompt. Whenever you receive a warning that a Rogue Wave is incoming, check its angle of approach on the mini-map and always try to steer into it before you brace. Moving away from it can lead to serious damage to the Aquila when the brace ends too quickly. That said, timing this maneuver perfectly can lead to the spectacular sight of the Aquila riding the crest of the wave.

Note that you can upgrade the Aquila over the course of the game, increasing the amount of damage that can be dealt to other ships, and making her less vulnerable to attacks. Once you reach Sequence 06, you can walk up to Robert Faulkner (who is standing on the landing stage of the Aquila), or books next to Harbormasters, and purchase upgrades (see page 253).

## NAVAL WARFARE

### General Advice

⊙ Approaching enemy ships head-on is often an inefficient solution as it limits your offensive possibilities. Instead, try to make diagonal approaches that will enable you to fire powerful broadsides.

⊙ In many battles, you should ensure that all enemy ships are on one side of the Aquila. Being pounded by multiple ships from both sides can be disorienting and, as a consequence, devastating. Whenever it is possible to do so, circle around enemy fleets in a wide arc. In situations where you do have enemies on both sides, however, you should note that the port and starboard cannons can be fired independently, and are subject to separate reload timers. While the dangers posed by sailing amidst enemy vessels are higher, this situation also increases your potential firepower.

⊙ When you fire a broadside, holding the button to "focus fire" will gradually narrow the white band that indicates the direction of fire. This can lead to a huge increase in accuracy over medium-to-long range. When the Aquila is extremely close to an opposing vessel, there is no need to focus the cannons. Just fire away immediately; this can save precious seconds.

⊙ Hitting larger vessels with an accurate broadside may cancel a shot

that they are preparing to fire. The same, alas, is true for the Aquila: damaging hits will briefly disable your attacking options.

⊙ The swivel guns have a much shorter reload time, but inflict negligible damage against larger vessels unless directed at a Weak Point. Their primary function is to eliminate small gunboats with a single shot, or schooners with up to three hits. Unless fired at point blank range, swivel gun fire will only hit ships if the hovering target reticule is red. When the Aquila is close to an opposing ship, the reticule will be primarily red, with occasional shifts to white. Over long distances, the opposite is true. Acquiring the ability to "snipe" at long range is something that takes practice and experience to perfect.

⊙ Some naval expeditions take place on rough seas, with waves further complicating engagements. Taking aim is then a lot more difficult; in many instances, you must focus your cannons and wait until you have a clear line of sight to fire. If you find yourself within a wave canal (⊚ 03), wait until the Aquila and the enemy ship are aligned and seize the opportunity to fire. If the Aquila and an enemy ship are instead separated by a wave (⊚ 04), focus your cannons in the direction of the ship (using its mast as visual reference), and open fire when your target is at the same elevation as the Aquila.

- Naturally, upgrades (see page 253) make it easier to complete Optional Objectives if you are keen to secure 100% Synchronization. We strongly advise that you obtain the Extra Cannon, Improved Rudder and Piercing Round upgrades at an early stage in the story. Though shockingly expensive, Hull Reinforcements may also help with the most difficult Optional Objectives. They can facilitate more aggressive strategies, as the extra durability means that it is slightly less important to regard the Aquila's hull integrity as something to be maintained at all costs.

- Checkpoints are common in the multi-stage Naval Missions, and can be exploited if you are determined to complete a perfect playthrough.

Cutscenes often indicate that your progress has been stored, which means that you can return to that checkpoint if your progress in an Optional Objective is less than satisfactory. The shorter Privateer Contracts, however, occur as a single "take", and must be repeated from the very beginning if events go awry.

- Before we continue, a little trivia for readers conversant with Assassin's Creed motifs: Aquila is the Latin word for "eagle", and the name of a constellation that features the star Altaïr – which is derived from an Arabic phrase meaning "the flying eagle".

## ENEMY VESSEL TYPE OVERVIEW

### Gunboat

**Notes**
- Smallest enemy vessels; low damage.
- Not a priority: take them out with swivel guns as you wait for cannon reloads.

### Schooner

**Notes**
- Attack you head-on in a right-angle with grapeshot.
- Fast and highly maneuverable, they can deal considerable damage; eliminate them quickly.

### Frigate

**Notes**
- Can fire their cannons with relatively short reloading intervals.
- Ram their bow or focus a broadside at their bow to expose their Weak Point.

### Man-of-War

**Notes**
- Largest enemy vessel.
- Use heat shot for maximum damage, or aim broadsides at their bow (or even ram it!) to expose their Weak Point.

### Gunboats

Gunboats are the smallest and weakest vessels that the Aquila will face, though they can be moderately dangerous in large numbers. The best tactic when you face them in fleets comprising multiple vessel types is to target them with swivel guns in moments where you must wait for the main cannons to reload while engaging larger ships. Hold ⬛/L1 to display the aiming reticule, wait until it turns red, then release to fire. A single shot will usually send a gunboat to the bottom of the sea.

Firing broadsides at a single gunboat is generally inefficient. However, if there are multiple gunboats (and schooners) congregated to port or starboard, you can eliminate multiple vessels with a single volley (📷 05).

### Schooners

These vessels are small and not particularly durable, but they can deal considerable damage to the Aquila if left unchecked. They favor grapeshot and will fire an initial flurry during their approach if adopting hit-and-run tactics (📷 06), and may turn into your wake to attack the Aquila from behind. Even a single schooner can inflict grievous damage over the course of a battle, so it always pays to make them priority targets.

Schooners require at least three shots to sink with the default swivel guns, but can be destroyed with only two once you obtain the (essential) Piercing Round upgrade. A single broadside is sufficient to send them beneath the waves.

You can destroy all small ships by ramming them at high speed (📷 07), though the accompanying loss of velocity means that this is only practical against one (maximum two) targets at a time. This tactic is even more efficient if you purchase the Naval Ram upgrade.

There are many instances where you will face a large fleet composed primarily of schooners and gunboats. A good way to defeat them efficiently is to circle around them in a broad curve (📷 08). Fire broadsides at schooners or multiple vessels in close proximity, and employ the swivel guns to eliminate targets during reloads.

III

QUICKSTART

THE STORY SO FAR

PRIMER

WALKTHROUGH

SIDE QUESTS

REFERENCE & ANALYSIS

MULTIPLAYER

EXTRAS

MAP LEGEND

INDEX

## Frigates

When you engage a frigate it will usually attempt to circle your ship (◎ 09). However, as the frigate is able to fire its cannons at very short intervals, this can lead to a situation where you must almost perpetually brace to avoid its shots. A better strategy is to break off and steer in the opposite direction (◎ 10). While you are steering your ship in a half circle, the enemy will now come at you perpendicularly (◎ 11). Focus your cannons and fire a broadside at the enemy ship's bow (◎ 12). Furthermore, firing at a frigate's bow often exposes its Weak Point, enabling you to destroy it with a single well-aimed swivel gun shot.

When you face multiple frigates, try to avoid situations where they surround you. Instead, try to circle them, keeping both on one side, ideally in a straight line (◎ 13). With this tactic, one of the enemy frigates will act as a shield for the Aquila, and may sustain damage from broadsides fired by its more distant ally.

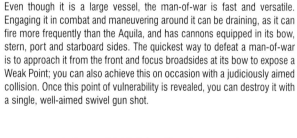

## Man-of-War

The man-of-war is the largest vessel you will encounter. Even if you use chain shot to destroy their masts, they are still able to shoot their cannons. For optimal results, measure your approach to pummel these leviathans while remaining outside their direct line of fire (◎ 14). The (extremely expensive) Heat Shot ammunition upgrade will increase the damage that you inflict with broadsides.

When you are very close to a man-of-war, there is no need to focus your broadsides (◎ 15). Just fire quickly and then steer the Aquila away from the inevitable counterattack.

Even though it is a large vessel, the man-of-war is fast and versatile. Engaging it in combat and maneuvering around it can be draining, as it can fire more frequently than the Aquila, and has cannons equipped in its bow, stern, port and starboard sides. The quickest way to defeat a man-of-war is to approach it from the front and focus broadsides at its bow to expose a Weak Point; you can also achieve this on occasion with a judiciously aimed collision. Once this point of vulnerability is revealed, you can destroy it with a single, well-aimed swivel gun shot.

## THE CHASE

| MISSION OVERVIEW | |
|---|---|
| **Unlocked** | **Optional Objectives** |
| ▪ Complete Sequence 05 | ▪ Limit the ship's damage to 50%.<br>▪ Use a mine to eliminate a gunboat.<br>▪ Limit damage from the Fort's mortars to 50%. |

Once you reach the first green zone, several enemy gunboats will attack your ally. In order to complete the related Optional Objective, you must destroy these targets (and those that follow) quickly and efficiently. Use broadsides for groups, if possible, and use swivel gun blasts to eliminate individual ships between reloads. Gunboats in the distance can be destroyed with the swivel gun if you have sufficiently quick reactions, which is the key to completing the Optional Objective.

Aim your swivel guns at a mine until the target indicator turns red. Destroying a mine will set off a chain reaction, creating a safe path.

In order to complete the related Optional Objective, simply shoot the three mines behind this rock – a gunboat is lurking right next to them.

Try to hit the Fort (or, more specifically, its three towers) with a precision broadside as soon as the introductory cutscene ends. You should then sail parallel to the Fort at Full Sail. When it fires its mortars, turn hard at Half Sail to steer away from the wash that indicates where the mortars are landing. With this tactic, you can usually land a broadside on a tower between each flurry of mortar fire. If you fail the Optional Objective, note that there is a checkpoint just prior to this final battle.

## THE BAHAMAS CONTRACTS

| NAME | AVAILABILITY | OPTIONAL OBJECTIVE | TIPS | EFFECT |
|------|--------------|--------------------|------|--------|
| Blistering Dawn | Complete Sequence 07 | Limit damage taken to 25%. | This is a very short and uncomplicated battle. Take care of the two schooners first, then eliminate the frigates. As long as you take care to brace, the Optional Objective should be easy to complete. | For each completed Contract: -25% Risk Rate for this route |
| A Call for Help | Complete Sequence 07 | Limit ally health loss to 75%. | Carefully navigate around the rocks. Some of the sharp turns necessitate a call for dead stop for a brief moment, before deploying Half Sail again. To save the Independence, you need to steer the Aquila right into the middle of the enemy groups to draw their fire. This will enable you to shoot both your port and starboard cannons alternately. Don't be too alarmed as your ally's life bar depletes at a rapid rate early in the fight: this is to be expected. As you eliminate enemy vessels, this will gradually slow to a crawl. | |
| Search for the Somerset | | Limit environmental damage to 25%. | Ram one of the two schooners while shooting your cannons at the other. Then fire your swivel guns at the small gunboats. With this strategy, you will destroy most of the Somerset's fleet during the opening approach. | |

## VIRGIN ISLANDS CONTRACTS

| NAME | AVAILABILITY | OPTIONAL OBJECTIVE | TIPS | EFFECT |
|------|--------------|--------------------|------|--------|
| The Sea Wolves | Complete Sequence 08 and all three Bahamas Contracts | Complete the Contract with no more than four allied casualties. | The eight merchant ships that you must escort will often get in your way during this Contract. Try not to ram them and pay attention to their positions; sometimes they will block your line of fire. The enemy frigates will concentrate most of their fire on the merchant ships, which enables you to be very bold and avoid wasting time by bracing for attacks. Upgrades to the Aquila's offensive capabilities will obviously make the Optional Objective easier to complete. | For each completed Contract: -25% Risk Rate for this route |
| A Midnight Engagement | Complete Sequence 08 and all three Bahamas Contracts | Limit environmental damage to 25%. | If you chart a course to the right of the rocks, taking the long route, you can hit the Greyhound with at least two full broadsides before she meets with her fleet – which, with the Extra Cannons upgrade, should be enough to sink her. You can then turn in to the left to deal with the four schooners. | |
| The Giant and the Storm | | Sink all ships by firing on the powder stores. | Don't be too casual with the schooners at the start of this mission: you will need your ship in robust shape for the battle that follows. Once you defeat them, the Orpheus and two frigates arrive. Having the Improved Rudder upgrade can be quite helpful in this Contract. To fulfill the tough Optional Objective, ramming the bow of the final three ships may prove useful to expose their Weak Points, as the rough sea makes aiming very difficult. One option is to use chain shot to disable them in advance – though even then, it's tricky to line up a broadside to the bow. | |

## ADDITIONAL CONTRACTS*

| NAME | AVAILABILITY | TIPS |
|------|--------------|------|
| Sinking a Secret | Complete Sequence 05 | As you reach a succession of green search zones, the camera will highlight ships to your left and right; left for the first two instances, right for the third. Wipe them out immediately with a single well-aimed broadside. In the final part of the mission, the Dartmoor has the advantage as you follow her through the rocks. Chart your pursuit carefully to avoid her guns until a cutscene begins; once this ends, the Aquila will be positioned right next to the man-of-war. Brace as prompted, then unleash a full, focused broadside at the Dartmouth's bow to reveal her Weak Point, and sink her immediately with a swivel gun shot. You can then finish off the gunboats and schooners in any fashion you please. |
| The Ghost War, Act 1 | Complete Sequence 05 | Carefully navigate the rocks and Rogue Winds to reach the green search zone, then eliminate the small privateer fleet of gunboats and schooners; you can actually sail into the middle of the fleet and decimate it with broadsides to the left and then right. Continue with the search until the Windermere attacks. Her angle of approach will enable you to aim two, perhaps three broadsides at her bow – and therefore eliminate this man-of-war by revealing her Weak Point. As in "Sinking a Secret", you then have the simple task of mopping up a collection of smaller vessels. |
| The Ghost War, Act 2 | Complete Sequence 05 and The Ghost War, Act 1 | After the short journey through the rocks, eliminate the small fleet that engages the Aquila, then set sail for the waypoint marker. Once the cutscene introduces your targets, wait until the Leviathan and the two frigates pass before you launch the ambush. This leads to an enjoyable battle on turbulent seas. With a deft hand at the wheel, you can actually lead the Leviathan to destroy her own allies. |

* These extra missions are only available if you have an appropriate preorder bonus or a Collector's Edition of Assassin's Creed III. They do not feature Optional Objectives or affect trade routes, though they each feature a man-of-war to fight – and are therefore extremely fun to play.

Introduced late in Sequence 05, Peg Leg is an elderly sailor who requests that Connor locate and deliver miscellaneous treasures called "Trinkets". The exact locations of these items, which are stored in tiny chests, are documented in the comprehensive Collectibles section at the end of this chapter. From the start of Sequence 06, you can collect and present Peg Leg with these objects. Once you reach specific collection milestones, you can access special Memories that take place in faraway Naval Locations.

After you speak to Peg Leg and unlock a Captain Kidd Memory, you can travel to the destination via the East Coast map, accessed via Robert Faulkner or any Harbormaster. We suggest that you do so at an early stage. The money that Connor can loot from Chests in each expedition adds up to a small fortune of over £20,000, while the final reward is a special item that can make it easier to complete damage-related Optional Objectives.

## FORT WOLCOTT

### OVERVIEW

| Unlock Conditions | Optional Objectives |
| --- | --- |
| ■ Complete Sequence 05 and receive Dead Man's Letter 1, obtained from Peg Leg in exchange for a single Trinket | ■ Perform three ledge assassinations.<br>■ Limit health loss to 33%.<br>■ Achieve a Kill Streak of three. |

**01**

You begin with a dizzying ascent to the top of the tower overlooking the ocean. When you reach the upper ledge, a guard will stand in place until you oblige with a ledge assassination. Climb up to trigger a cutscene. Press against the wall, whistle to attract the next guard, then perform a corner assassination when he moves within range.

**02**

Run onto the wooden balcony and perform an air assassination on the guard patrolling below. From your position on the lower level, follow the route shown here to find a Chest containing £1,250.

**03**

Move through the opening and climb to the upper level. From this point, stealth is mandatory.

**04**

In the next room, turn left and watch the guard below. When he turns away, dive into the hiding place and assassinate him when he returns.

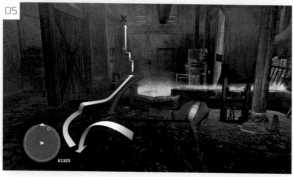

**05**

Remain in the hiding place and observe the second guard. When he turns away, run behind him to perform an assassination. Climb up to the balcony and dispatch a third guard with a ledge assassination when he strolls into position.

**06**

From the upper walkway, traverse via the hanging metal molds – using the Back Eject move when prompted – to reach an opening in the east wall. Jump through to reach the next room.

07

Use the lintels to traverse to the left, then Back Eject into the next room.

08

Use the light fixtures to cross the hall, ignoring the soldiers beneath, then jump through the open windows to reach a dormitory. Once inside, open the Chest on the table beside the third bed on the left to obtain £1,500.

09

Jump through the next open window and follow the course shown here. Kill the guard with a ledge assassination to complete the Optional Objective.

10

You must now kill the four guards in the prison, then scour the area for a clue in Eagle Vision (it's in the cell to the northeast, lower level). Before you perform the latter task, though, be sure to open the Chest inside the cell pictured here to obtain £2,000.

11

Connor is now confronted by a Grenadier; two successive Weapon Swipes followed by an attack while he lies prone will suffice. After the cutscene, run up the ramp formed by the collapse of the roof, then follow the route shown here to enter a building. Avoid the flames: these will cause you to fail the new Optional Objective.

12

Inside the building, run towards the opening until the floor collapses, then jump through the two windows to reach the position marked here. To complete the Optional Objective and achieve a Kill Streak of three, open the fight with a Counter Kill and then dispatch the next two soldiers without pausing. There is a checkpoint prior to this fight if you need to restart.

13

Follow the linear path, avoiding contact with the flames, until you reach the position marked here. Be sure to jump to the left – there is a dead-end to the right in the ruined building.

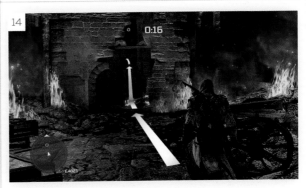

14

Finally, run through the tower and up the ramp. When you reach the end of this short path, Connor will automatically dive into the ocean below.

III

QUICKSTART

THE STORY SO FAR

PRIMER

WALKTHROUGH

SIDE QUESTS

REFERENCE & ANALYSIS

MULTIPLAYER

EXTRAS

MAP LEGEND

INDEX

COMPLETION TIMELINE

CITIZEN MISSIONS

ATTACKING CONVOYS

CLUBS

MINIGAMES

FORTS

LIBERATION MISSIONS

ASSASSIN'S GUILD

THE UNDERGROUND

NAVAL PRIMER

NAVAL MISSIONS

PRIVATEER CONTRACTS

NAVAL LOCATIONS

HOMESTEAD MISSIONS

BENEDICT ARNOLD MISSIONS

COLLECTIBLES

| OVERVIEW | |
|---|---|
| **Unlock Conditions** | **Optional Objectives** |
| ■ Receive Dead Man's Letter 2, obtained from Peg Leg in exchange for 6 Trinkets | ■ Perform three running assassinations.<br>■ Stay within 40 meters of your target.<br>■ Kill the target before he reaches the cave. |

Follow this path and loot the Chest to obtain £3,000 before you approach the cliffs.

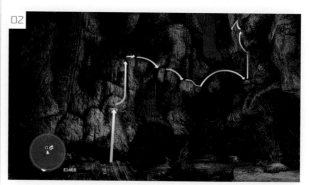

Start your climb, then perform a Back Eject when prompted. Climb as high as you can, then traverse to the left.

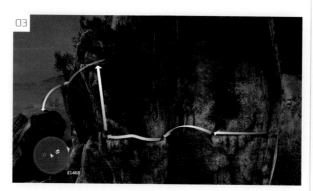

Climb up to reach a path above the cliffs, then follow it until you reach a ruined ship. Leaping to it triggers a cutscene.

When play resumes, Connor must pursue the mercenary. To complete the Optional Objectives, you must stay within 40 meters of the target and perform three "running assassinations". These are achieved by simply tapping ✖/⬜ just before Connor reaches a victim while sprinting.

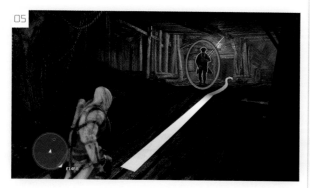

Connor's first running assassination target can be found in this position.

After the kill, duck through the gap and follow this course.

The second running assassination target is found in this location.

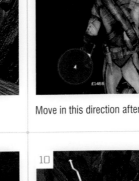

Move in this direction after Connor claims his second victim.

Climb above the obstruction to continue the pursuit.

At the top, follow this free run course. You can kill both mercenaries in the marked position simultaneously with a running assassination, completing the first Optional Objective.

**11**

This is the most complicated free running exercise in the chase. To add to the overall urgency, a new Optional Objective is introduced: you must kill the target before he reaches the cave. Don't panic when the mast falls: this is but a momentary setback.

**12**

As soon as Connor begins to slide down the deck, press ✖/□ to perform an air assassination on the mercenary as he runs beneath.

QUICKSTART
THE STORY SO FAR
PRIMER
WALKTHROUGH
SIDE QUESTS
REFERENCE & ANALYSIS
MULTIPLAYER
EXTRAS
MAP LEGEND
INDEX

COMPLETION TIMELINE
CITIZEN MISSIONS
ATTACKING CONVOYS
CLUBS
MINIGAMES
FORTS
LIBERATION MISSIONS
ASSASSIN'S GUILD
THE UNDERGROUND
NAVAL PRIMER
NAVAL MISSIONS
PRIVATEER CONTRACTS
NAVAL LOCATIONS
HOMESTEAD MISSIONS
BENEDICT ARNOLD MISSIONS
COLLECTIBLES

185

THE GHOST SHIP

## OVERVIEW

| Unlock Conditions | Optional Objectives |
|---|---|
| ■ Receive Dead Man's Letter 3, obtained from Peg Leg in exchange for 14 Trinkets | ■ Do not fall into the water.<br>■ Reach the Octavius within one minute. |

Follow the linear tunnel to reach a cutscene. Two Optional Objectives now appear: you must reach the Octavius within one minute, and do so without falling into the water. Start by sliding down the slope to Connor's right, open the Chest hidden behind the tent when you reach the bottom, then follow the route shown in this screenshot. There is a checkpoint just before this challenge, so you can restart if you fail.

The timed challenge ends when you reach this position, so stop to open the Chest behind the tents before you continue via the route shown here. Though another Chest appears on the mini-map, you cannot plunder it until later.

The prohibition on falling in the water remains in effect for the entire Memory, though this section of the climb presents no real danger.

Run down the pole to reach the deck.

There are two Chests to loot before you move below decks.

Run up through the opening to the south, then collect the treasure map. Once you leave the captain's cabin, another cutscene will begin.

07

Connor must now escape the Octavius. Start by sliding beneath this gap.

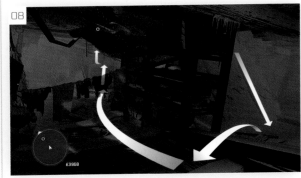

08

After you pass beneath the washing line, free run over the boxes to the right.

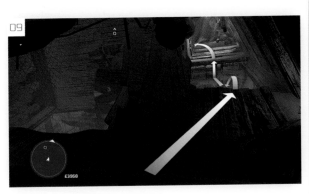

09

After the floor collapses, follow this path.

10

Approach the ladder. After Connor's fall, a time limit is introduced.

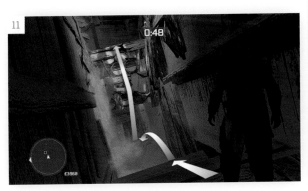

11

Start by climbing to the top of the surface shown here.

12

At the top, turn and use the fixtures to reach the far wall. At the end, climb to the top and perform a Back Eject when prompted.

13

Climb up the next wall and traverse to the right.

14

Finally, climb onto the frame of the door and scramble through the opening above to complete the Memory.

## OVERVIEW

| Unlock Conditions | Optional Objectives |
|---|---|
| ■ Receive Dead Man's Letter 4, obtained from Peg Leg after collecting all 24 Trinkets | ■ Reach the assailant's location within one minute.<br>■ Solve the riddle within one minute. |

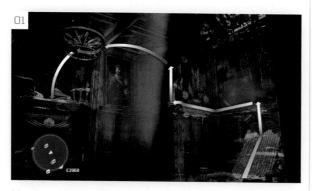

After the opening cinematic, run along the corridor and duck through the small opening. Follow this route to reach the upper level, performing a Back Eject to both reach the chandelier and then spring from it to land on the balcony.

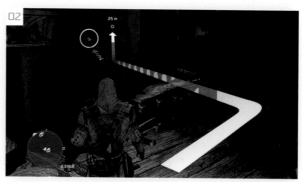

Open the Treasure Chest before you squeeze through the gap, then run through the next doorway to reach a balcony.

Use the pole to swing down to the lower level, then open the Chest situated a short walk to the north. You should then slide beneath the debris in front of the door to reach the next room.

Start by interacting with the clue in this position.

You can then analyze these two additional clues. Before you do so, examine the room to find a stuffed bear. Knowing its precise location will be useful in a moment.

The new Optional Objective must be completed within one minute. To reach the waypoint, follow this route by starting your climb at the stuffed bear. From the lower balcony, swing via the tusks to reach a hanging aviary, then Back Eject to reach another. At this point, climb up to the beam above, then hop onto another beam to the east.

From here, face the waypoint and jump to the pole directly ahead; Connor will then swing down. Open the Chest before you do anything else; note that you will need to perform a Back Eject from the beam above the display cabinet to reach it. Drop back down to continue. Examine the mask to find a mechanism behind it, then walk through the broken display case to examine a musket rack. After the cinematic, interact with the display cabinet to find a secret entrance.

Climb the pipe organ to reach the floor above.

Walk onto the beam, then turn to the right.

Just before you reach a V-shaped wooden rafter, drop to the floor below. Sprint at the small opening on the left side of the collapsed roof to find a Chest, then return to the upper area as directed.

Run along the beam, then drop to the room below.

Duck through the small opening in the wall and interact with the back of the painting (note the classic "haunted house" eyeholes) to enter the next room.

Analyze the clues in the area to trigger a cutscene. The solution to the riddle is to scrutinize the display cabinet filled with timepieces, and note that all hands are positioned to tell the same time: ten minutes to six, or 5:50. Approach the grandfather clock and press Ⓑ/◎ to interact with it, then align the hour and minute hands accordingly.

Enter the secret passage and follow the steps to the lower level, then enter the secret passage shown in the cutscene. Approach the waypoint marker to collect the final map portion. In a cinematic back at the Homestead, Connor and Faulkner intuit the precise location documented by the map portions. You can begin this Memory immediately, if you wish.

## OVERVIEW

| Unlock Conditions | Optional Objectives | Reward |
|---|---|---|
| ■ Complete Fort Wolcott, Dead Chest's Treasure, The Ghost Ship, and The Mad Doctor's Castle | ■ Solve the riddle within five minutes.<br>■ Do not use any ranged weapons against animals.<br>■ Limit health loss to 30%. | ■ Shard of Eden |

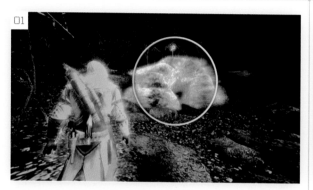

01

Walk with Faulkner until you reach a clearing, where the first Optional Objective appears. The first clue is found on this rock to the northwest. You can use Eagle Vision to make the search easier: the locations of the four clues are all highlighted at medium-to-close range.

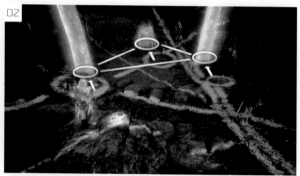

02

In the puzzle that follows when Connor analyzes the clue, align the overlay as shown here.

03

The second clue is in this tree, to the south of the previous clue. Climb to its upper reaches to find it at the end of a branch.

04

To solve the puzzle, align the overlay as follows, then perform a Leap of Faith to quickly return to the ground.

05

The third clue is on this pile of rocks.

06

The solution to the puzzle is illustrated here.

07

The final clue is in this tree. You can analyze this clue from the upper V-shaped position.

**08**

The final puzzle solution is shown here. If you have failed the Optional Objective, you can return to the previous checkpoint to retry after the benefit of an initial "trial run".

**09**

Approach the search zone marked on the mini-map. As Connor nears the position, a pack of three wolves will attack. To complete the accompanying Optional Objectives, you must defeat them with the timed button press minigame as they run in to attack, but without losing more than 30% health. Return to Faulkner at the green search zone and analyze the clue. After the cinematic, shoot one of the powder kegs shown here and perform a Leap of Faith into the water below.

**10**

Inside the limestone cavern, swim to the waypoint; dive beneath the obstruction when prompted. Free run over the limestone stalagmites, then climb the far wall.

**11**

At the top, traverse to the left to reach an opening, then climb up.

**12**

Swing via the supports to continue. Jump through the V-shaped limestone formation to reach a ledge beyond.

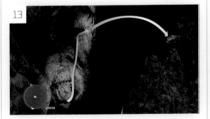

**13**

Climb up as shown here, then perform a Back Eject.

**14**

Run along the logs and wooden boards to reach this chamber, then jump straight ahead. When you land, slide beneath the gap.

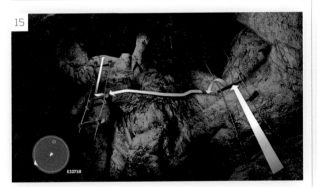

**15**

Climb via the decaying ladders to reach a hole above, then run straight ahead to discover Captain Kidd's treasure. You can only take the mysterious floating object: the other riches, alas, are not for Connor to plunder.

**16**

Connor then has twenty seconds to free run through the corridor before the countdown expires. After the closing cutscene, listen carefully when Connor disembarks from the Aquila to hear Shaun explain the origins and purpose of the Shard of Eden in a voice-over. This First Civilization device greatly reduces the likelihood that Connor will be hit by musket or pistol fire while fighting with armed opponents. You do not need to equip it: its effects are automatically and perpetually active.

# THE RUINS AT CERROS

## OVERVIEW

| Unlock Conditions | Reward |
| --- | --- |
| ▪ Available only as a preorder bonus or in Collector's Editions of Assassin's Creed III | ▪ Captain Kidd's Sawtooth Cutlass |

01

Run through the tunnel until you reach the opening shown here, then climb to reach the jungle above.

02

Head for the waypoint until you reach this tree, then follow the marked route to access the only path to the temple.

03

Follow the waypoint markers on the approach to the temple. The final marker is inaccessible from the south face, so move to the west side.

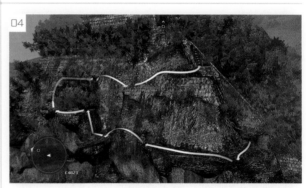

04

After Connor's brush with danger, follow the path shown here. Back at the south face of the structure, climb the exposed brickwork to reach a small opening.

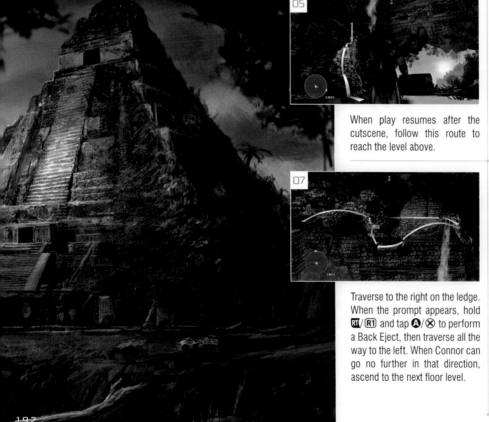

05

When play resumes after the cutscene, follow this route to reach the level above.

06

At the opening to the north, free run to reach the opposite side of the temple. In the next corridor, free run to the end and jump to the ledge directly ahead.

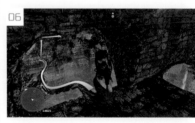

07

Traverse to the right on the ledge. When the prompt appears, hold **RT**/**R1** and tap **Ⓐ**/**Ⓧ** to perform a Back Eject, then traverse all the way to the left. When Connor can go no further in that direction, ascend to the next floor level.

08

On solid ground, slide under the small gap to the west, then swing via the tree roots to reach the corridor on the south side of the temple as shown here. Follow the corridor until it turns north, then climb the wall directly ahead. At the top, open the sarcophagus to obtain Captain Kidd's Sawtooth Cutlass, a unique sword. You can equip this at any time by visiting the basement in the Homestead Manor: see page 194.

# HOMESTEAD MISSIONS

Homestead Missions reveal a pastoral side to Connor's character as he gradually transforms the isolated Davenport Homestead into a thriving community. Though many of these Memories are short, they are vital steps that must be completed to access the full range of economic opportunities available via the Accounting Book interface (see page 244), and unlock a selection of extremely useful upgrades and weapons. They also make a large contribution to your actual (and potential) total Synchronization rating.

You can find a diagram that illustrates the unlock progression of all Homestead Missions on page 238.

## ACHILLES, THE HOUSEKEEPER

### ACHILLES MISSIONS

| MISSION | AVAILABILITY | NOTES |
|---|---|---|
| Encyclopedia of the Common Man | Sequence 06 | This long and surprisingly involved Homestead Mission cannot be completed until late in the main storyline. You only need to begin it – not complete it – to unlock any quests that follow. See the box-out below for details. |
| Manor Mysteries I | Sequence 07 | Talk to Achilles in front of the fireplace at the Manor. Follow him downstairs, then travel to talk to Norris inside the mine. Follow the miner to the cave entrance, and blow up the explosive barrel with a firearm. Follow the waypoint markers to reach your destination, then climb up the wall and free run to the Chest (⊙ 01). Once you have picked the lock, you have two minutes to escape the cave. Climb the wall to your right (⊙ 02), then retrace your steps, choosing the left-hand path every time you reach a fork. Finally, bring the contents of the Chest back to Achilles. |
| Manor Mysteries II | Sequence 09 | Talk to Achilles inside the Manor, then Fast Travel to New York and make for the ruined area on the west side of the city. Climb to the top of the building (⊙ 03), then retrieve the painting for Achilles and return it to him at the Homestead. |
| Legacy | Sequence 11 | You will find Achilles inside the Manor. Go talk to Father Timothy in the chapel. |
| Achilles' Painting | Sequence 11 | Examine the marked wall inside the Manor to complete Achilles' series of quests. |

### ENCYCLOPEDIA OF THE COMMON MAN

To begin this challenge, talk to Achilles inside the Manor. Your goal here is to create a record of individuals that will eventually come to live and work on the Homestead by "scanning" them in specific circumstances. This quest can therefore only be completed once you have recruited all possible Artisans and Harvesters.

The activities that will enable you to complete an entry to the Encyclopedia are related in the table below. You can check your in-game progress by studying the appropriate entry in the Logbook section of the Main Map menu.

⊙ To add an appropriate target to the Encyclopedia, press 🔘/🔘 to enter Precision Mode aiming, then move the cursor over the target.

⊙ There is an easy way to ascertain if a current activity can be scanned: just view the subject in Eagle Vision. If they appear with a gold highlight, this represents that a suitable activity is currently in progress. If they are blue they are not currently engaged in an appropriate pursuit.

⊙ You will need to visit the homesteaders often to see them performing relevant activities. Waiting or following them indefinitely will usually not work. The best way to pick up all possible entries is to visit all available subjects before and after you complete Homestead Missions. This will enable you to complete the Encyclopedia gradually, which is much easier than attempting to finish all entries late in a 100% playthrough.

### Encyclopedia Entries

| INHABITANT(S) | POSSIBLE ACTIVITIES TO SCAN |
|---|---|
| Big Dave (Blacksmith) | Adding a new metal ring; forging metal; horseshoeing; sharpening tools; splitting a log with the lumberers; unloading cart |
| Lyle White (Doctor) | Playing bowls; with a client; picking herbs; reading newspaper; taking measurements with Ellen |
| Warren & Prudence (Farmers) | Baking bread; keeping bees; feeding chickens; shoveling hay; making butter; milking cows; plowing a field; plucking a chicken; processing flax |
| Myriam (Huntress) | Cleaning musket; trading pelts; roasting hare; sharpening tools; skinning a deer; setting a trap |
| Oliver & Corinne (Innkeepers) | Butchering a pig; changing bottles; changing kegs; crushing apples; shoveling hay; idle behind bar; roasting deer; taking measurements; trampling grape |
| Godfrey & Terry (Lumberers) | Playing bowls; inspecting/loading lumber; reading newspaper; sawing; sharpening tools; splitting log; unloading cart |
| Norris (Miner) | Filling lantern; mining; repairing beam; sharpening tools; sifting rocks |
| Ellen (Tailor) | With a client; trading pelts; sewing; taking measurements |
| Lance (Woodworker) | With a client; inspecting fence; planning wood; repairing a beam; sawing; sharpening tools |

## THE MANOR

Not merely a set for narrative events in the main storyline and Homestead Missions, the Manor where Connor and Achilles both live has a number of interesting features.

⊙ The **basement** – accessed via a secret door opened by operating the nearby candelabra – is the storage room for all outfits and weapons acquired by Connor during his travels. The table in front of the "Templar Wall" is gradually filled with a number of keepsakes collected when Connor meets each target.

⊙ The **main floor** features an Accounting Book, where Connor can purchase resources from his friends on the Homestead, craft items once he has enlisted the services of artisans, and send convoys to deliver wares to merchants in Boston, New York and the Frontier, for healthy profits. You can also find a Fanorona board in Achilles' room, where the young Assassin can play games against his mentor.

⊙ The **upstairs floor** is filled with trophies and mementos as Connor overcomes challenges in the main storyline and completes objectives set in side quests. You can interact with many of these to learn of their origin whenever a prompt appears.

## GODFREY & TERRY, THE LUMBERERS

### GODFREY & TERRY MISSIONS

| MISSION | AVAILABILITY | LEVEL UNLOCKED | NOTES |
|---------|-------------|----------------|-------|
| River Rescue | Sequence 05 | 1 | This is the mission that enables you to recruit Godfrey & Terry. It is part of the main storyline (see page 90). |
| Burglar on the Homestead | Sequence 05 | 2 | Once this Memory begins, run to the lumberer's house and chase the thief; there is an obvious free run course to, and over, the river that will enable Connor to keep up with him. Kill or incapacitate the target; note that he will attack you if you stop to listen to his calls for mercy. |
| The Fight | Sequence 06 | 3 | After talking to the lumberer's children near their houses, follow them until you trigger a cutscene. Your goal here is to prevent the two colored cursors from reaching the Assassin icon in the center of the screen. To do so, use 🅛 and 🅡 respectively to adjust the position of the corresponding icons just "inside" each cursor (📷 04), in other words between the colored bar and the Assassin icon. Very slowly and incrementally tap each stick towards the outside of the screen, without ever letting the colored bars move towards the inside. Once you have separated the two lumberers, speak to them both at the waypoints to complete the mission. |
| Bowls Beginner | Sequence 07 | 4 | Meet the lumberers near the tavern and beat them at a Bowls game. See page 142 for assistance. |

## LANCE, THE WOODWORKER

### LANCE MISSIONS

| MISSION | AVAILABILITY | LEVEL UNLOCKED | NOTES |
|---------|-------------|----------------|-------|
| The Whittler's Weapon | Sequence 05 | 1 | This is the mission that enables you to recruit Lance. Simply save him from the thugs set to kill him near the exit to the Frontier. |
| Tools of the Trade | Sequence 09 | 2 | Talk to Lance outside his house. Fast Travel to Boston and meet him close to the North Port tunnel entrance. Follow him, then go talk to his apprentice, who is marked with a waypoint. When you tail him, use the various hay carts and Blending opportunities to remain undetected. Keep your distance, though, as Lance isn't always as discreet as you are. Finally, loot the Chest to recover Lance's tools. |
| Thousand-Pound Idea | Sequence 10 | 3 | Talk to Lance outside his house. Fast Travel to New York. Lance's contact is found near the Harbormaster in the southeast. Retrieve all three parts of Lance's plans by pickpocketing or looting the thugs. The former option may be preferable, as there are many guards in the area. The third thug is found on a boat that is part of a Restricted Area. Take him down while the guards are on the other end of the ship (📷 05), loot him and jump in the water to escape. Return the plan to Lance, who will be waiting for you on his house's rooftop. |

## WARREN & PRUDENCE, THE FARMERS

| MISSION | AVAILABILITY | LEVEL UNLOCKED | NOTES |
|---------|-------------|----------------|-------|
| **WARREN & PRUDENCE MISSIONS** | | | |
| **Abused** | Sequence 05 | 1 | This mission enables you to recruit Warren and Prudence. You will find them in Lexington. When you arrive at the scene, simply save them from the Redcoats. |
| **Prudence's Primrose** | Sequence 06 | 2 | Talk to Warren outside his farm. Walk with him towards the marker to the southeast and examine the clues in the green search zone, using Eagle Vision to highlight them if required. Once you have found all three clues, defend Prudence from the bear. Sprint over to intervene and follow the timed button prompts that appear onscreen to defeat it. You can then carry Prudence back to Warren. |
| **Happy Expectations** | Sequence 07 | 3 | Talk to Warren outside his farm. Fast Travel to Boston; your destination is on the east side of the Central District. Talk to the apprentice, then run to the green marker around the corner. Save the doctor by beating up the men attacking him. |
| **Pig Herder** | Sequence 07 | 4 | Talk to Prudence outside her farm. You now need to herd all three pigs into their pen. To do so, simply run behind them, then walk with them towards the pen. If they change direction or run away, make a quick dash in front of them to stop their escape, then move back behind them and repeat. The pigs you herd should be kept between Connor and the pen at all times. |

## MYRIAM, THE HUNTRESS

| MISSION | AVAILABILITY | LEVEL UNLOCKED | NOTES |
|---------|-------------|----------------|-------|
| **MYRIAM MISSIONS** | | | |
| **Silent Hunter** | Sequence 06 | 1 | This is the mission that enables you to recruit Myriam. She can be found a short walk to the southwest from the Manor. Carry her back to the house, then take care of the poachers. This actually acts as a tutorial to the Rope Darts. Make your way to each waypoint in turn and take down the first three poachers by following the onscreen prompts. Now retrace your steps to the south. You will find two poachers on a circular patrol. Dispatch them in any way you see fit. Finally, run to the waypoint to the east to trigger a cutscene, then return to Achilles to complete the mission. |
| **White Trophy** | Sequence 06 | 2 | After you have talked to Myriam, activate Eagle Vision and interact with the clues in the investigation zone. Once you have located the cougar, chase it down towards the mine entrance without worrying about the distance warnings. After talking to Norris, enter the mine and be ready to press Ⓑ/Ⓞ when the button prompt appears. |
| **Fool Me Once…** | Sequence 09 | 3 | You need to speak to Norris in the north of the Homestead to start this mission. Run to Myriam, then hunt the wolves marked by red waypoints. You can either start shooting them from afar with a ranged weapon, or follow the two onscreen button prompts to kill them when they attack. Skin the animals, then climb to the wooden platform highlighted with a green marker. Connor must now hurry to save Myriam. Free run through the trees to make sure that you reach her before her health is depleted (🎦 06). Once there, go after the poacher. Chasing him at branch level will enable you to perform a nice air assassination, though a standard chase will work just as well. |

06

## NORRIS MISSIONS

| MISSION | AVAILABILITY | LEVEL UNLOCKED | NOTES |
|---------|-------------|----------------|-------|
| The Brawler | Sequence 06 | 1 | This is the mission where Connor first meets Norris. He can be found right next to the North Port tunnel entrance in Boston. Dispatch the men attacking him to recruit the miner. |
| Norris Goes Courting | Sequence 07 | 2 | Talk to Norris in the middle of the river, on the southwest side of the map, then talk to Prudence outside her farm. Run to the northeast and follow the path shown on our reference screenshot (📷 07) to reach the flowers. You will be attacked by wolves during the journey, so it can help to have the pistol or bow at the ready. Collect and return the flowers to Norris. |
| Norris Tries Again | Sequence 07 | 3 | Talk to Norris outside his house, then travel to the marked area. You must then spy on Myriam without being spotted. If you are seen, run outside of the green zone before the timer expires. The best way to proceed is to approach Myriam's house from the west. Hide behind the corner of the building until Myriam walks south, and she will sit down with her back turned to Connor. While she does so, walk through the Stalking Zone and examine the clue (📷 08). Finally, retrace your steps and go back to Norris. |
| Raw Materials | Sequence 08 | 4 | Talk to Norris outside his house, then meet him in the Frontier, near the eastern edge of the Packanack region. Pick up and drop a powder keg on each of the three paths leading to the mine (📷 09). Position them at a sufficient distance to ensure that Norris will not be affected by an explosion. The Redcoats will arrive in three waves, one per path. Switch to Precision Mode aiming and destroy the powder kegs at the most opportune moments to eliminate groups of enemies with a single shot. You can then quickly dispatch any survivors. Don't forget to reload between each wave, and pay close attention to Norris' life bar on the left of the screen: if this is depleted, you will have to replay the fight from the start. |

## BIG DAVE, THE BLACKSMITH

## BIG DAVE MISSIONS

| MISSION | AVAILABILITY | LEVEL UNLOCKED | NOTES |
|---------|-------------|----------------|-------|
| Deserter | Sequence 08 | 1 | This is the mission that enables you to recruit Big Dave. He can be found at the southwestern edge of the John's Town region in the Frontier. Dispatch the Redcoats holding Big Dave prisoner. When only one assailant remains, a special set piece begins: Connor points a gun at the Redcoat, who holds Big Dave as a human shield. Wait for Big Dave to hit the Redcoat with his elbow, than fire. |
| The Proper Tools | Sequence 09 | 2 | Talk to Big Dave outside his house. Fast Travel to New York and enter the General Store to the east of the city. Buy the Ebony Hammer Handle and Hardened Steel Hammer Head (found in the Citizen Mission Items category), for a total of £50, and take them back to Big Dave. |
| An Eye for Trouble | Sequence 09 | 3 | Talk to Big Dave outside his house. As soon as the scout starts running, sprint after him in a straight line. If you're quick enough, you'll catch him before he has the time to mount a horse. Otherwise, you'll have to chase him down with a horse of your own. Once you have caught him, return to Big Dave. |
| The Comeback | Sequence 10 | 4 | Talk to Big Dave outside his house. Follow him until you reach the powder kegs. Pick one up and drop it at the bottom of the trail where the Redcoat platoon will arrive (📷 10). As the soldiers approach the keg, shoot it with your pistol to defeat them all instantly. You can then repeat this until you have cleared all enemy waves. Make sure that you position the kegs yourself, as throwing them will cause them to roll around and make the process more difficult. You should also place them so they are broadly level with the nearby tree, as the explosion can otherwise kill or injure your allies. |

## ELLEN, THE TAILOR

| | | | |
|---|---|---|---|
| **ELLEN MISSIONS** | | | |
| **MISSION** | **AVAILABILITY** | **LEVEL UNLOCKED** | **NOTES** |
| **Cutting Ties** | Sequence 09 | 1 | This Memory first introduces Connor to Ellen, who can be found in the center of New York. Talk to the young lady asking for help and follow her. Once you reach Ellen, beat up her assailant. |
| **Silk Errand** | Sequence 09 | 2 | Talk to Ellen outside her house. Fast Travel to New York and head toward the green marker. Examine the empty crate behind the wooden fence, inside the green search zone, and then retrieve the bolt of silk. You can now return it to Ellen. |
| **The Final Straw** | Sequence 09 | 3 | Talk to Godfrey outside the Mile's End tavern, then immediately run with the group towards Ellen. Your priority in the fight that follows is to protect Ellen's house, not your fellow Homesteaders. Dispatch any thugs attacking the house's door or windows as a priority, then focus on neutralizing those in the immediate area. |

## LYLE, THE DOCTOR

**LYLE MISSIONS**

| | | | |
|---|---|---|---|
| **MISSION** | **AVAILABILITY** | **LEVEL UNLOCKED** | **NOTES** |
| **Get Me a Doctor!** | Sequence 09 | 1 | Talk to Prudence near the Manor. You now have three minutes to get to Dr. Lyle White. Jump on the horse and rush to the waypoint to the south, using the spur move whenever you have the opportunity. The doctor will jump on a horse of his own and follow you. However, you must first stop to pick up Warren before you finally make it back to Prudence (11). Despite the countdown, don't panic: the time limit is actually quite generous, and your allies will struggle to keep up if you are too fast. |
| **Slander** | Sequence 10 | 2 | Talk to Lyle at his house and follow him. Fast Travel to Boston. The courier that you are looking for is at the south of the city. Talk to him, then walk to the southeast. You then need to find and bribe vendors in the area. Use Eagle Vision to identify them, then bribe them. Finally, pickpocket or beat up the overseer. Our reference screenshot shows you their exact positions on the map (12). |
| **Wait Times** | Sequence 11 | 3 | Talk to Lyle at his position near the Aquila. You have one minute to reach Diana, to the north, and bring her back to the doctor. Now go and heal the five nearby sailors, all marked with a green waypoint. You can then return to Lyle. |

## HOMESTEAD DAILY LIFE

| | | | |
|---|---|---|---|
| **OLIVER & CORINNE, THE INNKEEPERS** | | | |
| **MISSION** | **AVAILABILITY** | **LEVEL UNLOCKED** | **NOTES** |
| **Room at the Inn** | Sequence 07 | 1 | This Memory enables you to recruit Oliver and Corinne. To complete it, simply give £1,000 to Oliver to fund the construction of the Mile's End inn. |

| | | | |
|---|---|---|---|
| **FATHER TIMOTHY, THE PRIEST** | | | |
| **MISSION** | **AVAILABILITY** | **LEVEL UNLOCKED** | **NOTES** |
| **Finding his Flock** | Sequence 09 | 1 | This is the mission that enables you to recruit Timothy, who can be found inside the Mile's End. To complete the sole objective after the introductory cutscene, interact with Timothy to provide him with the £1,000 required to build a church. If you do not have this sum, you must raise it to complete the Memory. |
| **The Wedding** | Sequence 09 | 2 | Talk to Myriam outside the chapel. Follow Father Timothy, then talk to Norris inside the Manor. Go upstairs and interact with the clues in the room marked with a green waypoint. Run to the green search zone to the northeast, and you will find Myriam on a wooden platform above her house. Chase her at ground level by sprinting to the west and you will soon trigger a cutscene. Once in the tavern, listen to the conversations marked with the icon. |

## INVENTIONS

Benjamin Franklin's Inventions are items that you can craft via the Accounting Book interface from recipes obtained by collecting Almanac pages in Boston and New York. To read details on each Invention's recipe, as well as how to obtain the required ingredients, refer to page 245. Once crafted, Inventions appear on display in the Manor. You must craft all of them to reach 100% Synchronization. There is a small Easter egg if you approach the Glass Armonica during a post-story play session.

III

QUICKSTART

THE STORY SO FAR

PRIMER

WALKTHROUGH

SIDE QUESTS

REFERENCE & ANALYSIS

MULTIPLAYER

EXTRAS

MAP LEGEND

INDEX

COMPLETION TIMELINE

CITIZEN MISSIONS

ATTACKING CONVOYS

CLUBS

MINIGAMES

FORTS

LIBERATION MISSIONS

ASSASSIN'S GUILD

THE UNDERGROUND

NAVAL PRIMER

NAVAL MISSIONS

PRIVATEER CONTRACTS

NAVAL LOCATIONS

HOMESTEAD MISSIONS

BENEDICT ARNOLD MISSIONS

COLLECTIBLES

Exclusive to the PlayStation 3 release of Assassin's Creed III, the Benedict Arnold Missions are a stand-alone adventure that you can begin at any time after completing "Missing Supplies" at the start of Sequence 09. The Memory Start marker is situated close to the northwest Frontier exit in New York. To begin, simply interact with the individuals at the location marked by the ◈ icon. After Connor accepts the commission, travel to the same icon in the northwest of the map to visit West Point, a new and separate location where the events of this episode will take place.

## TRAITOR IN OUR MIDST

The first Memory Start position is just inside the West Point map, a short walk from the New York exit. Travel to the green search zone to the south. On arrival, a soldier at the back of a patrol is marked as the target that Connor must eliminate. After a short march, the patrol will reach an old red barn, which the target will patrol in a regular pattern. While there are several points of entry, the easiest is to slide through a gap close to the southeast corner of the barn, then hide in the hay cart inside (📷 01). When the target approaches, assassinate him, then leave by the same route.

You must then travel to a pair of search zones and identify and eliminate two spies; they appear with a gold highlight when viewed in Eagle Vision. In the most northerly area, your target is located inside a tent on the west side of the Patriot camp. A single soldier makes a short patrol that approaches his position. Wait until this potential witness moves away, and you can perform a simple Hidden Blade assassination and leave before the body is discovered.

In the southerly search zone, the target can be found taunting a Redcoat prisoner in the stocks. There is a Stalking Zone just south of his position; if you enter this and wait for his arrival, you can assassinate him without fear of discovery.

The final task requires that you visit the Fort to the south, but this is a Restricted Area where guards will not take kindly to Connor's presence. Walk through the gates and then turn immediately to the right to avoid detection; as you do so, the final target will jostle Connor as he runs past. Assassinate him before the other soldiers can react to end the Memory.

01

## SHOWING TRAITORS THE WAY

Speak to the Patriot soldier close to the south corner of the Fort to begin. Pick up a crate from the ground, then jog to the waypoint marker. On arrival, place the crate at the marked position. When the traitor breaks from the crowd of brawling soldiers, chase after him. He wears the Scout uniform, but is unusually leaden-footed. Just sprint behind him and press **Ⓑ/◎** in close proximity to perform the Tackle move for a non-lethal takedown. The next step is to escort the prisoner to the Vulture, a ship waiting on a dock to the east.

## A SPY AMONG US

This Memory once again begins inside the Fort to the southwest. After receiving orders, you should carry a Powder Keg to the Powder Reserve as directed. After placing the first at the entrance, however, a new objective is given. Move into the Stalking Zone to begin the eavesdrop and, when the subjects move on, follow them from a discreet distance by utilizing Stalking Zones while remaining within the circular boundary. Outside the walls, a large Stalking Zone enables you to stay close to them without fear of detection.

When John Anderson moves away, use the numerous Stalking Zones behind him to stay within range – at a sensibly reserved distance – until after he convenes with his Redcoat conspirators and orders them to leave. Enter the cornfield and move towards the center, where Anderson will leap into a hay cart to change his uniform. Move into the nearby Stalking Zone before he emerges, and adjust your position to avoid a roaming Redcoat if required. Connor cannot be seen while moving through individual rows of crops as long as you don't get too close to anyone.

Once you leave the cornfield and reach a point where Anderson turns to regard the path behind him (⊡ 02), climb the tree marked in our screenshot to continue the tail. Free run through the branches to reach the barn that featured in "Traitor in our Midst", then watch on as he is intercepted by a Patriot patrol.

## BATTLE OF WEST POINT

Return to the Fort for the final Memory of this side story. This features a lot of combat, so we advise that you have a full stock of consumables (particularly arrows) before you begin. The battle that ensues is rather chaotic, but you can emerge victorious by noting these simple tips:

- Follow the onscreen instructions whenever they appear. The most important directives are those that specify that you must kill a "sniper" before he destroys the powder reserve (⊡ 03). In these instances, disengage and eliminate the target marked by the ⬤ icon immediately. If you have a clear shot, a single arrow will neutralize them instantly.

- In the battles at each gate, try to set up Kill Streaks to eliminate opponents efficiently: your adversaries are primarily of the Soldier archetype, so have no special resistances. Combo attacks are a waste of valuable time: just wait for a Counter Kill opportunity, then defeat as many targets as you can.

- When instructions appear telling you to defend another gate, break away to comply even if there are hostiles remaining in your current location. Troops entering a new gate will form firing lines to shoot at Connor's allies. This will drain the meter on the left side of the screen at a greatly accelerated speed.

Once the final charge has been repelled, the closing cinematic of the Benedict Arnold Missions begins. You are then free to enter and explore West Point at any time, or replay individual Memories via the DNA Tracker. From a pure gaming perspective, West Point is a great area to complete many combat-oriented challenges for the Boston Brawlers and Thieves (see page 139). There are no Notoriety penalties in this small region, so you can enter combat with impunity.

### WEST POINT MISSIONS

Using the club challenges format, the West Point Missions are a collection of six bonus tasks that you can complete as and when you see fit. You can view your current progress via the Logbook entry in the Main Map menu. Note that you can complete these challenges anywhere in the game world, not just in the West Point area.

#### West Point Missions

| CHALLENGE | NOTES |
|---|---|
| Use all of the recruit abilities twice. | This simply requires that you obtain all six recruits via Liberation Missions, and use the unique abilities contributed by each apprentice twice. See page 155 for details. |
| Stealth assassinate guards while they're distracted by a riot on five occasions. | Simply start a riot by interacting with angry crowds found throughout Boston and New York, and then assassinate any guard that comes to investigate *before* they draw their weapons. This can only be accomplished during the opening moments of a riot. |
| Perform a double assassination with a musket. | Assassinate an opponent with a loaded musket, then immediately press Ⓨ/△ to shoot through the body to kill a second enemy. |
| Make five Snipers fall to their death. | Ledge assassinations and kills that subsequently lead to a Sniper falling from a roof do not count, so the best way to do this is to perform unarmed combos to kick or barge Snipers from high rooftops. |
| Kill a Snitch while he is escaping on five occasions. | Find a patrol that includes a Snitch, start a fight with the group, then disengage and kill the Snitch the moment he starts to run away. |
| Craft Artillery four times. | This can be accomplished from Sequence 10 onwards. The recipe requires the Blacksmith (Lv. 4), the Woodworker (Lv. 3), Flints (a crafted material), Iron Ore (from the miner) and Oak Lumber (from the lumberers). See page 244 for further information. |

In this section we offer detailed maps that show the locations of all collectibles in Assassin's Creed III. While many of these can be found in plain sight once you arrive in the marked area, some are fiendishly hidden or tied to an incidental challenge. In such instances, we offer instructions and illustrative screenshots to enable you to find objects with ease.

As an added bonus for dedicated hunters, we have also annotated the Frontier and Homestead maps with all locations where specific varieties of animal can be found. You can use this information to make a fortune by hunting and trapping to acquire pristine pelts to sell via convoys (see page 242).

There are four different varieties of collectible in Assassin's Creed III:

**Almanac Pages** are only found in Boston and New York, and will begin to float away once Connor moves within a certain range. You must time and direct your approach carefully to catch them before they disappear, which often entails free running over a specific route. If you fail to catch an Almanac, note that they will respawn in their original position once you move a couple of streets away. If you are close to a Fast Travel position, jumping there via the main map can be a quick way to reset the collectible. Once you collect all four pages in an individual Almanac, you obtain a crafting recipe for one of Ben Franklin's Inventions – a requirement for full game completion.

**Feathers** are more conventional static collectibles, and can be found only in the Frontier, usually in the upper reaches of trees. We offer special advice on Feathers that are particularly hard to reach or find. For all others, the route should be almost immediately obvious if you stand beneath them, then observe your surroundings to "reverse engineer" the required path to their position.

**Treasure Chests** (or, to be more precise, those that contribute to 100% Synchronization) are located in Boston, New York and the Frontier. The containers found in cities are secured, and require that Connor pick their locks to obtain their rich contents (usually comprising cash and crafting recipes). However, completing Liberation Missions (see page 154) furnishes Connor with keys to all strongboxes in the related district, which rather simplifies the process. The only exceptions are the Chests located inside Forts: these must always be opened via the lockpicking minigame, though the cash sums inside are considerable (£7,500 in all but one instance, which offers £10,000).

**Peg Leg's Trinkets** distributed throughout the game world (including the Homestead) are required to unlock Naval Locations in the hugely enjoyable and rewarding Captain Kidd's Treasure side story. See page 182 for further details.

Before you read any further, we suggest that you note the following short selection of pertinent tips and tricks:

◉ You can track outstanding collectibles via the Logbook. Note that you must collect at least one object in a category – for example, a Feather – for information to appear. Similarly, completed entries are removed: once you collect all Trinkets, they no longer appear in the list.

◉ All collectibles picked up when you use the Replay feature are automatically saved – even if you do not complete the Memory. This includes funds and crafting recipes found inside Chests.

◉ A useful feature of the Custom Marker function on the main map screen: selecting collectible items will not merely help you to travel to the object in question, but also provide information on its elevation relative to Connor. If you invest in all Maps that can be purchased from Sequence 06 (see page 252), you will be able to see and select any collectible – even those in "fogged" areas that you have yet to explore.

◉ If Connor catches even a glimpse of a new collectible, it will be permanently marked and subsequently appear on the main map and mini-map until collected.

◉ Finally, you should note that you cannot access all map areas (and, therefore, locate and pick up every collectible) until New York and the full Valley Forge area become available in Sequence 09.

## CHESTS: REWARDS PER REGION

| | BOSTON | FRONTIER | NEW YORK |
|---|---|---|---|
| **Total £** | 26,250 | 31,750 | 25,500 |
| **Special Item Recipes** | ▪ Lincoln's Sword (Replica)<br>▪ "Broken Sword" Knife<br>▪ Royal Navy Sea Service Flintlock<br>▪ Naval Duckfoot | ▪ Italian Flintlock<br>▪ English Flintlock Pistol<br>▪ War Tomahawk<br>▪ French Naval Axe | ▪ Royal Pistol<br>▪ Washington's Battle Sword (Replica)<br>▪ French Coat Pistol |

## LEGEND

| | | | | |
|---|---|---|---|---|
| 🦅 | Viewpoint | Ac | Achilles |
| | Fort | Go | Godfrey |
| | Almanac Page | Te | Terry |
| | Feather | La | Lance |
| | Chest | Wa | Warren |
| | Peg Leg's Trinket | Pr | Prudence |
| — | Animal Habitat Border | My | Myriam |
| | Fox | No | Norris |
| | Bear | Ol | Oliver |
| | Cougar | Co | Corinne |
| | Wolf | Da | Big Dave |
| | Bobcat | Ly | Lyle |
| | Hare | El | Ellen |
| | Beaver | Ti | Father Timothy |
| | Raccoon | | |
| | Deer | | |
| | Elk | | |

Though we show the route to the Trinket here, players attempting a time-efficient playthrough should note that Connor must make this exact same climb during the "Norris Goes Courting" Homestead Mission (see page 196).

The Trinket not far south from Peg Leg can be found in plain sight, but you should note that the area is usually teeming with wolves.

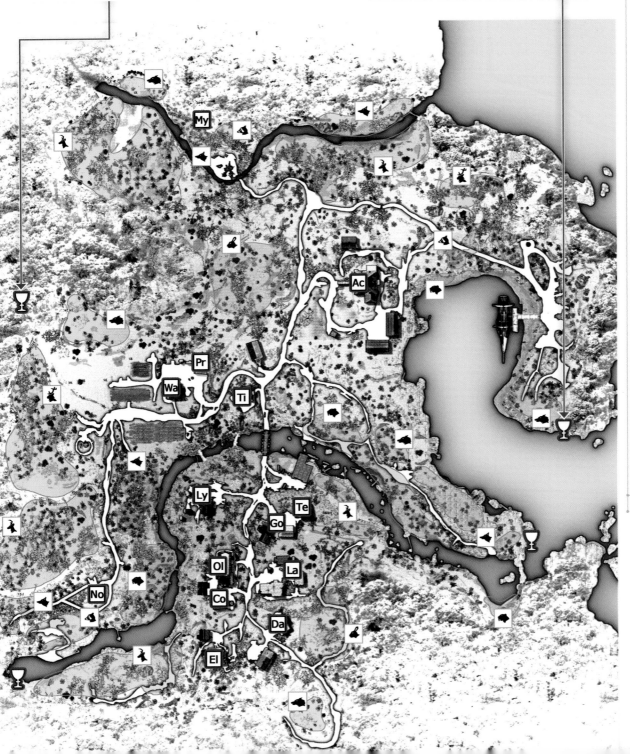

Approach from the southwest using the ladder. Free run straight to the north and you will intercept the page on the high rooftop.

Approach from the northeast. As soon as the page flies away, jump down at street level and run to the shop front shown here to intercept it.

Approach from the south. Sprint to the rope that runs over the street to intercept the page (jump vertically by holding **RT**/**R1** and pressing **A**/**X** if required). An alternative solution is to jump down to the street and climb up on the houses to the northwest to intercept it there.

Approach from the south. If you don't catch the page before the end of the first rooftops, jump to the next ones via the tree branch.

Approach from the south. Use the free run course starting from the canopy as it is faster than climbing all the way to the top (where, in addition, rooftop sentries would get in the way). Climb up to the rooftops of the houses across the small street to intercept the page.

Approach from the east. Jump down at ground level and run across the vegetable gardens. Climb up as shown here to intercept the page.

The Chest in Fort Hill is below ground, in a room close to the back entrance: see page 148.

There are four guards positioned to protect this Chest, and several more who may enter the fray if a fight breaks out. Either create a diversion to lure them away, or start with an air assassination from above to reduce the numbers against you.

Approach from the ladder to the northwest. If you haven't caught up by the time the page flies across the street, keep going forward: you'll intercept it once it comes back to your side of the street.

Approach from the northeast. If you don't catch the page immediately, run to the rope as shown here to intercept it (jump vertically by holding RT / R1 and pressing A / X if required).

Approach from the north. Run in a straight line and you will intercept the page as it goes round the fourth chimney.

Approach from the southwest. Free run on top of the chimney, and then directly to the rooftop across the alleyway. If you haven't collected the page at this stage, run to the rope that spans the main street.

This Chest is guarded, but you can easily bypass the sentries by swimming to it.

QUICKSTART

THE STORY SO FAR

PRIMER

WALKTHROUGH

SIDE QUESTS

REFERENCE & ANALYSIS

MULTIPLAYER

EXTRAS

MAP LEGEND

INDEX

COMPLETION TIMELINE

CITIZEN MISSIONS

ATTACKING CONVOYS

CLUBS

MINIGAMES

FORTS

LIBERATION MISSIONS

ASSASSIN'S GUILD

THE UNDERGROUND

NAVAL PRIMER

NAVAL MISSIONS

PRIVATEER CONTRACTS

NAVAL LOCATIONS

HOMESTEAD MISSIONS

BENEDICT ARNOLD MISSIONS

COLLECTIBLES

Approach from the east. Climb the church to cause the page to start flying, then jump to the north and climb to the rooftop of the house shown here to intercept the page.

Approach from the north. Run in a straight line and you should get the page before it even reaches the first beam.

Approach from the west. Don't use the free run course where the page is initially found. Instead, run at ground level and climb via the wooden boxes further down on the other side of the street. Wait on the small canopy for the page to come to you.

Approach from the north. Instead of following the page, jump down to the square southwest of the church, and climb in the second V-shaped section of the tree: the item will come to you.

Approach from the southwest. Immediately turn east and jump to the V-shaped tree, then to the ground. Run to the wooden boxes and use them to jump to the ledge with the potted plants above a shop sign, where you will intercept the page.

Boston's most well-hidden Chest is upstairs in the Green Dragon Tavern. This unique strongbox contains not only £750, but also any sum of money that Haytham had accumulated before the close of Sequence 03.

Approach from the east and cut the corner to intercept the page.

Wait for patrols to move away, then perform a running double assassination on the two guards. Quickly loot the Chest and make your escape before the nearby patrol runs to investigate.

Approach from the west and sprint in a straight line to catch up with the page.

Climb onto the ship from the southwest side to avoid conflict with the guards before you open this Chest.

Approach from the east and sprint to the rope that crosses the street: after a few seconds, the page will come straight at you.

Approach from the north, sprinting on the left side of the street. Climb on the small wooden structure and you will catch the page as Connor jumps on the pole.

Approach from the northwest. Run up the sloped cart but instead of following the page, climb up the building and intercept the collectible on the rooftop.

This is possibly the most well-hidden collectible in the entire game. Start by finding this distinct tree (with a log providing a bridge over the river below) approximately 80 meters south/southeast of the Trinket's position.

Climb down via the positions marked here to reach a cave entrance. The Trinket is inside. There is a corpse right next to the chest that you can loot to collect several pelts. Backtrack to the entrance and dive into the river to abbreviate the return journey.

This Trinket is hidden inside a cave, with the entrance located approximately 40 meters to the south of the item's position.

The sole free run course that leads to this Feather starts to the north.

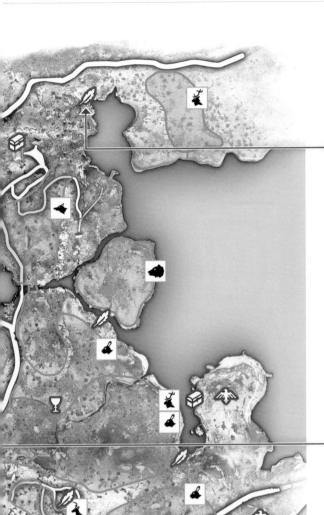

You should automatically pick up this Feather by following our suggested stealth route during "Hostile Negotiations" at the end of Sequence 06. If you missed it, the quickest way to get to its position is to walk south from the road to the Homestead further north, then climb down via the route shown here.

The entrance to the cave where this Trinket is stored can be found close to the last house in the north of Lexington.

The rock-and-earth mound at the center of Lexington has an open mine shaft that you can enter to find this Chest; just look for the trail that begins on the main north-south road that divides the settlement. After collecting the Chest, follow the dotted line here to collect the nearby Feather.

There is a lone tree that seems close enough to offer a route to this Feather, but it's actually a convenient stepping stone to return to the ground after making the real free run approach from the south.

You must perform a Back Eject (tap Ⓐ/✕ while holding RT/R1) after running up the trunk of the tree to reach the upper branch and, beyond it, the Feather.

The Chest is inside a barn, usually guarded by three Grenadiers and an Officer.

This Chest lies inside a Restricted Area in a small military camp.

This Chest is protected by a sizable contingent of troops, with a fairly significant patrol operating on the nearby road. Wait until the latter opponents leave before you engage the guards to reach the Chest.

You should uncover this Chest when you first Fast Travel here via the nearby Harbormaster. It usually features four Grenadiers by the Chest itself, two Soldiers guarding a nearby door, and a sizable patrol operating nearby. Wait for an opportune moment, drop a Smoke Bomb to incapacitate the immediate guards before they can attack, grab the goods, then turn tail and flee.

III

QUICKSTART

THE STORY SO
FAR

PRIMER

WALKTHROUGH

SIDE QUESTS

REFERENCE &
ANALYSIS

MULTIPLAYER

EXTRAS

MAP LEGEND

INDEX

The Trinket is actually inside a tunnel, with the most convenient entrance situated approximately 60 meters to the north of the icon. Exit from the opposite end to emerge through a waterfall: a glorious sight.

Testament to the incredible engine that underpins traversal in Assassin's Creed III, you must scale the moving sails of the windmill to reach this Feather.

This Feather is on a small, rocky island to the south of Fort St-Mathieu; leaping from the cliff beside the Fort is the quickest way to reach it.

This Chest is concealed within a cave. You can find the entrance directly to the southeast.

It's clear that there is only one free run route to the Feather on this island, but it's easy for one specific step to elude you: after hopping onto the stripped tree and jumping to the nearby branch, you need to wall run up the trunk of the next tree and perform a Side Eject: press **L** to the right and tap **Ⓐ**/**Ⓧ** before Connor drops. This island is close to a great hunting spot: the beach to the north can sometimes abound with raccoons and hares that you can easily kill from range with the bow while wading in the water.

This Trinket is in a small camp, protected by a handful of guards. In later Sequences, you may arrive to find Patriots and Loyalists fighting here.

Follow the path shown here to reach the lofty branch and collect the Feather.

This Trinket is guarded by troops in a camp defined by its lack of branches overhead or Stalking Zones. The area is also notable for the presence of bobcats, which makes it a good area to wait and watch if you have yet to obtain the "Eye Witness" Achievement/Trophy.

If you are hunting Feathers without buying the appropriate in-game Map, this collectible can be hard to see. Approach it from the rock to the north to find it hidden in the foliage.

QUICKSTART

THE STORY SO FAR

PRIMER

WALKTHROUGH

SIDE QUESTS

REFERENCE & ANALYSIS

MULTIPLAYER

EXTRAS

MAP LEGEND

INDEX

COMPLETION TIMELINE

CITIZEN MISSIONS

ATTACKING CONVOYS

CLUBS

MINIGAMES

FORTS

LIBERATION MISSIONS

ASSASSIN'S GUILD

THE UNDERGROUND

NAVAL PRIMER

NAVAL MISSIONS

PRIVATEER CONTRACTS

NAVAL LOCATIONS

HOMESTEAD MISSIONS

BENEDICT ARNOLD MISSIONS

COLLECTIBLES

This Feather is unique in that it is hidden underground. The cave entrance can be found to the east of the icon.

You should collect this Feather when you visit the nearby Viewpoint. Be wary in this area: this is a cougar habitat.

Though it may not be concealed, collecting this Feather requires a climb. On our screenshot, we present the ideal route if you approach from the south.

This Trinket is hidden inside a mine. You can find the entrance approximately 35 meters away from the item's location to the south.

Approach from the south as shown here, and free run straight to the north. Keep the page in view and you should be able to easily intercept it. If you miss it, jump down to the ground level and sprint to the wooden shelter for a second chance.

Approach from the northeast, climb the stairs and sprint to the wooden fence shown here. The page will come straight at you.

QUICKSTART

THE STORY SO FAR

PRIMER

WALKTHROUGH

→ SIDE QUESTS

REFERENCE & ANALYSIS

MULTIPLAYER

EXTRAS

MAP LEGEND

INDEX

COMPLETION TIMELINE

CITIZEN MISSIONS

ATTACKING CONVOYS

CLUBS

MINIGAMES

FORTS

LIBERATION MISSIONS

ASSASSIN'S GUILD

THE UNDERGROUND

NAVAL PRIMER

NAVAL MISSIONS

PRIVATEER CONTRACTS

NAVAL LOCATIONS

HOMESTEAD MISSIONS

BENEDICT ARNOLD MISSIONS

COLLECTIBLES

Though there are guards by the nearby door and at the corner of the building, you can actually just hop over the fence and loot this Chest without repercussions if you pay the sentries a wide berth.

Approach from the southwest and sprint in a straight line on the east slope of the rooftops. You will easily intercept the page as it floats through the air.

Approach from the northwest. As soon as the page starts flying to the southeast, jump down at street level and sprint to the southeast. Climb on top of the tavern's sign to intercept the incoming item.

Approach from the west and free run straight toward the rope to the east, where you will intercept the incoming page.

Approach from the east and climb on top of this chimney. The page will float straight at you.

Approach from the north and stand at the edge of the rooftop. The page will come straight at you.

This Chest is heavily guarded, with numerous additional troops situated in the immediate area, and more than one nearby patrol. Calling a recruit to start a riot is the perfect way to draw the closest guards out of position, though you will still need to time your approach carefully to avoid being drawn into the conflict.

Approach from the south until the page starts flying away. Immediately perform a Leap of Faith in the nearby hay cart and sprint to the position shown here where you will easily intercept it.

Approach from the west and climb on the rooftop as shown here. The page will float straight at you.

Climb up to the V-shaped section of the tree shown here, and jump to the branch closest to the page. It will come straight at you.

Approach from the north and run in a straight line to the south. You should intercept the page on the narrow wooden bridge.

Approach form the south and jump to the rooftops across the street. Sprint to the northeast, using the rope to intercept the page on top of the blue house.

Approach from the west and run straight to the east. You should intercept the page once you reach the rope, if not before.

Approach from the northwest and jump down to street level. Sprint to the empty cart shown here and you will easily intercept the page.

Approach from the northeast and run to the southwest in a straight line. You will intercept the page on the beams.

Approach from the southwest and free run in a straight line to the northeast. You can intercept the page after you jump from the beam, or at the end of the wooden terrace. Ignore the rooftop sentry and focus on the page until you collect it.

# REFERENCE & ANALYSIS

**SPOILER WARNING:** We strongly advise that you avoid reading this chapter until you have at least reached Sequence 04. Any challenges that Haytham faces in the story before that stage are covered by the advice and instructions we offer in the Primer (see page 32), or the appropriate sections of the Walkthrough chapter.

In this chapter, we take a more in-depth look at some of the systems that underpin the Assassin's Creed III experience, with a particular focus on unlockable items, combat and managing the Homestead. We also cover topics such as advanced free running, the Fast Travel network, and a breakdown of the steps required to obtain all Achievements/Trophies for players looking to conquer every last challenge.

From Sequence 04 to the end of Sequence 05, the Assassin's Creed III environments burst into life with a vast wealth of new activities and experiences. The routes that Connor travels between narrative engagements are littered with profitable diversions, from major side quests to simple optional tasks and challenges. Where Haytham effectively travelled in a straight line between main story Memories, Connor's path between objectives – for players who wish to enjoy as much of this world as they can – will soon come to resemble a vast and

intricate web that covers all corners and regions of Boston, the Frontier, the Davenport Homestead and New York.

For this reason, using and expanding the Fast Travel network to drastically cut travel times is an essential step. Before we examine this vital system, we will first take a look at the new free running moves and abilities introduced in Sequence 04.

## ADVANCED FREE RUNNING & CLIMBING

The Feathers and Trees Memory acts as a crash course in the art of free running through trees. Initially, this new feature is somewhat intimidating. Even dedicated players with years of free running experience honed through previous Assassin's Creed games may find their customary purposeful movement punctuated by uncustomary bouts of hesitancy.

If you are joining us from the Walkthrough chapter with a sense of bewilderment, we can reassure you immediately: free running in trees becomes second nature in almost no time at all. As we discussed in the Primer chapter earlier in the guide, the key to being truly accomplished at

climbing and free running in urban areas is learning to instinctively read and interpret the visual language of the world, planning each journey a few steps in advance. The same applies with free running in trees – it's just that the "language" of these lofty paths is written in a slightly different dialect that you must first learn to parse quickly and efficiently.

While practice really does make perfect, the following visual guide to the essential "building blocks" of tree-based free run courses will help you to more readily interpret routes and move with greater confidence.

Just as barrels, crates or upturned carts might mark the beginning of an urban free run route in Boston, many tree-based courses begin with a recognizable start point. The style of tree shown here – a stump where its trunk once stood, with a thick bough extending outwards – is a typical entry point. You might also begin by running up a trunk to reach a low branch, or by leaping from another platform, such as a rock outcrop or rooftop.

Though Connor cannot climb the vast majority of tree trunks directly, the type of tree shown here has a number of small hand-holds that enable him to scale them. These tend to appear when there is a free run course above, offering a convenient entry point.

Many trees feature V-shaped sections that Connor can leap through en route from one branch to another. While Connor can use combat abilities, such as firing ranged weapons and performing air assassinations, from branches, these are generally not available when he is positioned between boughs, or while at rest in the intersection between the tree trunk and a major branch.

Some larger trees may contain more than one V-shaped position. To ascend from a V-shaped section to another at a higher elevation, tap Ⓐ/Ⓧ. This is much more convenient than realigning the camera with Ⓡ to climb manually.

Perhaps the hardest part of tree-based free running, at least at first, is having faith in Connor's ability to swing around the outside of a tree trunk to reach a branch on the opposite side of a tree. If you know that there is a branch on the other side, it's just a simple matter of holding **RT**/**R1** and **L** to direct him into the trunk: Connor will do the rest.

Don't worry if a branch on the opposite side of a trunk appears to be at a slightly higher or lower elevation: Connor will still perform the maneuver with great precision.

Though Connor cannot stand on thin branches, they can be used to swing between two "solid" positions on a free run course.

This screenshot shows a typical free run route through trees, using many of the different steps we've described in this section. As with many such courses, there is no need to release **RT**/**R1** and **L** at any point: all you need to do is to point Connor in the appropriate direction.

A number of Viewpoints in the Frontier are situated in the upper branches of huge trees. These generally require that you jump between large branches at the base, then ascend via V-shaped sections and swing on sequences of smaller branches closer to the top to reach the official Viewpoint position. This is, of course, signposted by the customary eagle, who will take off as Connor approaches.

For a final tip as we leave the trees, note that any cliffs in the rugged Frontier can be scaled whenever you can espy recognizable hand-holds for Connor to grasp. While horizontal ledges are usually easy to spot, you should look carefully for narrow vertical crevices, as pictured here. Though it's not immediately obvious, these enable him to ascend with ease.

The "**Gateway**" icons between different regions highlight the first Fast Travel positions that you will have at your disposal. To travel from the Frontier to Boston via these Gateways, for example, you would need to open the Boston map via the East Coast map, then select the Frontier icon at the south of the Boston map. If you select the Boston icon on the Frontier map, Connor will instead travel to a position close to the Boston area transition point within the Frontier, necessitating a short walk and another break for loading to complete the journey.

Some standard **Fast Travel icons** are unlocked as you progress through the main storyline, or by "unfogging" their location on an area map to reveal them. For example, a Fast Travel icon automatically appears in Connor's village in the Frontier at the start of Sequence 06. To unlock two Fast Travel positions in Lexington and Concord to the south, however, you must explore the settlements to find them. In Boston and New York, you must explore their respective networks of underground tunnels to open up new Fast Travel opportunities. See the "Underground Tunnels" section for more details.

**Harbormaster icons** appear on all maps once you complete Boston's Most Wanted, the second Memory of Sequence 05. These also function as Fast Travel destinations. From the start of Sequence 06, you can also interact with Harbormasters to begin naval missions.

As far as the in-game chronology is concerned, Fast Travel is effectively instantaneous. Any timers that are active when you begin the journey (such as a clock charting the progress of a Convoy moving from the Homestead to a General Store, or Assassins assigned to missions) will be unaffected by the transition.

The Fast Travel network is one of the most vital systems in Assassin's Creed III, as it enables you to skip literally hours of time spent in transit between destinations. Though it is occasionally disabled during main story Memories and certain side quests, this should be your primary method of abbreviating journeys between different areas, or even to move from one side of an individual region to another.

To Fast Travel, press ◁/(SELECT) to bring up the main map screen, select your required Fast Travel position on the map (we'll document these in a moment) with Ⓐ/⊗, then confirm your choice. After a brief loading break, Connor will appear in your chosen destination. If you would like to transfer to a different region – for example, from the Homestead to Boston – use LT/L1 to zoom out from the area map to the East Coast map, target the new region that you wish to reach with the cursor, then press RT/R1 to zoom in to that map. You can now select an appropriate Fast Travel icon to make the journey.

There are several different icons that are used in the Fast Travel system:

| FAST TRAVEL ICONS | |
|---|---|
| **ICON** | **DESCRIPTION** |
| Ⓑ | Boston Gateway/Entrances |
| ⛰ | Frontier Gateway/Entrances |
| 🏠 | Homestead Gateway/Entrances |
| NY | New York Gateway/Entrances |
| ⬇ | Fast Travel Destinations |
| ⚓ | Harbormasters |

## UNDERGROUND TUNNELS

Boston and New York both have unique networks of tunnels that you can explore to unlock new Fast Travel positions. At first, each city has a single Fast Travel position marked by the ⬇ icon. This is also a Tunnel Entrance. By visiting this location and interacting with the highlighted doorway, you can enter these underground mazes to find and unlock new Tunnel Entrances, which then appear and function as Fast Travel destinations. There are ten of these – the initial Tunnel Entrance, then a further nine to unlock – in each city, and opening them can drastically cut the amount of time that you spend travelling.

The process of exploring these underground mazes and conquering their puzzles is covered in the Side Quests chapter: see page 164 for details.

Once introduced in the A Trip to Boston and Boston's Most Wanted Memories in Sequence 05, the Notoriety system acts as a powerful deterrent to dissuade players from acts of wanton violence. In effect, it encourages you to approach situations with the subtlety and stealth befitting a member of the Assassin Brotherhood, and to eschew atypical bloodthirsty rampages. While you can still cut a swath through opponents to complete an objective, unless expressly forbidden, the penalties introduced once Connor is Notorious make it harder to travel without further complications or confrontations, and demand payment of a toll (measured in cash and/or simple time and effort) to remove.

There are four levels of Notoriety:

⦿ **Incognito:** Potential hostiles will ignore Connor unless he performs an illegal act, or trespasses in an area deemed off-limits (such as free running over rooftops). Minor infractions at street level (such as colliding with a soldier) will lead to a rebuke. As long as you stand still to accept this scolding, the situation will not escalate into open conflict.

⦿ **Level 1:** Guards will begin to detect Connor whenever he enters their field of vision, as indicated by the yellow Social Status Indicators that appear over their heads, but will not move to investigate him until the meters are completely filled (▽➡▼). High Profile actions such as running or climbing will accelerate the detection time.

⦿ **Level 2:** Guards will move to investigate Connor as soon as he enters their field of vision, as indicated by red Social Status Indicators. Once these meters have been filled (▽➡▼), they will attack.

⦿ **Level 3:** Guards will practically attack on sight, though you may avoid open conflict if they only catch a fleeting glimpse of the Assassin. In Boston and New York, the powerful and versatile Jäger enemy archetype will join the search for Connor: see page 225.

Notoriety in Boston and New York is determined by Connor's recent actions, but may also be adjusted temporarily in accordance with narrative events or special conditions. Entering the Restricted Area that surrounds a Fort, for example, will immediately change Connor's Notoriety level; leaving the zone will restore his previous status. In most areas of the Frontier, Connor's Notoriety is fixed at level 1, which makes it necessary to pay patrols a wide berth whenever you encounter them. The Notoriety system is not active in the Homestead region.

In Boston and New York, killing opponents in combat or assassinating targets in front of civilian witnesses increases Connor's Notoriety by the following steps:

⦿ Connor will move from Incognito to Notoriety level 1 after 5 kills.

⦿ He will move from level 1 to level 2 after an additional 5 kills (10 total).

⦿ A further 10 kills will increase Connor's Notoriety to the maximum level 3 (20 total kills).

Notoriety can be reduced in the following ways. Note that the first three techniques also reset the active kill count that marks the transition between levels:

⦿ Ripping down Posters lowers Notoriety by one level.

⦿ Bribing Town Criers (£30-50) reduces Notoriety by two levels.

⦿ Entering a Printing Shop to bribe the proprietor will instantly restore Connor to Incognito, but costs £400 to remove maximum Notoriety. Unless such expenditure is of no consequence due to vast wealth, you may prefer to use the first two methods.

⦿ There are also situations where Notoriety is removed automatically. Desynchronization (due to death in combat, for example) resets it to the lowest possible level within the location where you restart. There are also certain Memories and side quests that restore Connor to Incognito on completion, and starting a new Sequence always offers the Assassin a blank slate.

The Notoriety Meter, which appears next to the mini-map, offers a simple indication of Connor's current combat status: red when opponents are actively seeking to engage him in battle, yellow when he is out of sight but still sought by pursuing aggressors, blue when he is safely concealed in a suitable hiding place, and green when the conflict is over.

## DETECTION TIMES & CONDITIONS

Though reading and reacting to Social Status Indicators becomes second nature, it's interesting to look at some of the figures behind the system.

### Enemy Detection Range

| CONDITION | RANGE (M) |
|---|---|
| Standard | 25 |
| Rain | 20 |
| Blizzard | 13 |
| In a tree (city) | 25 |
| In a tree (Frontier) | 10 |
| In conflict (irrespective of the other conditions) | 25 |

⦿ Detection time (▽➡▼) can take up to 10 seconds with Connor in plain view, while investigation time (▽➡▼) can last up to 12 seconds.

⦿ The fill rate of detection and investigation meters is doubled whenever Connor performs High Profile actions, when a guard moves to within 4 meters of him, and in Restricted Areas.

⦿ Moving within 2 meters of a suspicious target will automatically lead to open conflict.

⦿ As an aside, it's worth noting that attempting to hide in a tree in Boston or New York is clearly not a smart move.

⦿ Any potential opponent within 25 meters of an active battle will automatically join the fray.

All opponents in Assassin's Creed III belong to one of several enemy archetypes, and will exhibit behaviors, proficiencies and weaknesses specific to their class. In this section, we examine their strengths and weaknesses, and offer tips on how you can avoid their attacks and disable them without complications.

There are, broadly speaking, three distinct factions in Assassin's Creed III. Their archetypes are all effectively identical in terms of behavior, even though they wear different uniforms. In the early stages of the story, you might only encounter Loyalists, the British Redcoat forces. As time goes by, the blue-uniformed Patriots become more common. The third uniform style is employed by the mercenaries and brigands that you encounter during certain main story Memories and side quests.

## ENEMY ARCHETYPES

### Soldier

Loyalist

Patriot

Soldiers are by far the most abundant archetype type during the first half of the story, and remain common in later Sequences.

- ◉ Soldiers are extremely susceptible to projectiles: a single arrow is usually enough to put them on their backs. They have no specific resistances.

- ◉ Whenever they appear in mixed groups with more dangerous allies, Soldiers provide an easy way to start a Kill Streak. In battles where you face several opponents, removing the majority of Soldiers via a Kill Streak can make it easier to take control of a combat situation.

- ◉ Though they have a degree of free running prowess, Soldiers are slower than Connor in a straight-line sprint and have limited climbing ability.

- ◉ Pay close attention to Soldiers standing outside the main combat circle, and make note of their movements. This can give you advance notice of firing lines, enabling you to position Connor close to a suitable human shield in advance.

### Sniper

Loyalist

Patriot

Snipers are almost always encountered on rooftops, where they act as sentries commissioned to punish all trespassers severely. Unlike their peers in previous Assassin's Creed episodes, who trod lonely and vulnerable patrol routes, Snipers can be found stationed in groups of up to four on recognizable wooden platforms that afford them a clear view of their surroundings.

- ◉ While Snipers may wear the same uniform as certain Soldiers, they have very unique behaviors. Once they have detected Connor, Snipers will open fire at regular intervals while he remains within range. If you cannot avoid them entirely, try to move out of sight as quickly as you can. It also helps to use natural cover elements (sloped rooftops and chimneys in particular) to disappear from view. If Connor is hit by a sniper shot while climbing or free running, use the Catch Back move – press 🕹 towards the closest surface with an available ledge – to avoid plummeting to the ground.

- ◉ Snipers will engage Connor in standard melee combat at close range. In these situations, their behavior is functionally identical to that of generic Soldiers.

- ◉ If a single Sniper might be problematic, you can use the silent bow to kill him without raising the alarm. Try not to use a pistol or musket: this will alert all guards within a surprisingly wide radius.

- ◉ Though it's a fairly elaborate infiltration technique, you can throw a Sniper's body from a rooftop into the path of a patrol below to temporarily pause their advance as they investigate, or close to sentries to draw them away from their post.

QUICKSTART

THE STORY SO FAR

PRIMER

WALKTHROUGH

SIDE QUESTS

REFERENCE & ANALYSIS

MULTIPLAYER

EXTRAS

MAP LEGEND

INDEX

ADVANCED NAVIGATION

FAST TRAVEL NETWORK

NOTORIETY

ENEMIES

WEAPONS

TOOLS

ASSASSIN RECRUITS

COMBAT MISCELLANY

GENERATING INCOME

THE HOMESTEAD

RECRUITING WORKERS

GATHERING RESOURCES

HUNTING

GATHERING RECIPES

CRAFTING

CONVOYS

SHOPS

OUTFITS

ACHIEVEMENTS & TROPHIES

MOVES OVERVIEW

MISSION CHECKLISTS

## Officer

Loyalist           Patriot

## Snitch

Loyalist           Patriot

⊙ Officers are immune to Counter Kills, but will fall instantly during a successful Kill Streak. You must use the Counter Disarm or Weapon Swipe/Break Defense techniques to break their guard to perform a combo. Ranged weapons are an effective alternative.

⊙ Officers may draw and use their pistol at close range. The ▲ icon appears above these enemies when they are poised to attack in this manner, with a short delay before they aim and open fire. You can use the human shield move, or strike them (ideally with the Weapon Swipe ability) before they pull the trigger.

⊙ Officers march at the head of many patrols, and can search hiding places and detect Connor while he is Blending with civilians. If detection seems unavoidable, it makes sense to begin the battle with the assassination of this dangerous foe.

⊙ Though a relatively rare behavior, Officers can mount nearby horses and fire on Connor from horseback. They may also attempt to gallop over Connor if there is sufficient space to perform the maneuver. Should this happen, press the button that appears in the onscreen prompt (as with animal attacks) to evade their charge. You can either neutralize Officers on horseback with a ranged weapon, or run in close to knock them from the saddle with melee attacks. More often than not, however, the best technique is simply to focus on killing their allies: after a time, they generally leave the saddle to engage Connor on foot.

⊙ Snitches do not play an active part in combat encounters.

⊙ Instead, they will flee the scene in an attempt to locate reinforcements.

## Grenadier

Loyalist

Patriot

Slow but relentlessly aggressive, the Grenadiers are easily identified by their imposing stature.

⊙ Grenadiers are relatively uncommon during the opening Sequences of Connor's story, but become a regular fixture in patrols (and as sentries) during later Sequences.

⊙ Grenadiers are immune to Counter Kills and end Kill Streaks with ease.

⊙ The most time-effective way to kill a Grenadier is to perform the Weapon Swipe move twice to knock them from their feet, then finish them off instantly as they lie prone. In one-on-one situations, you can alternatively employ the Counter Disarm move to remove their resistance to Combo Kills.

⊙ Grenadiers can perform the Slam Attack – their special move – after a distinct wind-up animation telegraphed by the ⚠ icon; on impact, it knocks Connor to the ground and causes massive damage. Perform a Weapon Swipe to interrupt the assault before it is launched, or press **Ⓑ/◎** to roll and evade the blow. If Connor's evasive maneuver takes him behind a Grenadier, it is possible to kill them instantly with an attack from behind. If you are especially confident, you can quickly move Connor close to another opponent before rolling to avoid a Slam Attack. If the Grenadier hits an ally, he will kill them instantly.

⊙ Grenadiers can also throw grenades whenever the ⚠ icon appears, which cause high damage within a fixed radius. To avoid this, simply sprint towards them to avert the danger, or move out of range of the blast.

⊙ Grenadiers are 10% slower than Connor when running, and cannot climb. From a higher vantage point or a safe distance, you can attempt to shoot them with ranged weapons or make an easy escape.

## Scout

Loyalist

Patriot

Scouts are agile adversaries defined by their speed and unusual set of resistances.

⊙ These opponents are perhaps more dangerous when you have a pressing need to escape combat. Though a Scout's free running and climbing prowess is no match for Connor, they are 30% faster in a straight line sprint, and can therefore outpace him in a footrace. As they run behind Connor, they will lash out to stagger him. When you see a Scout moving in to strike, just tap **Ⓐ/Ⓧ** to perform a short jump to foil their attack.

⊙ Scouts are immune to normal attacks, Weapon Swipes and Counter Disarm which – cumulatively – makes them effectively invulnerable to Combo Kills. They fall instantly to Counter Kills and attacks during Kill Streaks, however: it's just a matter of waiting for the right opening.

⊙ Scouts have a special move – telegraphed by the ⚠ icon – where they vault over Connor before performing an attack immediately after they land. Though you cannot prevent the initial acrobatics, be ready to punish the assault that follows with a suitable counterattack.

# Jäger

- Jägers are immune to every combat technique other than ranged attacks, Counter Disarm or a Special Counter with a ranged weapon. Disarming them, however, renders them vulnerable to a combo and a killing blow at the end of the attack chain. This makes them relatively easy to beat in one-on-one confrontations, though you are unlikely to have the time to complete combos during larger brawls.

- Combo attacks performed by Jägers are the longest and most withering that Connor can potentially face, and will reduce a full Life Bar to a perilously low level if left unchecked. The opening blow is always the easiest one to counter; thereafter, each subsequent strike offers a relatively miniscule window for a potential Counter Disarm or Special Counter. In any given group of opponents, the closest Jäger is always the target you should be most wary of.

- Jägers possess the special abilities of the Officer archetype: they can draw a pistol at any moment, and may mount a horse if there is one nearby. They will also throw grenades, though this is rare unless there are Grenadiers or other Jägers nearby.

- Though Jägers can resist multiple projectiles before they fall (unless administered during the mighty Special Counter finish with a ranged weapon), a single Poison Dart will always incapacitate and then kill them. Another trick of note, especially with multiple Jägers, is to drop a Smoke Bomb to render them vulnerable to instant kills.

III

QUICKSTART

THE STORY SO FAR

PRIMER

WALKTHROUGH

SIDE QUESTS

REFERENCE & ANALYSIS

MULTIPLAYER

EXTRAS

MAP LEGEND

INDEX

ADVANCED NAVIGATION

FAST TRAVEL NETWORK

NOTORIETY

ENEMIES

WEAPONS

TOOLS

ASSASSIN RECRUITS

COMBAT MISCELLANY

GENERATING INCOME

THE HOMESTEAD

RECRUITING WORKERS

GATHERING RESOURCES

HUNTING

GATHERING RECIPES

CRAFTING

CONVOYS

SHOPS

OUTFITS

ACHIEVEMENTS & TROPHIES

MOVES OVERVIEW

MISSION CHECKLISTS

Loyalist

Patriot

Encountered when Connor is at maximum Notoriety in Boston and New York, the Jäger is the ultimate enemy archetype, and is effectively a composite of the Officer, Grenadier and Scout classes. Resistant to many combat techniques, these are the toughest enemies you will meet.

## ENEMY OVERVIEW

| MOVE | SOLDIER | SCOUT | OFFICER | GRENADIER | JÄGER |
|---|---|---|---|---|---|
| Attack | Weak | Immune | Immune | Weak | Immune |
| Combo Kill | Weak | Weak | Weak | Immune | Immune |
| Kill Streak | Weak | Weak | Weak | Immune | Immune |
| Weapon Swipe/Break Defense | Weak | Immune | Weak | Weak | Immune |
| Ranged Attack | Weak | Weak | Weak | Weak | Weak |
| Counter Kill | Weak | Weak | Immune | Immune | Immune |
| Counter Disarm | Weak | Immune | Weak | Weak | Weak |
| Counter Throw | Weak | Weak | Weak | Immune | Immune |
| Special Counter (Ranged Weapons Only) | Weak | Weak | Weak | Weak | Weak |

### Table Notes:

- "Attack" refers to the opening blow in a combo. If an archetype is immune, this will always fail unless they are off-balance or facing away from Connor (for example, after a Weapon Swipe).

- "Combo Kill" refers to the final blow in a combo attack. If an opponent is immune, they will repel Connor's attempt to deliver a *coup de grâce* after weathering the blows that precede it. However, they only possess this resistance if they are currently holding a weapon. If unarmed, Grenadiers and Jägers will die like any other enemy as the final strike lands.

- A Special Counter with a pistol, musket, bow, Poison Darts, Rope Darts or Trip Mine is the ultimate finishing move: only unique opponents with onscreen life gauges can resist these deadly attacks.

- Whenever an opponent is immune to a technique, with the exception of the opening attack of a combo, their counterattack will cause Connor to lose health.

Every melee weapon is rated in three categories: Damage, Speed and Combo. These stats define their overall effectiveness in combat.

- **Damage:** This attribute is used to determine the strength of each successful attack. With most combat deaths achieved through counterattacks and Kill Streaks, this stat is the least important of the three.

- **Speed:** Weapons with a high Speed rating enable Connor to attack faster and more frequently. Heavier weapons tend to have lower Speed ratings.

- **Combo:** Weapons differ in the number of hits required before Connor can deliver a finishing blow. Unlike Damage and Speed, lower totals represent a superior Combo stat.

You can switch between weapons in your existing collection via the "Buy" option at any General Store, or by collecting them from the display racks inside the Homestead Manor.

**Note:** Unless removed briefly by narrative constraints, Connor can always count on his fists and Hidden Blade. He has one inventory slot that can be occupied by a tomahawk or small blade, and a second slot that enables him to carry a single weapon selected from the "Normal", "Heavy" and "Blunt" categories.

## UNARMED

Unarmed fighting enables you to attack at speed, and can be an enjoyable way to fight against weaker assailants, but puts Connor at greater risk – especially as the Parry ability is unavailable. For those seeking a stern test of their abilities, though, it's definitely the most technically demanding fighting style.

The principal reason to use unarmed combat is to employ the Disarm move, as this will enable you to take your target's weapon from their hands. Fist fighting can also be employed when you must disable opponents without killing them. If stealth and mercy are called for, sneak up behind an opponent and tap ✗/□ to incapacitate them with a non-lethal finishing move.

| UNARMED ATTRIBUTES | | | | |
| --- | --- | --- | --- | --- |
| NAME | DAMAGE | SPEED | COMBO | AVAILABILITY |
| Fists | 1 | 5 | 6 | Available from the start |

III

QUICKSTART

THE STORY SO
FAR

PRIMER

WALKTHROUGH

SIDE QUESTS

REFERENCE &
ANALYSIS

MULTIPLAYER

EXTRAS

MAP LEGEND

INDEX

ADVANCED
NAVIGATION

FAST TRAVEL
NETWORK

NOTORIETY

ENEMIES

WEAPONS

TOOLS

ASSASSIN
RECRUITS

COMBAT
MISCELLANY

GENERATING
INCOME

THE HOMESTEAD

RECRUITING
WORKERS

GATHERING
RESOURCES

HUNTING

GATHERING
RECIPES

CRAFTING

CONVOYS

SHOPS

OUTFITS

ACHIEVEMENTS &
TROPHIES

MOVES
OVERVIEW

MISSION
CHECKLISTS

## SMALL WEAPONS

Small weapons enable Connor to attack with great speed and, with the Dirk dagger and War Tomahawk, achieve remarkably rapid Combo Kills before other adversaries have time to interrupt his onslaught. The drawback to this category of weapons is that they are only effective at short range, which makes them relatively ill-suited to long Kill Streaks. You can either equip a Tomahawk or a short blade: Connor cannot carry both at once.

The Hidden Blade, long the weapon of choice for Assassin's Creed purists, is available at all times (unless the demands of the story temporarily dictate otherwise). It functions as a small weapon in terms of its range. It is, however, an appalling choice for combos unless you are facing a solitary opponent. The number of individual blows required before the killing strike means that Connor will often be interrupted by other assailants long before he disables a target.

| SMALL WEAPON ATTRIBUTES | | | | | |
|---|---|---|---|---|---|
| NAME | DAMAGE | SPEED | COMBO | PRICE (£) | AVAILABILITY |
| Hidden Blade | 1 | 3 | 6 | – | Available from the start |
| Stone Tomahawk | 1 | 2 | 5 | – | Complete Sequence 05 |
| Assassin Tomahawk | 3 | 3 | 3 | – | Sequence 06 |
| Iron Tomahawk | 2 | 3 | 3 | 2,475 | Sequence 06 |
| Iron Dagger | 3 | 4 | 4 | 2,450 | Sequence 06 |
| Stone Dagger | 1 | 3 | 5 | 450 | Sequence 06 |
| Dirk | 2 | 5 | 3 | 3,750 | Sequence 06 |
| War Tomahawk | 5 | 5 | 3 | – | Through crafting |
| "Broken Sword" Knife | 5 | 5 | 4 | – | Through crafting |

## HEAVY WEAPONS

Heavy weapons are carried by Grenadiers, and can be collected after you kill them. From Sequence 06 onwards, you can purchase and equip one of these mighty axes.

Weapons in the Heavy category are ostensibly slow and cumbersome, but their phenomenal reach and – with the best axes – short combos can make them extremely effective. The primary drawback to using heavy weapons is that, being two-handed, they preclude the use of ranged weapons and related Special Counter abilities. In battles against the most dangerous and gifted enemy archetypes, this can be a massive drawback for players who are less adept in

combat situations. That said, the capacity to fell a disarmed Jäger with two or three blows is no trivial characteristic – if you have the composure to do so, that is.

Connor's Tools may be unavailable while holding an axe, but the button is not left redundant: it is instead assigned to the unique **"Slam Attack"** instant-kill move. Hold **Y**/**△** to charge the assault, then release the button. Connor will slam the axe at the targeted opponent, killing them instantly – but losing the weapon in the process. If you forget to retrieve the axe at the conclusion of the battle, you can reequip it at any General Store or the Homestead Manor.

| HEAVY WEAPON ATTRIBUTES | | | | | |
|---|---|---|---|---|---|
| NAME | DAMAGE | SPEED | COMBO | PRICE (£) | AVAILABILITY |
| Hessian Axe | 2 | 1 | 4 | 3,650 | Sequence 06 |
| French Naval Axe | 2 | 3 | 3 | 5,450 | Sequence 06 |
| Boarding Axe | 3 | 4 | 3 | 7,000 | Sequence 09 |
| Pirate Boarding Axe | 5 | 4 | 2 | – | In specific Collector's Editions or as a preorder bonus |
| Naval Axe | 4 | 4 | 2 | – | Through crafting |

## NORMAL WEAPONS

Normal weapons are standard medium-sized blades that offer a fair blend of range and speed, and combos of a tolerable length, which makes them a balanced (if perhaps unspectacular) choice for any combat situation.

### NORMAL WEAPON ATTRIBUTES

| NAME | DAMAGE | SPEED | COMBO | PRICE (£) | AVAILABILITY |
|---|---|---|---|---|---|
| Normal Sword | 1 | 2 | 3 | 700 | Sequence 06 |
| French Rapier | 2 | 1 | 4 | 3,955 | Sequence 06 |
| Light Cavalry Saber | 4 | 3 | 5 | 3,500 | Sequence 06 |
| Hanger Sword | 3 | 3 | 5 | 1,250 | Sequence 06 |
| French Cutlass | 3 | 4 | 5 | 1,575 | Sequence 06 |
| Cuttoe Sword | 2 | 2 | 4 | 4,100 | Sequence 06 |
| Officer's Sword | 4 | 1 | 4 | 5,000 | Sequence 06 |
| Captain Kidd's Sawtooth Cutlass | 5 | 4 | 4 | - | In specific Collector's Editions or as a preorder bonus |
| Washington's Battle Sword (Replica) | 4 | 4 | 4 | - | Through crafting |
| Lincoln's Sword (Replica) | 5 | 5 | 5 | - | Through crafting |

## BLUNT WEAPONS

Blunt weapons are functionally very similar to the axes in the Heavy Weapon category, though Connor's assaults are tailored to bludgeon opponents rather than shear through flesh and solid bone. Other than this primarily aesthetic variation, they have the same benefits and drawbacks as heavy weapons: the better clubs enable shorter combos, and easy counterattacks, but reduce your tactical options through the unavailability of Tools and Special Counters with ranged weapons. Instead of the Slam Attack, they offer a throw assault, the **Blunt Attack:** hold then release **Y**/**△** and you will hurl the weapon at the targeted opponent, incapacitating them instantly. Interestingly, this is actually a non-lethal attack: note how enemies continue to writhe on the floor long after the impact.

### BLUNT WEAPON ATTRIBUTES

| NAME | DAMAGE | SPEED | COMBO | PRICE (£) | AVAILABILITY |
|---|---|---|---|---|---|
| Wooden War Club | 2 | 3 | 3 | 2,650 | Sequence 06 |
| Gunstock War Club | 3 | 4 | 2 | 6,500 | Sequence 06 |
| Stonehead War Club | 3 | 1 | 2 | 3,850 | Sequence 09 |
| Obwandiyag's War Club | 5 | 5 | 1 | - | In specific Collector's Editions or as a preorder bonus |
| Iron Blade War Club | 4 | 5 | 1 | - | Through crafting |

## THE MUSKET

Though you cannot purchase or permanently equip muskets, these weapons are easily acquired in most battles. With their excellent range and a cartridge loaded for a "free" ranged shot, they can be collected, used and then discarded without hesitation. As with all weapons, there is a knack to picking them off the ground during active combat: wait for a quiet moment with Connor standing above one on the ground, then briefly hold **RT**/**R1** and tap **B**/**○**.

While ❌/□ is designated for melee attacks with Connor's primary weapon, ⓨ/△ enables you to use items in the Tools category. Six of these items have an application in combat situations, or can be employed to create chaos and confusion during infiltrations or impromptu bouts of anarchy, and are the sole focus of this section. You can read more about the Horse Whistle and Throw Money ability in the Primer (see page 38 and 45), and "Snares & Bait" in a dedicated Hunting section on page 242.

Use of ranged weapons and gadgets is limited only by Connor's current stock of ammunition for each item. You can replenish consumables in multiple ways: from looting, crafting, purchasing them from merchants, or even resupplying the saddle bags on Connor's horse once you have crafted them (see box-out).

## SADDLE BAGS

Once they become available through the Crafting system (see page 244), you can create Saddle Bags that are automatically placed on Connor's horse. These are then loaded with a stock of consumable items in the Tools category. Whenever you need to resupply, you can use the Horse Whistle to summon Connor's mount, then approach it and press ⓑ/◯ for an immediate inventory refill.

### Saddle Bags: Capacity & Upgrades

| NAME | AVAILABILITY | REFILLS |
|---|---|---|
| Small Saddle Bags | Through crafting after completing Sequence 09 | Cartridges, Arrows |
| Medium Saddle Bags | Through crafting after completing Sequence 10 | Cartridges, Arrows, Rope Darts, Smoke Bombs |
| Large Saddle Bags | Through crafting after completing Sequence 12 | Cartridges, Arrows, Rope Darts, Smoke Bombs, Poison Darts, Trip Mines, Snares |

## RANGED WEAPONS

The primary use of Connor's ranged weapons is to disable or wound targets from a distance. However, all four of these weapons can be employed at close range with the Special Counter move, which kills all but the strongest opponents instantly.

There is no stat that corresponds to the raw power of each bow or pistol shot. The damage output of these weapons is instead expressed in terms of amount of shots required to kill each archetype, as described in the accompanying table.

### RANGED WEAPONS: SHOTS PER ENEMY TYPE

| NAME | SHORT RANGE (0-17m) | | | LONG RANGE (17-25m) | | | WEAPON SHOTS PER RELOAD | AVAILABILITY |
|---|---|---|---|---|---|---|---|---|
| | SOLDIER/ SNITCH | OFFICER/ SCOUT | GRENADIER/ JÄGER | SOLDIER/ SNITCH | OFFICER/ SCOUT | GRENADIER/ JÄGER | | |
| Bow (Reflex Shot) | 1 | 2 | 3 | 2 | 2 | 3 | N/A | Connor's initial equipment |
| Bow (Charged Shot) | 1 | 1 | 2 | 1 | 2 | 3 | | |
| Musket | 1 | 1 | 2 | 1 | 1 | 2 | 1 | From guards or racks |
| Flintlock Pistol | 1 | 1 | 2 | 2 | 2 | 3 | 1 | General Stores, Sequence 06 |
| Duckfoot Pistol | 1 | 1 | 2 | 2 | 2 | 3 | 1 | General Stores, Sequence 06 |
| Double-Barrel Pistol | 1 | 1 | 2 | 2 | 2 | 3 | 2 | General Stores, Sequence 09 |
| Pitcairn-Putnam Pistols | 1 | 1 | 1 | 1 | 1 | 2 | 1 | Complete Sequence 07 |
| Italian Flintlock | 1 | 1 | 2 | 1 | 1 | 2 | 1 | Through crafting |
| Royal Pistol | 1 | 1 | 2 | 1 | 1 | 2 | 2 | Through crafting |
| English Flintlock Pistol | 1 | 1 | 1 | 2 | 2 | 3 | 1 | Through crafting |
| French Coat Pistol | 1 | 1 | 1 | 2 | 2 | 3 | 2 | Through crafting |
| Royal Navy Sea Service Flintlock | 1 | 1 | 1 | 1 | 2 | 3 | 1 | Through crafting |
| Naval Duckfoot | 1 | 1 | 1 | 1 | 2 | 3 | 1 | Through crafting |
| Pirate Flintlock | 1 | 1 | 1 | 2 | 2 | 3 | 2 | In specific Collector's Editions or as a preorder bonus |
| Scottish Flintlock | 1 | 1 | 2 | 1 | 1 | 2 | 1 | In specific Collector's Editions or as a preorder bonus |

##  Bow

This powerful and silent weapon is perfect for stealth kills from a safe distance or elevation. You can fire arrows in two different ways. To perform a reflex shot, with reduced stopping power and range, just tap **Y**/**△** to fire at Connor's highlighted target. To exploit the maximum potential of this weapon, you must hold **Y**/**△** until the bow string is fully taut, then release it to fire; note that you can cancel a "charged" shot by pressing **B**/**○** before you let the arrow fly. The maximum 25 meter range of the bow is only available if you use Precision Mode aiming.

When employed with the Special Counter move, Connor will block his opponent's attack, draw the bow, and kill them instantly with a point-blank reflex shot. Arrows used to kill adversaries can often be retrieved by looting their bodies once combat ends.

| BOW: QUIVER CAPACITY & UPGRADES | | |
|---|---|---|
| **NAME** | **CAPACITY/UPGRADE** | **AVAILABILITY** |
| **Default Quiver** | 8 | - |
| **Quiver Upgrade 1** | +4 | Through crafting |
| **Quiver Upgrade 2** | +4 | Through Uplay |

##  Firearms

When you purchase a new pistol, its relative strength is expressed with the following stats:

⊙ **Rate of Fire:** Governs the frequency of shots.

⊙ **Short Range:** A measure of the efficiency of the weapon from 0 to 17 meters.

⊙ **Long Range:** A measure of the efficiency of the weapon from 17 to 25 meters. Note that shots of this range require that you use Precision Mode aiming.

When choosing which pistol to carry, you should also take into account the number of shots it offers per reload, and the potential stopping power of each trigger pull: see the "Ranged Weapons: Shots per Enemy Type" table at the start of this section for details. The Duckfoot Pistol is loaded with three cartridges, for example, but it discharges its entire capacity at once. While this hand-held "shotgun" has its applications, a pistol that offers more than one shot per reload generally offers you greater tactical flexibility: loading cartridges into firearms in open conflict is an implausible course of action. Once you have the necessary artisans and resources at the Homestead, you can craft the Twin Holsters upgrade (see page 244) to enable Connor to carry two pistols at once, for a maximum of four potential shots before a reload is required.

As with the bow, a pistol is used by pressing or holding and releasing **Y**/**△** (with **B**/**○** cancelling aimed shots). More powerful than the bow,

pistols are particularly useful for killing Snitches as they run in search of reinforcements. However, this power and convenience must be weighed against attendant drawbacks. Pistols are astonishingly noisy, and will attract attention and close scrutiny over a wide radius. In open conflict, this may draw nearby patrols into the fray. It should go without saying that the pistol is not suited to stealthy infiltrations.

When employed with the Special Counter move, Connor will blast his opponent at point-blank range, killing them instantly. If the pistol is unloaded, Connor will attempt a standard Counter Kill – which will almost certainly fail against resistant archetypes.

| FIREARMS: CARTRIDGE POUCH CAPACITY & UPGRADES | | |
|---|---|---|
| **NAME** | **CAPACITY/UPGRADE** | **AVAILABILITY** |
| **Default Cartridge Pouch** | 8 | - |
| **Cartridge Pouch Upgrade 1** | +8 | Through crafting |
| **Cartridge Pouch Upgrade 2** | +8 | Through crafting |
| **Cartridge Pouch Upgrade 3** | +8 | Through crafting |
| **Cartridge Pouch Upgrade 4** | +8 | Through Uplay |

QUICKSTART

THE STORY SO
FAR

PRIMER

WALKTHROUGH

SIDE QUESTS

REFERENCE &
ANALYSIS

MULTIPLAYER

EXTRAS

MAP LEGEND

INDEX

ADVANCED
NAVIGATION

FAST TRAVEL
NETWORK

NOTORIETY

ENEMIES

WEAPONS

TOOLS

ASSASSIN
RECRUITS

COMBAT
MISCELLANY

GENERATING
INCOME

THE HOMESTEAD

RECRUITING
WORKERS

GATHERING
RESOURCES

HUNTING

GATHERING
RECIPES

CRAFTING

CONVOYS

SHOPS

OUTFITS

ACHIEVEMENTS &
TROPHIES

MOVES
OVERVIEW

MISSION
CHECKLISTS

##  Poison Darts

With the exception of a select few individuals who enjoy story-mandated immunity, Poison Darts incapacitate an afflicted target instantly – but it's what happens afterwards that is perhaps most interesting from a tactical perspective. To throw a Poison Dart, press **Y**/△ when your intended victim moves within range, or use Precision Mode aiming to throw it over slightly longer distances. The affected adversary will instantly lose all interest in Connor – even if they previously had an active SSI meter – and stagger in a given direction (following an existing patrol route, if applicable), attracting the attention of everyone within range. When the dart's payload finally overwhelms them, they will collapse to the ground, causing all guards within the vicinity to move to investigate. If you need to eliminate a target and move on without raising the alarm, or to create a localized diversion, Poison Darts are one of the most powerful weapons at Connor's disposal.

Using Poison Darts in combat disables a target instantly. If employed with a Special Counter, Connor will simultaneously stab the target and hurl them aside (in a manner identical to a Counter Throw) in a single movement. Though they will clamber to their feet, their effective presence in the battle will be over; after a time, they will collapse. If a poisoned target is still standing after you kill the final active enemy in a battle, note that open conflict will not officially end until they fall to the ground.

### POISON DARTS: POUCH CAPACITY & UPGRADES

| NAME | CAPACITY/UPGRADE | AVAILABILITY |
|---|---|---|
| Default Poison Dart Pouch | 3 | - |
| Poison Dart Pouch Upgrade 1 | +1 | Through crafting |
| Poison Dart Pouch Upgrade 2 | +1 | Through Uplay |

##  Rope Darts

The Rope Dart has five combat applications, though it's perhaps fair to say that this exotic weapon is best suited to situations where you can favor showmanship over speed and efficiency. Three of its five moves enable Connor to reuse a Rope Dart at a later date; we specify the two techniques where a unit of the item is consumed.

1. From a tree branch or a beam above a suitable target, hold **Y**/△ to strangle a target situated below.

2. From a tree branch or a beam, hold **Y**/△ and press **L** in the appropriate direction to hang a target within range (📷 01). This "Predator" move consumes one Rope Dart.

3. On the ground, while standing behind an oblivious target, hold **Y**/△ to use the Rope Dart to pull an opponent towards Connor; when they stumble within range, he will kill them instantly.

4. In combat, tap **Y**/△ to fire a Rope Dart at a target and pull them to the ground. If you are close enough, you can then perform an instant finishing move.

5. Last, but by no means least, employing a Rope Dart in a Special Counter is lethal against all archetypes. Using this attack consumes a Rope Dart for each kill.

01

### ROPE DARTS: POUCH CAPACITY & UPGRADES

| NAME | CAPACITY/UPGRADE | AVAILABILITY |
|---|---|---|
| Default Rope Dart Pouch | 3 | - |
| Rope Dart Pouch Upgrade 1 | +1 | Through crafting |
| Rope Dart Pouch Upgrade 2 | +1 | Through Uplay |

Smoke Bombs

Depending on the demands of your current situation, a Smoke Bomb can be employed to create confusion and paralysis, enabling effortless kills of affected opponents, or to facilitate an easier escape. If flight is a prerequisite, dropping a Smoke Bomb in a confined space will incapacitate all pursuers who enter its area of effect (📷 02).

Though Connor and his allies are immune to the effects of Smoke Bombs, opponents inside the cloud (or those who enter it) are blinded, stunned and unable to move until the smoke dissipates. Anyone knocked outside the cloud will recover immediately.

### SMOKE BOMBS: POUCH CAPACITY & UPGRADES

| NAME | CAPACITY/UPGRADE | AVAILABILITY |
| --- | --- | --- |
| Default Smoke Bomb Pouch | 3 | Complete Memory 03 in Sequence 06 |
| Smoke Bomb Pouch Upgrade 1 | +1 | Through crafting |
| Smoke Bomb Pouch Upgrade 2 | +1 | Through Uplay |

 Trip Mines

To plant a Trip Mine, hold 🅨/△ until the onscreen meter is filled. Potential hostiles who witness this act will immediately move to investigate, which may lead to undesirable consequences – so it's wise to ensure that enemies are facing elsewhere before you begin. Once a mine has been planted, you will see two concentric circles (📷 03). The solid inner circle represents the activation zone, while the outer ring indicates the potential blast radius.

The primary use of Trip Mines is to kill targets without being detected, especially if you know their precise patrol route. As a potential added benefit, the explosion will cause all nearby guards to run to investigate, which can be exploited as a decidedly indiscrete but effective way to infiltrate heavily guarded areas. If your intended target is stationary, you can attempt to lure them into the device by whistling from a corner or hiding place, or by moving Connor into the intended victim's line of sight to lead them in the required direction.

You can lay traps that consist of multiple Trip Mines, but we strongly advise caution in areas that feature civilian traffic. Any non-allied NPC can trigger these devices, which will lead to Desynchronization if you kill too many innocents in quick succession. You should also note that, while Connor and his allies cannot trigger these devices, they may be injured if caught in the blast radius. If required, you can retrieve unused Trip Mines: stand over a device and tap 🅑/◎ to pick it up.

Though it might seem foolhardy, Connor can employ Trip Mines for a Special Counter. Slapping the primed explosive to his opponent, he propels them away with force just moments before the device detonates. If Connor is surrounded, or fighting in close quarters, the resultant localized explosion can kill or knock down other hostiles – and yet fortune smiles upon the Assassin himself, who always escapes the effect.

### TRIP MINES: POUCH CAPACITY & UPGRADES

| NAME | CAPACITY/UPGRADE | AVAILABILITY |
| --- | --- | --- |
| Default Pouch | 3 | - |
| Trip Mine Pouch Upgrade 1 | +1 | Through crafting |
| Trip Mine Pouch Upgrade 2 | +1 | Through Uplay |

# ASSASSIN RECRUITS

III

QUICKSTART

THE STORY SO
FAR

PRIMER

WALKTHROUGH

SIDE QUESTS

REFERENCE &
ANALYSIS

MULTIPLAYER

EXTRAS

MAP LEGEND

INDEX

ADVANCED
NAVIGATION

FAST TRAVEL
NETWORK

NOTORIETY

ENEMIES

WEAPONS

TOOLS

ASSASSIN
RECRUITS

COMBAT
MISCELLANY

GENERATING
INCOME

THE HOMESTEAD

RECRUITING
WORKERS

GATHERING
RESOURCES

HUNTING

GATHERING
RECIPES

CRAFTING

CONVOYS

SHOPS

OUTFITS

ACHIEVEMENTS &
TROPHIES

MOVES
OVERVIEW

MISSION
CHECKLISTS

Liberating districts of Boston and New York from the baleful influence of the Templars provides Connor with up to six Assassin recruits and a total of eight special abilities. Though the process of liberating city districts to expand the New World Brotherhood and the specific function of each ability is covered in the Side Quests chapter (see page 154), this short section looks at the use of recruits in open conflict.

## ASSASSIN ABILITIES

| ICON | ABILITY | RECRUIT | AREA | PAGE |
|------|---------|---------|------|------|
| ⊙ | Call Backup | All | All | 155 |
| ✊ | Riot | Stephane Chapheau | Boston Central | 155 |
| ⚔ | Assassinate | | | |
| 🛡 | Bodyguard | Duncan Little | Boston North | 156 |
| ✕ | Marksmen | Clipper Wilkinson | Boston South | 155 |
| ⊗ | Ambush | Jamie Colley | New York West | 156 |
| 👥 | Covert Escort | Jacob Zenger | New York East | 156 |
| 🤝 | Lure Away | Dobby Carter | New York North | 156 |

Once Connor enlists the services of Stephane Chapheau at the conclusion of The Angry Chef in Sequence 06, you gain the option to press **LB**/**L2** at any time in combat to summon available recruits with the Call Backup ability. Though this will initially only offer the assistance of Chapheau alone, you can increase Connor's Brotherhood to a maximum of six recruits: a further two from fully liberating Boston during Sequence 06, with the final three available to enlist in New York from Sequence 09. All of your recruits gain levels gradually as you call them on the battlefield or send them on assignments (see page 163).

In open conflict, the Call Backup option overrides all other recruit abilities, which remain unavailable until Connor kills his final opponent or escapes. Tapping **LB**/**L2** summons a recruit into a fight immediately, where they will then engage your opponents to the best of their abilities. Each additional press of **LB**/**L2** will summon another Assassin trainee if available, up to a full six once all Liberation Missions have been cleared (📷 01).

Naturally, this has a huge effect on the difficulty of most combat encounters. Though the recruits are rather feeble at lower levels, their presence divides enemy forces and presents many opportunities for one-hit kills as you take adversaries concentrating on your allies by surprise. While recruits may fall quickly in early battles, they cannot die: the only penalty is a five-minute "cooldown" period as they convalesce. Once they gain experience through combat encounters, ability use and by completing contracts, however, they become incredibly effective warriors. At high ranks, you can often summon recruits into a fight and almost sit back and let them do the hard work.

01

Though most Assassin abilities available outside of open conflict are used for stealth, infiltrations and neutralizing specific targets, the Marksmen command warrants a special mention here. Select it by holding **LB**/**L2** and choose it from the list on the right, then target any opponent in range. After a short pause, all available recruits will open fire, killing your specified hostile and up to five of his nearby cohorts instantly, before diving into battle. If you need to eliminate priority targets, or face a large battle against numerous opponents, this can enable you to even the odds – or perhaps end a fight before it really begins.

Though Assassin recruits are unavailable in the Frontier and in certain main missions, we would describe them as an "easy mode" for the more demanding combat encounters. The extent to which you call upon their services during battles is very much a question of personal taste.

In this final combat-focused section, we offer a selection of useful tips and suggestions that will help you make the most of Connor's abilities, and adjust the difficulty of the combat system to suit your personal needs.

⊙ If you are finding combat too challenging in later Sequences, you can summon available recruits with the Call Backup ability every time you face formidable enemies (see page 233). If you would prefer to deal with opponents on your own, the Special Counter move is your salvation. Ensure that Connor is not equipped with a weapon in the Heavy or Blunt categories (that is, an axe or a club – these disable the technique), and select the bow (with a full stock of arrows) as your active Tool. After pressing 🅑/◎ to counter an opponent's attack, you can then press 🅨/△ to kill them instantly – irrespective of their innate resistances or strength (🎦 01). Though this doesn't work with the occasional special opponents who have onscreen life bars, it's devastating against all standard enemy archetypes. Special Counters only function if you have ammunition for the selected ranged weapon or gadget, but this is rarely a problem: in addition to the bow, the pistol, Rope Darts, Poison Darts and Trip Mines can also be used to complete this finishing move, which should give you plenty of opportunities to win a difficult battle. You can replenish your depleted stock of consumables by looting dead bodies at the end of a confrontation.

⊙ If you simply need a technique to defeat the more challenging Grenadiers and Jägers, but do not want to constantly rely on Special Counters or Assassin recruits, we strongly recommend that you experiment with the Rope Dart. Though it takes a little practice to master the timing and targeting, pressing 🅨/△ will cause Connor to pull *any* opponent to the ground (🎦 02), enabling you to perform a finishing move or attend to other threats before they clamber to their feet.

⊙ By contrast, if you find that the use of Special Counters and Assassin recruits makes combat a little too easy, we suggest self-imposed limitations to heighten the challenge. A fair task for experienced Assassin's Creed players would be to fight with the Hidden Blade as your only weapon, eschewing all Special Counters and using ranged weapons only when a mission requires you to do so.

⊙ For true experts, an unarmed, fists-only approach is even more exacting and, having mastered the combat system over months of play, is our favored style. If you decide that Connor is only allowed to use weapons stolen from enemies, all battles become far more technically demanding.

⊙ The very largest battles can feature several opponents forming a firing line and devastating the Life Bar with a single volley. This is probably the most dangerous attack you will face in any combat scenario, especially as it is easy to miss the warning notifications until the last second. If avoiding firing lines is not your forte, this can be a real problem. Whenever Connor faces more than eight opponents at once, you will find that there are two distinct enemy fronts (🎦 03): the *inner ring*, with opponents actively engaged in the battle, and the *outer ring*, where opponents are primarily (but not entirely) passive: having numerous enemies in the outer ring increases the likelihood that firing lines will form. Killing assailants in the inner ring of a battle will cause others situated in the outer ring to move forward to join the fray, reducing the probability of a firing line (or, at very least, the number of potential guns). The best way to negate potential firing lines, then, is to start a Kill Streak and focus exclusively on weeding out weaker enemies who are vulnerable to such attacks: primarily Soldiers and Scouts, but also Officers if they are within range. Ignore Grenadiers and, if present, Jägers: just foil their attacks and temporarily stun them with a Counter Disarm, then move back to your main targets. You should also notice that automatic "double kills" are far more common when you are facing a large enemy force. Do your utmost to take these opportunities as they arise by pressing 🅑/◎ whenever you see the △ icon above the heads of two enemies simultaneously.

⊙ When attempting to use the human shield move, one problem that some people will encounter with firing lines is a tendency to press 🅐/✕ too early or rapidly as gunmen move into position. This can lead to an inadvertent Weapon Swipe or, worse, two instances that knock a prospective human shield to the ground. If you can stay composed, try to hazard a glance to the contextual button display on the right-hand side of the screen as you approach your intended target. In the brief window when the human shield move is possible, a notification will appear in this position. To reach slightly more distant targets, ensure that you hold 🅛 in their direction. This ingredient is easy to forget, but it improves the success rate considerably.

⊙ Don't neglect the potential assistance offered by groups of Vigilantes (represented by the ⬠ icon) if you notice them nearby in Boston or New York. Sprinting to their position can make battles much easier, as they will reach out to restrain hostiles that move within range. This can allow easy one-hit kills, prevents opponents from properly surrounding Connor if he operates close to the ruck, and provides a wall of bodies to defend against firing lines. As an aside, it's worth mentioning that groups of civilians that can be encouraged to start riots with 🅑/◎ are also remarkably bold, refusing to move while their less hardy peers flee for cover. Though they do not seek to interfere with guards, they can serve a similar strategic purpose.

# GENERATING INCOME

The following summary offers a simple guide to the ways in which Connor can accumulate funds, with links to advice in other sections of the guide where applicable. As main story Memories and the majority of side quests do not offer financial rewards on completion, unlike previous Assassin's Creed adventures, you must look to the following techniques to finance major purchases.

**Citizen Mission Rewards:** You can obtain cash payments for completing the Courier, Delivery Request and Assassination Contract side quests when they appear (see page 136). The sums are not remarkable, though they can be a welcome bonus in earlier Sequences.

**Pickpocketing & Looting:** The sum of coins and items you obtain through pickpocketing and looting is dependent on the individual you target. See page 240 for details.

**Treasure Chests:** Chests offer variable contents, from recipes, to sums of money and occasional crafting items; they also contribute to your total Synchronization rating. You can purchase maps that reveal their locations (see page 252).

**Couriers:** Catching these fleet-footed individuals by tackling them after a chase (killing moves are inadvisable) leads to a nominal financial reward. Given the difficulty of the pursuit, and the likelihood that guards will become involved, this should be regarded as an amusing or challenging diversion – not a practical means of generating income.

**Assassin's Guild Contracts:** From early in Sequence 06, sending Assassin recruits on missions not only enables you to improve their standing, but also leads to rewards that include cash bounties (see page 162).

**Attacking Convoys:** In the Frontier, Connor can attack enemy convoys and loot them (see page 138).

**Selling Animal Products:** Hunting and skinning animals in the Frontier and Homestead provides Connor with pelts, meat and other products that can be sold directly to General Stores or Peddlers when encountered on their mobile wagons.

**The Homestead:** The Homestead is Connor's primary source of income, and enables you to generate immense profits through the crafting and convoy systems. Turn the page for a full guide to this lucrative metagame and its many interconnected systems.

# THE HOMESTEAD

The following diagram offers an overview of the entire economic landscape in Assassin's Creed III, showing how a wide range of related activities (including money-making opportunities and potential investments) are interconnected. It should be immediately clear that the Homestead lies at the heart of this system. It is the only realistic way to

generate large amounts of cash, and to access the best items and upgrades – either through buying them from General Stores, or by calling on the Homestead's artisans to craft them.

The majority of Homestead operations – purchasing raw materials, crafting and sale of

products through convoys – are performed via the Accounting Book interface. You can find the master Accounting Book inside the Manor, but there are also identical copies of it in all General Stores throughout the major game regions. To interact with the Accounting Book, simply press **Ⓑ**/**Ⓞ**.

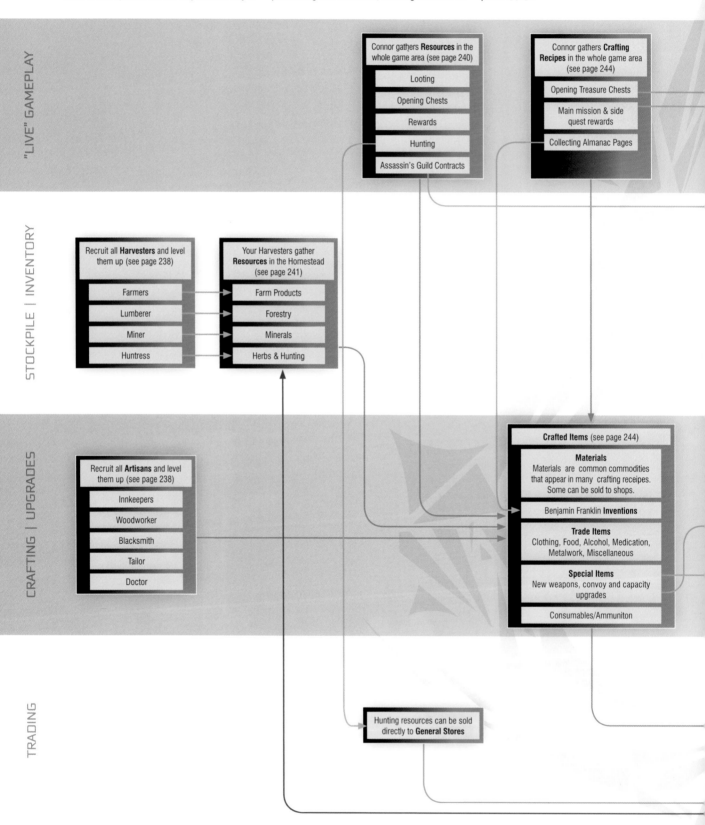

## LEGEND

| | |
|---|---|
| → | Crafting & Convoy System |
| → | Income |
| → | Expenditure |
| → | System Interaction |

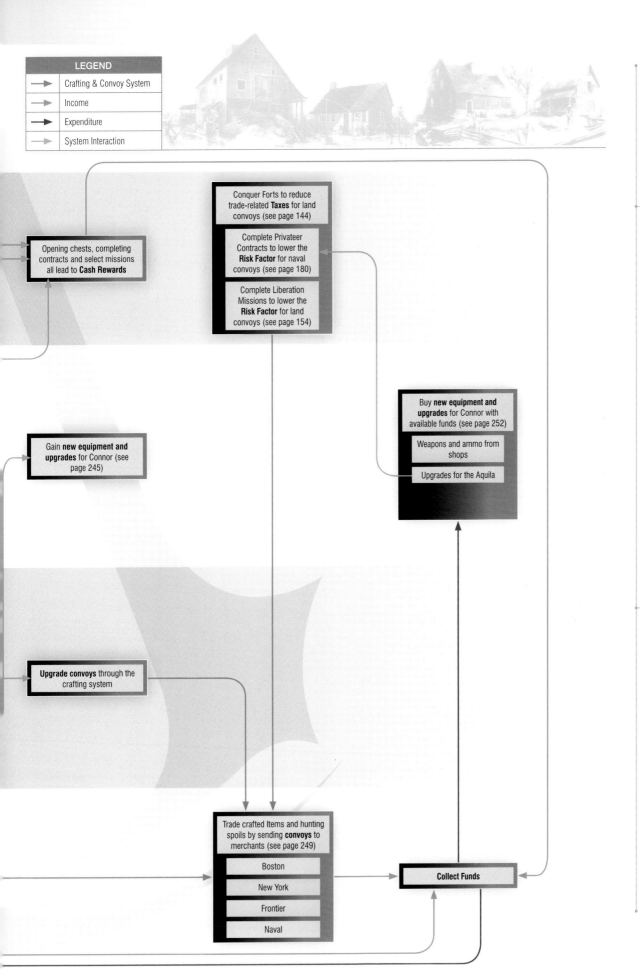

Conquer Forts to reduce trade-related **Taxes** for land convoys (see page 144)

Complete Privateer Contracts to lower the **Risk Factor** for naval convoys (see page 180)

Complete Liberation Missions to lower the **Risk Factor** for land convoys (see page 154)

Opening chests, completing contracts and select missions all lead to **Cash Rewards**

Buy **new equipment and upgrades** for Connor with available funds (see page 252)

Weapons and ammo from shops

Upgrades for the Aquila

Gain **new equipment and upgrades** for Connor (see page 245)

Upgrade convoys through the crafting system

Trade crafted Items and hunting spoils by sending **convoys** to merchants (see page 249)

Boston

New York

Frontier

Naval

**Collect Funds**

# RECRUITING WORKERS

Once the feature is unlocked towards the end of Sequence 05, you can gradually recruit two categories of workers at the Homestead:

**Artisans** are people who can craft items within their lines of expertise using resources that you must source and supply. Once again, this is achieved via the Accounting Book interface. There are five Artisans in total:

- ⊙ **Lance (Woodworker):** can craft weapons, and consumables.

- ⊙ **Oliver & Corinne (Innkeepers):** can craft food and alcohol.

- ⊙ **Big Dave (Blacksmith):** can craft weapons, metalwork, war supplies, consumables and inventions.

- ⊙ **Lyle White (Doctor):** can craft medication.

- ⊙ **Ellen (Tailor):** can craft capacity upgrades (such as pouches) and clothing.

**Harvesters** are people who grow or gather resources. You can then buy these resources from them via the Accounting Book. There are four Harvesters in total:

- ⊙ **Godfrey & Terry (Lumberers):** provide Forest products.

- ⊙ **Warren & Prudence (Farmers):** provide Farm products.

- ⊙ **Myriam (Huntress):** provides Hunting products and Herbs.

- ⊙ **Norris (Miner):** provides Minerals.

All workers can gain levels that facilitate access to better resources or more advanced crafting possibilities. They level up each time you complete one of their respective events or missions (see page 193 for details), which can only be done sequentially. The following diagram shows the unlock conditions for each of these side quests, with arrows representing when a completed mission unlocks a new one.

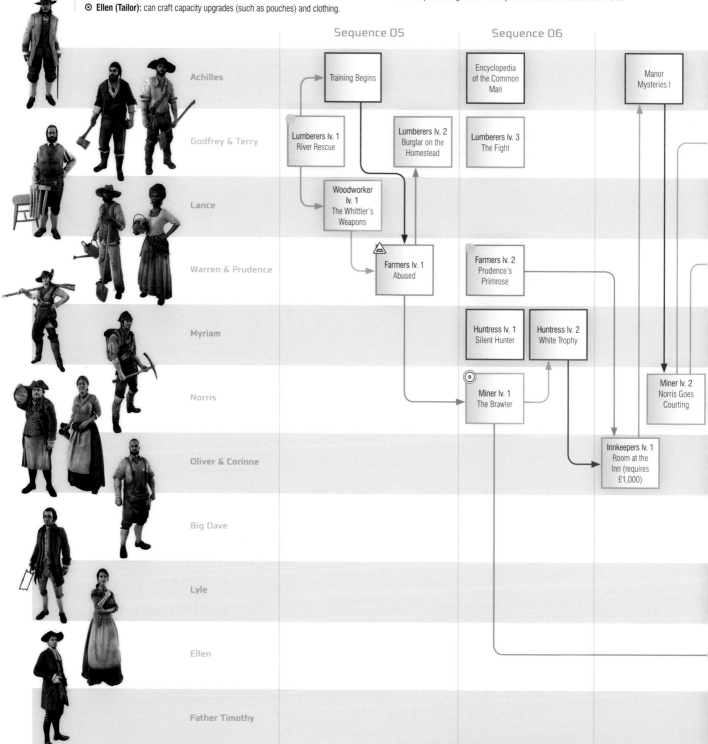

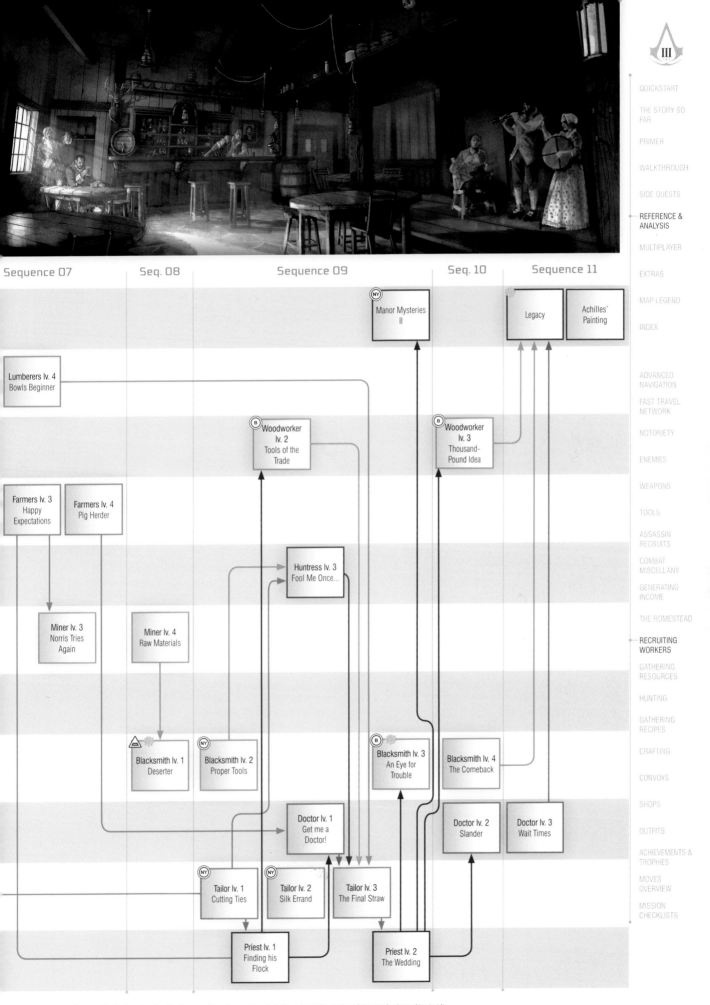

III

QUICKSTART

THE STORY SO FAR

PRIMER

WALKTHROUGH

SIDE QUESTS

REFERENCE & ANALYSIS

MULTIPLAYER

EXTRAS

MAP LEGEND

INDEX

ADVANCED NAVIGATION

FAST TRAVEL NETWORK

NOTORIETY

ENEMIES

WEAPONS

TOOLS

ASSASSIN RECRUITS

COMBAT MISCELLANY

GENERATING INCOME

THE HOMESTEAD

RECRUITING WORKERS

GATHERING RESOURCES

HUNTING

GATHERING RECIPES

CRAFTING

CONVOYS

SHOPS

OUTFITS

ACHIEVEMENTS & TROPHIES

MOVES OVERVIEW

MISSION CHECKLISTS

Note that you do not need to complete the Encyclopedia of the Common Man side quest to unlock Manor Mysteries at a later date: you simply need to start it.

## GATHERING RESOURCES

There are a wide variety of ways to gather resources, though some are markedly more efficient than others.

 Looting & Pickpocketing

You can obtain resources by pickpocketing civilians or guards. Every viable target can be pickpocketed at least twice. With each "lift" you perform on the same individual, the probability that they will react and cause a commotion will increase – unless you take steps to avoid discovery, such as Blending between attempts.

The items that you obtain depend on the class of the individual you target. With civilians, the quality of potential rewards is determined by the individual's wealth, which can be interpreted by their attire; rags for the poor, regalia for the rich. Naturally, guards are risky pickpocket targets and will react with violence if they catch Connor in the act. Potential hostiles only yield refills for Connor's consumables and small sums of cash; you can only obtain resources and crafted items from civilians.

The order in which you obtain loot is randomized: every time you perform a successful pickpocket, you can receive applicable rewards detailed in the accompanying table, in any order.

Which items you receive by looting dead or incapacitated NPCs is governed by the same rules as pickpocketing, though the direct prohibition on killing civilians means that this usually only applies to guards. However, there are occasional scripted instances where you can loot dead civilians, and occasions where firing lines, grenade volleys and general attacks performed by enemies can lead to the death of innocent bystanders.

### PICKPOCKETING REWARDS

| VICTIM | POSSIBLE REWARD #1 | POSSIBLE REWARD #2 | POSSIBLE REWARD #3 | POSSIBLE REWARD #4 |
|---|---|---|---|---|
| Civilian: Poor | One resource from "Group 1" | One resource from "Group 1" | £1-5 (50% chance) | - |
| Civilian: Medium | £8-15 | One resource from "Group 2" | £8-15 (50% chance) | - |
| Civilian: Rich | £8-15 | One resource from "Group 3" | £30-50 | Crafted item (50% chance) |
| Guards | Consumable | Cartridges (x3) | £8-15 | Cartridges (x3) |

### REWARD CATEGORIES

| "GROUP 1" RESOURCES | "GROUP 2" RESOURCES | "GROUP 3" RESOURCES | CRAFTED ITEMS | CONSUMABLES |
|---|---|---|---|---|
| Chicken Feathers, Charcoal, Oak Bark, Sand | Beeswax, Butter, Fresh Water, Milk, Bee Balm, Catnip, Lavender, Sage, Snakeroot, Clay | Apples, Honey, Eggs, Caraway, Rosemary, Roses, Glass Bottles, Flax, Hog Lard, Vegetables, Wheat, Madder, Barley, Rye, Wool, Salt | Stomach Ache Medicine, Snakebite Medicine, Hair Accessory, Paper, Digestive Tonic, All-Purpose Remedy, Deer Jerky, Cough Syrup, Bread, Ciders, Eye Drops, Toy Dolls, Cold Medicine, Skin Irritation Medicine, Ales, Spirits, Golden Rings, Tea, Buttons, Soap, Pomade | Smoke Bomb, Rope Dart, Arrows (x6), Trip Mine, Poisoned Dart |

Once you recruit the four available Harvesters (see page 238), you can buy the resources they produce. By completing their related side quests, you can increase their level – and, by doing so, gain access to new resources.

To purchase Harvester-produced resources, use the Stockpile entry in the Accounting Book. Connor can have a maximum of ten units of each item in his Stockpile at any given time (which is kept separate from his personal inventory). There is also a "cooldown" system for purchases made from Harvesters. With every unit that Connor purchases, you must wait approximately two minutes per item for the Harvester to generate replacement stock. Purchase ten valuable Beaver Pelts to immediately load onto Convoys, for example, and you must wait twenty minutes to purchase a full ten additional units.

QUICKSTART

THE STORY SO FAR

PRIMER

WALKTHROUGH

SIDE QUESTS

REFERENCE & ANALYSIS

MULTIPLAYER

EXTRAS

MAP LEGEND

INDEX

ADVANCED NAVIGATION

FAST TRAVEL NETWORK

NOTORIETY

ENEMIES

WEAPONS

TOOLS

ASSASSIN RECRUITS

COMBAT MISCELLANY

GENERATING INCOME

THE HOMESTEAD

RECRUITING WORKERS

GATHERING RESOURCES

HUNTING

GATHERING RECIPES

CRAFTING

CONVOYS

SHOPS

OUTFITS

ACHIEVEMENTS & TROPHIES

MOVES OVERVIEW

MISSION CHECKLISTS

## HARVESTER-PRODUCED RESOURCES

| CATEGORY | LEVEL | RESOURCE | PRICE (£) |
|---|---|---|---|
| **Farm Products (Farmer)** | 1 | Beeswax | 2 |
| | | Eggs | 5 |
| | | Honey | 5 |
| | | Milk | 4 |
| | 2 | Apples | 6 |
| | | Fresh Water | 5 |
| | | Vegetables | 8 |
| | | Wool | 10 |
| | 3 | Cow Hide | 15 |
| | | Pork | 17 |
| | | Poultry Meat | 16 |
| | 4 | Barley | 25 |
| | | Flax | 27 |
| | | Rye | 30 |
| | | Wheat | 24 |
| **Forest (Lumberer)** | 1 | Charcoal | 5 |
| | | Oak Bark | 3 |
| | | Oak Lumber | 8 |
| | 2 | Ash Lumber | 12 |
| | | Kindling | 5 |
| | | Walnut Lumber | 10 |
| | 3 | Pine Lumber | 15 |
| | | Spruce Lumber | 16 |
| | 4 | Hickory Lumber | 30 |
| | | Maple Lumber | 27 |
| | | Rosewood Lumber | 32 |
| **Herbs (Huntress)** | 1 | Catnip | 3 |
| | | Snakeroot | 5 |
| | 2 | Rosemary | 7 |
| | | St John's Wort | 9 |
| | 3 | Madder | 9 |

| CATEGORY | LEVEL | RESOURCE | PRICE (£) |
|---|---|---|---|
| **Hunting (Huntress)** | 1 | Beaver Pelt | 160 |
| | | Deer Pelt | 120 |
| | | Hare Meat | 20 |
| | | Hare Pelt | 30 |
| | 2 | Fox Pelt | 100 |
| | 3 | Bear Pelt | 240 |
| | | Wolf Pelt | 130 |
| **Minerals (Miner)** | 1 | Clay | 8 |
| | | Iron Ore | 12 |
| | | Sand | 3 |
| | 2 | Copper Ore | 15 |
| | | Limestone | 10 |
| | | Rock Salts | 8 |
| | 3 | Lead Ore | 16 |
| | | Sulfur | 22 |
| | 4 | Gold Ore | 35 |
| | | Silver Ore | 32 |

## Completing Assassins Guild Contracts

As you complete Liberation missions (see page 154), you obtain Assassin recruits that you can send on Contracts throughout the North American colonies (see page 162).

Each contract that your recruits successfully complete furnishes you with certain rewards, which are revealed in advance. Considering the time it takes to complete a contract, this is not an efficient way to gather resources. However, the cumulative sum of items that you will obtain while completing this metagame is not inconsiderable. If you ensure that you have Assassins engaged in missions while you attend to other activities from Sequence 06 onwards, this will help to increase your total resources available for crafting and trade.

Hunting

The hunting map (press ◁/SELECT to bring up the main map, then use L to select the appropriate entry) shows the various hunting regions of the Frontier, each of which is frequented by four indigenous species. These are represented by icons in the top-right corner of the screen; those that you have yet to encounter are marked by a paw print with a question mark (🐾). The Davenport Homestead counts as a single hunting region, and features seven creatures in total.

## HUNTING REGIONS

| NAME | ANIMALS | |
|---|---|---|
| Black Creek | | Bobcat, Elk, Hare, Beaver |
| Kanièn:keh | | Fox, Deer, Hare, Cougar |
| John's Town | | Bear, Fox, Elk, Hare |
| Valley Forge | | Elk, Hare, Raccoon, Beaver |
| Concord | | Raccoon, Hare, Beaver, Deer |
| Monmouth | | Hare, Raccoon, Elk, Fox |
| Davenport Homestead | | Elk, Deer, Fox, Beaver, Raccoon, Wolf, Hare |
| Diamond Basin | | Deer, Wolf, Cougar, Beaver |
| Great Piece Hills | | Bobcat, Hare, Wolf, Elk |
| Packanack | | Bear, Bobcat, Hare, Beaver |
| Scotch Plains | | Raccoon, Deer, Hare, Cougar |
| Troy's Wood | | Wolf, Hare, Deer, Elk |
| Lexington | | Hare, Raccoon, Deer, Fox |

Animals can be broadly divided into two categories: aggressive and passive.

⊙ **Aggressive animals** (primarily bears, wolves, bobcats and cougars) will stalk and attack Connor if they see him. They are represented as enemies on the mini-map. To kill them, you need to either use ranged weapons from a distance, take them by surprise with an assassination (particularly from above) or let them attack you and successfully complete the timed button-pressing minigame to kill them. The most dangerous animals (such as bears) may require longer and more involved chains of button presses to defeat, and there will be devastating consequences if you fail. Male elk may also charge and attempt to gore Connor if he startles or attacks them. Unlike natural predators, however, they will generally leave him be if a respectful distance is maintained.

⊙ **Passive animals** (such as hares and beavers) will flee the moment they see or hear Connor. To kill them, you can use a ranged weapon from a distance, a melee weapon at close range or plant snares to trap them. To lure animals to a specific position, distribute bait close to Stalking Zones or hiding places, then wait until they approach and strike from your place of concealment.

 SNARES & BAIT

Accessed via the Tool Wheel, bait and snares are employed solely for hunting. Bait is used to attract animals, which can be killed directly by Connor or caught in a pre-planted snare. You can also place snares (hold B/◎ until the meter is full) close to woodland clues in order to catch creatures. When a snare is set, wait for a notification that an animal has been caught, then hurry to retrieve the trapped animal before it escapes or is stolen.

You can refill your stock of bait and snares by crafting via an Accounting Book if you have the requisite resources and Homestead artisans, or by purchasing supplies from General Stores and Peddlers.

### Snares & Bait: Pouch Capacity & Upgrades

| NAME | CAPACITY/UPGRADE | AVAILABILITY |
|---|---|---|
| Default Bait Pouch | 10 | - |
| Default Snare Pouch | 10 | - |
| Snare Pouch Upgrade 1 | +5 | Through crafting |
| Snare Pouch Upgrade 2 | +5 | Through Uplay |

Animals slain while hunting can be skinned to obtain resources, which can be sold or used to craft new items. With practice, it's a highly lucrative diversion. Though securing the services of the Huntress at the Homestead will enable you to purchase a selection of animal products directly, there are certain animals that only Connor can kill and skin.

While hunting is not a particularly complicated activity, the following tips will nonetheless be of great service:

⊙ To increase the spawn rate of animals in a location, look for clues in Eagle Vision. Once you examine these, animals may appear in greater numbers, and the individual creature referenced when Connor scrutinizes the clue will be highlighted on the mini-map with the ◉ icon. Using bait near clues can attract multiple animals.

⊙ As a rule, animals will not see Connor if he is concealed within Stalking Zones, hiding places or situated out of sight in higher branches. A few animal types also have a blind spot directly behind them. As a general rule, though, most creatures will detect Connor immediately whenever he moves in the open.

⊙ Though Connor can obtain multiple resources from a single animal, the method employed to kill it determines the quality of the pelt obtained. Pristine pelts are by far the most valuable items that you will gather while hunting, while pelts damaged during the hunt – particularly if you use firearms – are worth significantly less. The cleanest kills are performed with the Hidden Blade via assassination moves. Aggressive animals slain with the Hidden Blade via the timed button press minigame always yield perfect pelts. Other suitable killing techniques are the Poison Darts, bow and snares.

⊙ One of the easiest hunting strategies is to find the start point of a tree-based free run course, examine nearby clues, then make your way to a high branch and remain still. You can then air assassinate animals that pass beneath Connor. If creatures are not moving within range, toss bait to the floor below to attract them. You can optionally set snares in suitable positions before you begin to potentially gather animal resources with maximum efficiency.

⊙ Inside hunting regions, you will find certain areas where a species is dominant and plentiful, with a remarkably high spawn rate. Try to make note of these whenever you encounter them. For example, the small island (and its surrounding area) on the far west side of the Packanack region is positively teeming with bears. Completing the Hunting Society side quests (see page 138) is a great way to discover such unique zones.

⊙ Some clues correspond to specific species: for example, there is a particular type of small bush that indicates the presence of deer. In time, you won't even need to examine them to know which animal you will find, which can enable you to move on if you are searching for a very particular type of creature.

⊙ Whenever you are travelling through the Frontier or Homestead, have the bow or Poison Darts and Hidden Blade equipped in anticipation of opportunistic kills. It's amazing how many animals will inadvertently move within range, and fast reactions can provide you with welcome bonuses.

Overall, hunting is an excellent way to gather hunting resources and generate income. It requires little investment (other than restocking Tools), it's never particularly demanding and, occasional attacks from predators and random guard encounters notwithstanding, rarely dangerous once you are accustomed to the challenges faced in the Frontier. The hunting spoils that offer the most profit when traded via convoys are the Bear Pelt and Beaver Pelt, which have a base value of £240 and £160 respectively. If you load a convoy with these items, you can make incredible profit – even at an early stage in the story. See page 249 for details.

| | HUNTING RESOURCES | | |
|---|---|---|---|
| **ICON** | **NAME** | **WEAKNESSES** | **POTENTIAL RESOURCES** |
| | Fox | Bait, snares | Fox Pelt (£100), Fox Tail (£20), Damaged Fox Pelt (£12) |
| | Bear | Bait, air assassinations | **Bear Pelt (£240)**, Bear Grease (£20), Bear Claws (£10), Damaged Bear Pelt (£40) |
| | Cougar | Bait, Poison Darts | Cougar Fangs (£10), Cougar Pelt (£90), Damaged Cougar Pelt (£4) |
| | Wolf | Bait, bow (while stalking) | Wolf Fangs (£10), Wolf Pelt (£100), Damaged Wolf Pelt (£10) |
| | Bobcat | Bait, snares, Poison Darts | Bobcat Claws (£10), Bobcat Pelt (£70), Damaged Bobcat Pelt (£4) |
| | Hare | Bait, snares, blind spot behind them | Hare Pelt (£30), Rabbit's Foot (£4), Damaged Hare Pelt (£2) |
| | Beaver | Bait, snares; they are also incredibly slow | **Beaver Pelt (£160)**, Beaver Teeth (£10), Castoreum (£30), Damaged Beaver Pelt (£12) |
| | Raccoon | Bait, snares, blind spot behind them | Raccoon Pelt (£60), Damaged Raccoon Pelt (£2) |
| | Deer | Bait, blind spot behind them | Deer Heart (£10), Deer Marrow (£4), Venison (£40), Deer Tail (£6), Deer Pelt (£120), Damaged Deer Pelt (£12) |
| | Elk | Bait, blind spot behind them, air assassinations | Elk Pelt (£140), Elk Antlers (£20), Elk Heart (£10), Elk Meat (£60), Damaged Elk Pelt (£16) |

## GATHERING RECIPES

Recipes reveal the ingredients required to craft items. There is one recipe for each of the items that can be crafted in the game, though you can also "blind craft" by using the tables in the Crafting section (see page 245) to choose the correct ingredients and artisans.

### From Treasure Chests

The most common way to obtain recipes is by opening chests, which are found in the Frontier, Boston and New York.

⊙ Chests in Boston and New York can be opened by picking their locks, unless you own a special key for the district where the chest is found. Chest keys are obtained by completing Liberation Missions (see page 154). In the Frontier, you automatically obtain a key to all regional chests at the start of Sequence 05.

⊙ General Stores sell maps that reveal specific collectibles, including chests. Once you have purchased a map, the chests will appear on your in-game main map – even in areas that you have yet to explore. If you are working on a tight budget, you can spare the expense by using our maps instead: see page 200.

### From Rewards

You can also obtain crafting recipes through main storyline progression and optional challenges.

| RECIPES: REWARDS | |
| --- | --- |
| **RECIPES** | **UNLOCK CONDITION** |
| Twin Holsters | Complete Sequence 05 |
| Consumables | Complete Sequence 03-06 |
| Small Saddle Bags | Complete Sequence 09 |
| Medium Saddle Bags | Complete Sequence 10 |
| Large Saddle Bags | Complete Sequence 12 |
| Benjamin Franklin Inventions | Complete Almanacs (see page 200) |
| Pouch Upgrades | Complete quests at the Homestead (see page 193) |

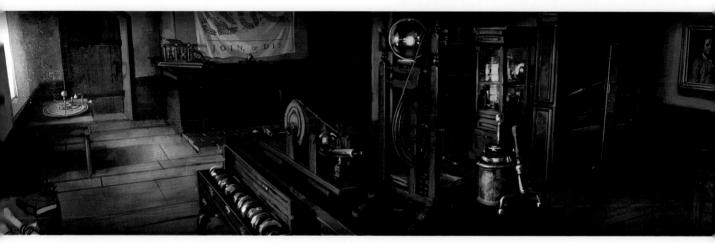

##  CRAFTING

### The Crafting Process

Crafting is accomplished via the Accounting Book interface. The "Crafting" entry of the Accounting Book features three sections:

⊙ **Recipes:** Shows the list of all recipes that you have already obtained (see page 244). If you select one, the required resources and artisans automatically appear in the appropriate slots. You can also "blind craft": that is, attempt to craft items without a recipe. However, if you attempt a combination that does not correspond to a possible recipe, the resources are lost. All items in our crafting tables except Special Items can be crafted without collecting the recipe beforehand as long as you have the required resources and suitably trained artisans.

⊙ **Artisans:** Each recipe requires the skills of one or two artisans, each at a specific minimum level. Refer to page 238 to find out how to recruit and level up each worker.

⊙ **Resources:** Resources are the physical ingredients used to create new items, and are sorted in categories. To find out how to gather or purchase resources, refer to page 240.

One you have selected a recipe, note the price in the bottom-left corner of the screen and press ◊/△ to craft a single unit of that item. As you create additional units, the price charged by the artisan will increase by steady increments. Depending on the object you are creating, there is a point where this rudimentary "supply and demand" system might seriously impact your potential profits. However, if you leave an individual item for a time, the base cost will be restored after a relatively short "cooldown" period.

### Crafted Items & Recipes

In the tables that follow, we document all crafting recipes, including the requisite artisans and resources.

⊙ **Consumables:** These are the items that appear in Connor's selection of Tools. Though they can be crafted, it is often easier (and less demanding) to replenish your stocks by looting corpses, or even by purchasing them from merchants.

⊙ **Inventions:** Once you have collected all pages from an individual Almanac (see page 200), you receive the recipe for one of Benjamin Franklin's inventions. There are no real rewards for this, though each object crafted will appear at the Manor, and crafting all inventions is required to reach 100% Synchronization.

⊙ **Special Items:** These are probably the most valuable items you can craft, and include new weapons, capacity upgrades and, to maximize your trade profits, convoy upgrades. Weapon recipes require an item called Special Iron Ingot. You can obtain seven of these by completing the Miner's quests (see page 196) and an additional five by opening a Chest behind the Manor.

⊙ **Materials:** Materials are crafted items whose main purpose is to be reused in other crafting recipes. Individually, they have very little value if you attempt to sell them via convoys. It's only once you reuse them in a second crafting recipe that they acquire their full value and enable you to make significant profit.

⊙ **Trade Items** (Alcohol, Clothing, Food, Medication, Metalwork, Miscellaneous, War Supplies, Woodworks): These items have no purpose other than to be sold using convoys to deliver them to merchants.

## CONSUMABLES

| RECIPE | INGREDIENTS | PRICE (£) |
|---|---|---|
| Arrow | Blacksmith (Lv. 1), Woodworker (Lv. 1), Iron Ore (from Miner), Kindling (from Lumberer) | 10 |
| Bait | Innkeeper (Lv. 1), Hare Meat (from Huntress or hunting), Poultry Meat (from Farmer), Vegetables (from Farmer) | 5 |
| Cartridge | Blacksmith (Lv. 1), Lead Ore (from Miner) | 15 |
| Poisoned Dart | Blacksmith (Lv. 1), Doctor (Lv. 2), Lead Ore (from Miner), Sulfur (from Miner) | 225 |
| Rope Dart | Blacksmith (Lv. 2), Tailor (Lv. 1), Cow Hide (from Farmer), Flax (from Farmer), Weapon Blades (crafted Material), | 125 |
| Smoke Bomb | Blacksmith (Lv. 3), Black Powder (crafted Material), Clay (from Miner), Dyes (crafted Material) | 50 |
| Snare | Woodworker (Lv. 2), Cow Hide (from Farmer), Kindling (from Lumberer) | 15 |
| Trip Mine | Blacksmith (Lv. 4), Black Powder (crafted Material), Clay (from Miner), Flints (crafted Material) | 150 |

## INVENTIONS

| RECIPE | INGREDIENTS |
|---|---|
| Busybody | Blacksmith (Lv. 2), Iron Ore (from Miner), Sand (from Miner) |
| Electrostatic Generator | Blacksmith (Lv. 4), Doctor (Lv. 3), Copper Ore (from Miner), Iron Ore (from Miner), Sand (from Miner) |
| Franklin Stove | Blacksmith (Lv. 3), Iron Ore (from Miner), Silver Ore (from Miner) |
| Glass Armonica | Blacksmith (Lv. 4), Charcoal (from Lumberer), Sand (from Miner) |
| Joseph Priestley Soda Apparatus | Innkeeper (Lv. 1), Fresh Water (from Farmer), Glass Bottles (crafted Material) |
| Kite and Key | Tailor (Lv. 2), Kindling (from Lumberer), Linsey-woolsey (crafted Material) |
| Leyden Jar | Blacksmith (Lv. 2), Copper Ore (from Miner), Fresh Water (from Farmer), Glass Bottles (crafted Material) |
| Orrery | Blacksmith (Lv. 1), Woodworker (Lv. 2), Copper Ore (from Miner), Rosewood Lumber (from Lumberer) |
| Watt Steam Engine | Blacksmith (Lv. 3), Fresh Water (from Farmer), Iron Ore (from Miner) |

## SPECIAL ITEMS

| RECIPE | INGREDIENTS |
|---|---|
| "Broken Sword" Knife | Blacksmith (Lv. 2), Special Iron Ingot (from Miner quest), Weapon Blades (crafted Material) |
| Cartridge Pouch 1 | Tailor (Lv. 1), Hare Pelt (from Huntress or hunting) |
| Cartridge Pouch 2 | Tailor (Lv. 2), Deer Pelt (from Huntress or hunting), Sewing Threads (crafted Material) |
| Cartridge Pouch 3 | Tailor (Lv. 3), Fox Pelt (from Huntress or hunting), Sewing Threads (crafted Material) |
| English Flintlock Pistol | Blacksmith (Lv. 2), Woodworker (Lv. 2), Flints (crafted Material), Oak Lumber (from Lumberer), Special Iron Ingot (from Miner quest) |
| French Coat Pistol | Blacksmith (Lv. 2), Flints (crafted Material), Iron Ore (from Miner), Special Iron Ingot (from Miner quest) |
| Iron Blade War Club | Blacksmith (Lv. 1), Woodworker (Lv. 2), Ash Lumber (from Lumberer), Special Iron Ingot (from Miner quest) |
| Italian Flintlock | Blacksmith (Lv. 3), Woodworker (Lv. 3), Flints (crafted Material), Maple Lumber (from Lumberer), Special Iron Ingot (from Miner quest) |
| Land Convoy | Woodworker (Lv. 1), Oak Bark (from Lumberer), Oak Lumber (from Lumberer) |
| Land Convoy Capacity Upgrade | Woodworker (Lv. 1), Kindling (from Lumberer), Pine Lumber (from Lumberer) |
| Lincoln's Sword (Replica) | Blacksmith (Lv. 4), Silver Ore (from Miner), Special Iron Ingot (from Miner quest) |
| Naval Axe | Blacksmith (Lv. 3), Woodworker (Lv. 3), Hickory Lumber (from Lumberer), Special Iron Ingot (from Miner quest) |
| Naval Convoy | Woodworker (Lv. 2), Bear Grease (from hunting), Oak Bark (from Lumberer), Spruce Lumber (from Lumberer) |
| Naval Convoy Capacity Upgrade | Woodworker (Lv. 3), Kindling (from Lumberer), Maple Lumber (from Lumberer) |
| Naval Duckfoot | Blacksmith (Lv. 3), Flints (crafted Material), Lead Ore (from Miner), Special Iron Ingot (from Miner quest) |
| Poison Dart Pouch Upgrade | Tailor (Lv. 1), Beaver Pelt (from Huntress or hunting), Hare Pelt (from Huntress or hunting), Sewing Threads (crafted Material) |
| Quiver 1 | Tailor (Lv. 1), Woodworker (Lv. 2), Ash Lumber (from Lumberer), Cow Hide (from Farmer) |
| Rope Dart Pouch 1 | Tailor (Lv. 1), Hare Pelt (from Huntress or hunting), Sewing Threads (crafted Material) |
| Royal Navy Sea Service Flintlock | Blacksmith (Lv. 4), Flints (crafted Material), Gold Ore (from Miner), Special Iron Ingot (from Miner quest) |
| Royal Pistol | Blacksmith (Lv. 3), Flints (crafted Material), Silver Ore (from Miner), Special Iron Ingot (from Miner quest) |
| Saddle Bags Large | Blacksmith (Lv. 4), Tailor (Lv. 3), Gold Ore (from Miner), Sewing Threads (crafted Material) |
| Saddle Bags Medium | Blacksmith (Lv. 4), Tailor (Lv. 3), Sewing Threads (crafted Material), Silver Ore (from Miner) |
| Saddle Bags Small | Blacksmith (Lv. 4), Tailor (Lv. 3), Copper Ore (from Miner), Sewing Threads (crafted Material) |
| Smoke Bomb Pouch Upgrade | Tailor (Lv. 1), Cow Hide (from Farmer), Sewing Threads (crafted Material) |
| Snare Pouch 1 | Tailor (Lv. 1), Sewing Threads (crafted Material), Wolf Pelt (from Huntress or hunting) |
| Trip Mine Pouch 1 | Tailor (Lv. 2), Cow Hide (from Farmer), Sewing Threads (crafted Material), Fox Pelt (from Huntress or hunting) |
| Twin Holsters | Tailor (Lv. 2), Rosewood Lumber (from Lumberer), Wolf Pelt (from Huntress or hunting) |
| War Tomahawk | Blacksmith (Lv. 2), Special Iron Ingot (from Miner quest) |
| Washington's Battle Sword (Replica) | Blacksmith (Lv. 4), Silver Ore (from Miner), Special Iron Ingot (from Miner quest) |

## MATERIALS

| RECIPE | INGREDIENTS | PRICE (£) |
|---|---|---|
| Barrels | Woodworker (Lv. 1), Oak Lumber (from Lumberer) | 35 |
| Belt Buckles | Blacksmith (Lv. 2), Copper Ore (from Miner) | 40 |
| Black Powder | Blacksmith (Lv. 3), Lead Ore (from Miner), Rock Salt (from Miner), Sulfur (from Miner) | 75 |
| Buttons | Woodworker (Lv. 2), Hickory Lumber (from Lumberer) | 55 |

## MATERIALS (CONTINUED)

| | | |
|---|---|---|
| Candles | Tailor (Lv. 1), Beeswax (from Farmer) | 27 |
| Disinfectant | Doctor (Lv. 1), Apples (from Farmer) | 31 |
| Dyes | Tailor (Lv. 2), Vegetables (from Farmer) | 35 |
| Flints | Blacksmith (Lv. 2), Iron Ore (from Miner), Lead Ore (from Miner), Limestone (from Miner) | 65 |
| Flour | Innkeeper (Lv. 1), Wheat (from Farmer) | 50 |
| Glass Bottles | Blacksmith (Lv. 1), Sand (from Miner) | 30 |
| Inks | Tailor (Lv. 2), Woodworker (Lv. 3), Madder (from Huntress) | 35 |
| Linsey-woolsey | Tailor (Lv. 1), Flax (from Farmer), Wool (from Farmer) | 65 |
| Nails | Blacksmith (Lv. 1), Iron Ore (from Miner) | 40 |
| Paper | Tailor (Lv. 1), Woodworker (Lv. 2), Flax (from Farmer), Oak Bark (from Lumberer) | 55 |
| Sewing Threads | Tailor (Lv. 1), Wool (from Farmer) | 35 |
| Weapon Blades | Blacksmith (Lv. 2), Charcoal (from Lumberer), Iron Ore (from Miner) | 45 |
| Weapon Handles | Woodworker (Lv. 2), Maple Lumber (from Lumberer) | 55 |

## ALCOHOL

| RECIPE | INGREDIENTS | PRICE (£) |
|---|---|---|
| Ales | Innkeeper (Lv. 1), Barley (from Farmer), Barrels (crafted Material) | 125 |
| Ciders | Innkeeper (Lv. 1), Apples (from Farmer), Barrels (crafted Material) | 106 |
| Spirits | Innkeeper (Lv. 1), Barley (from Farmer), Barrels (crafted Material), Rye (from Farmer) | 155 |

## CLOTHING

| RECIPE | INGREDIENTS | PRICE (£) |
|---|---|---|
| Belts | Tailor (Lv. 1), Belt Buckles (crafted Material), Cow Hide (from Farmer) | 120 |
| Boots | Tailor (Lv. 2), Belt Buckles (crafted Material), Fox Pelt (from Huntress or hunting) | 170 |
| Clothing | Tailor (Lv. 1), Buttons (crafted Material), Linsey-woolsey (crafted Material) | 210 |
| Coonskin Hat | Tailor (Lv. 2), Raccoon Pelt (from hunting), Sewing Threads (crafted Material) | 145 |
| Fine Clothing | Tailor (Lv. 3), Buttons (crafted Material), Linsey-woolsey (crafted Material), Wolf Pelt (from Huntress or hunting) | 305 |
| Fine Hats | Tailor (Lv. 3), Beaver Pelt (from Huntress or hunting), Hare Pelt (from Huntress or hunting) | 165 |
| Fine Shoes | Tailor (Lv. 3), Beaver Pelt (from Huntress or hunting), Belt Buckles (crafted Material) | 215 |
| Fox Tail Scarf | Tailor (Lv. 2), Fox Tail (from hunting), Sewing Threads (crafted Material) | 125 |
| Hats | Tailor (Lv. 2), Beaver Pelt (from Huntress or hunting) | 135 |
| Moccasins | Tailor (Lv. 2), Elk Pelt (from hunting), Sewing Threads (crafted Material) | 185 |
| Quilts | Tailor (Lv. 2), Dyes (crafted Material), Linsey-woolsey (crafted Material), Sewing Threads (crafted Material) | 265 |
| Shoes | Tailor (Lv. 1), Belt Buckles (crafted Material), Hare Pelt (from Huntress or hunting) | 120 |
| Tool Belts | Tailor (Lv. 2), Woodworker (Lv. 1), Belt Buckles (crafted Material), Cow Hide (from Farmer), Nails (crafted Material) | 175 |
| Wigs | Tailor (Lv. 2), Dyes (crafted Material), Sewing Threads (crafted Material), Wool (from Farmer) | 185 |

## FOOD

| RECIPE | INGREDIENTS | PRICE (£) |
|---|---|---|
| Bread | Innkeeper (Lv. 1), Eggs (from Farmer), Flour (crafted Material), Milk (from Farmer) | 124 |
| Deer Jerky | Innkeeper (Lv. 1), Rock Salt (from Miner), Venison (from hunting) | 120 |
| Deer Marrow Soup | Innkeeper (Lv. 1), Deer Marrow (from hunting), Fresh Water (from Farmer), Vegetables (from Farmer) | 55 |
| Jugged Hare | Innkeeper (Lv. 1), Hare Meat (from Huntress or hunting), Vegetables (from Farmer) | 58 |
| Meat Pies | Innkeeper (Lv. 1), Flour (crafted Material), Hare Meat (from Huntress or hunting), Pork (from Farmer) | 142 |
| Salt | Innkeeper (Lv. 1), Rock Salt (from Miner) | 35 |
| Salted Elk Meat | Innkeeper (Lv. 1), Elk Meat (from hunting), Rock Salt (from Miner) | 130 |
| Shepherd's Pie | Innkeeper (Lv. 1), Pork (from Farmer), Poultry Meat (from Farmer), Vegetables (from Farmer) | 81 |
| Smoked Elk Meat | Innkeeper (Lv. 1), Elk Meat (from hunting), Maple Lumber (from Lumberer) | 97 |
| Tea | Innkeeper (Lv. 1), Honey (from Farmer), Rosemary (from Huntress) | 52 |
| Venison Heart | Innkeeper (Lv. 1), Deer Heart (from hunting), Vegetables (from Farmer) | 53 |

## MEDICATION

| RECIPE | INGREDIENTS | PRICE (£) |
|---|---|---|
| All-Purpose Remedy | Doctor (Lv. 2), Glass Bottles (crafted Material), St John's Wort (from Huntress) | 119 |
| Bandages | Doctor (Lv. 1), Tailor (Lv. 1), Disinfectant (crafted Material), Linsey-woolsey (crafted Material) | 226 |
| Cold Medicine | Doctor (Lv. 1), Barley (from Farmer), Catnip (from Huntress), Glass Bottles (crafted Material) | 123 |
| Cough Syrup | Doctor (Lv. 2), Glass Bottles (crafted Material), Honey (from Farmer) | 115 |
| Daffy's Elixir | Doctor (Lv. 2), Barley (from Farmer), Glass Bottles (crafted Material), Rye (from Farmer) | 165 |
| Digestive Tonic | Doctor (Lv. 2), Flax (from Farmer), Glass Bottles (crafted Material) | 137 |
| Eye Drops | Doctor (Lv. 3), Glass Bottles (crafted Material), Rosemary (from Huntress) | 132 |

## MEDICATION (CONTINUED)

| Hysteria Medicine | Doctor (Lv. 4), Castoreum (from hunting), Glass Bottles (crafted Material) | 155 |
|---|---|---|
| Insect Repellent | Doctor (Lv. 1), Catnip (from Huntress), Glass Bottles (crafted Material) | 98 |
| Medical Charts | Doctor (Lv. 4), Inks (crafted Material), Paper (crafted Material) | 225 |
| Medical Equipment | Blacksmith (Lv. 2), Doctor (Lv. 4), Disinfectant (crafted Material), Iron Ore (from Miner) | 208 |
| Poisons | Doctor (Lv. 2), Glass Bottles (crafted Material), Sulfur (from Miner) | 132 |
| Pomade | Doctor (Lv. 1), Bear Grease (from hunting), Deer Marrow (from hunting) | 107 |
| Skin Irritation Remedy | Doctor (Lv. 3), Glass Bottles (crafted Material), Rosemary (from Huntress), St John's Wort (from Huntress) | 141 |
| Snakebite Antidote | Doctor (Lv. 2), Glass Bottles (crafted Material), Snakeroot (from Huntress) | 115 |
| Soap | Innkeeper (Lv. 1), Bear Grease (from hunting), Charcoal (from Lumberer), Rosemary (from Huntress) | 62 |
| Stiffness Remedy | Doctor (Lv. 3), Elk Antlers (from hunting), Elk Heart (from hunting) | 85 |
| Stomachache Medicine | Doctor (Lv. 1), Catnip (from Huntress), Charcoal (from Lumberer), Glass Bottles (crafted Material) | 103 |

## METALWORK

| RECIPE | INGREDIENTS | PRICE (£) |
|---|---|---|
| Brass Rings | Blacksmith (Lv. 3), Copper Ore (from Miner), Fresh Water (From Farmer) | 85 |
| Golden Rings | Blacksmith (Lv. 4), Gold Ore (from Miner) | 120 |
| Lanterns | Blacksmith (Lv. 2), Tailor (Lv. 1), Candles (crafted Material), Iron Ore (from Miner) | 159 |
| Mining Tools | Blacksmith (Lv. 1), Woodworker (Lv. 1), Iron Ore (from Miner), Maple Lumber (from Lumberer) | 119 |
| Plows | Blacksmith (Lv. 1), Woodworker (Lv. 1), Iron Ore (from Miner), Walnut Lumber (from Lumberer) | 102 |
| Silver Rings | Blacksmith (Lv. 3), Silver Ore (from Miner) | 102 |
| Woodworking Tools | Blacksmith (Lv. 1), Woodworker (Lv. 1), Hickory Lumber (from Lumberer), Iron Ore (from Miner) | 122 |

## MISCELLANEOUS

| RECIPE | INGREDIENTS | PRICE (£) |
|---|---|---|
| Bear Pendant | Blacksmith (Lv. 4), Tailor (Lv. 3), Bear Claws (from hunting), Elk Pelt (from hunting), Gold Ore (from Miner) | 260 |
| Bear Rugs | Tailor (Lv. 3), Bear Pelt (from Huntress or hunting) | 190 |
| Beaver Tooth Knife | Woodworker (Lv. 1), Ash Lumber (from Lumberer), Beaver Teeth (from hunting) | 57 |
| Blankets | Tailor (Lv. 2), Linsey-woolsey (crafted Material) | 145 |
| Bobcat Pendant | Blacksmith (Lv. 3), Bobcat Claws (from hunting), Copper Ore (from Miner) | 90 |
| Bricks | Woodworker (Lv. 1), Clay (from Miner) | 48 |
| Cougar Pendant | Blacksmith (Lv. 3), Copper Ore (from Miner), Cougar Fangs (from hunting) | 90 |
| Glass Windows | Blacksmith (Lv. 1), Woodworker (Lv. 2), Pine Lumber (from Lumberer), Sand (from Miner) | 113 |
| Hair Accessory | Tailor (Lv. 1), Deer Tail (from hunting), Sewing Threads (crafted Material) | 103 |
| Mounted Elk Antlers | Woodworker (Lv. 2), Beeswax (from Farmer), Elk Antlers (from hunting), Spruce Lumber (from Lumberer) | 100 |
| Playing Cards | Innkeeper (Lv. 1), Dyes (crafted Material), Paper (crafted Material) | 180 |
| Rabbit Foot Charm | Blacksmith (Lv. 3), Rabbit's Foot (from hunting), Silver Ore (from Miner) | 104 |
| Toy Dolls | Tailor (Lv. 2), Dyes (crafted Material), Wool (from Farmer) | 125 |
| Water Drum | Woodworker (Lv. 3), Ash Lumber (from Lumberer), Bear Grease (from hunting), Elk Pelt (from hunting) | 162 |
| Wolf Pendant | Blacksmith (Lv. 4), Tailor (Lv. 2), Elk Pelt (from hunting), Silver Ore (from Miner), Wolf Fangs (from hunting) | 210 |

## WAR SUPPLIES

| RECIPE | INGREDIENTS | PRICE (£) |
|---|---|---|
| Ammunition | Blacksmith (Lv. 3), Black Powder (crafted Material), Iron Ore (from Miner) | 182 |
| Artillery | Blacksmith (Lv. 4), Woodworker (Lv. 3), Flints (crafted Material), Iron Ore (from Miner), Oak Lumber (from Lumberer) | 260 |
| Firearms | Blacksmith (Lv. 3), Flints (crafted Material), Iron Ore (from Miner), Weapon Handles (crafted Material) | 252 |
| Horseshoes | Blacksmith (Lv. 1), Iron Ore (from Miner), Nails (crafted Material) | 117 |
| Officer Swords | Blacksmith (Lv. 4), Silver Ore (from Miner), Weapon Blades (crafted Material), Weapon Handles (crafted Material) | 267 |
| Saddles | Tailor (Lv. 3), Beaver Pelt (from Huntress or hunting), Cow Hide (from Farmer) | 165 |
| Ship Masts | Woodworker (Lv. 1), Spruce Lumber (from Lumberer) | 56 |
| Ship Sails | Tailor (Lv. 2), Linsey-woolsey (crafted Material), Sewing Threads (crafted Material) | 205 |
| Swords | Blacksmith (Lv. 3), Weapon Blades (crafted Material), Weapon Handles (crafted Material) | 220 |

## WOODWORKS

| RECIPE | INGREDIENTS | PRICE (£) |
|---|---|---|
| Buckets | Woodworker (Lv. 1), Pine Lumber (from Lumberer) | 55 |
| Crates | Woodworker (Lv. 1), Walnut Lumber (from Lumberer) | 50 |
| Fine Furniture | Woodworker (Lv. 3), Hickory Lumber (from Lumberer), Pine Lumber (from Lumberer), Walnut Lumber (from Lumberer) | 125 |
| Fishing Rods | Woodworker (Lv. 1), Sewing Threads (crafted Material), Spruce Lumber (from Lumberer) | 116 |
| Furniture | Woodworker (Lv. 2), Pine Lumber (from Lumberer), Walnut Lumber (from Lumberer) | 80 |
| Torches | Blacksmith (Lv. 3), Woodworker (Lv. 1), Black Powder (crafted Material), Pine Lumber (from Lumberer) | 208 |

## Optimal Crafting Strategy

The following table offers a selection of the most profitable trade items that you can craft in each Sequence. This takes into account the fact that most Homestead workers only gain levels as you progress through the Sequences, enabling you to craft more elaborate items gradually as you advance in the main storyline.

The profits are calculated with a mathematical formula that factors in the cost of the resources, the artisan fees, as well as the added value contributed by the labors of your artisans – all of which is computed to provide you with the best returns on investment.

To make the most of this table, cross-reference it with the "Merchant Multipliers" table in the section that follows: this will allow you to identify which merchants offer the best multipliers during each Sequence. Doing so will enable you to optimize your profit from the crafting and convoy systems.

### TRADE ITEMS: BEST RETURNS PER SEQUENCE

| | |
|---|---|
| **Sequence 05** | ▪ Crates (Woodworks) |
| **Sequence 06** | ▪ Bricks (Miscellaneous) |
| **Sequence 07** | ▪ Ales (Alcohol) <br> ▪ Salted Elk Meat (Food) <br> ▪ Bread (Food) |
| **Sequence 08** | ▪ Ales (Alcohol) <br> ▪ Salted Elk Meat (Food) <br> ▪ Bread (Food) |
| **Sequence 09** | ▪ Fine Clothing (Clothing) <br> ▪ Quilts (Clothing) <br> ▪ Swords (War Supplies) |
| **Sequence 10** | ▪ Artillery (War Supplies) <br> ▪ Officer Swords (War Supplies) <br> ▪ Bear Pendant (Miscellaneous) |
| **Sequence 11** | ▪ Artillery (War Supplies) <br> ▪ Medical Equipment (Medication) |
| **Sequence 12** | ▪ Artillery (War Supplies) <br> ▪ Medical Equipment (Medication) |

## Crafting: Summary

If you are at all confused by the relative complexity of the crafting system, here is a concise summary that offers a recap of the most important points we have discussed so far:

1. Crafting requires resources, raw ingredients that you can gather by hunting with Connor (for hunting resources only), or by purchasing them from your Harvesters at the Homestead (see page 240 for further details). You will also obtain resources from other activities, but these do not guarantee a regular supply.

2. Crafting requires recipes, which you can collect from chests and as rewards (see page 244), or recreate by consulting our tables on page 245.

3. Finally, crafting requires artisans, who will transform your resources into trade items. Each artisan advances in level as you complete their related side quests (see page 193), which enables you to craft more elaborate items.

4. Once you have all of the required ingredients, you can craft using the Accounting Book interface. The most lucrative goods to craft are trade items, which can be sold via convoys to make big profits. Crafting Special Items will offer you new weapons and capacity upgrades – and, to increase the profitability of trading, additional convoys and convoy upgrades. Finally, crafting is the only way to create inventions that are required to reach 100% Synchronization. See page 245 for details.

5. Never sell crafted items from the Materials category: the returns are negligible, as they are meant to be crafted a second time as part of more complex recipes.

6. Some trade items provide better returns on investment than others. Always try to craft the most lucrative items first (see the "Trade Items: Best Returns per Sequence" table), and stop crafting specific items when the gradual artisan cost increments become too expensive and reduce your potential profits (see page 244).

# CONVOYS

III

QUICKSTART

THE STORY SO FAR

PRIMER

WALKTHROUGH

SIDE QUESTS

REFERENCE & ANALYSIS

MULTIPLAYER

EXTRAS

MAP LEGEND

INDEX

## Main Features

Convoys enable you to sell your resources and crafted items via land and, later, naval routes to accumulate vast profits thanks to the wondrous effect of "multipliers".

To send a convoy, simply use the Trading entry of the Accounting Book. Every convoy features a default number of slots for cargo, which can each be filled with a single unit of an item (for example, Apples). You can craft additional convoys, as well as capacity upgrades for all convoys (both land and naval) to increase the amount of slots available. These upgrades belong to the Special Items crafting category (see page 245). Try to unlock all convoys and capacity upgrades as soon as you can: more convoys and greater quantities of cargo per convoy will enable you to increase your returns on each trade trip.

What makes convoys quite ridiculously profitable is that they enable you to sell your wares at a price point enhanced by multipliers. For obvious reasons, it is much more rewarding to sell items of high value (in other words, trade items – see page 235), rather than cheap raw materials such as basic resources. For example, a convoy filled with resources such as Walnut Lumber (£10 per unit) will net you very little, whereas a convoy filled with Crates (a crafted trade item made of Walnut Lumber) has a base value of £50. Six convoy slots filled with Walnut Lumber add up to a mere £60 (6x10), whereas six slots filled with Crates have a base value of £300 (6x50). Factor in a multiplier of 3 or 4, and you can see how huge the difference can be – hundreds, or even thousands of pounds per convoy.

However, it's worth noting that certain animal pelts that you can acquire by hunting (or even purchase from the Huntress) actually offer miraculous returns when traded via convoys. Unlike trade items (which require you to pay for resources and artisan fees), spoils that you acquire through hunting are free of charge, thus enabling you to secure maximum profits. While all unspoiled animal skins offer a fine return, the Beaver Pelt and Bear Pelt are the most valuable goods to hunt. With a base value of £160 and £240 respectively, they are extremely lucrative items.

## Merchant Multipliers

Merchant multipliers are determined by seasonal conditions that represent the law of supply and demand, and are only available when you trade with them via convoys. Essentially, every merchant will buy items from you with a multiplier that varies depending on your current Sequence. A "x3" multiplier means that the merchant will buy the goods for three times the standard shop price.

To make the best possible profits, therefore, your goal should always be to trade with merchants that offer the best multipliers in each Sequence. Of course, the more convoys and capacity upgrades you unlock through crafting, the greater your profits will be.

Note that most merchants apply lower multipliers to certain categories of items. For that reason, you should avoid selling them the types of goods referenced in the "Devaluated Item Categories" column.

### MERCHANT MULTIPLIERS

| MERCHANT | MULTIPLIER PER SEQUENCE | | | | | | | | DEVALUATED ITEM CATEGORIES |
|---|---|---|---|---|---|---|---|---|---|
| | 05 | 06 | 07 | 08 | 09 | 10 | 11 | 12 | |
| **Boston: Hancock's Store No. 5** | x3.8 | x3.7 | x3 | x3 | x3.5 | x3 | x2.8 | x3.5 | Alcohol, War Supplies, Metalwork |
| **Boston: Elizabeth Murray's Fineries** | x3.4 | x3.5 | x3.2 | x3.4 | x3.2 | x3.3 | x3 | x3.6 | Woodwork, Alcohol, Clothing |
| **Boston: Child's Still House & Dry Goods** | x4.5 | x3.3 | x3.8 | x3.3 | x2.8 | x3.5 | x3.5 | x3.4 | Medication, Food, Miscellaneous |
| **New York: Rhinelander's Sugars** | - | - | - | x3.8 | x4 | x4.7 | x4.5 | x5.2 | Medication, Food |
| **New York : De Lancey's Imports & Goods** | - | - | - | x4 | x4.2 | x4 | x4.6 | x5 | Woodwork, War Supplies, Metalwork |
| **New York : Van Brugh's Spices** | - | - | - | x2.7 | x3.8 | x3.2 | x3.6 | x4.8 | Alcohol, Food |
| **Frontier : The Walking Haberdashery** | x3 | x4 | x3.6 | x3 | x3.5 | x4.3 | x3.8 | x4.3 | Food, Metalwork, Clothing |
| **Frontier : The Milliner's Wares** | x3 | x3.5 | x3.5 | x3.5 | x3 | x4.5 | x3.4 | x4.2 | Medication, War Supplies, Metalwork |
| **Frontier : Murdoch's Barter** | x3 | x3.8 | x3.2 | x3 | x3.5 | x3.1 | x3.3 | x4.4 | Woodwork, War Supplies, Alcohol, Miscellaneous |
| **Louisbourg** | - | - | - | - | x5.2 | x4.8 | x4.6 | x6.1 | Medication, War Supplies, Metalwork |
| **The Bahamas** | - | - | - | - | x5.1 | x4.7 | x5.2 | x6 | Woodwork, Clothing, Alcohol, Food |
| **Saint-Augustine** | - | - | - | - | x4.8 | x4.4 | x4.8 | x6.5 | Clothing, War Supplies |
| **Virgin Islands** | - | - | - | - | x4.7 | x5.2 | x5.3 | x6.3 | Food, Alcohol, Miscellaneous |

LAND CONVOY — NAVAL CONVOY

To fully determine the most efficient way to make profits with convoys, you need to take three additional factors into account. The first is the total travel time, which determines how long it takes for a convoy to reach its destination, which triggers your immediate payment and enables you to restock the convoy for another trip. The first merchant you choose to trade with determines the base travel time of your convoy.

| CONVOYS: BASE TRAVEL TIME | | |
|---|---|---|
| | MERCHANT | BASE TRAVEL TIME (MIN.) |
| LAND CONVOY | Boston: Hancock's Store no. 5 | 12 |
| | Boston: Elizabeth Murray's Fineries | 12 |
| | Boston: Child's Still House & Dry Goods | 12 |
| | New York: Rhinelander's Sugars | 22 |
| | New York : De Lancey's Imports & Goods | 22 |
| | New York : Van Brugh's Spices | 22 |
| | Frontier : The Walking Haberdashery | 17 |
| | Frontier : The Milliner's Wares | 17 |
| | Frontier : Murdoch's Barter | 19 |
| NAVAL CONVOY | Louisburg | 38 |
| | The Bahamas | 35 |
| | Saint-Augustine | 32 |
| | Virgin Islands | 42 |

If you sell all goods in your convoy to a single merchant, the total travel time of the convoy remains unchanged. However if you trade with additional merchants, the journey is extended as follows:

| FIRST DESTINATION | ADDITIONAL DESTINATION | TRAVEL TIME ADDED (MIN.) |
|---|---|---|
| Boston | Boston | +2 |
| | New York | +12 |
| | Frontier | +7 |
| | Frontier (Murdoch's Barter) | +9 |
| New York | Boston | +2 |
| | New York | +2 |
| | Frontier | +2 |
| Frontier | Boston | +2 |
| | New York | +7 |
| | Frontier | +2 |
| | Frontier (Murdoch's Barter) | +4 |
| Frontier (Murdoch's Barter) | Boston | +2 |
| | New York | +5 |
| | Frontier | +2 |
| Louisburg | The Bahamas | +2 |
| | Saint-Augustine | +2 |
| | Virgin Islands | +6 |
| The Bahamas | Louisburg | +5 |
| | Saint-Augustine | +2 |
| | Virgin Islands | +9 |
| Saint-Augustine | Louisburg | +8 |
| | The Bahamas | +5 |
| | Virgin Islands | +12 |
| Virgin Islands | Louisburg | +2 |
| | The Bahamas | +2 |
| | Saint-Augustine | +2 |

Travel time is an essential variable to factor in when you are choosing a merchant with a high multiplier. For example, if a merchant in Boston has a x3 multiplier, whereas another from New York has a x4 multiplier, it may actually make more sense to trade with the store in Boston. Within a comparable duration, you will be able to send two convoys to Boston (12 minutes, twice, for a total effective multiplier of x6) against only one to New York (22 minutes, with a x4 multiplier). However, this is only true if you actually have the opportunity to access an Accounting Book after 12 minutes, which may not be the case if you're otherwise engaged in a mission.

The most profitable decision, then, should be determined by how close you will be to an Accounting Book for the foreseeable future. If you will be undertaking a major main story Memory, for example, a longer journey that offers a higher multiplier is the wiser choice.

## Additional Factor #2: Risk

Every time you send a convoy there is a risk, expressed as a percentage, that the convoy might be attacked. The risk directly depends on how many merchants you intend to trade with for a single convoy: the more merchants you involve, the greater the risk.

⊙ For land convoys, you can reduce the risk factor inherent to each merchant's route by completing Liberation Missions (see page 154). Each district that you free from Templar influence lowers the risk rate for all convoys sent to the local merchant.

⊙ For naval convoys, the risk tends to be higher than for land convoys. However you can reduce the risk factor for each sea route by completing Privateer Contracts (see page 180). Each of these missions directly lowers the risk percentage. If you finish all Privateer Contracts for a given route, this will enable you to reduce the risk significantly.

## Additional Factor #3: Taxes

Taxes only affect land convoys. The process governing how taxes are applied is actually quite simple. Every possible land destination is found either in Boston, New York or the Frontier. All three regions are under the influence of Forts: two in Boston, two in New York and three in the Frontier. Forts are initially commanded by forces sympathetic to Templar interests, but you can liberate them (see page 144) to reduce the tax penalties.

Whenever you send a convoy through a region that has at least one Fort under Templar control, a 15% tax is levied on your convoy for each active Fort, up to a maximum tax rate of 30% for Boston and New York, and 45% for the Frontier.

Make it a priority to liberate all seven Forts at a fairly early stage in the story – ideally in Sequence 06 or 07 for Boston and the Frontier, and in Sequence 09 for New York. This will enable you to make more substantial profits with land convoys for the rest of the game.

## Defending Convoys

01

For every convoy that you send, there is a chance that it will be attacked, even if you have completed all Liberation Missions. You will be notified by an onscreen message when hostiles attempt a heist, and you must then decide how to save your wagons and stock within the specified time limit.

Attacks on your land convoys only occur in the Frontier. If you are not in that area, you can finish your current business (time limit permitting) and then Fast Travel there instantly; note that this has no effect on the countdown. On arrival, look for the ⬤ icon that marks the location of a convoy under siege. When you approach this destination, you will see your convoy's escort in conflict with the attacking forces (📷 01). To save your investment, just kill all marked hostiles in the vicinity. You can then return to your business elsewhere, leaving the convoy to continue to its destination.

If you are busy, you can assign Assassin recruits to save the convoy via the Guild Menu (see page 162). Hold **LB**/**L2**, then press **Ⓧ**/**Ⓞ** to display the appropriate screen. You will see the Defend Convoy option in the bottom-right corner of the screen. Press **Ⓧ**/**Ⓞ** to check the details of the mission, which works just like a normal contract, with the Success Rate dependent on the current prowess of the recruits you assign to it. If your recruits succeed in their mission, you have the added benefit of receiving additional rewards; if not, they will be unavailable for their period of convalescence, and you will lose the entire convoy.

Naval convoys can be lost at sea suddenly and without warning or further recourse. Despite this danger, they will still turn a handsome profit over a long enough timeline, but you should always save your most lucrative trades for land convoys.

Should you lose a land or naval convoy, you will need to gather resources and craft a replacement. While this isn't a colossal expense, the value of the goods lost can be quite significant. If you decide to leave the game idling while land convoys are in transit, we would advise that you take the time to periodically check the Logbook on the map screen to ensure that your assets are not under attack. If they are, a new entry will reveal how long you have left to save them.

## Convoys: Summary

1. Sending a convoy is performed via the Accounting Book interface, which can be accessed at the Manor or inside any General Store.

2. To maximize your profits, make sure you unlock as many convoys and capacity upgrades as possible (see page 245): the more total slots available, the greater your profits will be.

3. Only ever sell trade items (see page 248) or expensive hunting resources (all pristine pelts are profitable, but Bear Pelts and Beaver Pelts especially so). Selling materials or raw resources is a waste, occupying slots that could be put to much better use. Ideally, choose the most profitable goods, and use them to fill a whole convoy.

4. Select the merchants that you trade with based on their multipliers, which vary depending on your current Sequence (see page 249). Try to avoid selling items from a category that a merchant consignee devalues.

5. To limit the risk factor, try to trade with as few merchants at the same time as possible – and ideally only one per convoy. For naval convoys, complete all Privateer Contracts on a route you intend to take to lower the risks (see page 180). For land convoys, you can achieve the same result by completing Liberation Missions (see page 154).

6. To eliminate taxes applied to land convoys, liberate the game's seven Forts (see page 144).

7. Finally, if a land convoy is under attack, defend it within the allotted time (see page 162) or send Assassin recruits via the Guild Menu.

III

QUICKSTART

THE STORY SO FAR

PRIMER

WALKTHROUGH

SIDE QUESTS

REFERENCE & ANALYSIS

MULTIPLAYER

EXTRAS

MAP LEGEND

INDEX

ADVANCED NAVIGATION

FAST TRAVEL NETWORK

NOTORIETY

ENEMIES

WEAPONS

TOOLS

ASSASSIN RECRUITS

COMBAT MISCELLANY

GENERATING INCOME

THE HOMESTEAD

RECRUITING WORKERS

GATHERING RESOURCES

HUNTING

GATHERING RECIPES

CRAFTING

CONVOYS

SHOPS

OUTFITS

ACHIEVEMENTS & TROPHIES

MOVES OVERVIEW

MISSION CHECKLISTS

This section provides the unlock progression and price lists for all items available from merchants. We also cover upgrades for the Aquila, available exclusively from Harbormasters.

## £ GENERAL STORES & PEDDLERS

With the exception of rare events where you must visit a specific merchant to purchase a scripted item for a side quest, all General Stores have identical inventories. These are gradually expanded as you progress through main story Memories. You can also use the "Buy" option while interacting with a vendor to equip previously purchased weapons or outfits, which can save a trip back to the Homestead. All General Stores feature an Accounting Book, which you can use to access the trading and crafting interface.

There are three General Stores apiece in Boston, New York and the Frontier. To trade with these merchants with convoys sent via the Accounting Book interface, you must have visited their establishments at least once. While you can sell items acquired by Connor in his adventures directly to store owners, such as animal products obtained by hunting, you will find that potential profits are significantly higher if you perform these transactions via convoys: see page 249 for details.

Peddlers can be found riding their carts through the streets of Boston and New York, and roaming primary routes in the Frontier. They offer an inventory limited to items in the Consumables category in the table to the right, but will buy any item that Connor can sell. Though they are perhaps made redundant with the advent of the Saddle Bags that you can create in later Sequences (see page 229), you may find that a serendipitous encounter with a Peddler will enable you to stock up on ammunition at an opportune moment, especially while completing Liberation Missions.

## SHOP SELECTION

| CATEGORY | NAME | PRICE (£) | AVAILABILITY |
|---|---|---|---|
| Normal Weapons | Normal Sword | 700 | Sequence 06 |
| | French Rapier | 3,955 | Sequence 06 |
| | Light Cavalry Saber | 3,500 | Sequence 06 |
| | Hanger Sword | 1,250 | Sequence 06 |
| | French Cutlass | 1,575 | Sequence 06 |
| | Officer's Sword | 5,000 | Sequence 06 |
| | Cuttoe Sword | 4,100 | Sequence 09 |
| Blunt Weapons | Gunstock War Club | 6,500 | Sequence 06 |
| | Wooden War Club | 2,650 | Sequence 06 |
| | Stonehead War Club | 3,850 | Sequence 09 |
| Small Weapons | Assassin Tomahawk | - | Sequence 06 |
| | Iron Tomahawk | 2,475 | Sequence 06 |
| | Stone Dagger | 450 | Sequence 06 |
| | Iron Dagger | 2,450 | Sequence 06 |
| | Dirk | 3,750 | Sequence 06 |
| Heavy Weapons | Hessian Axe | 3,650 | Sequence 06 |
| | French Naval Axe | 5,450 | Sequence 06 |
| | Boarding Axe | 7,000 | Sequence 09 |
| Firearms | Flintlock Pistol | - | Sequence 06 |
| | Duckfoot Pistol | 5,999 | Sequence 06 |
| | Double-Barrel Pistol | 8,250 | Sequence 09 |
| Consumables | Arrows | 10 | Sequence 06 |
| | Cartridges | 15 | Sequence 06 |
| | Rope Darts | 125 | Sequence 06 |
| | Poison Darts | 225 | Sequence 06 |
| | Trip Mines | 150 | Sequence 06 |
| | Smoke Bombs | 50 | Sequence 06 |
| | Snares | 15 | Sequence 06 |
| | Baits | 5 | Sequence 06 |
| Outfits | Assassin Outfit | - | Starting Equipment |
| | Boston Outfit | 500 | Sequence 06 |
| | Jamestown Outfit | 1,500 | Sequence 06 |
| | Charleston Outfit | 3,000 | Sequence 06 |
| | New York Outfit | 1,000 | Sequence 09 |
| | Philadelphia Outfit | 2,000 | Sequence 09 |
| | Baltimore Outfit | 2,500 | Sequence 09 |
| Maps | Frontier – Chests | 3,000 | Sequence 04 |
| | North Boston – Chests | 1,000 | Sequence 04 |
| | Central Boston – Chests | 1,500 | Sequence 04 |
| | South Boston – Chests | 1,000 | Sequence 04 |
| | NY North – Chests | 2,000 | Sequence 04 |
| | NY East – Chests | 2,500 | Sequence 04 |
| | NY West – Chests | 2,000 | Sequence 04 |
| | Black Creek – Feathers | 2,500 | Sequence 04 |
| | John's Town – Feathers | 2,500 | Sequence 04 |
| | Monmouth – Feathers | 2,500 | Sequence 04 |
| | Lexington – Feathers | 2,500 | Sequence 04 |
| | Page Map | 5,000 | Sequence 04 |
| | Trinket Map | 3,000 | Sequence 04 |

## ⚓ HARBORMASTER

The ledger that can be found next to any Harbormaster, including Robert Faulkner in the Homestead region, can be used to purchase upgrades for the Aquila from Sequence 06 onwards. These can increase your tactical options, raw damage-dealing potential and resistance to enemy attacks in naval missions. Though remarkably expensive – and essentially unaffordable unless you are exploiting the potential profits available through expanding the Homestead and trading via convoys – these enhancements make it easier to complete Optional Objectives tied to nautical-themed Memories for players aspiring to full 100% Synchronization.

### SHOP SELECTION

| UPGRADE | PRICE (£) | EFFECT |
|---|---|---|
| Wooden Hull Reinforcements | 13,000 | Increases the ship's resilience, reducing damage sustained during enemy attacks. |
| Extra Cannon | 2,500 | Increases the amount of damage dealt during broadsides. |
| Heat Shot | 19,000 | A new type of ammunition: burning cannonballs. Effective against the mighty Man-of-War vessels. |
| Grapeshot | 17,000 | Another special ammunition type for broadsides, used to destroy masts and deny enemy ships free mobility. |
| Improved Rudder | 11,000 | Improves the Aquila's maneuverability: a huge bonus in combat, but also a great upgrade for Memories where there are Optional Constraints that forbid collision damage. |
| Naval Ram | 8,000 | Increases the amount of damage dealt when the Aquila rams smaller vessels. |
| Piercing Round | 9,000 | An upgrade specific to the swivel guns, this type of ammunition travels faster and causes more damage. |
| Iron Hull Reinforcements | 25,000 | Offers a further enhancement to the Aquila's durability. Only available after you have purchased the Wooden Hull Reinforcements. |

## OUTFITS

The following table reveals the purchase price and/or unlock conditions for the different outfits that Connor can wear. Note that donning alternative attire is a purely cosmetic consideration: there are no outfits that offer any form of armor or an increase in Connor's natural hardiness.

| NAME | PRICE (£) | UNLOCK CONDITION |
|---|---|---|
| Assassin Outfit | - | Starting Equipment |
| Boston Outfit | 500 | Sequence 06 |
| Jamestown Outfit | 1,500 | Sequence 06 |
| Charleston Outfit | 3,000 | Sequence 06 |
| New York Outfit | 1,000 | Sequence 09 |
| Philadelphia Outfit | 2,000 | Sequence 09 |
| Baltimore Outfit | 2,500 | Sequence 09 |
| Altaïr's Outfit | - | Complete all main missions with all Optional Objectives |
| Captain Kidd's Outfit | - | Complete the Oak Island Naval Location (see page 190) |
| Achilles' Original Outfit | - | Complete the Achilles' Painting mission (see page 193) |
| Kanien'kehá:ka Outfit | - | Collect all Feathers (see page 200) |
| Ezio's Outfit | - | Through Uplay |

QUICKSTART

THE STORY SO FAR

PRIMER

WALKTHROUGH

SIDE QUESTS

REFERENCE & ANALYSIS

MULTIPLAYER

EXTRAS

MAP LEGEND

INDEX

The following tables offer a range of prompts and tips to help readers obtain a full haul of Achievements and Trophies. Where extended guidance is required or might prove useful, we've also supplied page references to relevant information elsewhere in the guide.

| ICON | NAME | Ⓖ | TROPHY | UNLOCK CONDITION |
|---|---|---|---|---|
| | | | MAIN STORY MILESTONES | |
| ◇ | Rude Awakening | 10 | Bronze | Enter the Animus at the start of the story. |
| ◉ | Mystery Guest | 20 | Bronze | Complete Sequence 01 and Sequence 02. |
| 🏵 | How D'ya Like Them Apples | 20 | Bronze | Complete Sequence 03. |
| 🏵 | Heroes are Born | 20 | Bronze | Complete Sequence 04. |
| 🏵 | The Day the Templars Cried | 20 | Bronze | Complete Sequence 05. |
| ◇ | Criss Cross | 20 | Bronze | Complete the Skyscraper mission as Desmond. |
| 🏵 | Tea is for Englishmen | 20 | Silver | Complete Sequence 06. |
| 🏵 | The Whites of Their Eyes | 20 | Silver | Complete Sequence 07. |
| 🏵 | Caged Wolf | 20 | Bronze | Complete Sequence 08. |
| ◇ | Daddy Dearest | 20 | Bronze | Complete the Stadium mission as Desmond. |
| 🏵 | Two if by Sea | 20 | Silver | Complete Sequence 09. |
| 🏵 | Grim Expectations | 20 | Bronze | Complete Sequence 10. |
| ◇ | The End is Nigh | 20 | Silver | Complete the Abstergo mission as Desmond. |
| 🏵 | Difficult End | 20 | Bronze | Complete Sequence 11. |
| ⚡ | The Sum of Truth | 50 | Gold | Complete Sequence 12. |
| ◈ | No Good Deed Goes Unpunished | 20 | Silver | Open the vault gate in the Grand Temple and learn Desmond's fate. |
| ☠ | Fin. | 30 | Silver | Complete the brief "Epilogue missions" that follow the end credits: see page 131. |

## SIDE QUESTS & OPTIONAL ACCOMPLISHMENTS

| ICON | NAME | G | TROPHY | UNLOCK CONDITION |
|------|------|---|--------|------------------|
| | **House Party** | 10 | Bronze | Recruit your first artisan on the Homestead. See page 193. |
| | **Monopoly Man** | 10 | Bronze | Send at least one convoy to deliver goods to a merchant in all possible destinations: Boston, New York and the Frontier. See page 249. |
| | **Blowing in the Wind** | 20 | Bronze | Retrieve every page of an Almanac. See page 200. |
| | **Patent Not Pending** | 10 | Bronze | Craft one of the Franklin-era inventions to decorate the Homestead Manor. See page 245. |
| | **Original Gamer** | 20 | Bronze | Win a game of Fanorona, one of Bowls and one of Morris, on the Homestead. See page 142. |
| | **A Complete Set** | 20 | Silver | See all the optional characters settled at the Homestead. See page 238. |
| | **An Extraordinary Man** | 10 | Bronze | Complete the Encyclopedia of the Common Man. See page 193. |
| | **Coureur des Bois** | 10 | Bronze | Sell an undamaged animal pelt at every General Store in the game. This can be achieved in Sequence 09 at the very earliest. |
| | **Magna cum Laude** | 20 | Bronze | Train a single recruit to the maximum rank. See page 162 for details. |
| | **By Invitation Only** | 20 | Bronze | Be invited to join a club. For most players, this will unlock in Sequence 04 or 05. See page 139 to learn more about clubs. |
| | **In Good Standing** | 30 | Silver | Complete all challenges for a single club. This can be a quite lengthy and demanding task, so it's wise to start working towards the many requirements at an early stage. See page 139 for further details. |
| | **Man of the People** | 20 | Silver | Liberate all districts in Boston or New York. This is rather easier to accomplish in the former city, as one of its three districts is freed of Templar influence automatically during a main story Memory. See page 157 for details. |
| | **Tumblehome** | 10 | Bronze | Obtained once you purchase a first upgrade for the Aquila via the ledger found next to each Harbormaster. The Extra Cannon enhancement costs a mere £2,500, and will satisfy this requirement. |
| | **Entrepreneur, not Pirate!** | 20 | Bronze | Complete all Privateer Contracts. See page 180 for details. |
| | **All Washed Up** | 40 | Silver | Complete all Naval Missions. See page 176 for details. |
| | **Bring Down the House** | 20 | Bronze | Obtain a trinket for Peg Leg (see page 200), then complete the Fort Wolcott Memory (see page 182). |
| | **Kidd Gloves** | 30 | Bronze | After collecting all 24 trinkets and finishing all other Peg Leg Missions, complete the Oak Island Memory (see page 190). |
| | **Perfectionist** | 50 | Silver | Complete all main story Memories with a 100% Synchronization rating. |
| | **Multitasking** | 20 | Bronze | Complete 50% of all DNA Tracker grid entries. |
| | **Completionist** | 50 | Silver | Complete *all* DNA Tracker grid entries. This requires 100% Synchronization in every Memory, including Optional Objectives. |
| | **Head in the Cloud** | 20 | Silver | Find all pivots and synch the Animus to the Cloud in the post-story online side quest. See page 297 for further details. |

## MULTIPLAYER

| ICON | NAME | G | TROPHY | UNLOCK CONDITION |
|------|------|---|--------|------------------|
| | **Personalized** | 10 | Bronze | Customize your Multiplayer profile and avatar. |
| | **Winning Team** | 20 | Bronze | Be on the winning team at the end of a Multiplayer game session. |
| | **Hunter/Killer** | 20 | Bronze | Reach Sequence 10 on a map in Wolfpack mode. |
| | **Abstergo Entertainment** | 10 | Silver | Reach Level 20. |
| | **The Truth Will Out** | 20 | Silver | Unlock a hacked version of an Abstergo video. |

## UNIQUE FEATS

| ICON | NAME | G | TROPHY | UNLOCK CONDITION |
|------|------|---|--------|------------------|
| | **Spit Roast** | 20 | Bronze | To achieve this feat, simply assassinate an opponent with a loaded musket, then immediately press Ⓨ/△ to shoot through the body to kill a second enemy. |
| | **Circus Act** | 10 | Bronze | Kill 15 guards with a single cannon shot. This can be achieved during the Battle of Monmouth mission (see page 122). |
| | **Prince of Thieves** | 10 | Bronze | Loot a convoy without killing any of its guards. This is just a simple matter of using unarmed combat throughout the fight. See page 138. |
| | **Predator** | 10 | Bronze | Hang five enemies by using Rope Darts. See page 231 for instructions on how to use this technique. It's much easier to accomplish in the Frontier, especially when there are branches that overlook an enemy patrol route. |
| | **Whit's fur ye'll no go by ye!** | 10 | Bronze | Block a firing line five times by using a human shield. This should be a milestone that you complete very early in the story. If for some reason you do not, create chaos in Boston or New York and accumulate a small army of angry patrols and guards. You should then play the fight purely to complete the requisite human shield moves when firing lines assemble. |
| | **Jager Bomb** | 20 | Bronze | After reaching maximum Notoriety, hunt and kill ten Jägers. This can only be accomplished in Boston or New York. See page 225 for advice on how to fight Jägers. |
| | **Eye Witness** | 10 | Bronze | Witness a predator (a bear, wolf, bobcat or cougar) killing an enemy. While this may occur automatically during many varied travels through the Frontier, especially if you enjoy hunting, it is something that you can engineer by luring aggressive animals into the path of a patrol. |
| | **Master Assassin** | – | Platinum | Get every trophy (PS3 only). |

## BASIC MOVES & FUNCTIONS

| MOVE | XBOX 360 | PS3 |
|---|---|---|
| Walk/Move | Hold (L) | Hold (L) |
| Fast Walk | Hold (L) + (A) | Hold (L) + (X) |
| Look/Control Camera | (R) | (R) |
| Run/Free Run | Hold (L) + (RT) | Hold (L) + (R1) |
| Manual Jump/Leap of Faith | Hold (L) + (RT) + (A) | Hold (L) + (R1) + (X) |
| Jump Up | Hold (RT), press and release (A) | Hold (R1), press and release (X) |
| Breaking A Fall (Forward Roll) | Hold (L) forward | Hold (L) forward |
| Stealth Assassinations | (X) | (□) |
| High Profile Assassinations | Hold (RT) + (X) | Hold (R1) + (□) |
| Precision Mode Aiming | (LT) | (L1) |
| Synchronize (on Viewpoint) | (B) | (○) |
| Eagle Sense | (R3) (Toggle On/Off) | (L3) (Toggle On/Off) |
| Interact | (B) | (○) |
| Steal/Pickpocket/Loot | Hold (B) | Hold (○) |
| Pick Up/Drop Weapon/Dead Body | (B) | (○) |
| Gentle Push | Hold (L) + (B) | Hold (L) + (○) |
| Shove | Hold (L) + (RT) + (B) | Hold (L) + (R1) + (○) |
| Throw Money | (Y) | (△) |
| Quick Inventory | ⬆, ⬇, ⬅, ➡ | ⬆, ⬇, ⬅, ➡ |
| Weapon & Tool Wheel | Hold (RB), select with (L) or (R) | Hold (R2), select with (L) or (R) |
| Customize Quick Inventory | Hold (RB), select item with (L)/(R), choose direction on ✛ | Hold (R2), select item with (L)/(R), choose direction on ✛ |

## CLIMBING AND LEAPING

| MOVE | XBOX 360 | PS3 |
|---|---|---|
| Start Climbing | Hold (L) + (RT) | Hold (L) + (R1) |
| Climb | (L) | (L) |
| Climb Ladder/Switch Side | (L) | (L) |
| Look Down From Raised Surface | Hold (L) forward | Hold (L) forward |
| Ledge Drop/Beam Drop | Hold (L), press (B) | Hold (L), press (○) |
| Drop/Let Go | (B) | (○) |
| Catch Back | Hold (L) towards surface | Hold (L) towards surface |
| Beam Shimmy | (L) | (L) |
| Vault/Drop | Hold (L) + (RT) + (A) | Hold (L) + (R1) + (X) |
| Back Eject | Release (L), hold (RT), press (A) | Release (L), hold (R1), press (X) |
| Side Eject | Hold (RT), tilt (L) left/right, press (A) | Hold (R1), tilt (L) left/right, press (X) |
| Wall Run | Hold (RT), tilt (L) in required direction | Hold (R1), tilt (L) in required direction |
| Back Eject/Side Eject While Wall Running | Hold (RT), tilt (L) in required direction, press (A) | Hold (R1), tilt (L) in required direction, press (X) |
| Swing On Pole | Hold (RT), push (L) | Hold (R1), push (L) |
| Turn On Pole | (L) backwards | (L) backwards |
| Leap Of Faith | (L) + (RT) + (A) | (L) + (R1) + (X) |

## COMBAT

| MOVE | XBOX 360 | PS3 |
|---|---|---|
| Attack | (X) | (□) |
| Combo | (X), repeat in sequence | (□), repeat in sequence |
| Tool/Ranged Weapon | Press or hold & release (Y) | Press or hold & release (△) |
| Cancel Shot/Throw | (B) | (○) |
| Special Attack | Hold (Y) | Hold (△) |
| Weapon Swipe | (A) | (X) |
| Parry/Deflect/Block | Hold (B) | Hold (○) |
| Counter | (B) | (○) |
| Counter Kill | After initiating a counter, press (X) | After initiating a counter, press (□) |
| Counter Throw | After initiating a counter, press (B) | After initiating a counter, press (○) |
| Special Counter | After initiating a counter, press (Y) | After initiating a counter, press (△) |
| Counter Disarm | After initiating a counter, press (A) | After initiating a counter, press (X) |
| Counter Grab | As an enemy grabs you, press (X) | As an enemy grabs you, press (□) |
| Finish Enemy On Ground | (X) | (□) |
| Escape Fight | Hold (L) + (RT) | Hold (L) + (R1) |
| Tackle | Hold (L) + (RT), press (B) | Hold (L) + (R1), press (○) |

## SWIMMING

| MOVE | XBOX 360 | PS3 |
|---|---|---|
| Swim | (L) | (L) |
| Front Crawl | Hold (L) + (RT) | Hold (L) + (R1) |
| Hide/Swim Underwater | Hold (B) (+ (L)) | Hold (○) (+ (L)) |
| Dive | (A) (while jumping towards water) | (X) (while jumping towards water) |
| Climb Out Of Water | (L) + (RT) | (L) + (R1) |

## HORSE RIDING

| MOVE | XBOX 360 | PS3 |
|---|---|---|
| Mount Horse | (A) | (X) |
| Dismount Horse | (B) | (○) |
| Trot | (L) | (L) |
| Gallop | (RT) + (L) | (RT) + (L) |
| Spur (while galloping) | (A) | (X) |
| Leap from Saddle | (B) | (○) |
| Rear | (A) | (X) |

## CAMERA & INTERFACE

| MOVE | XBOX 360 | PS3 |
|---|---|---|
| Center Camera/Switch Shoulder (Precision Mode Aiming) | (R3) | (R3) |
| Display Map | (BACK) | (SELECT) |
| Pause Menu/Access Database Entry | (START) | (START) |

# MISSION CHECKLISTS

## MAIN MISSIONS

| SEQUENCE | MEMORY | PAGE |
|---|---|---|
| 01 | 01 | 62 |
| | 02 | 64 |
| | 03 | 66 |
| 02 | 01 | 69 |
| | 02 | 70 |
| | 03 | 72 |
| | 04 | 74 |
| | 05 | 75 |
| 03 | 01 | 78 |
| | 02 | 80 |
| | 03 | 82 |
| 04 | 01 | 83 |
| | 02 | 84 |
| | 03 | 86 |
| | 04 | 86 |
| 05 | 01 | 87 |
| | 02 | 88 |
| | 03 | 89 |
| | 04 | 90 |
| | 05 | 91 |
| 06 | 01 | 94 |
| | 02 | 96 |
| | 03 | 97 |
| | 04 | 98 |
| 07 | 01 | 102 |
| | 02 | 104 |
| | 03 | 105 |
| | 04 | 108 |
| 08 | 01 | 111 |
| | 02 | 113 |
| | 03 | 113 |
| 09 | 01 | 116 |
| | 02 | 117 |
| | 03 | 118 |
| | 04 | 119 |
| 10 | 01 | 120 |
| | 02 | 121 |
| | 03 | 122 |
| 11 | 01 | 126 |
| | 02 | 127 |
| 12 | 01 | 128 |
| | 02 | 130 |

## SIDE MISSIONS

### CLUBS (SEE PAGE 139)

| ICON | NAME | REWARD |
|---|---|---|
| | The Hunting Society | |
| | The Frontiersmen | Mementos at the Manor |
| | Boston Brawlers | |
| | Thief's Club | |

### LIBERATION MISSIONS (SEE PAGE 154)

| NAME | REWARD |
|---|---|
| North Boston | |
| Central Boston | |
| South Boston | One Assassin recruit per liberated district; lower risk factor for convoys; a key to the chests of each district |
| North New York | |
| West New York | |
| East New York | |

### COLLECTIBLES (SEE PAGE 200)

| ICON | NAME | REWARD |
|---|---|---|
| | Almanacs | Invention recipes |
| | Chests | Recipes and cash rewards |
| | Feathers | Kanien'kehá:ka Outfit |
| | Peg Leg Trinkets | Dead Man's Letters (required to access the Naval Locations) |

### LIBERATE FORTS (SEE PAGE 144)

| NAME | REWARD |
|---|---|
| Fort St-Mathieu | |
| Fort Monmouth | |
| Fort Duquesne | |
| Fort Hill | Lower taxes for land convoys |
| Fort Independence | |
| Fort Division | |
| Fort Washington | |

### THE UNDERGROUND (SEE PAGE 164)

| NAME | REWARD |
|---|---|
| Boston | Additional Fast Travel positions |
| New York | |

### CITIZEN MISSIONS (SEE PAGE 136)

| ICON | FACTION | REWARD |
|---|---|---|
| | Assassination Contracts | |
| | Courier Missions | Cash rewards |
| | Delivery Requests | |

### NAVAL MISSIONS

| NAME | PAGE |
|---|---|
| The Chase | 176 |
| The Rescue | 177 |
| French Involvement | 178 |
| Biddle's Hideout | 179 |
| The Aquila | 253 |

### NAVAL LOCATIONS

| NAME | PAGE | REWARD |
|---|---|---|
| Fort Wolcott | 182 | |
| Dead Chest's Treasure | 184 | Oak Island's Map Fragments |
| The Ghost Ship | 186 | |
| The Mad Doctor's Castle | 188 | |
| Oak Island | 190 | Shard of Eden that deflects musket balls |
| The Ruins at Cerros | 192 | Captain Kidd's Sawtooth Cutlass |

### PRIVATEER CONTRACTS (SEE PAGE 180)

| NAME | REWARD |
|---|---|
| Henderson in Distress | |
| Paving the Way | |
| Dread of Night | |
| Troubled Waters | |
| Raiding the Prospector | |
| One of a Kind | |
| Blistering Dawn | Lower risk factor for the corresponding naval convoy routes |
| A Call for Help | |
| Search for the Somerset | |
| The Sea Wolves | |
| A Midnight Engagement | |
| The Giant and the Storm | |

### HOMESTEAD (SEE PAGE 193)

| NAME | REWARD |
|---|---|
| Achilles | |
| Big Dave | |
| Godfrey & Terry | |
| Lance | |
| Warren & Prudence | |
| Norris | Recipes and additional levels for all Homestead workers |
| Lyle | |
| Ellen | |
| Myriam | |
| Homestead Daily Life | |
| Homestead Inventions | |

QUICKSTART

THE STORY
SO FAR

PRIMER

WALKTHROUGH

SIDE QUESTS

REFERENCE &
ANALYSIS

MULTIPLAYER

EXTRAS

MAP LEGEND

INDEX

# MULTIPLAYER

With its multitude of features, game types and destinations, the Assassin's Creed III multiplayer suite may seem a little daunting to a first-time player. In this chapter, we provide a wealth of explanations, insights and techniques that will help you to play at a competitive level from your very first foray into this engrossing play mode.

# BASICS

## GAME PRINCIPLES

The most important thing to understand about the Assassin's Creed III multiplayer mode is that points, not kills, are used to determine winners. While a high kill count is certainly an accomplishment, performing well in each match is a matter of *how* you execute your assassinations – not your final body count. With special bonuses acknowledging worthy feats, particularly those that involve stealth and subtlety, there is a definite onus on playing the mode in the way its creators intended.

The Assassin's Creed III multiplayer mode is a very different experience than the single-player

adventure. The focus here is on free running, social stealth and assassinations, with a simplified combat engine. Instead of open brawls, you will acquire and use a range of unlockable skills to improve your ability to hunt and kill targets, or to evade aggressors.

Once a multiplayer session has been launched, your character will appear somewhere on the chosen map. You will notice that all citizens around you resemble one of the many playable characters, or "skins". In most Game Modes, some will look identical to you. All you know at

first is that other human players are out there, hiding among the crowds, and you will be assigned a contract to kill one of them.

However, you will regularly find yourself cast in the dual role of hunter *and* prey. As you walk the streets in search of your contract, other players are likely to be tracking you. Naturally, stealth is of paramount importance. A covert approach can be employed to evade the attention of your victims and potential executors, but you must always be ready to adapt your tactics and flee or hide if a rival assigned to kill you is closing in fast.

## THE MAIN MENU

You can cycle through the various tabs of the main menu with **LB**/**L2** and **RB**/**R2**.

**Progression:** Used to check your progression in the game, as well as statistics and ladders. Note that Abstergo Storyline entries are unlocked by leveling up (see page 268), whereas Erudito entries are unlocked by completing Challenges (see page 272).

**Customization:** This is where you can prepare yourself before each game session. Select this menu to edit your Ability Sets (see page 275), change your character's appearance and animations, and set up your player profile (emblems, pictures, titles, and so forth).

**Home:** This is the menu that allows you to play games. You will find a description of all game modes on page 278.

**Abstergo Social:** This tab covers all of the interactions you may have with Friends. "Ongoing Competition" challenges you and your friends to complete mode-based score objectives that are updated on a regular basis.

**News and Data:** This provides access to the Animus Database, where you will find information on all manner of topics, from the User Manual to score Bonuses. You can also modify game options and read news updates.

# ONSCREEN DISPLAY

III

QUICKSTART

THE STORY
SO FAR

PRIMER

WALKTHROUGH

SIDE QUESTS

REFERENCE &
ANALYSIS

MULTIPLAYER

EXTRAS

MAP LEGEND

INDEX

BASICS

CHARACTERS &
CUSTOMIZATION

SCORE &
PROGRESSION

ABILITY SETS

GAME MODES

ADVANCED TIPS

MAPS &
ANALYSIS

## 1 Player Data:

⊙ This shows your current rank and score. Victory is handed to the player with the most points at the end of the round.

⊙ The number of red markers indicates how many players are stalking you.

⊙ An Escape sequence begins once your pursuer has been revealed.

## 2 Target Data:

⊙ This portrait shows the skin of the character you must kill. Beware of lookalikes and disguises. It will take a little while to become acquainted with all characters, but you'll soon gain the ability to recognize your target with a brief glance at his or her picture.

⊙ The outline around the portrait turns blue when your target is in your line of sight – but this also means that your victim can see you as well. The background of the portrait becomes blue when you are close to your target.

⊙ The players hunting your target appear as blue markers below the picture. One arrow means that you are the only combatant in direct pursuit of this target.

⊙ The Approach Meter illustrates your level of discretion and directly affects your kill bonus. The more careful the approach, the greater the bonus. Subtle, Low Profile actions (such as walking or hiding) gradually fill up the Approach Meter – from Discreet, to Silent and then Incognito. Conversely, performing High Profile actions (such as running) will cause your Approach Meter to empty to the Reckless level. A Chase sequence will ensue when your Approach Meter is fully depleted.

## 3 Compass:

⊙ The primary function of this directional indicator is to show the approximate position of your target. The width of the "fill" arc

increases as you approach your target, becoming a full blue disc when you are in close proximity. It will turn bright blue whenever your target is in sight.

⊙ Arrows may also appear on the outer edge of the Compass, indicating secondary targets in team missions (blue), and enemy pursuers (red).

⊙ There is no Compass in Simple Deathmatch and Deathmatch modes.

## 4 Assassinate/Stun Button and Lock Button Icons:

⊙ A contextual visual button prompt over a character's head indicates when a kill or stun can be performed by pressing ✕/⬜.

⊙ You can also lock (🔒) on to a target by pressing LT/L1. The lock lasts while your target is in your line of sight, or until manually disabled. It will break if you lose sight of the target for more than a few seconds.

## 5 Abilities and Streaks:

⊙ Icons in these slots show which Abilities are currently available to you and, when applicable, which Streak bonuses you can trigger.

⊙ Abilities in Cooldown (that is, recharging after use) are replaced by a timer until available.

## 6 Session Information:

⊙ This shows the countdown to the end of the round.

⊙ You will also find information specific to your game mode here, such as team scores.

## 7 Players List:

⊙ Press ◀/SELECT to display a list of players in the current session, as well as their scores. The list will disappear after a few seconds.

## CONTROLS

| XBOX 360 | PS3 | COMMAND |
|---|---|---|
| L | L | Basic Movement |
| R | R | Camera Control |
| ✛ | ✛ | Taunt; switch Targets in Team modes; select Ability Set |
| A | ✗ | Fast Walk; Sprint/Jump (High Profile mode only) |
| B | ◯ | Shove (High Profile mode only); drop from a ledge; vault over obstacles |
| X | ▢ | Assassinate; Stun |
| Y | △ | Use Ability 3 (hold to aim) |
| LT | L1 | Lock Target |
| RT | R1 | High Profile Mode |
| LB | L2 | Use Ability 1 (hold to aim with abilities that can be thrown) |
| RB | R2 | Use Ability 2 (hold to aim with abilities that can be thrown) |
| R | R3 | Center Camera |
| START | START | Pause Menu |
| BACK | SELECT | Display extra information, such as the Players List and scores |

01

**Control Notes:**

⊙ The Fast Walk command (hold Ⓐ/⊗) enables you to increase your movement speed by a barely perceptible degree, which can be invaluable for closing the gap on a victim, or pulling away from a would-be aggressor. This incurs no Approach Meter penalties, but experienced players can identify you when you change pace.

⊙ If you are forced to flee, Ⓑ/◯ can be held to barge past civilians in your path as you run.

⊙ While walking through crowds, you will notice that the Assassinate/Stun button icon can appear above any civilian when you face them in close proximity. Killing innocents leads to the loss of your contract, so this is where the Lock function comes in useful. Press Lock when your suspected target is in your immediate sight, or hold to aim and release to Lock the target from a distance. A white padlock will then appear over your target's head (🔒). The advantage of the Lock function is that the Assassinate icon only appears for this individual, meaning that you cannot accidentally strike an innocent. The Lock will break if you lose sight of a target for more than a few seconds.

⊙ If an enemy makes a High Profile move while in plain sight, a red icon (🛡) will appear over their heads to enable you to focus your attention with ease.

⊙ When running away from an enemy, press Ⓑ/◯ to vault (rather than jump) over small obstacles, or to quickly drop from a rooftop (📷 01). This might surprise your pursuer, who will usually expect you to perform a jump, whereas this move can make you suddenly disappear from their line of sight.

# CHASES AND ESCAPE

In most modes, a Chase sequence begins when a pursuer's Approach Meter is fully depleted (thus preventing them from getting any Approach Bonus). This is usually caused by performing High Profile actions while in the target's line of sight.

⊙ **Pursuer:** Once you trigger a Chase, the Chase Timer appears on your HUD. You must now kill your target before they can hide from you. If you can keep your target in sight, they will be unable to hide. However, as soon as they turn a corner or disappear from view, the Chase Timer will begin to deplete. If it is completely depleted, they will have achieved an Escape – and you will have lost both the Chase sequence and the contract.

Once a Chase begins, it's often a good idea to start free running and ascend to higher ground. Not only will your target have to work harder to hide, but you'll also increase the effective range of assassination through free running tackles and aerial kills. You could also try to use shortcuts whenever you have a good idea of where your target intends to run next (📷 02), or employ relevant Abilities at your disposal, such as Closure. You only have to regain sight of your target for a moment to reset the Chase Timer completely. As exhilarating as a Chase can be, note that protracted pursuits will waste valuable match time.

⊙ **Target:** When you are made aware that an assailant is closing in to assassinate you, a red Escape Timer appears and the race begins. You must now attempt to leave your opponent's line of sight by turning corners, entering buildings or dropping out of view. Use Chase Breakers to gain distance (📷 03). If you succeed, the Escape Timer will turn yellow and begin to fill. When this occurs, you can slip into a hiding place to turn the bar blue. The blue bar will fill up rapidly while you are hidden. If the assigned killer fails to catch you before the Escape Timer expires, you will have achieved an Escape and your hunter will lose the contract on your head. Successful Escapes earn extra points.

Even if a pursuer is hot on your heels, hope remains right up until they hit the Assassinate button. With a little luck, good reflexes or tactical sense (if you lure them to a hiding place, for example), you can strike them first with your character's stun move. This will incapacitate them for a few seconds and end the Chase, earning you extra points.

III

QUICKSTART

THE STORY
SO FAR

PRIMER

WALKTHROUGH

SIDE QUESTS

REFERENCE &
ANALYSIS

MULTIPLAYER

EXTRAS

MAP LEGEND

INDEX

BASICS

CHARACTERS &
CUSTOMIZATION

SCORE &
PROGRESSION

ABILITY SETS

GAME MODES

ADVANCED TIPS

MAPS &
ANALYSIS

**Carts filled with hay (or leaves or hides), bushes and straw piles** are the most obvious hiding places featured in the multiplayer game, and completely remove you from view when you jump inside. All kills made from such places of concealment lead to generous bonuses (📷 04), but with the obvious drawback that you must remain stationary while a rival may be closing in on your position. Furthermore, entering and leaving these hiding places is clearly not the behavior of a civilian: such acts telegraph your intentions to anyone who happens to glance in your direction.

Social stealth is the most common method of finding a hiding place, either by blending with a crowd of bystanders or by sitting on a bench (📷 05). It

is easy to make Low Profile transitions from one group to another, and you need only move briefly through a passing crowd when closing in on your target to earn a related kill bonus. Use the Fast Walk move to catch up with groups of citizens walking ahead of you.

A good hiding place is the fastest way to end a Chase. Your judgment on whether to stay put or flee in such situations should be dictated by the time left on the Escape Timer, and the likelihood of whether your opponent can reach your hiding place before it expires. If you successfully escape after a pursuit, it will not matter if your pursuer knows your location or even approaches you, as they will have lost the contract on your head.

04

05

## CHASE BREAKERS

Each map features a number of Chase Breakers to enable competitors to briefly evade opponents in pursuit. There are four types to look for, readily identified by the white shimmer of their Animus matrix outline. As Chase

Breakers are triggered by any High Profile activity such as running, you can pass them stealthily without incident. They also reset after a short period of time, so always make good use of the valuable seconds of grace they offer.

**Lifts:** Collide with the front of these devices to trigger them, and the counterweight will propel you instantly to roof level. Note that you can also drop onto a Lift from above – a tactic of great merit when a rival is almost directly behind you.

**Corner Helpers:** As you bound over beams and balconies, these swinging handholds will not only break a vital element of the free running route behind you, but will often slip you immediately into the yellow "out-of-sight" status as you round the corner. Alternatively, you can press 🅱/⭕ in midair just before reaching a Corner Helper to perform a Long Jump and be propelled forwards.

**Closing Gates:** Running through these passages will cause doors to swing shut or portcullis grates to fall. Time your entry carefully, and these Chase Breakers will slam shut in the face of your would-be assassin and force them to take another path.

**Falling Platforms:** These wooden stepping stones fall free of their ropes shortly after you step on them, giving you (but not your pursuer) just enough time to jump off.

# CHARACTERS & CUSTOMIZATION

Though weapons and animations may differ between each avatar, there is no functional difference between them. Your choice of character, therefore, is very much a matter of personal preference – and, as you unlock further options, an opportunity to show off your experience with items that aren't immediately available. Level progression rewards you with custom packs that allow you to alter the in-game appearance of every character with different costumes and colors.

Use the Characters menu in the Customization tab to change or customize weapons (some of which are unique to particular characters), appearance, costume, colors and animations – including taunts and stun moves.

THE LADY MAVERICK

THE INDEPENDENT

THE PIONEER

THE PREACHER

THE NIGHT STALKER

THE MOUNTEBANK      THE CARPENTER      THE COMMANDER      THE RED COAT

THE HIGHLANDER      THE HUNTSMAN      THE ROBBER      THE SILENT SHADOW

III

QUICKSTART

THE STORY
SO FAR

PRIMER

WALKTHROUGH

SIDE QUESTS

REFERENCE &
ANALYSIS

MULTIPLAYER

EXTRAS

MAP LEGEND

INDEX


BASICS

CHARACTERS &
CUSTOMIZATION

SCORE &
PROGRESSION

ABILITY SETS

GAME MODES

ADVANCED TIPS

MAPS &
ANALYSIS

THE COYOTE MAN      THE HESSIAN      THE BEAR

THE GOVERNOR      THE STRONG MAN      THE SHARPSHOOTER

## SCORING SYSTEM & BONUSES

To repeat our earlier advice, it is your score that matters – not kills. If you sprint over to a target in the street and brazenly execute them at the first opportunity, you might score a paltry 100 points. However, if you exercise a little restraint and incorporate just a few additional stalking techniques for bonuses, you could increase your points haul significantly. In essence, one good kill is worth several bad ones. With a time limit on the session, maximizing each kill score will enable you to make the most of a finite number of contracts.

Familiarize yourself with the following bonus tables, then think about how you can incorporate them into your playing strategies.

## LEVELS AND PROGRESSION

The points you earn from participating in multiplayer matches are converted into experience points (or "XP") that are recorded in your online profile. You can earn XP by:

⊙ Finishing game sessions. Your score in most sessions is converted to XP – so if you end the session with 1,800 points, you will receive 1,800 XP. The only exception is Wolfpack, where a ratio is applied to your score

⊙ Completing Challenges

Whenever your total XP reaches a new threshold, your Templar trainee will "level up" and gradually advance from Level 1 to Level 50 – and beyond, with Prestige Mode. A Level increase usually grants a reward of one or more of the following:

⊙ New Abilities, Perks, Kill Streaks or Loss Bonuses

⊙ A new custom Ability Set

⊙ New Abilities to craft

⊙ Profile elements (emblem, patron picture and title) and character customization parts (such as body parts and colors, weapons, stun and taunt animations). These are cosmetic upgrades and have no effect on gameplay

⊙ Storyline files and videos, which offer information and propaganda from Abstergo, as well as hacked revelations from the (pro-Assassins) Erudito group

Level progression improves your character's capabilities and increases your chance of success against other players online. You will find that opponents with greater experience have the advantage in terms of Abilities and score bonuses.

Rewards and items are not automatically awarded when you level up. To obtain newly unlocked features, you must purchase them using Abstergo Credits (▲). You can earn credits in the following ways:

⊙ Leveling up

⊙ Completing game sessions

⊙ Finishing in the three first ranks of a competitive session

⊙ Being the best player on your team

⊙ Winning a team session

⊙ Obtaining accolades

⊙ Receiving Loyalty Gifts (rewards given for regular play)

The diagram overleaf reveals which elements are unlocked throughout the course of your leveling progression.

### KILL BONUSES

| NAME | CONDITION | SCORE |
|---|---|---|
| Basic | Kill your target from the ground. | +100 |
| Aerial | Kill your target from rooftop to ground. | +100 |
| Acrobatic | Kill your target while climbing or crouching. | +200 |
| Hidden | Kill your target while hidden in a crowd, on a bench or in a haystack. | +300 |
| Grab | Kill your target from below while your target is on a rooftop. | +450 |
| Contested | Kill your target at the same time your target stuns you. | +100 |
| Gun | Kill your target with the Pistol Ability. | +100 |
| Poison Dart | Kill your target with the Poison Dart Ability. | +200 |

### ACTION BONUSES

| NAME | CONDITION | SCORE |
|---|---|---|
| First Blood | Perform the first kill of the session. | +50 |
| Execution | Kill your target with the Pistol Ability while he or she is running. | +100 |
| Mid-Air | Kill a jumping target with the Pistol Ability. | +100 |
| Chain | Perform two main actions in 10 seconds (kill, escape, stun). | +50 |
| Multiple Escape | Escape from 2 or more pursuers at the same time. | +100 |
| Close Call | Empty the Escape Timer with your pursuer in a range of 10 meters. | +50 |
| Revenge | Kill your previous pursuer before he's killed by another player. | +50 |
| Ambush | Kill or stun your target with less than 1 second of line of sight with them. | +100 |
| Savior | Kill your target when they're less than 10 meters away from their own target. | +50 |
| Poacher | Kill your target while another of their pursuers is in a range of 10 meters. | +50 |
| Ground Finish | Perform a finish move on a target killed by another player. | +50 |
| Poison | Kill your target with the Poison Ability. | +200 |
| Grounded | Kill your target while he or she is stunned. | +50 |
| Lure | Have an opponent kill or stun a civilian lookalike that you spawned using an ability. | +100 |
| Intercepted | A poisoned target is killed by another player. | +50 |
| Variety | Earn 5/10/15 different bonuses in a session. | +200/ +400/ +600 |

### DEFENSE AND ESCAPE BONUSES

| NAME | CONDITION | SCORE |
|---|---|---|
| Stun | Stun a pursuer. | +200 |
| Honorable Death | Try to stun a pursuer and at the same time your pursuer kills you. | +100 |
| Basic Escape | Successfully escape while the Escape Timer is red. | +100 |
| Out of Sight | Successfully escape while the Escape Timer is yellow. | +150 |
| Hidden | Successfully escape while the Escape Timer is blue. | +200 |
| Brutal | Escape on a stun. | +200 |

The values in these tables may be adjusted in post-release updates.

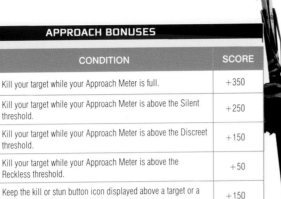

## APPROACH BONUSES

| NAME | CONDITION | SCORE |
|---|---|---|
| Incognito | Kill your target while your Approach Meter is full. | +350 |
| Silent | Kill your target while your Approach Meter is above the Silent threshold. | +250 |
| Discreet | Kill your target while your Approach Meter is above the Discreet threshold. | +150 |
| Reckless | Kill your target while your Approach Meter is above the Reckless threshold. | +50 |
| Focus | Keep the kill or stun button icon displayed above a target or a pursuer for 3 seconds. | +150 |

## TEAM BONUSES

| NAME | CONDITION | SCORE |
|---|---|---|
| Revive | Help a stunned ally stand up. | +50 |
| x2 Multi Kill | 2 kills are performed in a period of 3 seconds by the player or a teammate. | +100 |
| x3 Multi Kill | 3 kills are performed in a period of 6 seconds by the player or teammates. | +250 |
| x4 Multi Kill | 4 kills are performed in a period of 9 seconds by the player or teammates. | +400 |
| Knock-Out | Your team stuns 2 pursuers in a period of 3 seconds and you are involved in at least one of them. | +100 |
| Assist | A teammate kills/stuns a target/pursuer locked by the player. | +50 |
| Assist Stun | Stun a pursuer locked by a teammate. | +50 |
| Assist Kill | Kill a target locked by a teammate. | +50 |
| Opportunist | Kill a target chased by a teammate. | +50 |
| Diversion | A teammate killed the target you were chasing. | +50 |
| Rescuer | Stun a pursuer who was chasing a teammate. | +50 |
| Rescued | The player's pursuer has been stunned by a teammate. | +50 |

## MODE BONUSES

| NAME | CONDITION | MODE | SCORE |
|---|---|---|---|
| Hidden Alone | Earned when the player is hidden (blend, bench, haystack) as a prey. | Manhunt | +10 |
| Team Hidden | Earned when the player is hidden with 1 to 3 teammates in range. | Manhunt | +20-50 |
| Artifact Stolen | Earned when the player steals the opponent's artifact. | Artifact Assault | +150 |
| Artifact Score | Earned when the player carries back the opponent's artifact in his/her own base. | Artifact Assault | +500 |
| Support | Earned when the player kills/stuns an opponent in a range of 20 meters from a teammate carrying the artifact. | Artifact Assault | +50 |
| Recovery | Earned when the player returns a stolen artifact to the player's base after picking it up or killing the carrier. | Artifact Assault | +50 |
| Capture | Earned when the player captures an enemy-controlled territory. | Domination | +250 |
| Defense | Earned when the player kills the last attacker in a territory with the capture gauge below 25%. | Domination | +50 |
| Zone Secured | Earned when the player refills the capture gauge to 100%. | Domination | +50 |
| Domination | Earned every 5 seconds when the team owns all the territories. | Domination | +50 |

The values in these tables may be adjusted in post-release updates.

III

QUICKSTART

THE STORY
SO FAR

PRIMER

WALKTHROUGH

SIDE QUESTS

REFERENCE &
ANALYSIS

MULTIPLAYER

EXTRAS

MAP LEGEND

INDEX

BASICS

CHARACTERS &
CUSTOMIZATION

SCORE &
PROGRESSION

ABILITY SETS

GAME MODES

ADVANCED TIPS

MAPS &
ANALYSIS

# LEVELING PROGRESSION CHART

## GAMEPLAY REWARDS

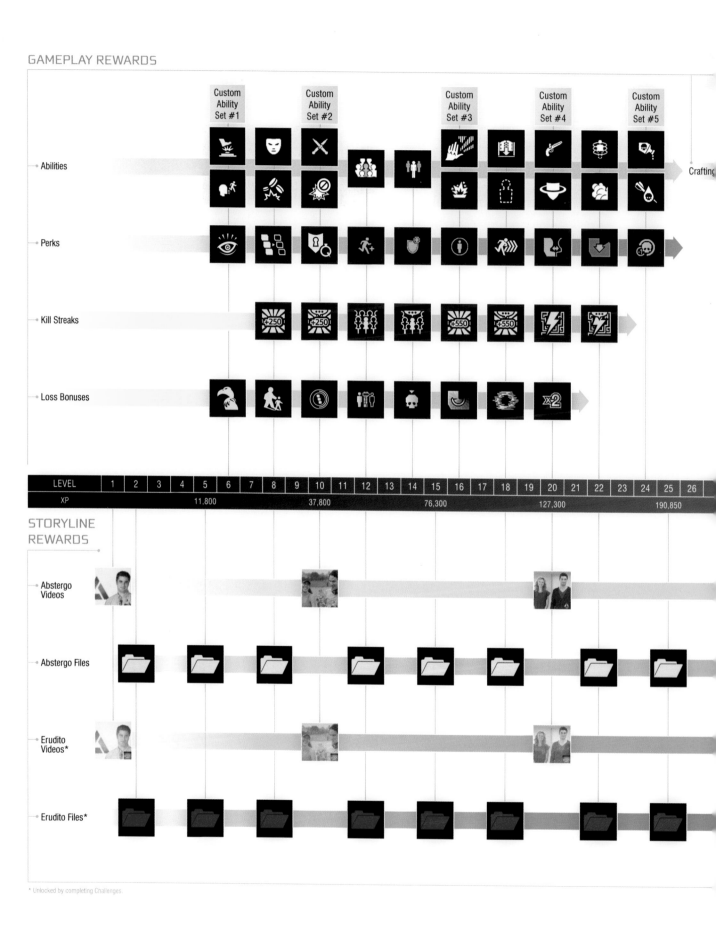

| LEVEL | 1 | 2 | 3 | 4 | 5 | 6 | 7 | 8 | 9 | 10 | 11 | 12 | 13 | 14 | 15 | 16 | 17 | 18 | 19 | 20 | 21 | 22 | 23 | 24 | 25 | 26 |
|---|---|---|---|---|---|---|---|---|---|---|---|---|---|---|---|---|---|---|---|---|---|---|---|---|---|---|
| XP | | | | | 11,800 | | | | | 37,800 | | | | | 76,300 | | | | | 127,300 | | | | | 190,850 | |

### STORYLINE REWARDS

* Abstergo Videos
* Abstergo Files
* Erudito Videos*
* Erudito Files*

* Unlocked by completing Challenges.

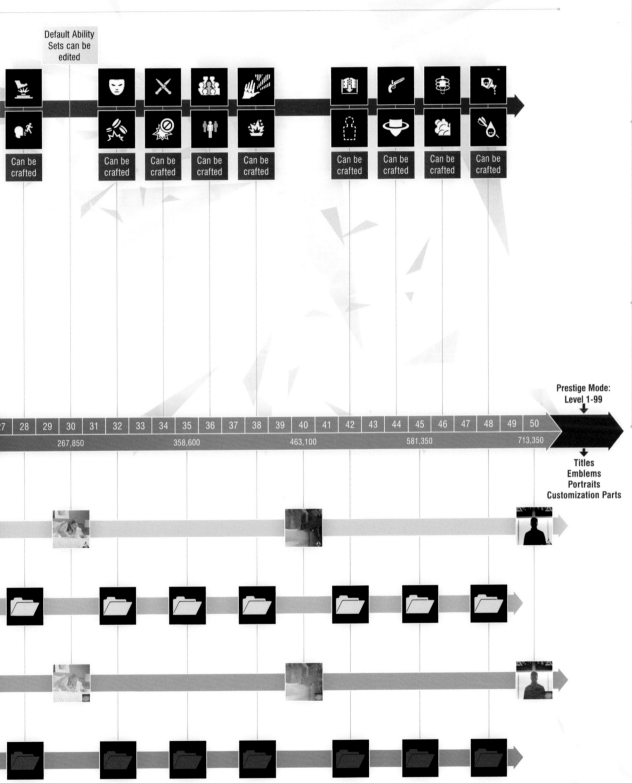

Default Ability Sets can be edited

Can be crafted

Prestige Mode: Level 1-99

Titles
Emblems
Portraits
Customization Parts

| 27 | 28 | 29 | 30 | 31 | 32 | 33 | 34 | 35 | 36 | 37 | 38 | 39 | 40 | 41 | 42 | 43 | 44 | 45 | 46 | 47 | 48 | 49 | 50 |

267,850   358,600   463,100   581,350   713,350

The values in these tables may be adjusted in post-release updates.

## CHALLENGES

Four types of Challenges are recorded in the Progression menu. These are unlocked by repeating the corresponding feat a certain number of times (specified in each table's Total column). Each Challenge has three milestones that reward you with an XP bonus when completed (the values we specify here correspond to the first milestone). Completing the first milestone of certain Challenges also unlocks Erudito Files and Videos. When you complete a milestone, a segment of the outline surrounding the corresponding icon becomes highlighted.

| ABILITIES | | | |
|---|---|---|---|
| **ABILITIES** | **CONDITION** | **TOTAL** | **XP** |
| The Apothecary | Use Poison after focusing a target. | x5 | 1,500 |
| The Artful | Use Knives to knock down a climbing player. | x5 | 1,000 |
| The Chameleon | Perform a stun while in morphed crowd. | x10 | 750 |
| The Cleaner | Use Wipe and kill a target or stun a pursuer. | x5 | 1,000 |
| The Clear Sighted | Use Disruption to confuse and kill a target. | x5 | 1,000 |
| The Clever | Use Closure to block your pursuer. | x1 | 1,000 |
| The Deceiver | Stun a pursuer while using Disguise. | x5 | 1,000 |
| The Defensive | Use Animus Shield to block another player's ranged weapon. | x1 | 1,500 |
| The Distractor | Use Disruption to confuse and stun a pursuer. | x5 | 1,500 |
| The Evader | Use Teleport while less than 10 meters away from a pursuer. | x5 | 1,000 |
| The Fierce | Perform a kill or a stun while being poisoned. | x5 | 1,000 |
| The Generous | Use a Money Bomb to reveal and kill a blended target. | x5 | 750 |
| The Ghost | Use Glimmer to kill a target. | x5 | 750 |
| The Herbalist | Poison one target and kill another before the poison takes effect. | x1 | 1,500 |
| The Impassive | Use Animus Shield to block a bomb then kill a target or stun a pursuer. | x5 | 1,000 |
| The Knife Thrower | Use Knives to slow down and kill a target. | x10 | 750 |
| The Liar | Kill a target while using Disguise. | x5 | 750 |
| The Magician | Use a Smoke Bomb to stop and stun a pursuer. | x10 | 750 |
| The Marauder | Use a Smoke Bomb to stop two or more players. | x5 | 1,500 |
| The Master Hunter | Use a Tripwire Bomb to stop and kill a target. | x1 | 1,500 |
| The Noble | Use Bodyguard to stun a locked pursuer. | x5 | 1,000 |
| The Observant | Use Morph or Mass Morph to reveal and kill a target. | x1 | 1,000 |
| The Pistolier | Use the Pistol to kill a jumping or running target. | x5 | 1,000 |
| The Precise | Use the Pistol to kill a target from afar. | x5 | 750 |
| The Puppet Master | Make another player kill your Decoy or Bodyguard. | x5 | 1,000 |
| The Pyrotechnician | Use Firecrackers and kill a blinded target. | x5 | 750 |
| The Quick Thinker | Use Wipe to counter a ranged weapon, a Bomb or Teleport. | x1 | 1,500 |
| The Shaman | Use Teleport to cross the frontier in team game modes. | x5 | 750 |
| The Sly | Use a Tripwire Bomb to stop a pursuer. | x5 | 750 |
| The Spiritualist | Use Glimmer to stun a pursuer. | x5 | 1,000 |
| The Trapper | Use Closure to block and kill a target. | x1 | 1,000 |
| The Trouble Maker | Use a Money Bomb to form a crowd and slow down your pursuer. | x1 | 1,000 |
| The Vanquisher | Use Firecrackers and stun a blinded pursuer. | x1 | 1,000 |

The values in these tables may be adjusted in post-release updates.

III

QUICKSTART

THE STORY
SO FAR

PRIMER

WALKTHROUGH

SIDE QUESTS

REFERENCE &
ANALYSIS

MULTIPLAYER

EXTRAS

MAP LEGEND

INDEX

BASICS

CHARACTERS &
CUSTOMIZATION

SCORE &
PROGRESSION

ABILITY SETS

GAME MODES

ADVANCED TIPS

MAPS &
ANALYSIS

## STYLE

| NAME | CONDITION | TOTAL | XP |
|---|---|---|---|
| The Artist | Perform a kill worth at least 700 points. | x5 | 750 |
| The Bird of Prey | Earn an Aerial Kill bonus. | x20 | 750 |
| The Good Samaritan | Revive a teammate. | x10 | 1,000 |
| The Inventive | Kill or stun a target using the environment. | x10 | 750 |
| The Killing Machine | Perform 2 kills in less than 7 seconds. | x5 | 1,000 |
| The Medium | Kill a target that is close to at least 2 lookalikes. | x10 | 750 |
| The Perfectionist | Earn a Greater Variety bonus. | x20 | 1,000 |
| The Resourceful | Earn an Extreme Variety bonus. | x5 | 1,500 |
| The Serial Killer | Play a game session with every character. | x1 | 2,000 |
| The Silent Master | Earn a Focus bonus. | x5 | 1,000 |
| The Unseen | Earn a Hidden Kill bonus. | x10 | 750 |
| The Vengeful | Earn a Ground Finish bonus. | x50 | 750 |
| The Versatile | Earn a Variety bonus. | x50 | 750 |

## ASSASSINATION*

| NAME | CONDITION | TOTAL | XP |
|---|---|---|---|
| The Ambitious | Earn the First Blood bonus. | x5 | 750 |
| The Audacious | Survive at least 15 seconds while hearing whispers. | x5 | 1,500 |
| The Changeling | Trigger a Mass Morph or a Silent Mass Morph. | x10 | 1,000 |
| The Competitor | Activate 2 Kill Streaks in a single game session. | x5 | 1,500 |
| The Crafty | Perform 2 stuns in less than 7 seconds. | x5 | 1,500 |
| The Fighter | Perform 4 stuns without dying. | x1 | 1,000 |
| The Gatekeeper | Use a Chase Breaker to escape. | x10 | 1,000 |
| The Inquisitor | Taunt then kill or stun another player. | x1 | 1,500 |
| The Mass Murderer | Kill 10 targets in a single game session. | x1 | 1,000 |
| The Patriot | Score at least 6,000 points in a single game session. | x1 | 1,000 |
| The Provoker | Taunt a target you have just stunned or killed. | x10 | 750 |
| The Psychic | Trigger an Animus Hack or a Silent Animus Hack. | x5 | 1,500 |
| The Runaway | Earn the Multiple Escape bonus. | x1 | 1,500 |
| The Sagacious | Stun your pursuer and kill your target within 7 seconds. | x10 | 1,500 |
| The Stealth Master | Earn 3 Incognito bonuses in a single game session. | x5 | 1,000 |
| The Usurper | Take the lead in the last 20 seconds and keep it until the session ends. | x1 | 1,500 |
| The Vigilant | Stun a pursuer who is near 1 teammate. | x20 | 1,000 |
| The Wrestler | Stun a pursuer. | x50 | 1,500 |

* These challenges cannot be completed in Wolfpack.

## MODES

| NAME | CONDITION | TOTAL | XP |
|---|---|---|---|
| The Collaborator | Complete 10 sequences in a row in a Wolfpack game session. | x5 | 750 |
| The Conqueror | Have all territories captured in Domination for at least 10 seconds. | x1 | 1,500 |
| The Conquistador | Capture a zone occupied with at least 2 opponents in Domination. | x5 | 1,000 |
| The Cool-Headed | Successfully complete a Sync-Kill in a Wolfpack game session. | x5 | 1,000 |
| The Dark Bear | Win a Wolfpack session playing as the Bear. | x1 | 1,000 |
| The Dark Carpenter | Win a Wolfpack session playing as the Carpenter or on Virginian Plantation. | x1 | 1,000 |
| The Dark Commander | Win a Wolfpack session playing as the Commander. | x1 | 1,000 |
| The Dark Hessian | Win a Wolfpack session playing as the Hessian or on Fort Wolcott. | x1 | 1,000 |
| The Dark Huntsman | Win a Wolfpack session playing as the Huntsman or on Animus Core. | x1 | 1,000 |
| The Dark Independent | Win a Wolfpack session playing as the Independent. | x1 | 1,000 |
| The Dark Lady Maverick | Win a Wolfpack session playing as Lady Maverick or on New York Brewery. | x1 | 1,000 |
| The Dark Mountebank | Win a Wolfpack session playing as the Mountebank. | x1 | 1,000 |
| The Dark Night Stalker | Win a Wolfpack session playing as the Night Stalker or on Boston Harbor. | x1 | 1,000 |
| The Dark Pioneer | Win a Wolfpack session playing as the Pioneer. | x1 | 1,000 |
| The Dark Preacher | Win a Wolfpack session playing as the Preacher. | x1 | 1,000 |
| The Dark Robber | Win a Wolfpack session playing as the Robber or on Boston North End. | x1 | 1,000 |
| The Dark Strong Man | Win a Wolfpack session playing as the Strong Man or on the Northwest Passage. | x1 | 1,000 |
| The Deathless | Stay alive for 60 seconds in Deathmatch. | x10 | 1,000 |
| The Enduring | Earn a Multi-Kill bonus in any team mode or Wolfpack. | x25 | 750 |
| The Eradicator | Kill a target that is holding the Artifact. | x5 | 1,000 |
| The Highwayman | Score an Artifact in an Artifact Assault game session. | x5 | 1,000 |
| The Infiltrator | Earn 200 points of Hidden Bonuses in Manhunt. | x10 | 1,000 |
| The Punisher | Stun, acquire and kill a pursuer within 10 seconds in an Assassinate game session. | x5 | 1,000 |
| The Show-Off | Taunt an opponent from across the frontier in team game modes. | x10 | 750 |
| The Vulture | Kill a target that has just performed a kill in an Assassinate game session. | x5 | 1,000 |
| The Wolfpack Leader | Win a Wolfpack session on all maps. | x1 | 1,000 |

The values in these tables may be adjusted in post-release updates.

## ACCOLADES

Accolades are rewards given at the end of each session that acknowledge special feats; they reveal a great deal about your play style. By claiming Accolades, you can earn additional .

### ACTION ACCOLADES

| ICON | NAME | CONDITION |
|------|------|-----------|
| | The Drunkard | Was stunned most often. |
| | The Escape Artist | Escaped the most. |
| | The Expert | Had the best single kill score. |
| | The Master | Earned the most Incognito bonuses. |
| | The Professional | Had the best kills/deaths ratio. |
| | The Savage | Had the most contested kills. |
| | The Savior | Revived the most allies. |
| | The Slayer | Had the most kills. |
| | The Stalker | Earned the most Focus bonuses. |
| | The Stunner | Performed the most stuns. |
| | The Unstoppable | Had the longest Kill Streak. |
| | The Vicious | Performed the most Ground Finishes. |
| | The Wingman | Earned the most Assist bonuses. |

### STYLE ACCOLADES

| ICON | NAME | CONDITION |
|------|------|-----------|
| | The Gargoyle | Spent the most time on rooftops. |
| | The Hacker | Performed the most Animus Hacks. |
| | The Immortal | Stayed alive the longest. |
| | The Improviser | Used the greatest variety of Abilities. |
| | The Mimic | Was morphed or disguised the longest. |
| | The Poisoner | Poisoned the most targets. |
| | The Sacrificial Lamb | The first to die. |
| | The Shadow | Spent the most time hidden. |
| | The Sniper | Had the most Pistol kills. |
| | The Survivor | Died the least. |
| | The Target | Died the most. |
| | The Untouchable | Was never killed. |
| | The Victim | Spent the most time afflicted by Abilities. |
| | The Wanderer | Spent the most time walking. |

### MODES ACCOLADES

| ICON | NAME | CONDITION |
|------|------|-----------|
| | The Alpha Wolf | Had the best kill score in Wolfpack. |
| | The Despot | Captured the most Territories. |
| | The Elusive | Was acquired the least. |
| | The Glutton | Scored the most Artifacts. |
| | The Lurker | Spent the most time blended with an ally. |
| | The Mole | Got the most Defense bonuses. |
| | The Monster | Score the most Multi-Kills. |
| | The Practiced | Had the most kills without being stunned. |
| | The Sneaker | Was revealed the least by targets. |
| | The Stalwart | Killed the most Artifact thieves. |
| | The Visionary | Revealed the most pursuers. |

The values in these tables may be adjusted in post-release updates.

# ABILITY SETS

Ability Sets grant your character additional skills, weapons or bonuses, all of which are detailed over the pages that follow. Each set is composed of:

⊙ Three Abilities
⊙ Two Perks (only one with Default Sets)
⊙ One Streak
⊙ One Loss Bonus

Initially you only have two default sets to play with. As you gain levels, you will unlock up to five custom sets, which you can freely define in accordance with your preferences or the challenges that lie ahead in a particular play mode. The default sets can also be customized once you reach Level 30.

Once you have unlocked many skills and perks, be sure to prepare several Ability Sets that you can use in various situations or game modes.

|  | DEFAULT SET 1 | DEFAULT SET 2 |
|---|---|---|
| **Abilities** | Disguise | Wipe |
|  | Money Bomb | Tripwire Bomb |
|  | Knives | Disruption |
| **Perks** | Sixth Sense | Sentry |
|  | *Unavailable* | *Unavailable* |
| **Streak & Bonus** | Streak +250 | Silent Streak +250 |
|  | Scavenger | Vision |

## ABILITIES

Abilities can be used at any time, but are then unavailable for a Cooldown period as they recharge. Some of them can be thrown by holding and releasing the corresponding button. The eighteen Abilities can be improved through Crafting, which enables you to improve two parameters of the chosen Ability.

### ABILITIES

| ICON | NAME | UNLOCKED | EFFECT | NOTES |
|---|---|---|---|---|
| | **Tripwire Bomb** | Level 6 | Explodes when a target or pursuer steps on it, preventing them from moving and performing any action during a short period. | ⊙ You can drop the bomb at your feet or aim and throw it. The bomb takes a few seconds to activate, which is when the Cooldown begins.<br>⊙ Place a bomb in a narrow corridor (the entrance to a Domination territory, for instance) for an easy stun opportunity. |
| | **Decoy** | Level 6 | Changes the appearance of a civilian to mimic your own, and causes them to run away, tricking your pursuers. | ⊙ Good for misleading both pursuers and targets.<br>⊙ Can be used to simply divert an approaching pursuer, or to set up a stun opportunity once they have been distracted. |
| | **Disguise** | Level 8 | Temporarily changes your appearance to surprise opponents. | ⊙ Use this when you are out of a pursuer's line of sight for better results. Most effective when you stand close to a lookalike of your true skin.<br>⊙ During an Escape, activate it right as you round a corner and turn around to surprise your pursuer.<br>⊙ There's a risk of being revealed when the effect expires. This exposure factor can be reduced through crafting. |
| | **Money Bomb** | Level 8 | Attracts civilians within a fixed radius, but has no effect on other characters, which reveals any player in the vicinity. | ⊙ You can drop the bomb at your feet or aim and throw it. The bomb blows up immediately, but the Cooldown begins only when the coins disappear.<br>⊙ Useful to reveal a target blended in a crowd or to impede the progress of an aggressor during an Escape. |
| | **Knives** | Level 10 | Throws Knives that slow down your target. | ⊙ Lock your target before throwing the Knives. A target that you have hit with Knives can still stun you, so don't approach them recklessly.<br>⊙ Knives prevent a victim from climbing and limit their range of action. Being hit by a Knife will cause a target to fall while climbing. |
| | **Wipe** | Level 10 | Reveals all players in the ability radius, prevents them from using their abilities, and silences their whispers and heartbeats. | ⊙ Essentially, this turns targets into defenseless victims, giving you free reign to kill them.<br>⊙ Useful to reveal targets blended in crowds. |
| | **Morph** | Level 12 | Transforms civilians inside the area of effect into your duplicates. | ⊙ This is very useful to hide from pursuers, but make sure that you use it while hidden in a crowd.<br>⊙ Offensive use: Morph a crowd from afar to reveal a blended target. |
| | **Bodyguard** | Level 14 | Creates a duplicate of your character who will protect you from pursuers. | ⊙ Can only be used when you are being pursued.<br>⊙ A very effective way to confuse your pursuers. Stay close to your duplicate for maximum efficiency and defensive stun opportunities. |
| | **Disrupting** | Level 16 | Scrambles the vision of a target. | ⊙ This can be used both offensively and defensively.<br>⊙ This is a great ability to employ to elude a pursuer, or to turn the tables and stun them. |
| | **Firecrackers** | Level 16 | Scare civilians and blind opponents, revealing their presence. | ⊙ Can be used to identify opponents; watch the movements of all affected individuals carefully.<br>⊙ You can drop Firecrackers at your feet or aim and throw them. The latter can be an efficient way to identify and/or stop a distant target. |
| | **Glimmer** | Level 18 | Makes you almost invisible. | ⊙ Can be used to escape a pursuer or approach a target unnoticed.<br>⊙ The slower you move, the more invisible you get. If hidden, you're almost completely invisible. If you run, an "aura" can be seen by experienced opponents. |
| | **Closure** | Level 18 | Triggers all the Chase Breakers around you. | ⊙ The Chase Breakers will all reopen after a few seconds.<br>⊙ They will also open if you (or your teammates) approach them: the point is to put your opponents at a temporary disadvantage. |
| | **Pistol** | Level 20 | Shoot down the targeted character after securing a Lock. | ⊙ There is no Incognito, Silent or Focus bonus for kills, but other specific bonuses apply (Execution and Mid-Air).<br>⊙ Good for rooftop chases, and for swiftly dispatching targets who lose their nerve and break cover to flee. |
| | **Animus Shield** | Level 20 | Makes you immune to Poison, Bombs and ranged weapons. | ⊙ Can be used both offensively (for example, to resist the effect of a Smoke Bomb dropped by a target that spotted you) and defensively (to survive when a pursuer uses Abilities against you).<br>⊙ Increases your chances to survive longer, especially as a sound effect reveals when someone aims at you.<br>⊙ By default, the shield can only negate one Ability, but this can be upgraded through crafting (up to three shield "charges"). |
| | **Teleport** | Level 22 | Teleports you to a different position on the map. | ⊙ Perfect to escape an incoming pursuer.<br>⊙ Can be used in Artifact Assault mode to increase your chances to quickly bring back the Artifact to your base. |
| | **Smoke Bomb** | Level 22 | Throw a Smoke Bomb to confuse civilians and opponents alike. | ⊙ You can drop the bomb at your feet or aim and throw it.<br>⊙ Offensive use: score Silent and Focus bonus on target; prevent Chase.<br>⊙ Defensive use: paralyze one or more pursuers for a follow-up stun. |
| | **Poison** | Level 24 | Poison a target to slowly kill them. | ⊙ You can only poison a target in close proximity. The Cooldown begins when the target dies.<br>⊙ There is no kill animation, so you can escape flashpoints stealthily. |
| | **Poison Dart** | Level 24 | Poison a target from afar. | ⊙ The Cooldown begins only after the Poison kills the target.<br>⊙ You can be spotted as you aim. |

The values in these tables may be adjusted in post-release updates.

QUICKSTART

THE STORY
SO FAR

PRIMER

WALKTHROUGH

SIDE QUESTS

REFERENCE &
ANALYSIS

MULTIPLAYER

EXTRAS

MAP LEGEND

INDEX

BASICS

CHARACTERS &
CUSTOMIZATION

SCORE &
PROGRESSION

ABILITY SETS

GAME MODES

ADVANCED TIPS

MAPS &
ANALYSIS

Crafting is the process by which you can customize every Ability by modifying and tweaking its parameters. This enables you to upgrade your Abilities in a way that best suits your strategy, but can only be achieved as you reach specific level milestones. You can upgrade an Ability twice through Crafting, each upgrade costing Abstergo Credits.

| CRAFTING ABILITIES | | | | | |
|---|---|---|---|---|---|
| ICON | NAME | PARAMETER | DEFAULT VALUE | UPGRADE #1 | UPGRADE #2 |
| | Tripwire Bomb | Range | 1.8m | 1.9m | 2.0m |
| | | Activation Time | 5s | 4s | 3s |
| | | Cooldown | 80s | 70s | 60s |
| | Decoy | Duration | 5s | 10s | 15s |
| | | Cooldown | 60s | 55s | 50s |
| | | Behavior | Normal | Discreet | Disguised |
| | Disguise | Duration | 15s | 17.5s | 20s |
| | | Cooldown | 60s | 55s | 50s |
| | | Exposure | Strong | Medium | Light |
| | Money Bomb | Civilians Attracted | 6 | 8 | 10 |
| | | Range | 5m | 7.5m | 10m |
| | | Cooldown | 70s | 65s | 55s |
| | Knives | Speed Decrease | 20% | 25% | 30% |
| | | Duration | 2.5s | 3s | 3.5s |
| | | Cooldown | 70s | 65s | 55s |
| | Wipe | Range | 8m | 10m | 12m |
| | | Duration | 5s | 7.5s | 10s |
| | | Cooldown | 80s | 70s | 60s |
| | Morph | Range | 3.5m | 4.5m | 5.5m |
| | | Civilians Morphed | 3 | 4 | 5 |
| | | Cooldown | 70s | 65s | 55s |
| | Bodyguard | Range | 5m | 7.5m | 10m |
| | | Duration | 5s | 7.5s | 10s |
| | | Cooldown | 70s | 65s | 60s |
| | Disruption | Aiming Time | 1s | 0.6s | 0.3s |
| | | Duration | 5s | 7.5s | 10s |
| | | Cooldown | 60s | 55s | 50s |
| | Firecrackers | Range | 5m | 5.5m | 6m |
| | | Duration | 4s | 4.5s | 5s |
| | | Cooldown | 80s | 70s | 60s |
| | Glimmer | Cooldown | 80s | 70s | 60s |
| | | Duration | 8s | 10s | 12s |
| | | Exposure | Strong | Medium | Light |
| | Closure | Range | 20m | 25m | 30m |
| | | Duration | 5s | 6s | 7s |
| | | Cooldown | 60s | 55s | 50s |
| | Pistol | Aiming Time | 2s | 1.5s | 1s |
| | | Initial Accuracy | 30% | 45% | 60% |
| | | Cooldown | 100s | 90s | 80s |
| | Animus Shield | Duration | 4.5s | 6s | 7.5 |
| | | Charges | 1 | 2 | 3 |
| | | Cooldown | 100s | 90s | 80s |
| | Teleport | Activation Time | 3.5s | 3s | 2.5s |
| | | Range | 35m | 40m | 45m |
| | | Cooldown | 100s | 90s | 80s |
| | Smoke Bomb | Range | 3.2m | 3.4m | 3.6m |
| | | Duration | 3s | 3.4s | 3.8s |
| | | Cooldown | 100s | 90s | 80s |
| | Poison | Delay | 6.5s | 5s | 3.5s |
| | | Score Bonus | 200 | 250 | 300 |
| | | Cooldown | 100s | 90s | 80s |
| | Poison Dart | Delay | 8s | 7s | 6s |
| | | Range | 12m | 14m | 16m |
| | | Cooldown | 100s | 90s | 80s |

The values detailed in this table may be adjusted in post-release updates.

# PERKS

You can further customize your character by choosing two Perks, additional powers that remain active throughout each match. Perks are also unlocked through Level progression.

## PERKS

| ICON | NAME | EFFECT | UNLOCKED |
|------|------|--------|----------|
| | Sixth Sense | Reveals notorious pursuers behind you and decreases the time needed to escape pursuers during a chase. | Level 6 |
| | Copycat | Allows you to copy the Ability Set of the opponent who just killed you. | Level 8 |
| | Sentry | Increases the time a target will remain locked when you lose sight of him or her. | Level 10 |
| | Hot Pursuit | Increases your speed when chasing a target and slows down the depletion of your Approach Meter. | Level 12 |
| | Resistance | Reduces the duration of stuns or Contested Kills. | Level 14 |
| | Overall Cooldowns | Reduces all Ability Cooldown periods. | Level 16 |
| | Resilience | Decreases the duration of Abilities used against you. | Level 16 |
| | Unstoppable | Opens all recently closed Chase Breakers and allows you to charge through civilians without falling. | Level 18 |
| | Blender | When you blend with a crowd, one of the civilians is automatically Morphed into your character's skin. | Level 20 |
| | Kill Buffer | Decreases your Kill Streak by 1 instead of resetting it when you die. | Level 24 |

# STREAKS

Streaks are performance-based bonuses earned through cumulative accomplishments or successive failures within each round.

⊙ A **Kill Streak** of successfully completed contracts will reward the player with extra points or a temporary play bonus.

⊙ Players who consistently die or lose contracts will incur a **Loss Bonus**, which actually helps them to arrest their poor form by granting small advantages. Loss Bonuses occur after five contract losses in a row, or after five deaths or stuns in a row.

## KILL STREAKS

| ICON | NAME | DESCRIPTION | UNLOCKED |
|------|------|-------------|----------|
| | Streak +250 | Receive 250 points when you kill or stun 5 targets without being killed. | Level 8 |
| | Silent Streak +250 | Receive 250 points when you silently kill or stun 3 targets without being killed. | Level 10 |
| | Mass Morph | If you perform a Kills Streak of 6, up to 15 surrounding civilians will be morphed into your lookalikes. | Level 12 |
| | Silent Mass Morph | If you perform a Silent Kills Streak of 4, up to 15 surrounding civilians will be morphed into your lookalikes. | Level 14 |
| | Streak +550 | Receive 550 points when you kill or stun 7 targets without being killed. | Level 16 |
| | Silent Streak +550 | Receive 550 points when you silently kill or stun 5 targets without being killed. | Level 18 |
| | Animus Hack | If you perform a Kills Streak of 8, this enables you to kill whomever you want from a distance. The sum of points you earn increases with each opponent you kill in this manner. | Level 20 |
| | Silent Animus Hack | If you perform a Silent Kills Streak of 6, this enables you to kill whomever you wish from a distance. The amount of points you earn increases with each opponent you kill in this manner. | Level 22 |

## LOSS BONUSES

| ICON | NAME | DESCRIPTION | UNLOCKED |
|------|------|-------------|----------|
| | Scavenger | Rewards you with 200 points for each Ground Finish until you perform a kill or stun. | Level 6 |
| | Shadow Approach | Fills up your Approach Meter faster when hunting your main target until you perform a kill or stun. | Level 8 |
| | Ability Switch | Allows you to change your current Ability Set each time you lose or miss your contract until you perform a kill or stun. | Level 10 |
| | Vision | Reveals targets in your line of sight or their location through walls until you perform a kill. | Level 12 |
| | Revelation | Reveals all pursuers in your line of sight until you perform a kill. | Level 14 |
| | Minor Hack | Allows you to kill your next target from a distance. | Level 18 |
| | Score x2 | Doubles the points earned by your next kill or stun. | Level 20 |
| | Boost Cooldowns | Resets and decreases the duration of Cooldowns until you perform a kill. | Level 22 |

The values in these tables may be adjusted in post-release updates.

QUICKSTART

THE STORY
SO FAR

PRIMER

WALKTHROUGH

SIDE QUESTS

REFERENCE &
ANALYSIS

MULTIPLAYER

EXTRAS

MAP LEGEND

INDEX

BASICS

CHARACTERS &
CUSTOMIZATION

SCORE &
PROGRESSION

ABILITY SETS

GAME MODES

ADVANCED TIPS

MAPS &
ANALYSIS

## INTRODUCTORY SESSIONS

| Mode: | Non-competitive | Duration: | ∞ |
|---|---|---|---|
| Objective: | Practice kills, stuns, and Escape sequences. | | |

### Notes & Tips:

- ⊙ These three sessions are only intended as one-off tutorials. However, you can replay them as many times as you like to experiment with different approaches.

## PLAYGROUND

| Mode: | Non-competitive | Duration: | ∞ |
|---|---|---|---|
| Objective: | Find and kill assigned targets in any way you see fit. | | |

### Notes & Tips:

- ⊙ Use it to explore maps and practice your Abilities.

## SIMPLE DEATHMATCH

| Mode: | Competitive | Duration: | 1 round of 10 minutes |
|---|---|---|---|
| Objective: | Achieve the highest score by killing assigned targets. | | |

### Notes & Tips:

- ⊙ This is a simplified version of Deathmatch. The rules are broadly the same, though you cannot access your Ability Sets.

- ⊙ Simple Deathmatch is the best mode for new players to familiarize themselves with basic multiplayer concepts. Complexities such as the Compass and Abilities are disabled, the maps are tiny, and each competitor is assigned a unique character, which means that targets are very easy to identify.

- ⊙ With no Abilities or Perks at your disposal, blending with moving groups is the key to success on these small, congested maps.

## DEATHMATCH

| Mode: | Competitive | Duration: | 1 round of 10 minutes |
|---|---|---|---|
| Objective: | Achieve the highest score by killing assigned targets. | | |

### Notes & Tips:

- ⊙ Each player's skin is the only one of its kind in this mode, though you can use Abilities or Perks that create duplicates.

- ⊙ You are both predator and prey, and can only kill your assigned target.

- ⊙ You cannot trigger Chases, but your Approach Meter still allows you to earn Kill Bonuses.

- ⊙ There is no Compass for any player in this mode. This means that Deathmatch is all about line of sight and paying attention to your target's portrait outline. If the portrait outline is not blue (meaning your target is not in your line of sight), run to a new large open area and slow down. If the outline turns blue, use low profile actions to approach your target. If the outline doesn't turn blue, run to a different area and try again. Once you are close to your target, the background of the portrait becomes blue too, which will help you identify it.

- ⊙ Deathmatch maps are very small, so it pays to get into moving cover as soon as you spawn. Your pursuer is never very far away.

- ⊙ The higher your rank, the more pursuers will hunt you.

- ⊙ Blender is a useful Perk in Deathmatch. Creating a lookalike of your character whenever you blend offers a more-than-welcome life insurance – though beware that pursuers might identify you if they see you in the process of creating a duplicate (⊙ 01).

- ⊙ Animus Hack can be lethal in this game mode, as there are no lookalikes. The moment you activate this Streak, and provided you've spent enough time in the session to identify each unique character, you can rack up kills at an incredible rate.

- ⊙ When you think you have spotted your target, be aware that they could be Disguised.

- ⊙ Smoke Bombs are great to use defensively. The moment you spot an incoming pursuer, watch them approaching and throw your bomb when they're close for an easy stun.

### Sample Ability Set

| Abilities | Animus Shield |
|---|---|
| | Smoke Bomb |
| | Knives |
| **Perks** | Kill Buffer |
| | Blender |
| **Streak & Bonus** | Animus Hack |
| | Scavenger |

01

QUICKSTART

THE STORY
SO FAR

PRIMER

WALKTHROUGH

SIDE QUESTS

REFERENCE &
ANALYSIS

► MULTIPLAYER

EXTRAS

MAP LEGEND

INDEX

BASICS

CHARACTERS &
CUSTOMIZATION

SCORE &
PROGRESSION

ABILITY SETS

GAME MODES

ADVANCED TIPS

MAPS &
ANALYSIS

## WANTED

| Mode: | Competitive | Duration: | 1 round of 10 minutes |
|---|---|---|---|
| Objective: | Achieve the highest score by killing assigned targets. | | |

### Notes & Tips:

- You are both predator and prey, but you may only kill your contracted target.

- It's harder to hide in Wanted than in Deathmatch as your pursuer has a Compass. However, there are duplicates of your character wandering around, making it easier to blend and lure your pursuer into killing a civilian.

- Use your Compass to anticipate a target's route through an arena, and you may be able to catch him or her out as they round a corner.

- When you blend with a group, try to select one with at least one duplicate of your character.

- It can sometimes be more efficient to take the time to identify and escape a pursuer before tracking your own target. Staying alive enables you to complete Streaks and earn more points. This is especially true when you're trying to activate the Animus Hack Kill Streak.

- If you manage to approach your target from behind an obstacle, jump on the obstacle and perform the kill from there for an easy bonus.

- When you're following a target that hasn't noticed you, don't always rush to get a cheap kill. Silently fast walking behind them may enable you to kill them as they're performing a kill themselves, which will net you more points.

- In this very hectic mode, defensive Abilities can enable you to survive longer and get more kill opportunities. The Animus Shield often proves particularly useful in this sense.

- When you use a Chase Breaker to escape a pursuer, consider stopping and Blending immediately as you exit. Your pursuer will expect you to run away frantically and may lose you completely ( 02).

- If you are first with a high score, you will usually be pursued by two or three characters at the same time. In such instances, consider playing defensively. Blend in a group with at least one lookalike (more, ideally), and your rivals will need to employ Abilities to identify you – something that they won't always have access to.

- Don't run away after you kill a target. You will often be pursued yourself, and sprinting will only make you easier to identify.

### Sample Ability Set

| | | |
|---|---|---|
| **Abilities** | Morph | |
| | Poison | |
| | Pistol | |
| **Perks** | Sentry | |
| | Blender | |
| **Streak & Bonus** | Streak +550 | |
| | Score x2 | |

---

## ASSASSINATE

| Mode: | Competitive | Duration: | 1 round of 10 minutes |
|---|---|---|---|
| Objective: | Identify, acquire and assassinate the target of your choice to achieve the highest score. | | |

### Notes & Tips:

- There is no pre-assigned target in this mode. The key is to acquire one, simply by pressing 🎮/L1. However you can acquire anyone you encounter, including civilians. Therefore your goal is to be very cautious, keep a low profile and watch your surroundings. Every time you notice someone behaving strangely, running or performing other High Profile actions, quickly acquire them and try to make a discrete approach to achieve a kill with the best possible bonus.

- As a rule, you will perform fewer kills than usual in this mode. It takes time to acquire your target, so be cautious: discretion and keen observation are pivotal. Maximizing your points haul for each kill is vital, as you will enjoy fewer opportunities to score.

- Identifying your pursuer with a Lock exposes them and empties their Approach Meter.

- You do not have a proper Compass in this mode; however, up to four arrows show you the general direction of nearby players (📷 03). As you approach your target, the arrow turns into a thin arc, then a full circle, so you can rarely use it to determine the exact position of your potential target. As an indicator of where you should begin a hunt, though, these prove invaluable. A very effective strategy is to use the arrows to travel directly towards a target. As soon as an arrow turns into an arc or a circle, be stealthy and blend until you spot a target that you can acquire.

- Acquiring and killing a civilian reveals you to others, though there are no further penalties.

- Always acquire your target before you attempt anything else. You won't be able to use your moves or Abilities efficiently until you have acquired a target.

- Disguise is not as useful in this mode (since there are no portraits representing pre-assigned contracts), unless you know someone is stalking you. In that case, go round a corner, Disguise and turn around to surprise them.

- Decoy and Bodyguard can be combined for some effective defensive strategies. Activate either whenever you know that a pursuer has identified you to lure them away, giving you a chance to acquire them. If you add the Pistol for ranged kills, this can prove to be a very balanced Ability Set.

- If a target is stunned in front of you, consider acquiring it immediately (even if you had acquired someone else beforehand), as this will give you the time to secure the Focus bonus before you perform the kill.

### Sample Ability Set

| | | |
|---|---|---|
| **Abilities** | Decoy | |
| | Bodyguard | |
| | Pistol | |
| **Perks** | Resistance | |
| | Overall Cooldown | |
| **Streak & Bonus** | Mass Morph | |
| | Shadow Approach | |

## MANHUNT

| Mode: | Team-based | Duration: | 2 rounds of 5 minutes |
|---|---|---|---|
| Objective: | Achieve the highest team score, hiding together as targets, and performing valuable kills as hunters. | | |

### Notes & Tips:

- Both teams take a turn as hunters and hunted.

- While hunted, blend with a crowd of civilians that includes at least one lookalike. Otherwise, use Morph or Bodyguard to confuse your pursuers with lookalikes. You can even fortify your position with a well-placed Tripwire Bomb, or employ a Smoke Bomb instead.

- Hiding with your team is the best way to rack up noteworthy points totals. If one of you is killed, there will always be someone on hand to score an easy stun before fleeing.

- When on the offensive, coordinate with your allies to perform multiple kills.

- Wipe works very well in Manhunt to reveal targets that are hidden among lookalikes, and to prevent them from knocking you down with Abilities. Money Bombs and Firecrackers can be used for the same purpose.

- Morph is also a fantastic choice, as you can use it remotely. When you suspect a target is hidden in a group of civilians, Morph the entire group from afar and your target will be revealed as the odd one out (⚟ 04).

- You will usually have opportunities to perform high-score kills with Poison Darts in Manhunt games, as you'll often be facing two or three enemies at a time. Add the Hot Pursuit and Unstoppable perks for a well-rounded offensive Ability Set.

- An amusing strategy is to hide in a haystack and create a lookalike (with Blender) right next to your position. A pursuer will be likely to attack your doppelganger, allowing you to perform an easy stun.

### Sample Ability Set

| | Offense Set | Defense Set |
|---|---|---|
| **Abilities** | Firecrackers | Morph |
| | Wipe | Disguise |
| | Poison Dart | Knives |
| **Perks** | Hot Pursuit | Blender |
| | Unstoppable | Overall Cooldown |
| **Streak & Bonus** | Mass Morph | Silent Mass Morph |
| | Minor Hack | Revelation |

04

05

## ARTIFACT ASSAULT

| Mode: | Team-based | Duration: | 1 round of 10 minutes |
|---|---|---|---|
| Objective: | The team with the highest number of captured artifacts wins. | | |

### Notes & Tips:

- You will score by stealing the other team's artifact from their base and carrying it back to yours.

- You are a pursuer while in your territory, but become a target once in enemy territory. When you are carrying the artifact, enemies can kill you even in your own territory.

- When your team's artifact has been stolen, your Compass will blur each time you move close to your home base, rendering it useless.

- It is vital that you learn the safest route back to your base after stealing the artifact. Using Chase Breakers can be crucial to your success.

- Knives are particularly useful when defending, as they enable you to stop a fleeing enemy in their tracks and recover your artifact.

- When defending, consider camping close to your Artifact and intercept any opponent who steals it.

- Use Tripwire Bombs to protect your Artifact; these will knock down any opponent who triggers them. Place your Bomb in the middle of an obvious entry/exit point or at the nearest Chase Breaker to your base to increase your chances of success (⚟ 05).

- Use the Disguise or Morph Abilities to blend in before making a dash for the enemy artifact. Drop a Firecracker or Smoke Bomb to facilitate your escape.

- While attacking, it's best not to use the Blender Perk – if you inadvertently brush against a crowd your opponents may spot one of the civilians transforming, revealing your position.

- Look out for Tripwire Bombs when you approach the enemy artifact, and while escaping the immediate vicinity.

- The Unstoppable and Hot Pursuit Perks are particularly useful, especially if you adopt a defensive role, giving you an edge while chasing a fleeing enemy.

- If a rival manages to steal an Artifact, use Closure to temporarily seal all Chase Breakers and stop the thief.

- A great strategy is to have two people trying to steal the enemy team's artifact, and two others defending your team's Artifact. If you have a strong lead, you can consider focusing most of your team on defense to ensure victory.

- Closure can also be used offensively. After you've stolen the Artifact, run towards your objective and activate Closure to stop pursuers. If you can also activate Animus Shield, this protects you from ranged attacks, maximizing your chances to score.

- Hide behind a wall or an obstacle near the enemy team's Artifact, and use Glimmer to become invisible. You can then steal the Artifact and return to your base.

- Another effective strategy is to steal the Artifact and then activate Teleport to quickly bring it back to your base.

### Sample Ability Set

| | Defense Set | Offense Set |
|---|---|---|
| **Abilities** | Tripwire Bomb | Disguise |
| | Closure | Glimmer |
| | Pistol | Disruption |
| **Perks** | Hot Pursuit | Overall Cooldown |
| | Unstoppable | Resilience |
| **Streak & Bonus** | Shadow Approach | Silent Streak +250 |
| | Vision | Minor Hack |

## DOMINATION

| Mode: | Team-based | Duration: | 1 round of 10 minutes |
|---|---|---|---|
| Objective: | Achieve the highest score by capturing territories and defending them. | | |

### Notes & Tips:

- Your team's priority is to capture as many territories as possible at the same time. To capture a territory, all you have to do is step inside the marked area and remain there until the capture gauge is fully filled. The more allies that are in a territory at the same time, the faster a capture occurs. The team that fills the scoring gauge or obtains the highest score at the end of the countdown wins.

- When you defend a territory that you have captured, you are considered a pursuer and can kill any member of the opposing team that is contesting your capture. Conversely, when you contest a territory controlled by the opposing team, you are their prey. This means that you can only stun your rivals, who will often have the time to regain consciousness before you have finished capturing the territory.

- When you attack an enemy-controlled territory, your sole priority is to remain alive for as long as possible while in the marked area. Use abilities to increase your chances.

- The members of each team have the same skin, so Abilities that enable you to change your appearance can be extremely useful.

- A good way to defend a territory is often to use stealth. Blend within a crowd or use a hiding place inside the territory and rotate the camera to keep an eye on all possible points of entry. You will easily spot any member of the opposing team that rushes towards the objective. Abilities that create lookalikes of your character are quite useful, as they enable you to survive longer.

- The Pistol is of great benefit while defending a territory. You only need to briefly leave a place of concealment to fire it, and it removes the need to cross open ground to intercept an interloper.

- If you notice a rival closing in for a kill, consider dropping a Smoke Bomb, as this has an area of effect that can neutralize multiple targets.

- If you happen to encounter a member of the opposing team on your way to a territory, feel free to stun them for the benefit of your entire team.

- You can sprint or free run to reach a territory as long as you are not in the line of sight of anyone inside. As you get close and become visible to a potential defender, walk and try to act as civilians do in order to allay suspicions. Use an Ability if you don't want to take any chances. For example, use Disguise just before you reach a territory. This means any enemies defending it won't identify you as you change skins.

- If you stun a target inside a territory, keep that target in sight until they revive.

- If an unidentified opponent enters your territory, stay blended and watch everyone within the area to detect clues on who the interloper might be. Abilities that reveal targets are especially useful for players focusing on defense.

- Don't automatically respawn (by pressing Ⓨ/△) if you get stunned, as you will regain control of your character faster if you just wait. Respawn only if you're sure that you have lost the territory that you were defending, as this will usually teleport you to a position closer to another territory.

- Coordinate with your allies to have one character defending each captured territory, and the others trying to conquer new ones. Not only do you score points by doing so, but you also prevent the opposing team from scoring. Teams that cooperate will almost always enjoy an overwhelming advantage over those that act as a ragged collection of individuals.

- Resilience is very useful when you defend a territory as it enables you to recover faster when enemies use Abilities against you.

- Use Glimmer when you are on the periphery of a territory, ideally around a corner or behind an obstacle (📷 06). This will enable you to capture the territory without being spotted by your enemies. If they look at your position from a distance, they will simply not see anything.

| Sample Ability Set | | |
|---|---|---|
| Abilities | Disguise | |
| | Glimmer | |
| | Disruption | |
| Perks | Overall Cooldown | |
| | Resilience | |
| Streak & Bonus | Silent Streak +250 | |
| | Scavenger | |

# WOLFPACK

| Mode: | Cooperative (1-4 players) | Duration: | Up to 25 sequences | Objective: | Achieve the highest score by killing targets in timed sequences. |
|---|---|---|---|---|---|

## Notes & Tips:

- Your priority in every timed sequence is to reach the score threshold before the end of the countdown. This can be achieved by killing AI-controlled targets. For each sequence, you will usually have as many targets as there are members in your team.

- To save time, which this game mode is all about, run as long as your target cannot see you, then complete your approach by fast walking.

- The usual Bonuses apply, but you can also get extra points by killing a target at the same time as your teammates. In addition, you can get more bonus points by completing secondary objectives that appear onscreen.

- Discuss the selection of Abilities with your teammates. Choose Ability Sets that complement each other well or expand your tactical options.

- More generally, this game mode is all about communication. This is especially true in Hardcore. You need to speak with your teammates at all times to act as an efficient unit while synchronizing your kills, identifying the team member best positioned to intercept a fleeing target, and so forth.

- It is essential to synchronize your kills to maximize your score with every wave of enemies. Use the OSD in the top left of your screen as a visual guide. All members of your team are represented with their portrait. If you see a padlock icon below a portrait, it means that player has locked their target. If you see a sword icon, it means the player is within killing range of the target. If you see an orange outline blinking around the portrait, it means that player is being detected by their target. When all team members have locked their targets, a "Go!" prompt appears onscreen, allowing you to synchronize the kills and maximize your score (📷 07).

- You get special Sync Kill opportunities for waves 10, 16, 22, and 25. Synchronize your kills as usual to get a massive kill bonus (📷 08).

- Every once in a while, you will have a chance to kill an extra target. There's no penalty for missing this opportunity, but it offers you a way to secure additional points.

- Press ◀/SELECT or ♦ to display the characteristics of your targets. Each has specific traits that will enable you to determine how best to approach them. For example, the Alert enemy type will detect you when you are in their line of sight, forcing you to approach stealthily. Conversely, those described as Short Sighted or Fools will only detect you if you perform obvious High Profile actions in front of them. You can find a detailed description of all traits in the Animus Database menu.

- At the end of each session, you will receive an additional score bonus based on time remaining: 10 points per second in Standard, 30 points per second in Difficult, and 75 points per second in Hardcore.

- In Hardcore, you really need to maximize your score to reach milestones. One essential step to fulfill is to secure Variety bonuses, which requires that you obtain 15 different Kill bonuses throughout the session. Make sure to start by performing all types of approaches (from Reckless to Incognito), then try to use other forms of kills (such as Poison, Aerial Kills and so forth). If every participant manages to get all Variety Bonuses, this will be a massive boon for the team.

- Try to Ground Finish all of the targets before they disappear. You can do this multiple times by locking the targets that have been killed by your allies (📷 09). If every teammate does this consistently, you will accumulate plenty of additional points throughout each session. This is especially important in Hardcore.

- In Hardcore, it's essential to make sure that every target is taken care of by a single team member. If you make the mistake of having two allies on one target, you will lose time tracking the final victim, which you simply cannot afford in this difficulty level. To ensure that you avoid this mistake, use the OSD in the top right corner of the screen. Ideally, there should be one blue triangle (each representing a teammate) per target. For advanced waves of enemies, consider switching targets with a teammate when you are closer to each other's current quarry.

- On all difficulty levels, but especially on Hardcore, only pay attention to the additional objectives if they will net you more points than a normal kill. For example, if the additional objective requirement is to perform an Aerial Kill for 100 points, it makes sense to stick to a more profitable high-yield stealth finish. You will usually get other chances later on to use similar kills (in our example, Aerial Kill) which will reward you with an improved points haul, or which will help you to reach the Variety Bonuses more efficiently.

- Your team should avoid using all of its abilities in a single wave of enemies. This enables you to react more efficiently during an emergency, such as a when a target is fleeing.

- Smoke Bombs can enable you to kill multiple targets simultaneously (within the same radius/area of effect) and get big scores (📷 10).

- Craft Poison Darts to reduce the Cooldown and make the ability available as often as possible. The Pistol is also useful for killing targets that run away.

- Abilities that reveal targets (such as Wipe) are very useful for later waves where enemies disguise themselves. For experienced players who can identify their targets without any help (using the line of sight and portrait outline), it makes more sense to favor Abilities that make it easier to approach targets undetected, such as Disguise and Glimmer.

| Sample Ability Set | | |
|---|---|---|
| | **Standard** | **Difficult/Hardcore** |
| **Abilities** | Firecracker | Disguise |
| | Wipe | Glimmer |
| | Poison Dart | Pistol |
| **Perks** | Resilience | Overall Cooldown |
| | Resistance | Kill Buffer |
| **Streak & Bonus** | Streak +250 | Streak +550 |
| | Boost Cooldowns | Scavenger |

| Wolfpack-specific Icons | | | |
|---|---|---|---|
| | Wary | | Fighting Target |
| | Suspicious | | Extra Target |
| | Detected | | Revive |
| | Fleeing Target | | |

07

08

09

10

QUICKSTART

THE STORY
SO FAR

PRIMER

WALKTHROUGH

SIDE QUESTS

REFERENCE &
ANALYSIS

MULTIPLAYER

EXTRAS

MAP LEGEND

INDEX

BASICS

CHARACTERS &
CUSTOMIZATION

SCORE &
PROGRESSION

ABILITY SETS

GAME MODES

ADVANCED TIPS

MAPS &
ANALYSIS

## GAME CATEGORIES

Game Categories are Game Modes or combinations of Game Modes linked thematically.

| NAME | THEME/RULE | GAME TYPES | LIMITATIONS |
|---|---|---|---|
| Free For All | Solo play | Wanted, Assassinate, Deathmatch | - |
| Team Objectives | Team play | Manhunt, Artifact Assault, Domination | - |
| Simple Deathmatch | Learn the basics | Simple Deathmatch | No abilities |
| Wolfpack | Co-op play | Wolfpack | * |
| Private | Custom games with friends | All | No XP or ▲ awarded |

* In "Invite Only Wolfpack", you can only play with your friends. Other players cannot join the game session.

## GOLDEN RULES

- Stay on the move. You have a target to track down and you are being hunted constantly. You should only remain still in very specific instances, such as when you are hiding from a pursuer or poised to spring an ambush.

- Aim to complete your contracts with a high score bonus. Securing more kills than your rivals isn't helpful if they consistently accumulate twice the points.

- Avoid surrendering points to other players by allowing yourself to be killed or |stunned. Be patient! Running towards a target will get you to them more quickly, but will also increase the likelihood you will be noticed (or, worse, Locked) by other players.

- A player with higher XP and character resources will always have an advantage, so just keep playing. Your progression curve will flatten out, with higher Levels coming more slowly, but the advanced Abilities are worth striving for.

- Improvise, don't strategize. Concentrate on finding your target as quickly as possible, but remain alert and be ready to switch tactics in an instant.

- Try to Lock your targets whenever you identify them. Locking enables you to keep track of opponents, even when they move out of view (though only briefly), and helps to avoid situations where you execute civilians by mistake.

- It makes sense to use Abilities sooner rather than later. Even with default Cooldown periods, the assignment of contracts and tracking time with a full Ability Set roughly equates to one Ability per kill.

## ABILITY SET TIPS

- As you level up, you will need to define tactical custom sets to get the best use of your Abilities, Perks and Streaks. These sets enable you to activate two Perks, whereas the default sets only feature one initially.

- Through advancement, you will acquire up to five custom sets for a range of strategic options, enabling you to choose various sets of complementary powers. You can switch sets between rounds, after dying, by pressing **◀**/(SELECT) + **Ⓐ**/**Ⓧ** during a game (though this costs **Ⓐ**), or by activating the Ability Switch Loss Bonus. Give each set a unique descriptive name to facilitate quick choices before respawns.

- If your opponents take to the rooftops, a focus on ranged Abilities may catch them out. If they act aggressively, defensive Abilities will humiliate them. If you suspect that the other participants are more experienced than you, choose a favorite Loss Bonus (such as Score x2) to remain competitive.

- Remember that Abilities are not 100% reliable. The fog of a Smoke Bomb can be avoided during the explosion delay; the trap of a Tripwire Bomb can be negotiated by walking carefully around it; you can even escape the effect of Wipe by staying out of your opponent's range for a second or two.

- Some Abilities have a counterpart that undermines them. For example, Firecrackers can reveal a Disguised or Morphed target; Knives will slow down a target even if they have the Hot Pursuit Perk.

- To get you started on ideas for good combinations, here are a few selections of skills that complement each other well:

| DEFENSIVE SETS | | | |
|---|---|---|---|
| | **Set 1** | **Set 2** | **Set 3** |
| **Abilities** | Animus Shield | Decoy | Tripwire Bomb |
| | Smoke Bomb | Bodyguard | Closure |
| | Knives | Pistol | Pistol |
| **Perks** | Kill Buffer | Kill Buffer | Hot Pursuit |
| | Blender | Blender | Unstoppable |
| **Streak & Bonus** | Animus Hack | Mass Morph | Shadow Approach |
| | Scavenger | Revelation | Vision |

| OFFENSIVE SETS | | | |
|---|---|---|---|
| | **Set 1** | **Set 2** | **Set 3** |
| **Abilities** | Morph | Disguise | Decoy |
| | Wipe | Glimmer | Bodyguard |
| | Poison Dart | Disruption | Disruption |
| **Perks** | Hot Pursuit | Overall Cooldown | Blender |
| | Unstoppable | Resilience | Kill Buffer |
| **Streak & Bonus** | Mass Morph | Silent Streak +250 | Mass Morph |
| | Revelation | Scavenger | Revelation |

## SCORE & BONUS TIPS

- When your target is hiding in hay, jump in yourself. This will force him or her out, setting up an easy Hidden Kill bonus.

- In any given round, try to mix up your kills. There are big points bonuses for variety.

- After you perform a kill, close proximity to other players will delay the assignment of another contract. Move to the outer edge of the map to reduce the waiting time.

- When another player kills your target, don't forget to finish them off for a Ground Finish bonus.

- Crafting (see page 276) is a good way to improve your favored Abilities, which will make it easier to score more points in each session.

- The better your approach is, the shorter the kill animation will be. This will help you to remain unnoticed and move on immediately to your next target.

# OPPONENT IDENTIFICATION

⊙ When a player moves his camera to look behind, his character moves his head – use this distinct "tell" to locate your rivals (📷 04).

⊙ Take a moment to stop and look at which way the arc is moving on your Compass. By interpreting its width and direction, you may be able to intercept your target at the nearest intersection.

⊙ If your target is constantly running around on rooftops, you can either chase him up there for a Reckless kill, or save your time and earn a bonus by shooting them in the back with the Pistol or a Poison Dart.

⊙ Once you hear whispers, you know that your pursuer is drawing near. Conversely, once you hear your heartbeat, you know that your target is nearby. If you are finding it difficult to hear the whispers, try adjusting sound levels on your TV, or use headphones.

⊙ An arrow inside the Compass reveals you when your target is at a different elevation, perhaps striding over rooftops while you stalk the streets, or walking on a different floor level (📷 01). Use this to plan ahead your approach and know where to look when tracking down your target.

⊙ Blending with moving crowds enables you to approach your target without being spotted.

⊙ Blending isn't half as effective as standing next to a civilian with an identical appearance. This leaves the sticky problem of deciding who to strike, which should at the very least slow an opponent down.

⊙ If you're trying to kill a target that has a lookalike in a Blend group, you can use the line of sight to identify which one is your target. Position yourself behind an obstacle or around a corner, and inch slowly to have only one character at a time in your line of sight: the outline around your target's portrait will reveal which lookalike to kill (📷 02 & 📷 03). Conversely, when you use a lookalike defensively (with Blender, for instance), try to position your character in such a way that you will appear in the line of sight of your pursuer at the same time as your clone.

⊙ When you have spotted a target that has also identified you, the outcome of the duel is often determined by Abilities. Use the Ability that has the most profound and long-lasting effect: for example, a Smoke Bomb incapacitates its target for a longer duration than Knives.

⊙ Moving at a higher elevation increases your chances of targeting your contract. If you are on a rooftop above them, the range of an air assassination while in pursuit exceeds the proximity you would need to reach them at street level – and you won't take damage from falling. At the same time, rooftop activity marks you out to all other players.

⊙ Some characters are harder to spot at a distance than others, particularly for new players. If there is one you find troublesome, simply choose that skin as your own to avoid this problem. There is a chance, of course, that your pursuers may have the same trouble identifying you.

⊙ Watch how AI-controlled civilians move and attempt to imitate them. Other players are just as busy as you, so a rough approximation will let you pass for an NPC on most occasions.

⊙ If your pursuer performs a High Profile action while in your line of sight, a red icon will appear above their head, making them very easy to spot (🔻).

⊙ The moment you locate your target and assassinate them, even if striking from a hiding place, you break your cover for the entire world to see. You are never more likely to be killed than at this moment, so you may benefit from a swift getaway rather than blending or hiding.

⊙ Use Poison or Poison Darts to avoid creating a disturbance, then make a discrete departure – the ensuing commotion may distract any opponents closing in on your approximate position.

- When in close pursuit of a target, don't forget to regularly look around to identify opponents zeroing in on you.

- You cannot be assassinated by normal moves while climbing or jumping. However ranged Abilities make short work of anyone scaling walls or free running.

- Chases favor the escapee, as they can use Chase Breakers and hiding places to accelerate a time-out. For this reason, don't

attempt to follow your target's exact footsteps: attempt to cut them off instead. Chases cost potential killing time, so a 50/50 gamble on whether they'll turn left or right will conclude the matter sooner rather than later. It's often better to ditch an adept opponent than enter a protracted pursuit.

- Always climb in steps, using beams and poles, and make distance on flat ground or free running surfaces. Scaling a wall leaves you open to ranged attacks.

- If you have your pursuer Locked, press the stun button rapidly as they close in for the kill and you have a greater chance of incapacitating them and ending their pursuit. Worst-case scenario, you will get an Honorable Death bonus for your troubles.

- When you are chased, you can use the Disruption Ability as you go round a corner or behind an obstacle, then suddenly turn around and stun your pursuer.

## TEAM TACTICS

- Cooperative actions boost scores. Before rushing to complete a kill, check if you can't maximize the return by involving teammates. Plan your Ability Sets together for offense or support roles.

- Whenever you are close to an ally who has just killed a target, run to the victim and perform a Ground Finish for an easy bonus. This can be achieved by all teammates and is a great way to maximize your score if you move in formation.

- If you see a teammate being stunned while standing in close proximity, try to kill their target and then immediately revive your ally. You will not only save your cohort precious seconds, but also earn more points; remind him or her to perform a Ground Finish on the vanquished target.

- When you Lock a target, your partners see them Locked too (🛡), which helps to coordinate your actions.

- If a partner is killed or stunned, their assassin is ripe for a counterattack (📷 05). Cover each other when close, as you will be drawing both of your hunters to the same location.

- Press 🅱/⭕ to revive a stunned ally and earn a bonus (📷 06).

- Use your Target HUD (see page 261) to switch between targets, then go for the opponent who is closest, or in the most interesting location. Don't necessarily settle for the first assigned target.

- Animus Hack isn't as effective in team modes, as you only have a maximum of four targets.

- Use your teammate to drive a target towards your location. Setting a trap with Disguise is effective, as many opponents will expect to recognize their pursuers.

- Adjust your solo and cooperative efforts to suit the situation. When trailing, work together on one target for quality kills and Team Bonuses. Once you take the lead, it can be advantageous to split up and take a target each.

- Remember that a Chase Breaker that was closed by a teammate will automatically reopen for you.

# MAPS & ANALYSIS

To help you to familiarize yourself with each arena, the maps that follow reveal the layout of the destinations you will visit. They also include the positions of all points of interest, such as Chase Breakers and elements exclusive to certain game modes.

## Legend

| | |
|---|---|
|  | Lift |
|  | Corner Helper |
|  | Closing Gates |
|  | Falling Platform |
|  | Territory (Domination only) |
|  | Artifact & Base (Artifact Assault only) |

## BOSTON HARBOR

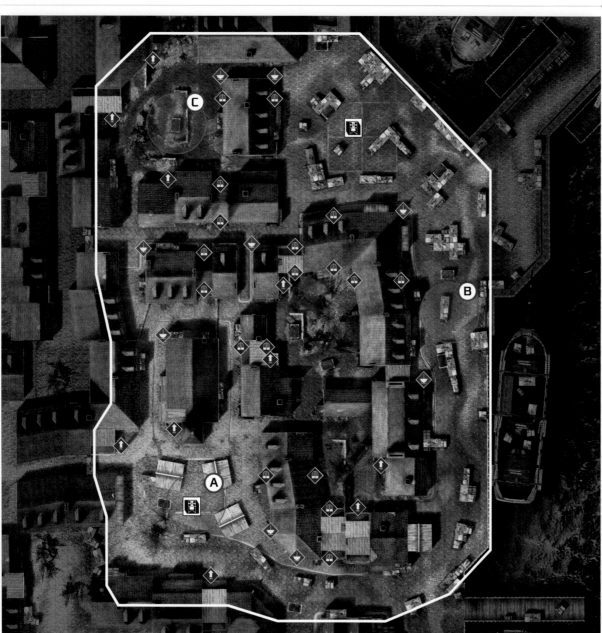

- ⊙ When attempting to escape a pursuer, avoid running along the quay. The entire area is rather linear and offers few opportunities to break line of sight.

- ⊙ The busy square on the steps of the church offers plenty of blending spots and moving crowds for social stealth, but is open and exposed when your cover is broken.

- ⊙ Aerial kills, Pistol exchanges and even assassinations from ledges are a frequent feature of the upper routes, so watch the skyline.

III

QUICKSTART

THE STORY
SO FAR

PRIMER

WALKTHROUGH

SIDE QUESTS

REFERENCE &
ANALYSIS

MULTIPLAYER

EXTRAS

MAP LEGEND

INDEX

BASICS

CHARACTERS &
CUSTOMIZATION

SCORE &
PROGRESSION

ABILITY SETS

GAME MODES

ADVANCED TIPS

MAPS &
ANALYSIS

## NEW YORK BREWERY

- This map can be incredibly hectic in Deathmatch, as it's small and features two floor levels. This means that it's easy to establish the general location of your opponent, but without necessarily knowing where they are. The Blender Perk is vital here: use it while you blend on the upper floor as a defensive precaution.

- The many gangways and balconies make perfect spots for Focused assassinations and aerial kills on targets below and nearby.

- You will often find that your target is at a different elevation on this map. Don't be impatient: if you climb a wall to take a

shortcut, you will draw unnecessary attention to yourself.

- This map is possibly easier than others in Wolfpack because of the numerous angles and obstacles that can potentially mask your approach.

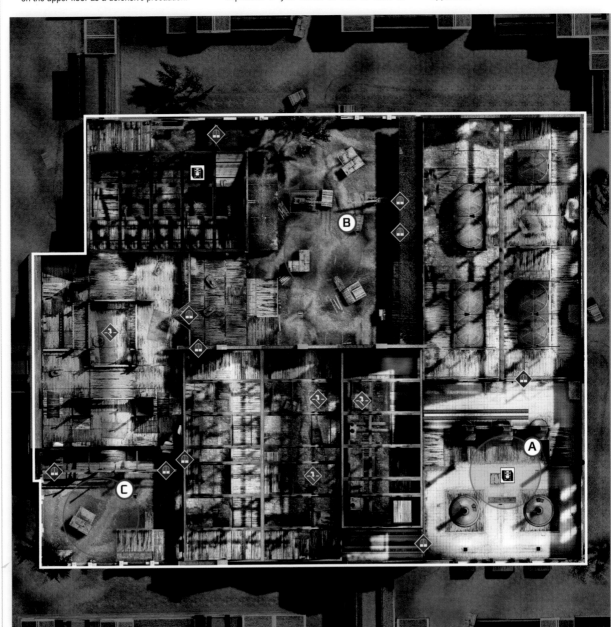

- If you reach a vantage point on this map, you can have a clear view of almost the entire map. This can be good to identify incoming pursuers, for instance, but the downside is that you may have a hard time knowing for sure who your target is if you have more than one lookalike in your line of sight.

- Games played on this map can be very intense in Deathmatch and Simple Deathmatch modes. Use the various hiding places, benches and static blend groups to pounce on passing targets for Hidden Kill bonuses.

- You do not have access to any rooftops per se on this map, which keeps the action largely

on the ground. Even without rooftops, you may learn to lose your pursuer by squeezing through the crowds. It is faster to weave between civilians than to use the Shove move.

- This map is fairly difficult in Wolfpack because of the many open areas that make stealthy approaches problematic.

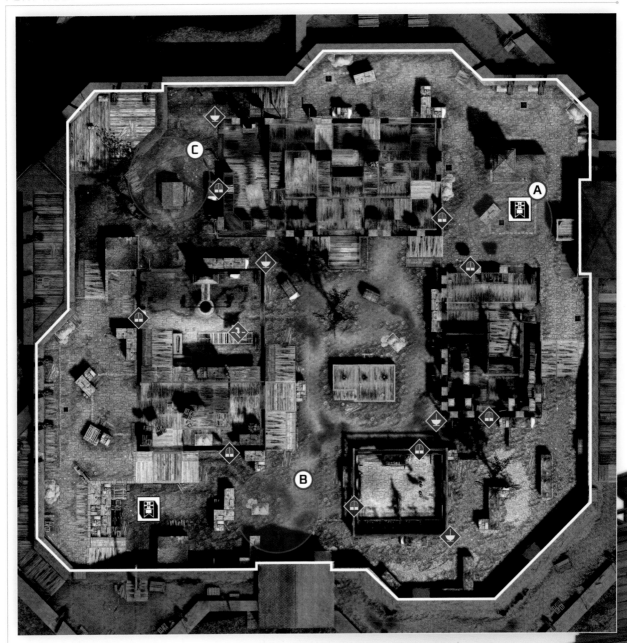

⊙ Use the many gangways and balconies to your advantage. While this might provide opportunities to air assassinate your target, being on high ground will sometimes help you to spot pursuers. A citizen halting for no reason below your position is most likely a rival attempting to ascertain your exact location.

⊙ This map features haystacks that are handily located near closing gates. Running through these Chase Breakers and hiding immediately as you arrive on the other side can be very effective, and may offer an opportunity to stun your pursuer. However, it should go without saying that experienced players will often anticipate this...

⊙ Any high profile action on the gallows plaza is likely to lead to immediate detection, though incoming pursuers are very easy to identify in such an open space. Rush inside one of the surrounding buildings to shake off anyone on your tail.

- Moderately high buildings are found on either side of most streets on this map, granting an excellent vantage point for spotting your prey. Use the Lifts to reach these elevated positions if the coast is clear: climbing, while comparatively silent, makes you too easy to see.

- The width of the streets sometimes makes it difficult to navigate efficiently at rooftop level.

- This map may be easier than others in Wolfpack because of the numerous angles and obstacles that protect potential approach routes.

## ANIMUS CORE

- The Animus-like portions of the map offer plenty of opportunities to escape a pursuer. Not only can you easily break their line of sight by taking advantage of corners and multiple floor levels, but you also have access to all kinds of Chase Breakers.

- On the plaza with the lanterns, try to use the hiding places that are close to groups of citizens. Nearby lookalikes will make it harder for other players to be certain as they attempt to intuit your location.

- With both a hiding place and a blending opportunity, as well as many possible exit points via the archways, the inside of the city hall building is a great place to set a trap.

- If you take to the rooftops, don't forget that this map features many small indoors sections. If your target is inside one of them, do not be confused by the fact that you cannot see them even though your compass is filled.

- This map is rather difficult in Wolfpack, as its many open areas make it hard to stalk your targets discretely.

III

QUICKSTART

THE STORY
SO FAR

PRIMER

WALKTHROUGH

SIDE QUESTS

REFERENCE &
ANALYSIS

MULTIPLAYER

EXTRAS

MAP LEGEND

INDEX

BASICS

CHARACTERS &
CUSTOMIZATION

SCORE &
PROGRESSION

ABILITY SETS

GAME MODES

ADVANCED TIPS

MAPS &
ANALYSIS

# EXTRAS

**SPOILER WARNING:** IF YOU HAVE YET TO COMPLETE THE MAIN STORYLINE OF ASSASSIN'S CREED III, THEN **DO NOT READ THIS CHAPTER**. THE FOLLOWING PAGES CONTAIN SPOILER MATERIAL AND PLOT REVELATIONS THAT WILL DIMINISH YOUR EXPERIENCE IF STUDIED PREMATURELY.

After a short recap of all secrets and unlockable extras in Assassin's Creed III, this chapter offers an extensive analysis of the central storyline – including hints and speculation on potential developments in future episodes…

## UNLOCKABLES

Use this checklist to identify any rewards that you have yet to unlock.

| | UNLOCKABLES OVERVIEW | | | |
|---|---|---|---|---|
| **CATEGORY** | **UNLOCKABLE** | **UNLOCK CONDITION** | **NOTES** | **PAGE** |
| **Outfits** | Boston Outfit | Start of Sequence 06 | Unlocked in Shops. | 252 |
| | Jamestown Outfit | Start of Sequence 06 | | |
| | Charleston Outfit | Start of Sequence 06 | | |
| | New York Outfit | Start of Sequence 09 | | |
| | Philadelphia Outfit | Start of Sequence 09 | | |
| | Baltimore Outfit | Start of Sequence 09 | | |
| | Altaïr's Outfit | Complete all main missions with all Optional Objectives | Unlocked in the Manor; interact with the outfit racks. | 66 |
| | Captain Kidd's Outfit | Complete the Oak Island Naval Location | | 190 |
| | Achilles' Original Outfit | Complete the Achilles' Painting mission | | 193 |
| | Kanien'kehá:ka Outfit | Collect all Feathers | | 200 |
| | Ezio's Outfit | Through Uplay | | - |
| **Maps** | Boston North Chests | Sequence 04 | Once unlocked, purchase these Maps from shops. | 252 |
| | Boston Central Chests | | | |
| | Boston South Chests | | | |
| | New York North Chests | | | |
| | New York West Chests | | | |
| | New York East Chests | | | |
| | Frontier Chests | | | |
| | Lexington Feathers | | | |
| | John's Town Feathers | | | |
| | Monmouth Feathers | | | |
| | Black Creek Feathers | | | |
| | Almanac Pages | | | |
| | Trinkets | | | |
| **Chest Keys** | Frontier | Sequence 05 | Each key opens all Chests located in the corresponding region (with the exception of those situated in Forts, where you must always pick the lock). | 252 |
| | Boston Central | Complete Memory 02 in Sequence 06 | | 96 |
| | Boston North | Complete the Boston Central Liberation Mission | | 158 |
| | Boston South | Complete the Boston South Liberation Mission | | 157 |
| | New York North | Complete the New York North Liberation Mission | | 159 |
| | New York East | Complete the New York East Liberation Mission | | 161 |
| | New York West | Complete the New York West Liberation Mission | | 160 |
| **Naval Locations** | Fort Wolcott | Obtain 1 Trinket and receive Dead Man's Letter 1 from Peg Leg | Each Naval Location is accessed from the East Coast map. | 182 |
| | Dead Chest's Treasure | Obtain 6 Trinkets and receive Dead Man's Letter 2 from Peg Leg | | 184 |
| | The Ghost Ship | Obtain 14 Trinkets and receive Dead Man's Letter 3 from Peg Leg | | 186 |
| | The Mad Doctor's Castle | Obtain 24 Trinkets and receive Dead Man's Letter 4 from Peg Leg | | 188 |
| | Oak Island | Complete the 4 previous Naval Locations and thereby obtain all 4 Oak Island Map Fragments | Completing this rewards you with a Shard of Eden that deflects bullets. | 190 |
| | The Ruins at Cerros | Available only as a preorder bonus or in Collector's Editions of Assassin's Creed III | Completing this rewards you with Captain Kidd's Sawtooth Cutlass. | 192 |
| **Multiplayer** | The Huntsman Outfit & Spiritwalker Title | Complete the single player adventure | These can be accessed via the Customization menu in the Multiplayer mode. | 131 |
| | William Johnson Patron & Title | Unlock the corresponding Mementos by completing main story missions | | -* |
| | John Pitcairn Patron & Title | | | |
| | Thomas Hickey Patron & Title | | | |
| | Charles Lee Patron & Title | | | |
| | Benjamin Church Patron & Title | | | |
| | Haytham Kenway Patron & Title | | | |
| | Israel Putnam Patron & Title | | | |
| | The Black Bear Hunter Title & Emblem | Obtain the Bear Memento | | |
| | The Wolf Hunter Title & Emblem | Obtain the Wolf Memento | | |
| | The Cougar Hunter Title & Emblem | Obtain the Cougar Memento | | |
| | The Elk Hunter Title & Emblem | Obtain the Elk Memento | | |
| | The Bobcat Hunter Title & Emblem | Obtain the Bobcat Memento | | |
| | The Deer Hunter Title & Emblem | Obtain the Deer Memento | | |
| | The Master Hunter Title & Emblem | Complete all Hunting Challenges | | |
| **Recruits and Abilities** | Stephane Chapheau & Riot/Assassinate abilities | Complete Sequence 06, Memory 02 | | 96 |
| | Clipper Wilkinson & Marksman ability | Complete the Boston North Liberation Mission | | 158 |
| | Duncan Little & Bodyguard ability | Complete the Boston South Liberation Mission | | 157 |
| | Dobby Carter & Lure Away ability | Complete the New York North Liberation Mission | | 159 |
| | Jamie Colley & Ambush ability | Complete the New York West Liberation Mission | | 160 |
| | Jacob Zenger & Covert Escort ability | Complete the New York East Liberation Mission | | 161 |
| **Mementos** | Ben Franklin Painting | Complete Sequence 12 | Decoration unlocked in the Manor. | 128 |
| | The Battle of Trenton Newspaper | | | |
| | The Great Fire of New York Newspaper | | | |
| | Pitcairn's Memento | Complete Sequence 07 | | 102 |
| | Johnson's Memento | Complete Sequence 06 | | 94 |
| | Hickey's Memento | Complete Sequence 08 | | 110 |
| | Charles Lee's Memento | Complete Sequence 12 | | 128 |
| | Kaniehtí:io Memento | Complete Sequence 04 | | 83 |
| | The Boston Massacre Newspaper | Complete Memory 02 in Sequence 05 | | 88 |
| | First Expedition Painting | Complete Memory 05 in Sequence 05 | | 91 |
| | The Boston Tea Party Newspaper | Complete Memory 03 in Sequence 06 | | 97 |
| | Robinson Tea Chest | Complete Memory 03 in Sequence 06 | | 97 |
| | Paul Revere's Ride Newspaper | Complete Memory 01 in Sequence 07 | | 102 |
| | The Battle of Lexington Concord Newspaper | Complete Memory 02 in Sequence 07 | | 104 |
| | The Second Continental Congress Newspaper | Complete Memory 02 in Sequence 07 | | 104 |

| CATEGORY | UNLOCKABLE | UNLOCK CONDITION | NOTES | PAGE |
|---|---|---|---|---|
| **Mementos** | The Battle of Bunker Hill Newspaper | Complete Memory 04 in Sequence 07 | Decoration unlocked in the Manor. | 108 |
| | The Declaration of Independence Newspaper | Complete Memory 03 in Sequence 08 | | 105 |
| | Valley Forge Newspaper | Complete Memory 01 in Sequence 09 | | 116 |
| | Brewery Memento | Complete Memory 03 in Sequence 09 | | 118 |
| | Naval Painting | Complete Memory 04 in Sequence 09 | | 119 |
| | Benjamin Church's Memento | Complete Memory 04 in Sequence 09 | | 119 |
| | The Battle of Monmouth Newspaper | Complete Memory 03 in Sequence 10 | | 122 |
| | The Battle of Chesapeake Newspaper | Complete Memory 01 in Sequence 11 | | 126 |
| | The Battle of Chesapeake Naval Map | Complete Memory 01 in Sequence 11 | | 126 |
| | Haytham's Memento | Complete Sequence 11 | | 126 |
| | Scale Model of the Aquila | Complete the Oak Island Naval Location | | 190 |
| | Privateer Memento | Complete all Privateer Contracts | | 180 |
| | Nicholas Biddle Memento | Complete the Biddle's Hideout Naval Mission | | 179 |
| | Boston Brawlers Memento | Complete all Brawler Challenges | | 141 |
| | Thief's Club Memento | Complete all Thief's Challenges | | 142 |
| | Hunting Society Memento | Complete all Hunting Challenges | | |
| | Bear Memento | Complete the The Man-Eater Hunting Society mission | | 138 |
| | Bobcat Memento | Complete the Feline Feet Hunting Society mission | | |
| | Deer Memento | Complete the The Patriarch Hunting Society mission | | |
| | Wolf Memento | Complete the The Pack Leader Hunting Society mission | | |
| | Cougar Memento | Complete the Acute Cat Hunting Society mission | | |
| | Elk Memento | Complete the The Elk Bachelor Hunting Society mission | | |
| **Manor Trophies** | Know it All | Complete all Sequences with a 100% Synchronization rating | All Trophies can be examined in the Manor. | 66 |
| | More Than Stories | Complete all Side Missions with a 100% Synchronization rating | | 134 |
| | Anchors Aweigh | Complete all Naval Locations with a 100% Synchronization rating | | 182 |
| | New York Liberation | Complete all Liberation Missions in New York | | 159 |
| | Boston Liberation | Complete all Liberation Missions in Boston | | 157 |
| | Free the People | Liberate all Forts | | 144 |
| | The Art of Conversation | Complete all ambient conversations with Connor | | 193 |
| | A Place Called Home | Upgrade all workers to their maximum level | | 193 |
| | Shipshape | Purchase all Ship Upgrades | | 253 |
| | Spoils of War | Attack 10 Convoys | | 138 |
| | Friends in High Places | Get all Recruits to Assassin rank | | 162 |
| | Boston Exploration | Unfog the map of Boston | | 202 |
| | New York Exploration | Unfog the map of New York | | 212 |
| | Frontier Exploration | Unfog the map of the Frontier | | 206 |
| **Uplay Rewards** | 10 ⊕ | Complete Sequence 02 | ⊕ points are earned by reaching certain key milestones in the game if you have a Uplay account connected to your profile. | |
| | 20 ⊕ | Complete Sequence 06 | | |
| | 30 ⊕ | Complete Sequence 12 | | |
| | 40 ⊕ | Reach level 20 in Multiplayer mode | | |
| | Assassin's Creed III Theme | Purchase for 10 ⊕ through Ubisoft's Uplay service | Unlocks PlayStation 3 XMB or Xbox 360 Dashboard theme. | – |
| | Pouch Upgrades | Purchase for 20 ⊕ through Ubisoft's Uplay service | Increases the maximum capacity of consumables that Connor can carry. | |
| | Ezio's Outfit | Purchase for 30 ⊕ through Ubisoft's Uplay service | Unlocked in the Manor. | |
| | Multiplayer Pack | Purchase for 40 ⊕ through Ubisoft's Uplay service | Customization options in the Multiplayer mode. | |

## ANIMUS SYNCHING

⊙ The introduction to this minigame can be viewed if you are offline, but you must be online to find the first Pivot and proceed. The game itself will prompt you on the participation requirements for your individual format.

⊙ You are given three Pivots during the tutorial: Tau, Zeta and Rho. Note that the Animus Synching game is connected to your gaming profile, not your current playthrough. After completing the Assassin's Creed III storyline with a profile, the Animus Synching entry on the main map menu will appear automatically in all new games started with that profile.

⊙ Planting Pivots that you have collected enables you to triangulate the position of new Pivots. To do so, visit the Animus Synching Map screen. To pick up a Pivot, hover over its icon and press Ⓐ/⊗. Though you can remove them from the map at any time, you can only plant Pivots at Connor's current position. To do so, select his icon on the Animus Synching map and press Ⓐ/⊗.

⊙ The search area for each Pivot is highlighted in green on the Animus Synching map. When you plant your Pivots, you can eliminate entire map areas and narrow down your search. By reducing the green search zone to a small portion of land (▣ 01), you can then scour that area until you espy the 📲 icon on the mini-map. You can then approach and run into the Pivot to collect it.

⊙ New Pivots appear one by one, with a base spawn time of once every 15 minutes while the game is active. For Pivots to appear, you must be inside the Animus and not in a menu screen – with the exception of the Pivots Info screen, which shows the active countdown until a new Pivot appears. If you have people in your friends list who have collected the first Pivot, each qualifying friend increases the speed at which new Pivots appear by 20%. If you have no such friends, one second of play time counts as one second of Pivot spawning time. If you have one qualifying friend, one second of play time counts as 1.2 seconds of Pivot spawning time. If you have five qualifying friends, the overall waiting time is halved.

⊙ The Pivots that you search for in the game world have been planted by other gamers, and are assigned to you randomly. In turn, Pivots that you place may be assigned to someone else. This generally means that you will find them in the open – though you must be prepared for eventualities where they have been planted in hard-to-reach locations. If one of your Pivots is collected by another gamer, it is removed from your Animus Synching map. You do not lose the Pivot itself: just its current placement.

⊙ Once you have collected all Pivots, open the main map and pay close attention as you open the Pivots Info entry. After the voice-over ends, press any button to receive the Head in the Cloud Achievement/Trophy.

01

## ANIMUS HACKS

Once unlocked by collecting Pivots, Animus Hacks can be activated from the Options menu. Game progress is not saved while these cheats are active.

| CHEAT | EFFECT |
|---|---|
| Made of Steel | You can't get hurt. |
| Infinite Ammunition | You have infinite ammunition. |
| Sun and Moon | You can manually choose between day and night. |
| Killing Spree | You can assassinate your targets even when in open conflict. |
| Semi-Automatic | No more reload time for ranged weapons. |
| Ninja | Guard detection and investigation is disabled. |
| Recruit | You have infinite Recruit Tokens. |
| Weather Man | You can set the weather. |
| Thunder Kill | Every kill is accompanied by a peel of lightning and ominous thunder. |
| Season Changer | You can manually set the season to summer or winter. |

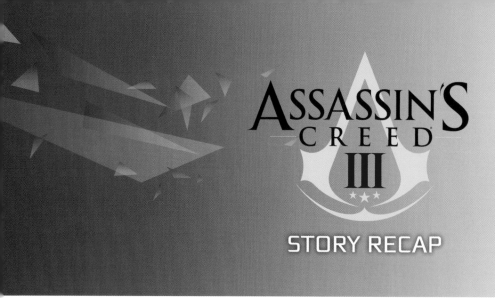

# ASSASSIN'S CREED III

## STORY RECAP

This section offers a concise recap of the Assassin's Creed III story, followed by an extensive analysis of established facts, and lively speculation on future developments. It should be clear that these pages contain **major spoilers** for those who have not yet reached the final credits.

HAYTHAM'S ALLIES

CHARLES LEE

JOHN PITCAIRN

BENJAMIN CHURCH

THOMAS HICKEY

WILLIAM JOHNSON

HAYTHAM KENWAY

The Assassin's Creed III story begins on October 30, 2012, and follows directly – almost to the second – from the conclusion of Revelations. Desmond and his colleagues enter a long-sealed vault, the Grand Temple, chosen by the First Civilization as the storehouse for their accumulated knowledge. Shortly after their arrival, the awaiting Juno triggers a reaction in Desmond that causes him to experience moments in the life of a new ancestor: Haytham Kenway. We learn that Haytham performed an assassination at a London opera and, in doing so, obtained an unusual amulet, which is the key to the Grand Temple's locked inner chamber – so Desmond explores further into Haytham's life to learn of its location.

Haytham also understands that the amulet is a key to a First Civilization vault. He is commissioned – by what we presume at this point to be a member of the Assassin Brotherhood hierarchy – to travel to the New World, both to open the vault and secure its contents, and to establish a foothold for the organization. On arrival in Boston in 1753, Haytham enlists the services of local allies, and comes to the conclusion that he requires the assistance of Native Americans, and their more intimate knowledge of the region, to locate the vault. To that end, he frees a group of Kanien'kehá:ka slaves, hoping to win their gratitude – and, more pertinently, a favor.

This tactic is proved a success when, after further persuasion and assistance, a Kanien'kehá:ka woman known as Kaniehtí:io agrees to escort Haytham to a sacred site that bears markings similar to those on his amulet. Disappointment awaits, however, as Haytham recognizes First Civilization script at the cave, but finds that his amulet apparently doesn't unlock anything within. Haytham relays this setback to his companions, but resolves to continue the search. As Haytham formally introduces Charles Lee to his Order, Desmond comes to an unexpected realization: Haytham was not an Assassin, but a Templar.

Haytham and Kaniehtí:io share a brief and passionate relationship. Their entanglement ends abruptly when, though the precise catalyst is unclear, she rejects the Templar on coming to understand his motives and methods. Unbeknownst to Haytham, who promises never to return, their union bears a child. From Desmond's perspective, his focus (more specifically, his ancestral link) shifts to Kaniehtí:io and, in turn, her son: Ratonhnhaké:ton.

In 1760, at five years of age, Ratonhnhaké:ton is brutally assaulted by Charles Lee and told to relay a message to his kind. When the spirited boy threatens to one day find and kill Lee, the Templar and his companions retort with condescension – and the boy is bludgeoned with the butt of a rifle as they turn to depart. Ratonhnhaké:ton regains consciousness to find his village in flames and his mother dead, believing it to be the handiwork of Lee and his cohorts. Lee had sought information on the location of the precursor temple; when rebuffed, he reacts with remorseless violence.

KANIEHTÍ:IO

III

QUICKSTART

THE STORY
SO FAR

PRIMER

WALKTHROUGH

SIDE QUESTS

REFERENCE &
ANALYSIS

MULTIPLAYER

→ EXTRAS

MAP LEGEND

INDEX

SECRETS

→ STORY RECAP

ANALYSIS &
SPECULATION

RATONHNHAKÉ:TON, LATER KNOWN AS CONNOR

The story shifts forward by almost a decade. Aged 14, Ratonhnhaké:ton must take part in a rite of passage and, in doing so, interact with an object that we recognize as a Piece of Eden. During the (to his eyes, supernatural) journey that ensues, he is addressed by Juno who instructs him to protect the "sanctuary" – the Grand Temple where Desmond lies on the Animus in the present day. Juno shows the boy a future in which his nation is overrun and erased from all memory, and presents an alternative: the Assassin symbol. Ratonhnhaké:ton is directed to seek out a man who once helped his mother, and

has a particular connection with the symbol from his dream. On arrival, he is forcefully rebuffed by the petulant Achilles, an episode repeated for days in succession. After he demonstrates his courage while fighting a band of thieves set on robbing his reluctant would-be mentor, the older man agrees to train the boy – who, in order to integrate more successfully with others in the New World, is told to adopt the name Connor.

Following years of intensive training and study, Connor, now deemed fit to wear the Assassin garb and use their iconic tools, sets out to fight

the Templars who threaten his village. Joining forces with new allies, Connor gradually revives the Assassin Brotherhood during the events of the American Revolution as he eliminates the Templars loyal to his father. Connor's path leads him to a direct confrontation with Haytham, who reveals the Templars' *true* agenda: they do not cast their lot with the British, as Connor presumed, nor those who oppose them. They simply seek to manipulate events to ensure that, come the time, true power would rest with their Order alone.

ACHILLES                    WILLIAM MOLINEUX                    PAUL REVERE

THE AMULET

QUICKSTART

THE STORY
SO FAR

PRIMER

WALKTHROUGH

SIDE QUESTS

REFERENCE &
ANALYSIS

MULTIPLAYER

EXTRAS

MAP LEGEND

INDEX

SECRETS

STORY RECAP

ANALYSIS &
SPECULATION

Haytham and Connor agree to a temporary truce and cooperate while their interests are aligned: a desire to support the fight for independence is something they share. Though they both harbor a hope that they might each persuade the other of the validity of their respective ideologies, theirs is a fragile alliance. Haytham is determined to see George Washington dead or disgraced, and have Charles Lee assume his command; Connor, in turn, is fervent in his desire to make good on his promise to kill Lee, avenge the attack on his tribe, and secure their future.

Connor is forced to kill Haytham when his father's aggression – and desire to protect Lee – leaves him no alternative. His course locked, he sets out to face his mortal enemy, the final Templar of significance in Haytham's chapter. When his initial attack leaves Lee gravely wounded, the exhausted Connor tracks him to an ale house, where the two foes share a brief moment of silent reflection. Resigned to his fate, Lee does nothing to resist Connor's killing blow – and the Assassin finally claims the First Civilization amulet.

There is no triumph for Connor in this moment. His people assailed and driven from their lands by Washington for their cooperation with the British, and many of those once dear to him dead or estranged, he heads back to his ruined and deserted village to find the Piece of Eden seemingly placed for his return. Using it to convene with Juno, he finds her unmoved by the plight of his people: she is merely satisfied that they served their purpose. Her final command, with no trace of sentiment, is that Connor place the amulet where no one might happen upon it by chance. His choice of a burial mount rather encapsulates his feelings – and the terrible price paid to transfer the amulet to its future owner.

GEORGE WASHINGTON

DANIEL CROSS

## THE POWER SOURCES

As Desmond explores the past, the present-day Assassins pull him from the Animus at regular intervals to retrieve First Civilization devices required to power the Grand Temple. The hunt for each power source takes Desmond on expeditions that lead him into confrontations with the Templars.

⊙ **November 15-18, 2012:** Desmond retrieves the first power source by infiltrating a skyscraper in Manhattan. This is his first meeting with Daniel Cross, a former Assassin who – albeit against his will – killed the Mentor of the Brotherhood before defecting to the Templars.

⊙ **December 2-6, 2012:** Desmond obtains the second power source after infiltrating a stadium in Brazil surrounded by a tight web of Abstergo security. His second confrontation with Cross reveals the beleaguered (and clearly psychotic) Templar to be suffering the worst ravages of the Bleeding Effect.

⊙ **December 13-17, 2012:** Desmond travels to Italy to mount a rescue after his father's attempt to retrieve the third power source fails. This leads Desmond to the Abstergo facility where he was imprisoned many months before. While retrieving the artifact, Desmond kills Daniel Cross and deploys the Apple of Eden to engineer Warren Vidic's demise. With this, he and his father return to the Grand Temple.

Every time Desmond obtains a power source, he places it inside a receptacle within the Grand Temple. Each of these "activates" rooms where he learns about potential methods of salvation developed by the First Civilization to forestall or mitigate the effects of the Catastrophe. To summarize, these were presented as:

⊙ **Method #1** – Building towers that would absorb the solar flare.

⊙ **Method #2** – Erecting an energy shield that would protect the Earth from the solar flare.

⊙ **Method #3** – Using the suggestive power of Pieces of Eden to enjoin all sentient minds to prevent the Catastrophe.

⊙ **Method #4** – Divination: predicting the future with advanced mathematical machines to learn of a future solution and, later, to communicate with generations that might follow. (This was Minerva's project.)

⊙ **Method #5** – Bio-engineering: transforming themselves physically to resist the cataclysm. (One test subject who volunteered for this project was Aita, Juno's husband; she was later forced to kill him to relieve his intense suffering.)

⊙ **Method #6** – Transcendence: transferring the mind from a body to another vessel. This is how Juno is still "alive", living within the temple's walls.

WARREN VIDIC

III

QUICKSTART

THE STORY
SO FAR

PRIMER

WALKTHROUGH

SIDE QUESTS

REFERENCE &
ANALYSIS

MULTIPLAYER

←EXTRAS

MAP LEGEND

INDEX

SECRETS

←STORY RECAP

ANALYSIS &
SPECULATION

In the present day, as December 20, 2012 becomes December 21, Desmond retrieves the amulet hidden by his forebear. After the Grand Temple's inner chamber has been unlocked, Juno informs Desmond that she possesses the means to save the world from the imminent cataclysm – though it would necessitate his death and her rebirth. A projection of Minerva, cast through time late in her life (long after her interaction with Ezio), materializes to warn Desmond of the dire consequences of liberating Juno.

While Minerva and other First Civilization scientists and leaders sought to avert the previous Catastrophe, we learn that Juno exploited the chaos and confusion as an opportunity to try and conquer the world, not save it. When her betrayal was revealed, she and her co-conspirators were condemned to death, their bodies interned in the final sealing of the Grand Temple – but Juno survived. After transferring her consciousness to the Grand Temple with the "transcendence" technology, Juno plotted for thousands of years, subtly directing events in human history to reach the point where Desmond stands before her. Acceding to her wishes, Minerva cautions, leads to a future where mankind will be enslaved. The alternative, however, is to allow the Catastrophe to occur, and have Desmond emerge into a toxic wasteland to sow the seeds of society's rebirth in a distant future. It is implied that this will lead the cycle to repeat, with mankind once again destined to meet near-extinction in a subsequent Catastrophe.

With the weight of the immediate consequences at the forefront of his mind, Desmond chooses to comply with Juno's wishes. As the other Assassins retreat from the vault, Desmond lays his hand on the First Civilization pedestal. His body is consumed by fire – and, simultaneously,

the escalating apocalyptic effects of the heightened solar activity dramatically subside. The world, we are led to understand, has been saved by his decision.

With the image of the triumphant Juno and Desmond's sacrifice fresh in our minds, let's consider what the true cost might be – among other burning questions…

JUNO

MINERVA

Many of the more tantalizing mysteries in Assassin's Creed III will only be resolved by future games in the series. That said, there are plausible answers to be found for those who care to look closely – and, moreover, clues on potential developments in forthcoming episodes.

### What did the Templars hope to achieve in the War of Independence?

The Templars had no affection for the Tories – those who would see the nation remain a colony of Britain – nor, for that matter, the Patriots. Independence was an opportunity, little more: indeed, we see that Haytham placed agents in both camps. Their goal was to ensure that the Templars might shape and command the political landscape formed by the upheaval.

However, it is important to remember that Haytham's original commission was to seek out a "precursor" vault unlocked by the amulet that we recognize as the key to the inner chamber of the Grand Temple. As has been revealed in previous episodes, the Templars have exploited the power of First Civilization technology (particularly the potent Pieces of Eden) throughout history to control minds in a more subtle and deceptive fashion. While the efforts of Haytham and his associates to locate the site and exploit the technology inside were fruitless, his Templar chapter laid the groundwork for their future dominance in a more conventional fashion.

QUICKSTART

THE STORY
SO FAR

PRIMER

WALKTHROUGH

SIDE QUESTS

REFERENCE &
ANALYSIS

MULTIPLAYER

→ EXTRAS

MAP LEGEND

INDEX

SECRETS

STORY RECAP

→ ANALYSIS &
SPECULATION

**How is it that Desmond, an Assassin, has an ancestor who was a Templar? Why did Haytham betray the Assassins?**

We know that Haytham was, to a certain age, an Assassin: his use of the iconic Hidden Blade and certain aspects of his professional technique betray his Brotherhood training. However, people are not born with an innate affiliation to either the Assassin or Templar cause. The respective ideologies must be first taught, embraced over time, and then upheld throughout the lifetime of any given individual.

The Templars ultimately aspire, through political machinations and First Civilization technology, to elevate their hierarchy to the status of a ruling elite capable of commanding the minds of its subjects. The rationale behind this varies from one noteworthy Order figure to another. Some claim a motivation of compassion (Prince Ahmet in Revelations aspired to eliminate all racial, religious and cultural boundaries to foster lasting peace), whereas others are more inspired by the allure of power (such as Rodrigo Borgia and his venal kith and kin in Assassin's Creed II and Brotherhood). Haytham, for his part, appears to have been seduced by a perceived pragmatism in the Order's goals – as this exchange during his climatic fight with Connor reveals:

*Haytham: The people never have the power. Only the illusion of it. And here's the real secret: they don't want it. The responsibility is too great to bear. It's why they are so quick to fall in line as soon as someone takes charge. They want to be told what to do. They yearn for it. Little wonder, that, since all mankind was built to serve.*

*Connor: So because we are inclined by nature to be controlled, who better than the Templars? It is a poor offer.*

*Haytham: It is truth! Principle and practice are two very different beasts. I see the world the way it is – not as I wish it would be.*

*Connor: No, father... You have given up – and would have us all do the same.*

Haytham views himself as a realist, and is contemptuous of his son's (to him, naïve) idealism. We see a distinct shift in the Templar's moral code over the course of his life. Earlier in the story, Haytham expresses disdain and disgust at the brutality of an Order peer, Braddock. He takes particular exception to his willingness to murder without qualm or reflection. Later, though, Haytham himself begins to use similar methods and – in his unwavering patronage of Charles Lee, for example – overlook such behavior in others.

That said, as Assassins and Templars alike commit murder for the sake of expediency, this cannot be where the philosophical line between the two factions – and, therefore, Connor and Haytham – is drawn.

As established in previous storylines, and as the events of Assassin's Creed III have shown, it is simplistic to characterize the Assassin versus Templar conflict as a battle between good and evil. The true point of contention is free will. What the Templars ultimately propose, on an increasing scale over time, is to *enforce* a new world order: to eschew the imperfect and difficult process of gradual social engineering in favor of a form of collective submission. In the past, Pieces of Eden could only be used to bewitch minds within their immediate vicinity, limiting the most malevolent form of Templar manipulation to regions and regimes. In the present day, Abstergo aspires to expand the range of such mind control to include the entire globe.

Though the end result and methodology may differ, it could be said that the Assassins and Templars actually embrace a common goal: both aspire to protect mankind from itself. It is this, perhaps, that enables the likes of Haytham, Lucy Stillman and Daniel Cross to revise their affiliation without great compunction.

HAYTHAM

What might also be appealing for Assassins who defect is that, for the Templars, victory would be absolute: they only need to win the war. Those who envisage the creation of a better world might also hope to live in it. For the Brotherhood, each individual battle is fought to ensure that the war has no end. Haytham, shortly before his death, has a decidedly unsentimental explanation for this stark reality:

*"It is because the Order is born of a realization. We require no creed. No indoctrination by desperate old men. All we need is that the world be as it is. This is why the Templars will never be destroyed!"*

### What is the significance of the amulet?

The amulet is a First Civilization artifact that was created as a key to an inner vault inside the Grand Temple, where Desmond and his Assassin cohorts reside during the events of Assassin's Creed III. This location was chosen as a storage facility for the knowledge accumulated by the precursor race during their efforts to avert the Catastrophe.

While the Piece of Eden secured and stored by Ezio was enough to allow Desmond to open the Grand Temple, the contents of the inner chamber were sufficiently valuable or dangerous to require additional security. Like other First Civilization items, the amulet fell into the hands of humans and, in time, the custody of the Assassins – until stolen by Haytham in the opera assassination scene.

If we take a step back from the Assassin's Creed III fiction for a moment, the amulet is actually an ingenious MacGuffin. Superficially a plot device that exists only to motivate the story's principal players, its actual purpose in the narrative is to ensure that the *real* key that Juno seeks is delivered to her on schedule, and oblivious to her agenda…

### What does Desmond mean when he says he "chose" to kill Lucy?

Prior to Assassin's Creed III, it had been implied that Desmond stabbed Lucy Stillman against her will, compelled by an unseen force presumed to be Juno. However, in a conversation with his father in the Grand Temple, he reveals that her death was his decision – a rational, conscious, calculated choice. Juno, Desmond reveals, merely showed him a future in which Lucy stole the Apple and returned it to Abstergo. In Juno's vision, the Templar corporation attempted to transport it on board the Eye-Abstergo satellite, the culmination of plans unveiled in the original Assassin's Creed… and yet the launch was a failure.

The mystery here is why Desmond, in a move that seems entirely out of character, would deem a summary execution as the only resolution. If we assume that Ezio's Piece of Eden was required to open the Grand Temple – and that Juno could not simply admit chosen visitors from inside – then we can at least understand the need for keeping it safe. But as Desmond's father suggests, did Desmond actually make the decision, or was he merely made to feel like he did?

That Juno manipulated events in human history to serve her own ends is abundantly clear. The death of Lucy – no matter whose will plunged the blade into the triple agent's abdomen – definitely suggests that Juno has the ability to actively control individuals, and not merely indoctrinate.

***Are the First Civilization entities, such as Minerva, Juno and Tinia, alive or dead?***

As physical beings, the First Civilization became extinct long ago. Though their genetic code lives on in their human creations (the product of a last desperate attempt to preserve their kind through interbreeding), they no longer exist as a distinct species.

As is currently understood, all First Civilization entities encountered so far – with the exception of Juno, who we will return to shortly – do not actually exist in the time in which they appear. They are dead. Many thousands of years ago, the individual known as Minerva led a project that attempted to forestall the Catastrophe by means of "divination". With computational devices of almost incomprehensible processing capacity, they sought to peer into the most plausible futures in order to learn of their ultimate salvation. This failed not because time and space were defined by a stochasticity that they could not decipher – their machines were perfectly capable of interpreting time's myriad variables – but because every line of inquiry led to the same conclusion: their civilization was doomed.

Though many abandoned this work, Minerva chose to persist, albeit with a different objective: to pass messages to the far future, to a time when their human

successors might possess the technological sophistication to continue their work and avert a subsequent Catastrophe. Though the complexity of such a feat beggars belief, it is by these means that Minerva (and others of her kind) conveyed messages along Desmond's bloodline.

Given the nature of the interactions, it is possible that Desmond is not confronted by simple recordings, but AI "constructs", each a partial facsimile of the sender with greater functionality than a mere message. This might explain the constructs' capacity to converse and react (as with Minerva's terse rebuke for Ezio in Assassin's Creed II, when she makes it clear that her words were not directed at him), and the interactions between Minerva and Juno at the close of the current story.

Though Minerva, Tinia and others are seemingly long dead, Juno's consciousness lives on within the Grand Temple, stored and maintained by First Civilization computer hardware. When she discusses the development of this "transcendence" technology (the sixth method of potential salvation developed by her kind) with Desmond, Juno's physical projection runs a hand over the surface of a glowing device. Juno's mind resides within these machines.

III

QUICKSTART

THE STORY
SO FAR

PRIMER

WALKTHROUGH

SIDE QUESTS

REFERENCE &
ANALYSIS

MULTIPLAYER

EXTRAS

MAP LEGEND

INDEX

SECRETS

STORY RECAP

ANALYSIS &
SPECULATION

## How did Juno come to transfer her consciousness to the First Civilization machines?

Minerva's intervention at the close of the story reveals that Juno deceived her scientific peers and, with the help of co-conspirators, attempted to foment a minor rebellion in her own time. Though the precise manner and magnitude of her betrayal is not clear, we at least know that Juno used the divination device in the Grand Temple to send the message that Desmond receives at the conclusion of Assassin's Creed Brotherhood: a distinctly bitter address, lest we forget, that culminated in the death of Lucy.

When Minerva and Tinia discovered the conspiracy, they attacked and killed Juno and her followers. After transmitting another message across the ages (Tinia's rather more specific address to Desmond at the climax of Revelations), they smashed the Grand Temple's divination sphere – the interface through which the technology could be used. They then sealed the vault, leaving the bodies of the traitors inside. Unfortunately, and in much the same way that a killer for hire might not readily comprehend

the concept of a peer review, the scientists neglected to complete the classic "triple tap" – and Juno survived the attempt on her life.

Whatever Juno's initial goals may have been in her time, the act of uploading herself into the First Civilization machines granted her the luxury of thousands of years to formulate a plan for her eventual rebirth. During the quasi-eternity that separates the death of her race from Desmond's time, it seems that she guided individuals (such as Desmond, Subject 16, and Connor's entire tribe) along multiple paths that ultimately converge at the point where Desmond lays his hand on the pedestal.

Minerva's words suggest that Juno's message to Desmond at the end of the Brotherhood episode (concerning Eve and the First Civilization's interbreeding attempt) were essentially sabotage born of contempt for the rebellious slave race – to lead Desmond on a fool's errand and damn humanity to endure the second Catastrophe. However, certain lines in her message, with hindsight, may reveal an incalculably elaborate plan that took her discovery, death and transcendence into account. For example:

*"It is hard to stay contained. Knowing as we do. We wait for you, Desmond. You will come here. You will activate it. You will know only when it is too late."*

More pressingly, it could be that her exhortation that Desmond find Eve was, in actual fact, a veiled allusion to Juno's resurrection by Desmond's (literal) hand. At the end of Brotherhood, Juno talked of the full power of the First Civilization "sixth sense", and insisted that he unlock its potential. What is interesting, though, is that Juno introduces the First Civilization devices in a specific order during her discussions with Desmond in AC3. The "transcendence" method, tellingly, is the sixth – which lends a very different weight to the final cryptic words of her address at the end of Brotherhood:

*"It is done. The way lies all before you. Only she remains to be found. Awaken the sixth."*

III

QUICKSTART

THE STORY
SO FAR

PRIMER

WALKTHROUGH

SIDE QUESTS

REFERENCE &
ANALYSIS

MULTIPLAYER

EXTRAS

MAP LEGEND

INDEX

SECRETS

STORY RECAP

ANALYSIS &
SPECULATION

### How can Juno manifest herself outside the Grand Temple?

As Minerva cautions (and, for the purposes of this question, confirms) at the climax of AC3, Juno was effectively imprisoned in the Grand Temple after the fall of the First Civilization. The ancient computer system that acts as the vessel for her consciousness confers remarkable longevity – but rather less scope for mobility. In a physical sense, Juno has never left the underground vault.

What she could do, it seems, was use the technology within the Grand Temple "hub" to convene with Pieces of Eden throughout the world – and, by extension, those who interact with them. Though their effects may seem fantastical, the primary purpose of these First Civilization devices appears to be the transmission of data. Humans, a slave race engineered by Juno's long-departed breed, are receptive by design to their broadcasts. As we have seen in previous episodes, they can alter human perception (individually or collectively), and transmit impulses that compel those affected to act against their will. Consider the enforced suicide of the Abstergo guards during Desmond's confrontation with Vidic. This was not a case of the Apple seizing and moving arms and trigger fingers

by force, but a broadcast of an irresistible instruction that might be measured in trivial bytes. Why move a mountain when you can simply adjust the mind's perception of it?

In a sense, you could liken Juno's ability to interact with the outside world as a telephone call: she can communicate directly wherever there is a receiver (a Piece of Eden) and a suitable subject. As a puppeteer – an arch manipulator with many

millennia to perfect her craft – the strings she uses to guide those in her grasp are primarily words and visions, compelling suggestions that few appear to resist. Her influence may spread far beyond Desmond's direct lineage. Connor's tribe, for example, was enjoined by Juno to protect a "sanctuary" (the Grand Temple) for an indeterminate number of years prior to his birth; Subject 16 was persuaded to lay down his life to guide Desmond. There certainly are many others.

### Why does Juno choose to focus so intently on Desmond?

In Assassin's Creed Brotherhood Juno revealed that the First Civilization, in its twilight hours, committed elements of their DNA to posterity through a "union" with their more durable human creations. History remains quiet on the particulars of this interbreeding experiment, but those with a sufficient concentration of precursor genes, such as members of Desmond's lineage, can command aspects of the Sixth Sense possessed by their distant ancestors.

If we (with a fair degree of confidence) assume that the pedestal at the heart of the Grand Temple is a First Civilization biometric device, Juno's efforts to guide Desmond to that place and point in time make perfect sense. What makes Desmond unique, as we currently understand, is that he exists at a specific convergence of genetic stock that gives him an unusually high concentration of First Civilization genes. So it's not Desmond that Juno wants – his death rather underlines this fact – but his DNA.

As touched upon earlier, there is a somewhat perverse irony to this. The events of Assassin's Creed III focus on Desmond's attempts to locate and retrieve the amulet that would allow access to the inner vault – but *he*, ultimately, was the key that Juno sought.

### Does Desmond really have no alternative at the end of the story?

Once Desmond enters the Grand Temple's inner vault, the myriad variables in his life to that point culminate in a stark binary decision: a yes or no; Juno's offer accepted or refused. To recap, his choices were:

⊙ To live – and, in doing so, allow the Catastrophe to occur, but prevent Juno from leaving her digital cell to enslave mankind. In this future, human civilization is brought to its knees by the effects of the Coronal Mass Ejection. Over 99.9% of people die, with small pockets of survivors – and their eventual offspring – reduced to a Bronze Age level of existence for many hundreds (perhaps thousands) of years.

⊙ To sacrifice his life to free Juno and trust in her ability to deploy First Civilization technology to avert the Catastrophe, but potentially damn humanity to perpetual servitude – or, perhaps, worse.

In that moment, on December 21, 2012, Desmond and his companions have no opportunity to explore alternative actions or lines of inquiry: as the cutscenes that accompany the conclusion of the story show, the end is well and truly nigh. Juno's

plan was not to lead Desmond to the Grand Temple, but to engineer his arrival at a very specific point in time, when the Catastrophe would represent a gun that she could hold to the head of the world.

Had mankind (whether through Desmond or another) entered the Grand Temple prior to this point, it might have found a way to separate Juno from the technology within; to secure safe passage beyond December 21, 2012 without paying her toll. In short, it may be that those subject to Juno's manipulation throughout history have worked not to protect the vault from the Templars, but from *everyone* – irrespective of affiliation or intent.

III

QUICKSTART

THE STORY
SO FAR

PRIMER

WALKTHROUGH

SIDE QUESTS

REFERENCE &
ANALYSIS

MULTIPLAYER

EXTRAS

MAP LEGEND

INDEX

SECRETS

STORY RECAP

ANALYSIS &
SPECULATION

### Why does Desmond so readily accept Juno's offer? Aren't Assassins supposed to preserve free will at all costs?

The consequences of the unchecked Catastrophe are abhorrent: several billion guaranteed deaths, the immediate dissolution of society, and the threat – articulated without reserve by Minerva – that mankind might be damned to repeat the cycle. By contrast, the prospect that Juno might take a metaphorical whip to the bioengineered slave species that supplanted their First Civilization creators is infinitely less tangible. Even Minerva's assertion that Juno is by far the greater of the two evils fails to dissuade Desmond from a decision that he appears to have already made.

Desmond's rationale appears to be that there *might* be a chance, however slim, to stop Juno; that his choice means that there will at least be something more to save than bloody and beaten survivors scratching a meager existence in post-apocalyptic ashes. It is a powerfully persuasive argument – and one that Haytham Kenway, Warren Vidic and other Templar luminaries might heartily endorse.

It could be argued that free will, the capacity to make any decision – right or wrong – is the basis of individuality. The desire to preserve this, perhaps at any cost, certainly lies at the very core of the Brotherhood's creed. With her command of First Civilization technology, and mankind's inherent susceptibility to their devices, we might assume Juno capable of transforming all minds within her grasp into an undifferentiated gestalt, acting on her specific instructions without hesitation. This was, of course, precisely what the Templar Order sought to achieve with a Piece of Eden and the Eye-Abstergo satellite.

This is not to suggest that Desmond (or, for that matter, Juno) has a secret Templar affiliation, but rather that his final decision is one that corresponds more closely with their ideology. In his last act, Desmond may "save" humanity by potentially sacrificing the ability of every last man, woman and child to act entirely of their own volition.

Even if we imagine Juno's part of the bargain as a form of tithe, a ten percent, with civilization permitted to function as previously – or even thrive and grow in meaningful ways – under her auspices, the fact that she might govern without protest is a terrifying prospect. For a dictator to order the execution of a dissident is an unpleasant proposition; to have the power to compel them to commit suicide from a remote location is quite terrifying; but what if dissonance itself were impossible? Juno's apparent attitude to her society's former slave race – irrespective of her long-term goals – suggests that she might not preside over her indentured subjects with even a fraction of the benevolence that Templars such as Haytham Kenway might have aspired to.

### How does Juno stop the Catastrophe?

The precise method by which Juno holds up her part of the bargain with Desmond is in fact revealed during one of their early conversations in the story. It is the first method of salvation devised, tested but dismissed as an impossibility by the First Civilization – but, as she clearly states, never truly discarded:

*"In the beginning, when we thought we could be saved, we sought to face the sun's wrath and contain it. Four towers would be built – to pull her fury into this place, where it would be dispelled. But even with all we knew, with all we had, it would take too long. A thousand years we could labor and still the work would not be done. The first tower was never completed. The project abandoned. We moved on. But while we labored on other endeavors, a few returned. They thought they might automate the process. Metal might finish what flesh could not."*

Juno's final line in her monologue is actually a candid admission – and the sight of the improbably deep chasm that the four towers lie in, a confirmation. Though the incredible device could not be finished in time to preserve the First Civilization, the process of building it continued long after the first Catastrophe. This lends weight to the idea that Juno sought to keep the Temple and its secrets sealed until the moment of her choosing. Had mankind gained entrance beforehand, Juno would have lost her bargaining chip: the leverage she uses to make Desmond lay down his life. And on that note…

### Why does Juno need Desmond's DNA?

The pedestal in the inner vault of the Grand Temple is clearly a biometric device, and Juno is quite explicit that Desmond be the one to lay his hand upon it. While the most obvious interpretation is that this is the activation switch for the First Civilization towers, which requires Desmond's DNA, there is another theory. When Desmond explores the room dedicated to the sixth method of salvation – transcendence, the method behind Juno's digital divinity – she, once again, offers a frank appraisal of the technology that might contain more than a hint of foreshadowing:

*"So we forged a new vessel. One that might endure. It proved easy enough to enter. But to leave... to leave required something more. Something wrong."*

As Juno presided over (or at very least abided) the completion of the energy-absorbing towers, it could be that she in fact possessed the capacity to trigger these independent of external assistance. Though Desmond's death may be a direct consequence of the towers and their activation, perhaps his death is… well, *"something wrong"*: the catalyst for Juno's release and rebirth.

### Who is the man who talks about hacking after the final credits? What could this mean?

Although we'll have to wait for a future installment of the series to answer this question, we do understand this to be an Abstergo technician working to interpret, disassemble and upload the memories of Desmond's ancestor Connor – and, possibly, everyone within his lineage – to "the Cloud". We already know that, through Desmond's enforced stay at Abstergo (and Lucy's later treachery – see page 27), their technicians have access to a great deal of data on their erstwhile test subject. This almost certainly includes full genetic sequencing.

On one level, this plot device enables us, as players, to continue with events in Haytham and Connor's lives after Desmond's death. On the assumption that Desmond's "true" performance was of the 100% Synchronization variety, we can later use an Animus to better align our success with his… or, just pick random fights, play checkers and enjoy other recreational pursuits against the striking backdrop of a birth of a nation.

Of course, this cryptic conclusion could suggest that the Templars now possess the technology to read genetic memories and package them in a format that anyone can experience – not only direct-line ancestors. The bearing that this might have on future developments in the Assassin's Creed story is profound.

### What does Juno hope to achieve?

One thing is certain: Juno is revealed to be the true villain of Desmond's story arc, and will return to cast a broad shadow in the chapters that follow – no matter which protagonists, past or present, occupy the starring roles.

Following the activation of the towers and the aversion of the Catastrophe, the Grand Temple appears to be more brightly illuminated, *more* active, than before. This suggests that it has attained full power after years of relative dormancy. Prior to this, Desmond and his Assassin companions lacked the time, support and expertise to study what else may lie within its rooms and chambers (or adjoining caverns, not to mention networked vaults elsewhere in the world), so there is no theoretical limit to what Juno might attempt. We can only speculate on her intentions.

**Revenge:** Juno blames humanity for the extinction of the First Civilization – the war between the slave and master races is believed to have precipitated the fall of the latter after the first Catastrophe. Moreover, she may view the death of her husband Aita as a direct consequence of that conflict. One thing is certain: charges of misanthropy would not be wildly inaccurate.

**Rebirth:** She may have the means to transfer her mind to another vessel, be it flesh and bone or more durable metal. Given that the events of Assassin's Creed III cast Juno as being capable of considering far more variables than those who might seek to oppose her, it is doubtful that she would limit herself to a single (and therefore vulnerable) point of existence. As a digital being, she may have the capacity to interact with global telecommunications networks to achieve virtual omniscience. Combine such prospective feats and weapons with the First Civilization tech at her disposal (particularly Pieces of Eden), and Minerva's final warning appears almost restrained.

**Restoration:** Juno utters the line "What once was shall be again" in conversations with both Connor and Desmond which, with the benefit of hindsight, might be more threat than deity-grade platitude. Could it be that she has the knowledge and means to resurrect her species? And is she actually alone within the First Civilization device where she resides?

Juno, then, only represents an "enemy of my enemy" scenario – and not a tableau for epiphanies that lead to Templars expounding the formation of transparent and accountable democracies, or Assassins advocating the virtues of mind-control devices.

Of course, it could be that both have actually served, however indirectly and unknowingly, to facilitate Juno's rebirth. The Assassin and Templar factions have both waxed and waned in terms of power and eminence throughout history. In one reading of her motives, Juno may have in part orchestrated these almost rhythmic fluctuations, playing one side against the other. The Assassins police the Templars and, in doing so, reduce their numbers and becalm their ambitions; the Templars, in turn, are periodically successful in "crusades" that force surviving members of the Brotherhood back into the shadows.

In the modern day, the dominant Templar Order controls the multinational Abstergo corporation, which might offer Juno vital resources – a head start, if you will, in a bid for global domination. The diminished Brotherhood, operating in small cells below the radar, provides the means by which Juno can transfer Desmond to a very particular place and time. After all: if Connor's only role was to locate and store the amulet, his story might not have ended with the elimination of the Templar chapter that sought to locate and exploit the Grand Temple, but with a simple theft.

## Might the Templars and Assassins unite to fight Juno?

Juno's rise to a potential position of global dominance, invisible to most, means that an uneasy alliance isn't an impossibility. However, we can safely say that this would be temporary, as the differences conveyed in the story of Connor and Haytham demonstrate – not least its conclusion.

If we agree that free will is the true point of dispute in the struggle between the two factions, the respective ideologies, in their purest form, are as distinct as black and white – and yet the manner in which they are interpreted and acted upon is often grey. Both groups claim to be humanity's custodians, and to represent its best interests, but there is perhaps a more elementary, human component to their differences. The archetypal Assassin, in wholeheartedly embracing the Brotherhood's cause, is prepared to sacrifice his or her self to preserve individuality and, by extension, humanity. The Templar, by contrast, would shackle individualism and preserve mankind through the sacrifice of others.

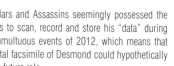

QUICKSTART

THE STORY
SO FAR

PRIMER

WALKTHROUGH

SIDE QUESTS

REFERENCE &
ANALYSIS

MULTIPLAYER

EXTRAS

MAP LEGEND

INDEX

SECRETS

STORY RECAP

ANALYSIS &
SPECULATION

### Is Desmond really dead?

Insofar as the body of the "real" Desmond is charred, devoid of a pulse and poised to putrefy? Almost certainly. In terms of Desmond making further contributions to the story? That remains to be seen.

The continued existence of Subject 16 – or a simulation thereof – following his death prior to the events of Assassin's Creed indicates that Desmond's digital resurrection is not an impossibility. Both the Templars and Assassins seemingly possessed the means to scan, record and store his "data" during the tumultuous events of 2012, which means that a digital facsimile of Desmond could hypothetically play a future role.

Based on what we know of the sixth method of salvation, it could also be speculated that the biometric device in the Grand Temple's inner chamber allowed a transfer of consciousness, and that Desmond now exists within the Temple's walls – just as Juno did before him for thousands of years.

### Who can we expect to stand out in a future installment?

The concept of the Abstergo Entertainment division packaging and selling memories through consumer iterations of its Animus tech also offers Juno (or the Templars, if operating beyond her control) a possible means to access a wide audience – from simple propaganda and historical revisionism, to implanting secret "impulses" in the minds of each user. This would almost certainly initiate a new and distinct chapter in the Assassin versus Templar war.

If Juno is to be the primary focus, we may find both Assassins and Templars engaged in a desperate struggle to develop new weapons to combat her. As we know, Desmond (and specific ancestors) are defined by their high concentration of First Civilization DNA, which equips them to more successfully operate the ancient yet powerful devices at Juno's disposal. Desmond's daring attack on Abstergo's Italian facility makes this apparent. It may be that similar individuals will need to be identified, recruited and trained via the Animus to stand at the vanguard of the fight.

A shift in focus to the Templar side of the war is also an intriguing prospect. Though the Assassins have the advantage of exclusive intelligence (the events witnessed by William, Rebecca and Shaun in the Grand Temple), it may be that the resources and influence of Abstergo could be pivotal in the battle against Juno.